# THE GUI STYLE GUIDE

### Susan L. Fowler

### Victor R. Stanwick

## AP PROFESSIONAL

Boston   San Diego   New York
London   Sydney   Tokyo   Toronto

This book is printed on acid-free paper. $\infty$

AP PROFESSIONAL
955 Massachusetts Avenue, Cambridge, MA 02139

An Imprint of ACADEMIC PRESS, INC.
A Division of HARCOURT BRACE & COMPANY

*United Kingdom Edition published by*
ACADEMIC PRESS LIMITED
24–28 Oval Road, London NW1 7DX


**Library of Congress Cataloging-in-Publication Data**
Fowler, Susan L., 1953–
    The GUI style guide / Susan L. Fowler, Victor R. Stanwick.
       p.   cm.
    Includes index.
    ISBN 0-12-263590-6 (pbk.)
    1. Graphical user interfaces (Computer systems)  I. Stanwick,
Victor R., 1958–    II. Title.
QA6.9.U83F69   1995
005.4'2--dc20                 94-32560
                                  CIP


Printed in the United States of America
94 95 96 97 98 IP 9 8 7 6 5 4 3 2 1

# THE
# GUI
# STYLE
# GUIDE

# Contents

# PART II  TEXT

## 4  Messages

## 5  Online Help

# PART III   DESIGN   213

## 6   International Software   215

# Foreword

Put two species in contact. Each possesses a treasure house of experience, a perceptive point of view, powerful abilities of comprehension, and habitual skills of expression. Each experiences the world from a fundamentally and irrevocably different point of view. Yet both have a mutual need and interest in sharing and exchanging experience. (Think of woman and man, parent and child, human and Klingon.) Put these two species in contact, and what do you get? A failure to communicate.

One party is quick, careful, painstaking, accurate, tireless, and eager to accomplish a million tasks. The other party has excellent perceptual and physical coordination, an attraction to grand but vaguely specified concepts, a slow reaction time, a short attention span, and an inability to remember or handle more than seven things at once. What do you get? A failure of computers and humans to communicate. (And you thought I was describing woman and man.)

The user interface is the unbreakable glass barrier on which humans and computers scribble in their struggle to communicate. Failure in this struggle means at least frustration and waste, at worst loss and danger. Success in this struggle means that humans and computers can collaborate to get good and useful things accomplished. If you are responsible for this success, you need skill to make it happen.

This skill depends on many levels of knowledge and experience. You need to understand the goals of each side—what the human is trying to do and what the computer is trying to do. You need to understand the abilities of each side—what the human can do and what the computer can do. You need to understand the terms of a common language—the signs and signals that humans and computers can exchange. You need to learn a style and discipline in manipulating the terms of this language, so that unfamiliarity and misuse do not cloud the communication. And, finally, you need to put goals, abilities, language, and style together to make successful communication.

The book that you have in your hands (if you are a human) or in your memory (if you are a computer) is a unique, organized guide to these needs for communicating through the glass barrier. It starts from a basis of the elements of the language—the text, numbers, tables, menus, graphs, icons, helps, buttons, bars, windows, cursors, pop-ups, desktops, and so on. It furnishes style and discipline in assembling and using these elements. It justifies style and discipline not according to arbitrary rule books but according to the cognitive, human, and social factors on which they are based. And, finally, it links the stylish and disciplined use of the communication language to the purposes of communication, showing how to enable the human and computer to say to each other what they need to say.

When a human uses a program and when a program uses a human, their communication should be easy, responsive, fluent, and productive. When people observe such successful communication, they make comments such as, "My nine-year-old kid could do that" and "What was so complex about that?" If you are the one who made the communication successful, you should not boast or enumerate the problems that you solved. You should just nod and smile and say "It was nothing," and silently thank the human and computer authors of this book.

And after these authors and you have solved human-computer communication, perhaps you will help us with woman and man, parent and child, human and Klingon?

Nicholas Zvegintzov[1]
Software Maintenance News, Inc.
141 St. Mark's Place
Staten Island, NY 10301 USA
e-mail: 72050.570@compuserve.com

---

[1] Nicholas Zvegintzov is the author of *Software: The Maintenance Manual* and the annual *Software Management Technology Reference Guide,* published by Software Maintenance News, Inc. In 1983, Zvegintzov founded the newsletter *Software Maintenance News* (*Software Management News* as of 1992), and in 1985, he and other stalwarts founded the Software Maintenance Association. Together, they gave a name and professional respectability to what most programmers do—supporting and extending existing programs rather than developing new ones.

# Preface

## SHOULD YOU BUY THIS BOOK?

You should buy this book if you are:

- A developer who feels strongly that your application's user interface should be efficient and attractive, but you don't have a lot of time to research interface design. *The GUI Style Guide* puts much of the information you need at your fingertips.

- A developer who hates working on interfaces because it takes time away from *real* programming (the code behind the interface that is the actual application). However, you no longer have to choose between good interfaces and good code. With the arrival of easy-to-use interface generators, the universe of potential interface developers expands beyond the programming staff to graphic designers, technical writers, and human interface professionals. In other words, buy *The GUI Style Guide* and give it to someone else.

- A developer who is about to transform a character-based interface into a graphical interface. Whenever possible, we annotate the differences between the two types of interfaces and mark the areas of difficulty.

- A developer of programming systems and tools who wants to see the various platform standards, rules of thumb, and screen-object styles all in one place. Throughout *The GUI Style Guide*, we compare and contrast various aspects of the standard graphical user interface platforms.

- A technical writer or graphic artist who is tired of fixing the interface in the documentation—in other words, explaining how something works when it should be self-explanatory. With the availability of so many software and intellectual tools (as described in this and other recommended books), you can fix the interface yourself.

- A human-factors professional who knows how to make an interface usable but could use a quick reference guide to the whys and wherefores of good interface design.

- A student or teacher of programming, technical writing, or human factors.

Do *not* buy this book if you need an interface programming cookbook. *The GUI Style Guide* contains no subroutines or code samples. It simply helps you make interfaces that make sense.

## STRUCTURE

The book is divided into three parts:

- Part 1, Widgets, describes the standards for developing windows, dialog boxes, icons, buttons, and menus.

- Part 2, Text, explains how to write messages and online help.

- Part 3, Design, covers three topics you have to design into your applications from the beginning, not just slather on at the end—internationalization, charts and graphs, and color and pattern. Also included is a chapter on multimedia design and development.

At the end of each chapter is a "Resource" section (except for the multimedia chapter, which is nearly all resources). In the fast-moving field of software development, conferences, periodicals, and online forums are often the best way to stay current. We have included as many people, organizations, and resources as we could find for each topic, but we would be happy to hear about additional ones.

# Acknowledgments

We didn't write this book alone. We had lots of help, some in the form of hardware and software, some in the form of advice and criticism, and some in simple understanding from our friends and families when we had to leave early or miss events altogether because we had to work on THE BOOK.

Special thanks to the friends and colleagues who reviewed the manuscript and who saved us from some horrible mistakes: Clint Goss and the lovely Vera Shanov, Gayle Gustafson, Katy Murphy, Mark Smith, Paula Valentine, and Robert Wimpfheimer. The authors take full responsibility for any remaining errors, mistakes, gaffs, blunders, typos, and inaccuracies.

Thanks to the many people who found information for us, even when they couldn't imagine what we wanted it for. We especially want to thank Harry Blanchard, Yuri Engelhardt, Chris Quain of the IBM Design Program, Martin Sheerin, Tom Siliato, and Sylvia Woodard.

We also want to thank the developers, managers, and technical communicators at The Small Computer Company, Comware Systems, EJV Partners, L.P., and other software houses who, over many years, graciously taught us almost everything we know about user interface design. At EJV Partners, special thanks to Tom McDonald for making it possible to finish the book *this* year instead of next year.

We would like to thank everyone who had a hand in the development and design of this book: Kim Fryer, now at Random House, who originally proposed that we do this book; Alan Rose, who rescued it when it was about to disappear from the original publisher's balance sheets; David Pallai and his colleagues at AP PROFESSIONAL for taking on the book; Katherine Antonsen for her excellent editing and Lauralee Reinke for her excellent formatting and desktop publishing; and Jack Putnam, whose encouragement and expertise kept us going during this long and difficult process.

Finally, we want to thank our parents, Arlene and Richard Stanwick and Jane and Edward Fowler, not only for encouraging us to follow what must have seemed like odd career paths ("Cartooning? You can make a living cartooning?" "Writing? You can make a living writing?") but for being artists, humorists, research historians, and writers themselves. Role models are important.

## CORRESPONDENCE

Please feel free to write to us with comments, additions, and corrections: AP PROFESSIONAL, 955 Massachusetts Avenue, Cambridge, MA 02139, or via CompuServe at 76266,3131 (Internet: 76266.3131@compuserve.com).

Susan L. Fowler and Victor R. Stanwick
August 1994

# Introduction

Many computer users today do not appreciate what a revolution interactive computing is. Those of us who once stood in line at system operators' desks to hand in stacks of punch cards can now sometimes be found in the halls of corporate America, smiling to think we lived in such a time.

Of course, the transition from batch processing to time-sharing using computer terminals was only the start of direct interaction between a computer and an end user. First, the personal computer arrived, with its command line and character-based screen. Finally, Xerox PARC's developers came up with the first graphical user interface (GUI).

Although the GUI was invented at Xerox PARC, Apple Computer popularized it. Apple Computer successfully marketed the transition from a command-line and menu-driven interface to one in which the user directly manipulated objects represented as icons. This type of GUI can be viewed as the very beginning of an "object-oriented" user interface. However, the notion of applications was not completely hidden from the user—in other words, users had to open an application to work on a file, rather than selecting a file and working on it with any number of applications.

The move toward a complete object-oriented user interface is currently embodied in the notion of the "documencentric" view, in which users will work with documents instead of applications. Documents are to be composed of various components: text, graphics, spreadsheets, data links, sound, animated graphics, and minimovies. Most of the computer platforms are moving toward this documencentric view and, in fact, today's software developers are expected to embrace this idea and produce releases with a profusion of these capabilities.

## THE DESIGN FUTURE

So document-centered applications are the new wave in user interface style. But what's next? For developers and designers working on current software projects, this may appear to be a philosophical question of just passing interest. However, given the tremendous growth in the computer industry, the issue takes on great importance for professionals involved in the development and implementation of software. Too narrow a focus on a single approach can leave you ill prepared for changes.

A scene in the future:

> I'm walking to my car when my personal communication device (PCD) goes off. Since a call on my PCD can mean many things (voice, data, paging, simple message), I pull the device out of my shirt pocket and glance at the symbol at the top of the small screen. The symbol is a graphical representation of a small human head with an open mouth, which tells me that I have a voice call. I press a small button on the device and say "hold." This voice command causes the system to answer the call and announce to the caller that I will be on the line within a minute or two and to please hold. If the caller does not wish to hold, he or she can leave a voice message.

The technology to implement such a system exists today, although it is still quite costly. However, tremendous technological and marketing forces are working not only to drive down the cost of this technology, but also to convince the general public that such communication devices and services are as essential as electric lights.

Yet many exciting new technologies are not immediately seen as essential. The reason for the delay has been simple lack of usability. For example, video tape recorders for home use have been around for some time. But until the cassette version of video tape was developed, the general usability of the product was not high enough to drive the marketability of the product.

A second example, again having to do with the videocassette recorder (VCR), is the difficulty that people have setting them up to tape TV shows. Apparently, the word *finally* reached the ears of the designers: Today, virtually all VCRs are programmed (should we simply say "set"?) by means of a menu on the TV screen. This theme continues today: The more usable products make their own markets, leaving their less-usable competitors behind.

## TWO POSSIBLE PARADIGMS

Two trends today strongly indicate that the document orientation of application software is soon going to be outdated. The first is the explosion of information-gathering technology. Articles in the popular press about the Internet and the information highway appear almost daily. The second is the continued increase in computer power and the reduction in cost and size.

Together, these two trends suggest that computers will be used for many purposes having nothing to do with documents. In fact, the next user paradigm may very likely be "intent driven" instead of object driven—using computer appliances and computer-based technology to "do something."

For example, instead of manipulating an icon that represents an object or even a set of steps, an intent-driven user interface will let the user communicate the "end result" or "intention" to the computer. The computer will then analyze the various options and, perhaps without further prompting, carry out the individual actions necessary to reach the desired end result—the "intent" of the user.

## INTENT-DRIVEN INTERFACE

Implementation of an intent-driven user interface would entail elimination of the keyboard as a primary input device. It would be replaced by voice commands, hand or finger gestures, and true three-dimensional displays—either a landscape on the screen or, eventually, a holographic display in space.

Need information on various species of tigers? Touch the library object, and say, "Tigers: What are the different species?" The computer responds, "Do you want information on extinct species or just nonextinct species?" "Nonextinct."

The conversation could go on like this for some time, but it would be strictly under the control of the user. Again, it is the user's intention that drives the conversation. This interface style is exactly how humans find out about the world in real life—by interacting with real objects and by asking questions and getting responses.

## BACK TO THE PRESENT

"But," you might be saying to yourself, "I've never designed *any* type of GUI before, much less a three-dimensional one! What does this have to do with me?"

This discussion is meant to give you a context for designing *any* user interface, computer-based or not. It all comes down to a very simple concept: The "thing" you're designing will be used for *someone* to *do something*. More than anything else, good design means keeping the "*do something*" always in focus.

GUI implementations certainly make it easier for people to do the kinds of things that computers are good for—spreadsheets, word processing, databases, information services, and so on. However, the notion of the intent-driven user interface is as useful in designing contemporary systems as it will be in the future. A clear focus on the end-user's intention can often be the difference between getting most of the interface right and having to redesign and reimplement unusable sections of the application.

In short, always remember the cardinal rule of good user interface design: "Someone is going to use this thing as part of the job he or she is doing. *My* job is to make it as easy as possible for that person to get that job done."

Mark W. Smith
Human Factors User Interface Designer
Spinnaker Reach Ergonomics Consulting
spinreach@delphi.com

## RELATED READING

Cringely, Robert X. *Accidental Empires: How the Boys of Silicon Valley Make Their Millions, Battle Foreign Competition, and Still Can't Get a Date.* Reading, MA: Addison-Wesley, 1992.

Gause, Donald C., and Gerald M. Weinberg. *Exploring Requirements: Quality Before Design.* New York: Dorset House, 1989.

Morse, Alan, and George Reynolds. "Overcoming Current Growth Limits in UI Development." *Communications of the ACM*, vol. 36, no. 4, April 1993, pp. 73–81.

Norman, Donald A. *The Psychology of Everyday Things.* New York: Basic Books, 1988. (Also published as *The Design of Everyday Things.*)

Nussbaum, Bruce, and Robert Neff. "I Can't Work This Thing!" *Business Week,* April 19, 1991, pp. 58–66.

# PART I

## WIDGETS

# 1

# Windows and Dialog Boxes

"Once I understood that the automatic teller machine's program was a conversation, everything fell into place. 'Hello, what would you like today? How can I help you?' Most people understand how to have a conversation."

Sylvia Woodard, Two Twelve Associates.[1]

One of the pleasures of programming is that you can turn a computer into anything at all. The same computer can be, from one moment to the next, an arcade game, a scientific calculator, a fax machine, a typewriter, a virtual room, an airplane cockpit, a psychotherapist . . .

However, the computer screen is two-dimensional, not three-dimensional. At a minimum, windows can be designed to contain the desired objects, flattened as they may be. In inventive applications, however, windows can also act as portholes into the object's space—or, in the case of games and multimedia adventures, into entirely other worlds.

This chapter explains window-design basics—the different kinds of windows, parts of windows and dialog boxes, how to transform character-based applications into window applications, and so on. There is a warning, however: To develop a system that users like, or will at least accept, you must

---

[1] Two Twelve Associates helped design the interface for Citibank's automated teller machines (ATMs). Contact them at 596 Broadway, Suite 1212, New York, NY 10012-3224; 212-925-6885.

involve them. You have probably heard this advice before and decided to disregard it because of time, financial, or management constraints. Nevertheless, there are now so many usability testing methods that you should be able to find one that suits your corporate culture, time frame, and budget. Plus, it costs hardly anything to educate yourself about joint application design, usability testing, really rapid prototyping, and so on—see Designing for and with Users for a list of recommended books and resources.

## TYPES OF WINDOWS

A window, according to the Motif style guide, is "an area of the screen (usually rectangular) that provides the user with the functional means to communicate with an application and through which an application can communicate with the user" (OSF, 1992, p. 7-2).

There are three types of windows—primary window, secondary window, and toolbar. These windows exist on the desktop. Definitions for these windows follow.

### Desktop

The "desktop," "workplace," or "root window" is the physical screen itself. The desktop is a background to, and is often completely covered by, the application windows.[2]

Companies that develop turnkey systems (a computer dedicated to a single specialized application like land surveying or professional typesetting) may take over the entire computer, overlaying or replacing the default desktop with their own proprietary desktops.

However, the software industry is moving away from captive computers to more open systems. In most GUI systems, the desktop's primary role is to give users access to the programs installed on the computer by displaying each program's—or, on object-oriented systems such as OS/2, each object's—icon.

---

[2] When you add "wallpaper" to a system, you're changing the look of the desktop rather than any individual window.

## Application versus Object Orientation

IBM—and, so far, only IBM—differentiates between "application-oriented interfaces" and "object oriented interfaces." However, as the PowerPC and Taligent, IBM's and Apple Computer's joint projects, become more popular, and as IBM joins the effort to update the Motif guidelines, object-oriented interface ideas may become more common.

An "application-oriented" interaction means that the user opens an application, then picks a file or other object to work on. For example, the user opens a word-processing program, then selects a file.

"Object orientation" means that the user picks an object, then selects an application. For example, the user picks a document (in icon form) and drops it on the printer icon to print it. Object-orientation aficionados use the analogy of a hammer and a nail—you don't pick up a hammer, then look for something to nail. Instead, you have a board that needs nailing, then you look for a hammer and a nail.

Keep in mind, however, that object-oriented *interfaces* are not necessarily the same thing as (or even attached to) object-oriented *programs*. In object-oriented programming, the objects are blocks of code that:

- Use classes organized in a hierarchy, with each object being an instance of a class of similar objects. In a warehouse management system, for example, the software version of 8,000 red-coated paper clips in a box might be an instance of the class OFFICE-STUFF.

- Inherit the behavior and characteristics of their parent objects (the objects higher in the hierarchy). This means that if you have defined your parent OFFICE-STUFF object as red office supplies, then all children objects will be red office supplies as well (unless you override "red" with "blue" for a particular instance of OFFICE-STUFF). To change the characteristic of all related objects, you simply change the color of the parent.

- Encapsulate data and/or instructions in a single block of code. Each object is the programmatic equivalent of a black box—you send it information and you get back results, and how the object does this is irrelevant (unless it does it wrong, in which case you have to find the author and make him or her fix it).

But, as IBM points out, "the [interface] objects that a user works with do not necessarily correspond to the objects, or modules of code, that a programmer used to create the product." Inheritance and hierarchy are more subtle in object-oriented interfaces than in object-oriented programming, since inheritance is based on similarities in look and feel, not on classes of objects. Also, an object-oriented interface uses the idea of "containment"— putting objects (documents, say) inside other objects (file folders)—which has no parallel in object-oriented programming (IBM, 1992, p. 9).

For more information about the differences and similarities of the two types of interfaces, see Chapter 1 of IBM's *Object-Oriented Interface Design* (IBM, 1992, pp. 4–10), and Chapter 8 in Theo Mandel's *The GUI-OOUI War, Windows Versus OS/2* (Mandel, 1994, pp. 225–294).

## Primary Windows

The primary window, which is generally called the application window or main window, is the place in which the main interactions between a user and a program or object occur.

Other characteristics of an application window are:

- It appears when the user opens an object or application by selecting its icon or menu option.
- It remains open until the user takes a specific action to close it.
- It is movable and resizable. Everything happens inside it, except that movable dialog boxes (see Types of Dialog Boxes) can be moved outside (but not underneath) its borders (Microsoft, 1992, p. 49).

For more on application windows, see How to Design Main Windows.

### *Secondary Application Windows*

A single software package may have as many independent primary windows as it needs. For example, database generators with creation and run-time modules probably require two main windows, one for creating the database and the other for the finished end-user version.

However, sometimes you want to contain a set of primary windows within the frame of your application. On the Microsoft Windows development platform, you can embed "document windows" within an application window (Microsoft, 1992, pp. 50–51). Document windows can be resized, even iconized, within an application window (see Figure 1.1). However, the document window cannot be moved outside the application window. If moved far enough, it seems to slip under the application window's edge.

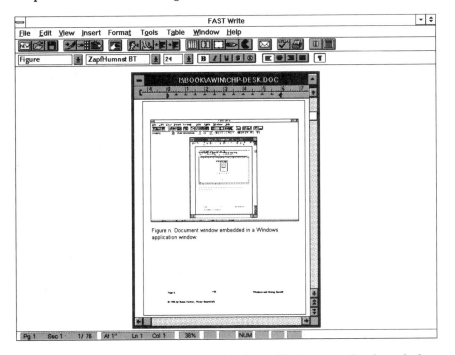

**Figure 1.1  Document window embedded in a Windows application window**

## Secondary Windows

Secondary windows are usually called dialog boxes or panels. A dialog box is a window in which the computer can present several alternatives, ask for more information, or warn the user that an error has occurred.

A dialog box is always associated with a parent window, but its parent can be either an application window or another dialog box. If the parent window is closed, hidden, or minimized, all of its dialog boxes are closed, hidden, or minimized as well.

Most dialog boxes are accessed from pushbuttons on the application window or from menu options. Message dialog boxes, however, appear automatically when the application requires more information or discovers a situation that merits the user's attention. (See Chapter 4 for help writing messages.)

Other characteristics of dialog boxes are:

- They can be movable or fixed.
- They always sit on top of their parent windows. They cannot be put behind their parent windows.

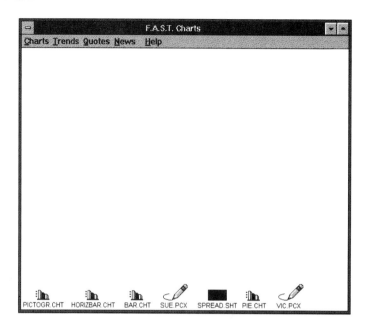

**Figure 1.2  Iconized subwindows in a Windows application window**

- They can be any size as long as they are smaller than their parent window.

- They can be modal (not allowing interaction with other windows) or modeless (allowing interaction with any other window).

For more information on the varieties of dialog boxes, see Types of Dialog Boxes.


## Toolbars and Palettes

Toolbars and palettes (see Figure 1.3) are small windows or boxes that:

- Provide constant access to important tools—for example, a set of text-formatting buttons for a word-processing program.

- Contain buttons labeled with pictures rather than labels—toolbars and palettes are generally used for graphics.

- Provide quick access to tools that require mouse interaction. For example, although circle and rectangle drawing tools should be accessible from a menu, the user has to use the mouse to shrink or enlarge the figure.

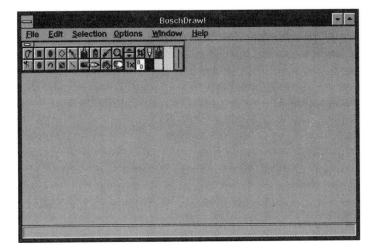

**Figure 1.3  Toolbar for a drawing program**

- Float above the application window at all times (as long as the user doesn't close them).

Stand-alone toolbars and palettes generally have a close button and a border that you can use to drag them around the window, but no other window controls. Toolbars and palettes can also be embedded in control panels—see Control Panels for more details.

## PARTS OF A MAIN WINDOW

The parts of a window (see Figure 1.4) are:

- Window frame, which defines the window's boundaries, separates each window from others that it may overlap, and lets users resize the window.
  *Exceptions:* Macintosh windows put a resize button at the bottom right corner. NeXTStep windows put a resize bar at the bottom of the window.

- Title bar with a control menu at the left, minimize and maximize/restore buttons at the right, and the title in the middle. (The maximize button is replaced with a restore button when the window is already maximized.) For more on titles, see Title Recommendations.
  *Exceptions:* The OS/2 guidelines recommend that you include a "small icon," which is a picture of the window's regular icon, next to the

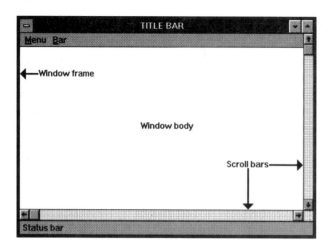

**Figure 1.4  A generic main window**

control-menu button. Users can use the small icon in the same way as they use the normal one—for example, they can print a file by dragging its small icon to the printer icon (IBM, 1992, p. 300). Macintosh windows replace the control-menu button with a close button; the minimize, maximize, and restore buttons with a zoom box; and put a resize button at the bottom right corner. NeXTStep windows have a "miniaturize the window" button instead of the control-menu button and a "close" button instead of minimize, maximize, and restore buttons.

- Menu bar. See Chapter 3 for information about developing menus. *Exceptions:* The menu bar is not used on Macintosh windows, since all menus appear on the top line of the desktop.

- Control panel (optional), described in Control Panel.

- Scroll bars, if the data in the window can exceed the size of the window. In OS/2 and Microsoft Windows systems, each scroll bar can contain a split box, which lets users divide windows into two panes (separate views, scrollable separately, of the same window).

- Window body, "workspace" (Microsoft), or "client area" (Motif), which contains data, labels, section headings, controls, buttons, onscreen prompts, and anything else the designer wants to put in it. Windows may also have "views," in which different aspects of a particular object come to the forefront—for example, a document might have normal and outline views, or a set of files might have icon and text-description views.

- Status, message, or information bar. The status bar contains, at a minimum, page or window identification. It can also contain status messages, mode indicators (CAPS, NUM, etc.), and running commentary on the buttons and menu options that the user highlights. *Note:* The OS/2 guidelines put a status area just below the menu bar and a message area as the last item at the bottom of the window. The guidelines for the other platforms put the status and/or message bars as the last items; sometimes the message bar overlays the status bar.

- Command line (optional). See Chapter 3 for more on command lines.


## Title Recommendations

The title is a navigation aid, not just a bit of fluff at the top of the window. Users need titles to orient themselves in the system: "I thought I chose BoschPaint. Is that where I am?" Therefore, make sure that the title on the window matches the label on the icon or menu option from which the users access it.

If your application has files, append the name of the selected file to the application name. However, each platform handles file names a bit differently.

*Macintosh* systems put only the file name in the window title. Make sure that the file name (as it appears in the Finder icon) and the window title match (Apple, 1992, p. 143).

*Microsoft Windows:* Use a space, a hyphen, and another space between the application name and the file name. Use uppercase letters for the file name (Microsoft, 1992, pp. 55–56). For example:

```
Microsoft Word -- CHP-WIN.DOC
```

*Motif* guidelines say that applications with a single main window should use the application name. Applications with more than one main window should use the purpose of each window as the title (OSF, 1993, pp. 7–8).

*NeXTStep* guidelines state that if a window contains a file, the title bar should display the name of the document, followed by two spaces, an em dash, another two spaces, and the path of the folder where the file is located (NeXT, 1992, p. 69). For example:

```
JobRecords  --  /Net/machine/home/records
```

Otherwise, the title of the window is the application name.

*OS/2* has two orientations, application and object, as described in Applications Versus Object Orientation (IBM, 1992, pp. 510–511). For application-oriented windows, use *Application Name - Object Name:*

```
Editor - Chp-Win
```

For object-oriented windows, use *Object name - view name:*

```
Customer List - Icons
```

*Note:* OS/2 titles are left-justified rather than centered like titles on all other platforms.

When more than one view of the same object is open, IBM recommends appending a colon and a number to the view name—for example, `Customer List - Icons:2`—and changing the first view's title from:

```
Customer List - Icons
```

into

```
Customer List - Icons:1 (IBM, 1992, p.511).[3]
```


## Titles for Unnamed Windows

If the window doesn't contain a file or the current file is as yet unnamed, the title should contain a placeholder file name:

- The recommended Macintosh style is to use `untitled` (all lowercase) for the first new window, then `untitled 2`, `untitled 3`, and so on, for all additional windows. Add numbers only where there is more than one open untitled window on the screen and don't retrofit a "1" to the first `untitled` window (Apple, 1992, pp. 142–143).

- The recommended Windows style is to use a word such as `Document`*n*, `Spreadsheet`*n*, or `Chart`*n*, where *n* is a number. Or you can simply use `(Untitled)`. Use upper- and lowercase rather than the usual uppercase as a visible cue that the placeholder is not an actual file name (Microsoft, 1992, p. 56).

---

[3] Although the Microsoft guidelines are silent on this issue, Microsoft programs also use ":n" for multiple copies of the same window.

## Control Panels

A control panel or bar is an array of options designed to be accessed quickly and repeatedly (Galitz, 1994, p. 146). It is generally used to hold toolbars, palettes, rulers, and ribbons.[4]

A control panel can be fixed to the edges of the main window or float above it in a dialog box or secondary application window. Floating control panels require a title bar (with or without title, since it's only used as a drag point) and a window-control menu (so the user can close it).

A well-behaved application lets users:

- Hide or close all components of a control panel, so that users have more working space when they need it.

- Access all controls from menus or the keyboard as well as the mouse. (Access to controls should always be obvious and explicit—don't require manual-hostile users to somehow stumble upon an important palette or tool set.)

---

## HOW TO DESIGN MAIN WINDOWS

Application windows can be divided into three functional types:

- *Form-based data-entry windows*, in which the user types data from a paper form into the computer. The typist generally looks at the paper form rather than the monitor and, in fact, uses the field labels only to find his or her place again after an interruption.

- *Conversational windows*, in which the user interacts with the computer. Activities that fall into this category range from CAD/CAM, games, and automatic teller machines, in which the user interacts only with the software, to airline reservation and telemarketing systems, in which the user interacts with a customer and the software at the same time.

---

[4] The term "palette" usually refers to a set of color- or pattern-selection buttons. A "toolbar" usually contains tools—pencil, eraser, selection lasso, rectangle drawing tool, and so on. "Rulers" are simply onscreen measurement aids. Most programs with rulers let users change the unit of measurement (from inches to picas, say, or from miles to meters). "Ribbons" are second-string toolbars—they contain additional settings and commands.

- *Inquiry windows*, in which the user searches for and retrieves specific information. Applications in this category range from telephone operators' databases to CompuServe libraries to CD-ROM encyclopedias.

The different functions require different window layouts.

- The most important design factor for form-based windows is matching the window to the form, line for line. Visual design is irrelevant.

- Conversational windows require careful visual organization and should include complete, unabbreviated labels and onscreen instructions. Status and informational messages, prompts, and context-sensitive help are useful here.

- Sophisticated visual design is important on inquiry windows, both because users need to see the desired information immediately and because inquiry applications tend to be market-oriented.

Each type of layout is described below.

## Form-Based Data-Entry Windows

The most sophisticated form-based data-entry windows are found in high-volume mainframe and minicomputer applications at insurance companies, hospitals, and banks. Many of these applications are being further automated with document imaging technology and machine-readable forms.

However, not all database applications require mainframe and minis and high-volume data-input techniques. In fact, consultants using database development systems and fourth-generation languages have created a cottage industry of small PC databases. If you are such a consultant, you can carry the mainframe designer's tradition of efficient data entry into the GUI environment—provided that you design the windows correctly.

The most important design problems for form-based windows are:

- Fitting all of the fields in the relatively limited space of the window
- Organizing the data
- Speeding up data entry

### Fitting the Data

Since the source of the form is a paper document (see Figure 1.5), the most effective form-based data-entry window is an exact image of the document.

| PART 1: EMPLOYEE INFORMATION | | | |
|---|---|---|---|
| Employee name (last, first, middle initial)<br>Please print | | ¤ Active<br>¤ Long-term disability | ¤ Retired<br>¤ COBRA |
| Your Social Security number | Date of birth<br><br>MM I DD I yy | ¤ Male<br>¤ Female | Marital status<br>¤ single    ¤ married<br>¤ widowed  ¤ divorced |
| Home address<br>Street | City | State | Zip Code |

| PART 2: COMPLETE ONLY IF CLAIM IS FOR A DEPENDENT | | | |
|---|---|---|---|
| Patient's name (last, first, middle initial) if a dependent | | | Dependent Status<br>¤ spouse    ¤ other<br>¤ child |
| ¤ Male<br>¤ Female | Marital Status<br>¤ single    ¤ married<br>¤ widowed  ¤ divorced | Date of birth<br><br>MM I DD I yy | Dependent's Social<br>Security Number |
| For a child 19 years or older,<br>is child is full-time student?<br>¤ Yes        ¤ No | Is the child employed?<br><br>¤ Yes ¤ No | Date of graduation: | Name and address of<br>school/employer: |

| PART 3: CO-INSURANCE INFORMATION | | | |
|---|---|---|---|
| Was your spouse employed at<br>the time of treatment?<br>¤ Yes        ¤ No | If yes, name and address of employer | | |
| Social Security Number | Date of Birth<br><br>MM I DD I yy | | Co-insurance?<br>¤ Yes ¤ No |
| Name and address of co-insurer | | Policy number | |

**Figure 1.5  Sample paper form from which the window was developed**

When the source and target match line for line, the data-entry employee can simply type from the form, filling in the entire screen without glancing at it or, at most, looking at it to check for typographical errors and to correct errors detected by software edits (Galitz, 1989, p. 121).

However, a paper form can have a dozen fields on a single line. To fit the fields horizontally, shorten the labels: If done correctly, abbreviating the labels won't change the usability of this type of window.

*Labeling:* Studies of abbreviation methods have found that truncating words is the best method for creating abbreviations. However, since you often end up with the same abbreviation for more than one word, you need backup methods.

- Contracting words to the first and last letters, deleting vowels, and phonic puns—FX for effects, XQT for execute—are good backup methods (Schneiderman, 1992, p. 163).

- Using the abbreviations found in commercial abbreviation dictionaries may help users who move often between jobs in the same industry. See Abbreviation Dictionaries for some of the most common dictionaries.

- Creating ad hoc abbreviations doesn't work well, because people have different ideas about the "natural" abbreviation for any one word— "meeting" might be "mtg" or "meet," for example (Galitz, 1989, p. 115).

When you use abbreviated labels, teach users the full word or words first, then its abbreviation. Novices who used full command names before being taught two-letter abbreviations made fewer errors than those who were taught only the abbreviations or who made up their own abbreviations (Schneiderman, 1992, p. 162).

It is necessary, but not sufficient, to list all of the abbreviations in onscreen selection sets—also let users know what your abbreviations stand for. Put the definitions online in the help system or hand out commercial abbreviation dictionaries or your own quick-reference guides.

*Paging and scrolling:* A paper form can have 60 or more lines on an 8 1/2-by-11 inch sheet of paper. Although you can't fit the same number of lines on one screen, you can display the entire form using the correct scrolling or paging strategy.

Apple suggests that when a user is at the edge of the window, the system should automatically scroll one line of text for word processing applications, one field for databases or spreadsheets, and one object (if possible) for graphics programs (Apple, 1992, p. 167).

For form-based windows, however, you might want to scroll by full screens. In other words, when the user fills all of the fields on the first window, pressing [Tab] or [Enter] on the last field moves him or her to the next page. (Depending on the system, you might want to save the entries automatically between window changes. Multimate and Radio Shack's Scripsit word-processing programs used to save your work whenever you changed pages, which was a lifesaver in the days of unreliable hardware.)

Better yet, let the user page up and down. Although expert users do well with either paging or scrolling, novices prefer paging, since it is familiar and less disorienting (Galitz, 1989, pp. 75–76).

Paging or scrolling by full screens works best if you divide the set of screens into logical sections. For example, an insurance claim form might be divided into its standard sections—insured name and address, claim information, information on dependents, doctor's information, and so on.

Although you don't want to use valuable screen real estate for titles and other cues, you can put them in the status bar. Here are some recommendations.

- When an application has more than one page or screen per form, show a page or screen number in the status bar. Use the "Page n of n" format to give users a sense of where they stand in the record.

- You might also put the screen number on the paper form—use an inconspicuous spot such as near the right margin.

- If you've broken the form into logical sections, put a subtitle in the status bar. The subtitle should match the title of the same section on the paper form.

Make sure that users can move backward as well as forward through the windows. This is especially important for systems in which corrections to already saved data are difficult and time-consuming—for example, when the data entries are referenced by a number of databases, such as in double-entry accounting systems, or when saved data are sent by modem to a mainframe in batch and cannot be retrieved, only overwritten. When users can't go back to correct an error, they will often abort the job, losing pages of work, and start over.

### Organizing the Data

Paper forms grow in unorganized ways—a legal requirement changes or marketing needs more information, so another question gets added to the end of the current form. After a few years, page 2 or 3 of the form is a mishmash of unrelated information.

Although data-entry clerks don't, strictly speaking, need to understand the information on the forms, they have no way to correct or even recognize errors if they don't understand it. Since repairing errors is far more expensive than doing it right in the first place, ensuring that the forms make sense is more cost-effective than training, job aids, or online help.

Therefore, for an understandable system, organize the form before you try to program the window against it. For help, see Wilbert O. Galitz's *Handbook of Screen Format Design*, which contains a chapter on form design. Graphic artists regularly design forms—ask them for advice as well.

The primary organization styles are:

*Sequence:* Arrange information in its natural order. An address, for example, is usually written as street, city, state or province, and postal code. If your system has a built-in zip code lookup, however, you might have the data-entry employees enter the zip code first, so that the system can automatically fill in the city and state. (Make sure that they can override the system when necessary, however—commercial zip code databases contain errors.)

*Frequency:* Put the information most often needed at the top. For example, since everyone who fills out a medical claim form enters his or her name, address, employer, and insurance ID number, this information appears at the top of the form.

*Function:* Group items according to their functions. On the federal tax forms, for example, all income appears in one section, all exemptions in another section, and what you owe (or are owed) in the last section.


## Speeding Up Data Entry

There are many ways to speed up data entry without forcing data-entry personnel to type faster, which leads to carpal tunnel syndrome, repetitive strain injuries, anger, frustration, and depression. Some of them are: expanding partial entries, using defaults, avoiding the mouse, and creating good data-entry codes.

*Expansion:* One of the most effective ways of speeding up data entry is to use the power of the computer to expand sets of letters into full words or phrases. For example, if your company has offices in a limited number of locations, when the user types a one-letter office code, the system can expand it to the full name—N for New York, say.

Another strategy is to create new entries based on earlier entries. For example, you can enter defaults in new fields based on the entries in earlier fields—"if Y, then skip to Sex and enter F." One clever reinsurance system generated entire paragraphs by embedding names, dollar amounts, and other data from earlier entries into boilerplate legal text. Except for the earlier entries, the text was guaranteed free of typographical errors.[5]

---

[5] For more information about intelligent databases, contact IMTI Systems, 355-33F South End Avenue, New York, NY 10280; 212-488-9400.

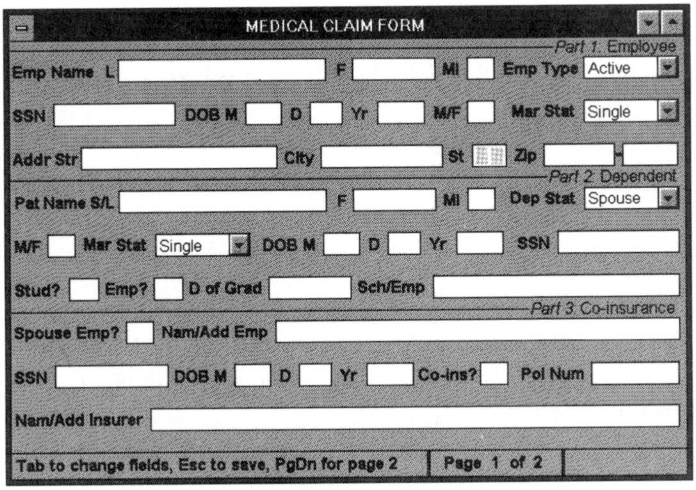

**Figure 1.6 Typical form-based data-entry window**

*Defaults:* In Figure 1.6, note the default entries ("Active," "Single," "Spouse,") and the grayed state field ("St")—the cursor skips over it, then the program fills it automatically when the typist enters the zip code. The "S" in front of the patient last name field is an onscreen hint that if the patient and the employee are the same, typing S will automatically move the typist to the next relevant section of the form. In general, using defaults is a time-saver. If 80 percent of entries are the same, then let users type only the 20 percent that don't fit the usual pattern.

*Typing is faster than mousing:* Codes can speed up data entry, provided that you put them in combination boxes.[6]

Combination boxes (see Figure 1.7) let users type the entire code or word, but also lets them select the correct code from a list if they forget which one to use. Cognitive psychologists have found that people are better at recognizing familiar patterns than remembering them, which is what makes lists such helpful tools. For form-based data entry, however, being able to type a known code is better than having to select it from a list. Why? Because you don't have to take your hands off the keyboard—most data-entry personnel are touch typists and do not like to switch from keyboards to mice and back again.

---

[6] Microsoft calls these boxes "combo boxes" (Microsoft, 1992, pp. 114–116). IBM calls them "drop-down combination boxes" (IBM, 1992, p. 266).

Employee Status:

| Longterm disability |   |
|---|---|
| Active | ▲ |
| COBRA | |
| **Longterm disability** | |
| Retired | ▼ |

**Figure 1.7  A sample combination box**

Mouse use is slower than keyboard use. Average times for keyboard and mouse use are (Lewis, 1993, p. 4.2.1):

- One keystroke on a standard keyboard: 0.28 second (ranges from 0.07 second for skilled typists doing transcription to 0.2 second for average 60-wpm typists to over 1 second for unskilled typists)

- Move hand to mouse: 0.36 second

- Use mouse to point at a screen object: 1.5 second (may be slightly lower for a small screen; increases for a larger screen or smaller object).

*Buttons for check-offs?* Printed forms often have check-off boxes for such items as sex, employee status, and various yes/no questions. Since they look like checkbuttons or radio buttons, you may be tempted to translate them into buttons. However, unless the data-entry clerk can turn the button on with a keystroke, he or she may be happier with a combination box or even a text-entry field with a good edit check (in a yes/no field, for example, the edit check accepts only Y, N, y, or n).

*Developing good codes:* Recommendations for developing effective data-entry codes are:

- Use common letter combinations. Because a good typist develops a body memory for certain letter combinations, he or she will type common combinations—TH and IN, for example—more quickly than uncommon ones such as YX or JS (Galitz, 1989, p. 117).

- The characters in the pairs I-1, O-0, B-8, and Z-2 are often confused. Try to eliminate them from your codes (Galitz, 1989, pp. 117–118).

- The letters Y, N, V, Z, Q, U, and G are most likely to be printed illegibly. On forms that will be filled in by hand, try not to use these letters for codes (Galitz, 1989, pp. 118–119).

- Long codes or numbers are easier to remember and enter if they are broken into three- or four-character groups. This is one of the reasons that phone numbers and Social Security numbers are written in chunks rather than as long strings of numbers.[7]

*Long-cut:* A popular input shortcut has been found to slow down users. "Auto-skip" or "automatic return" makes the cursor move automatically to the next field as soon as the last character in the previous field is completely filled. Theoretically, since this feature eliminates keystrokes ([Tab] or [Return]), it should be faster than manually tabbing between fields. Instead, it usually slows the user down. The reason for this is that since fields are rarely completely filled, the user has to stop, check the screen to find out whether the cursor is still in field 1 or if it has jumped to field 2, then either tab from field 1 or start entering data in field 2, depending on the cursor location. Although pressing [Enter] or [Tab] for each field seems like extra work, the user has no decisions to make and the typing is rhythmic and consistent. In a study of manual versus automatic tabbing, researchers found that manual tabbing led to faster performance and fewer keying errors (Galitz, 1989, p. 108).

## Conversational Windows

The conversational-window category (see Figure 1.8) includes everything from Sega and Nintendo games to desktop-publishing systems to telemarketing applications. What makes them "conversational" is that users look at and interact with the window itself—they are not tied to a data source.

Since the user's attention is on the window, more information is better than less. Field labels should be long and detailed; adding onscreen help and prompts (provided that users can turn them off) is recommended.

Conversational windows can become crowded, however, and highly complex. Without careful design, they can become confusing. Wilbert O. Galitz, in his most recent book, *It's Time to Clean Your Windows,* has a simple test for whether a conversational window is designed correctly: "Can all screen elements (field labels, data, title, headings, types of controls, etc.) be identified

---

[7] Each chunk of a phone number or Social Security number is meaningful. Phone numbers are broken into area code (state or province, except in high-population areas), exchange (neighborhood), and local number. The first three digits of a Social Security number represent the state in which the holder applied for the number, the next two are a code representing the year in which it was issued; and the last four are assigned at random (Blocksma, 1989, pp. 162–164).

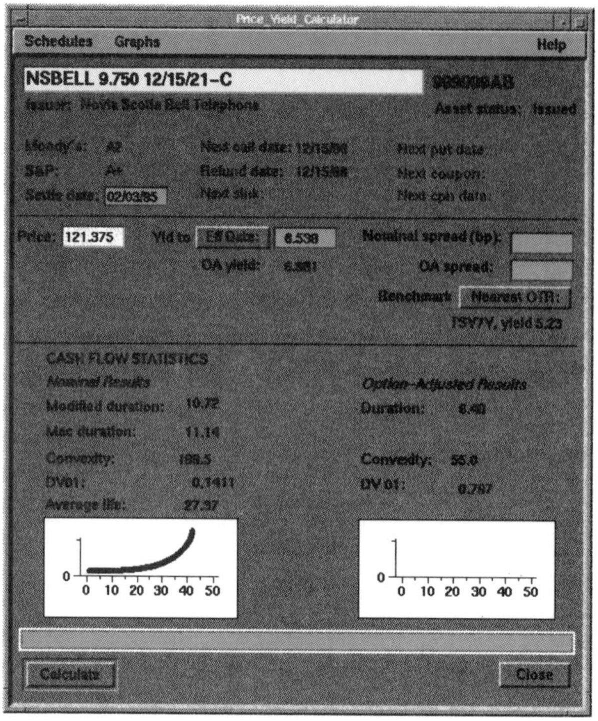

**Figure 1.8  Typical conversational window**

without reading the words that make them up?" (Galitz, 1994, p. 58). Designing windows that pass this test takes work. It is not, however, hard if you:

- Lower the density—see How to Reduce Density
- Align fields and labels well—see How to Align Fields
- Write labels correctly—see How to Write Labels

## How to Reduce Density

The overall density of a conversational window should be between 25 and 30 percent (Galitz, 1994, p. 75). In other words, 70 to 75 percent of the window should be empty space. This is not wasted space, however—the blank areas draw the user's eye to what you want him or her to notice—in the same way that advertisements draw your eyes to the car or the eyeliner the advertiser is trying to sell you.

Studies support these recommended densities. For example, NASA researchers found that densely packed screens (70 percent full) took an average of 5 seconds to scan, while sparsely filled screens (30 percent full) took only 3.4 seconds. By improving the labeling, clustering related information, using indentation and underlining, aligning numbers, and eliminating unnecessary characters, the researchers reduced task time by 31 percent and errors by 28 percent for inexperienced users. Experienced users did not improve their task times, but they did become more accurate. A study of telephone operators found that maintaining a 25 percent density and suppressing redundant family names reduced search times by 0.8 second per search (Schneiderman, 1992, pp. 318–319).

Measure density by counting the total number of characters on the window and dividing by the total number of characters available on the window. This number was easier to calculate on character-based screens, which were always 80 characters across and 26 lines deep (minus a few lines for status bars and other screen apparatus). However, you can count the number of characters on the window by typing "1234567890123 . . ." across the top and down the side. For the total, multiply the horizontal and vertical counts. To simplify a complicated window, start with these recommendations:

*Organize the information:* Put the most often entered or referenced information at the top and the least often used information at the bottom or in dialog boxes. See Organizing the Data for more ideas.

*Position buttons correctly:* Put buttons related to the entire window at the bottom of the window. Put buttons related to sections of the windows inside those sections.

*Create functional groups of information:* For example, put names and addresses at the top, billing information in the middle, sales data at the bottom. Break up the groups by putting them in boxes or by separating them with blank lines or rules. If there are no functional breaks, then break the screen every five to seven rows (Galitz, 1994, p. 78).

*Provide only need-to-know information:* If the user is looking for price relative to yield, then show him or her price and yield at the top of the window. Information about the company issuing the stock, the number of shares outstanding, the broker recommending the stock, and so on can go at the bottom of the window.

*Put nice-to-know information in dialog boxes:* For instance, a lab analyst needs to know whether a test result was positive or negative—therefore, this information goes on the main window at the top left. However, he or she might also like to know the statistical likelihood of a false positive using this batch of reagent, this level of humidity, and so on. This information can go in a separate dialog box.

Keep in mind that expert users (stock brokers, air traffic controllers, and so on) prefer denser displays because more information per screen means fewer computer-related operations. Since these users are familiar with the data, they can find what they need even on a screen with 70 to 80 percent density. You can, however, reduce overall complexity by organizing the data well, as described in Organizing the Data, and by reducing the number of alignments.

### How to Align Fields

Figure 1.9 illustrates unaligned fields on a window. However, minimizing the number of columns and rows—the number of alignment points, in other words—we can reduce window complexity. To test the complexity of your windows, use this formula (Galitz, 1994, pp. 72–73):

- Count the number of fields, labels, titles, buttons, boxes, and so on on the window.
- Count the number of different row alignment points.
- Count the number of different column alignment points.
- Add them up.

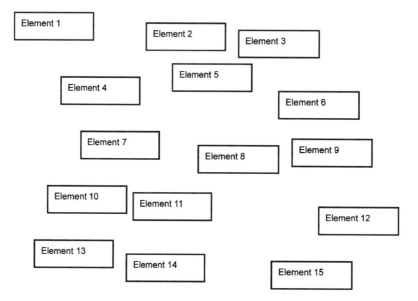

**Figure 1.9  Unaligned fields on a window**

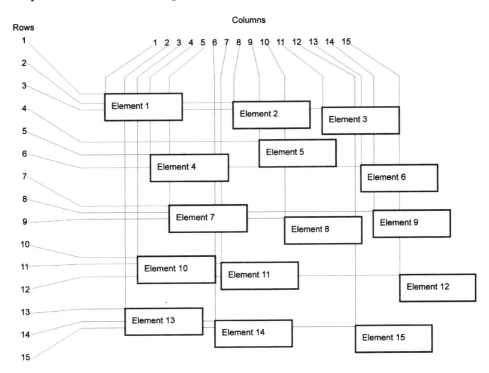

**Figure 1.10 Starting points for rows and columns**

Using this measure, Figure 1.10 has a complexity of 45 (15 elements, 15 starting points for rows, and 15 starting points for columns). The revised version in Figure 1.11, however, has a complexity of 23 (15 elements, 5 rows, 3 columns), which means that it is about 49 percent simpler.

*What labels should look like:* Field labels should be a word or phrase followed by a colon and a space:

```
Label:_Data
```

*Where to put labels:* Put labels for columns above the column. For example:

```
Names    Birthdays
Lucy     10/06/53
Sally    11/03/51
Mud      12/05/58
```

Put labels for individual fields in front of the fields. For example:

```
Price: 123.45    Yield: 6.78
```

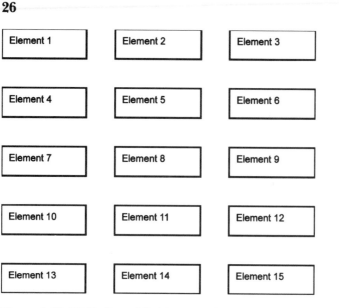

**Figure 1.11 Well-aligned fields on a window**

Don't put labels *above* individual fields—as well as using two lines per field instead of one, the labels tend to become visually detached from their fields:

```
Price:     Yield:
123.45     6.78
Spread:    Benchmark
10 bp      TSY10Y
```

*Justification:* Labels should be as close as possible to their fields and line up vertically in unobtrusive but organized columns. The best way to fulfill both requirements is to use either of the following to alignment methods.

*Left-justify the labels and the fields separately:* To figure out the spacing, find the longest label and add one space between it and the set of fields. Align the rest of the labels with the first letter of the longest label (see Figure 1.12).

This style works best in two situations:

1. When the data in the fields don't align well—for example, when some fields contain left-justified alphanumeric characters and others contain decimal-aligned numbers.

2. When the window has a mixture of input and protected (view-only) fields. Since protected fields don't have text-entry boxes, you can only align the labels.

Modified duration:   **10.72**

Mac duration:        **11.14**

Convexity:           **189.5**

DV01:                   **0.1411**

Average life:        **27.37**

**Figure 1.12  Left-justified labels and left-justified fields**

*Right-justify the labels and left-justify the fields:* This style works well when the data themselves are aligned (all alphanumeric or all decimal) or when the field edges are obvious (see Figure 1.13).

### How to Write Labels

Labels can't just look good—they have to read well, too. Recommendations for writing labels are:

- Use symbols—$, #, %—only if all users will understand them. Remember that "all users" may include international users. See Chapter 6 for more information.

- Try to use short, familiar words—"Cut" instead of "Reduce," for example. As well as being more readily understood, short words tend to be more punchy and authoritative. However, keep in mind that a long, familiar word is better than a short, unfamiliar one (Galitz, 1989, pp. 74–75).

- Try to use positive terms, which are generally better understood than negative terms. For example, use "Growing" instead of "Not Shrinking."

- When comparing objects, use the "more" rather than the "less" dimension if you have a choice. In other words, concentrate on the element

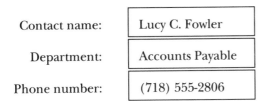

**Figure 1.13  Right-justified labels and left-justified fields**

that is becoming larger rather than the one that is becoming smaller (Galitz, 1989, p. 74).

- Don't stack letters to label a column or a table:

  C
  o
  l
  u
  m
  n

  Most readers read words whole, not one letter at a time, making the stacked style difficult to read. Instead, put the label above the column or table or turn the entire word sideways.

- For better readability, don't break words between lines.

- Show abbreviations, mnemonics, and acronyms without punctuation. Periods and other punctuation marks take up valuable window real estate without adding anything to readability.

## Inquiry Windows

At a minimum, inquiry windows let users search for and look at information. However, the idea of "inquiry" goes far beyond answering simple questions. Inquiry can also mean quickening a child's curiosity about dinosaurs or sending an adult on a chase from "wild goose," for example, to "Chinese cuisine" and "influenza epidemics."

The recommendations in earlier sections of this chapter—careful organization, easily scannable text and instructions, and the right amount of information per window—are just as important in inquiry applications as they are in database applications. However, the abundance of tools available—color, photographs, sound and video clips, Internet access, and so on—can make you lose your head and your users lose their ways. Therefore, this section concentrates on the basics, or, in other words, how to create readable, understandable, and consistent inquiry windows. For truly extraordinary interfaces, however, consider hiring a professional design team—see How to Find Designers.

### How to Design an Inquiry Window

Designing a sophisticated inquiry window is more like designing a magazine page than a software window—shape, color, and typography are paramount.

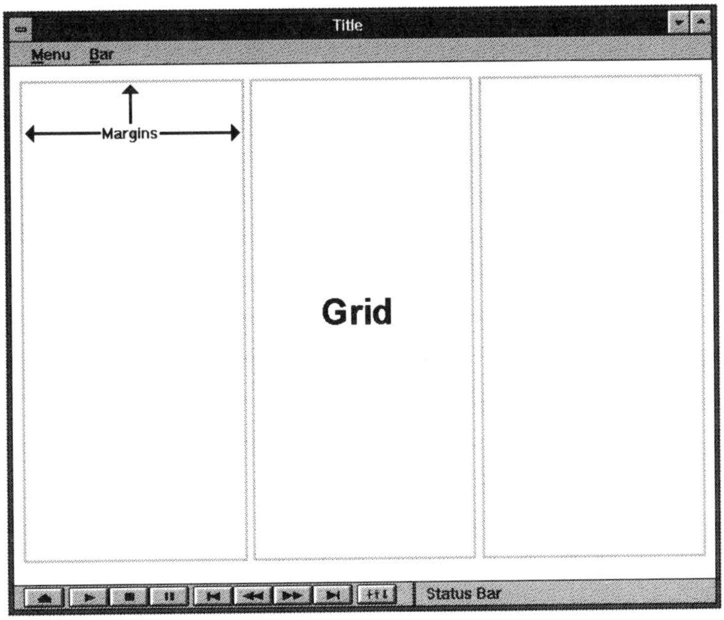

**Figure 1.14  A three-column grid**

To create an easily understood window, however, remember just three ideas: consistency, placement, and proportion.

*Consistency:* Define a standard window for the entire application. Magazine designers use the "grid system" to define pages and simplify layout, and this system works just as well for window design. (See Figure 1.14)

The first step in defining a grid system is selecting margins and, within the margins, a number of columns (Hurlburt, 1978, pp. 47–64). The columns can contain either text or pictures. Chunks of text and pictures can remain within the confines of the columns or break out across multiple columns, as shown in Figures 1.15 and 1.16)

Since all window elements remain within the grid, the windows look consistent as the user moves from one to the next. Since the elements are not rigidly restricted to one column, however, you can accommodate a variety of picture shapes and sizes. *Note:* The grids in Figures 1.14, 1.15, and 1.16 are visible as gray boxes around the columns. However, the grid in the finished product can be visible or invisible.

*Placement:* Can the user find what he or she is looking for immediately? Or, in a marketing presentation, does the user see what you want him or her to see immediately? You can satisfy either criterion by knowing two facts: People look at pictures first, and (in Western societies, at least) their eyes move

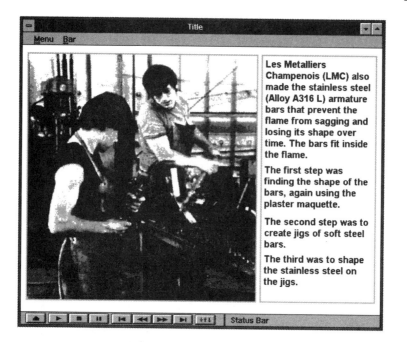

Figure 1.15  Picture, text (© 1994 by John D. Watson, Brooklyn, NY)

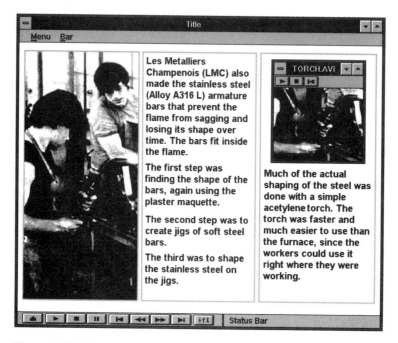

Figure 1.16  Picture, text, video

**Figure 1.17 Point towards the text**

from the upper lefthand corner to the lower righthand corner. Therefore, on a straight inquiry window, put your most important piece of information at the top left. In a marketing presentation or multimedia application, put your pictures or headlines at the top left, the text to the right. If you can, try to have something in the picture point to the text, as shown in Figure 1.17. Controls (buttons, sliders, and so on) generally go on the bottom of the window.

*Proportion:* For graphic elements such as photographs and illustrations, certain proportions are more pleasing than others. The "golden rectangle," whose proportions are 1 to 1.618, has intrigued Western artists, designers, and philosophers since antiquity. If you draw a line through the golden rectangle to create a square, the remaining area is another golden rectangle—a most interesting property. Another popular rectangle, especially in Japan, is the double square (Marcus, 1992, pp. 7–8). (See Figure 1.18.)

Typography requires a good sense of proportion as well. Luckily, there is a simple rule of thumb for the correct relationship between line length and type size for optimum readability: *A line of text should be about one and a half alphabets long* (39 characters, in other words). Actually, most of the type books say 40 to 60 characters per line is fine, depending on how wide or narrow the letters in the typeface are (Romano, 1984, pp. 86–87). Forty to sixty characters is about five to eight words (an average word is eight characters long). The easiest way to find the right size is to create a "ruler" in your chosen typeface by typing 1 to 0 four times:

```
12345678901234567890123456789012345567890
```

Change the type size of the ruler until it fits the desired line length.

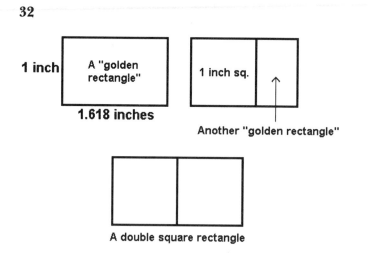

Figure 1.18  A golden rectangle and a double square

## A Popular Navigation Method

Even though most Americans cannot program their videocassette recorders, multimedia presentations often use VCR buttons for navigation. Figure 1.19 illustrates the most common buttons and their meanings (IBM, 1992, pp. 38–41).

| Play forward | Play backward | Fast forward | Rewind | Stop | Pause | Record | Load | Unload |
|---|---|---|---|---|---|---|---|---|
| ▶ | ◀ | ▶▶ | ◀◀ | ■ | ▌▌ | ● | ▼ | ▲ |

Figure 1.19  Common VCR buttons and their meanings

## How to Find Designers

Say that you have an idea that you're *sure* will be a best-seller—so sure that, to pay for its development, you're willing to mortgage the company's office building, your house, your parents' house, your boyfriend's house, and to apply for a dozen credit cards with large credit lines. Get a professional interface designer. A professional can give your product its own unmistakable look and feel, as well as save you from making serious color, shape, style, and legal errors.

There are at least four ways to find a designer.

- *Contact designers' professional organizations.* Ask for the names of designers in your area, the name and address of the local chapter's newsletter in which you can advertise, and the name and phone number of the local meeting manager, who may be willing to mention your project at the next meeting. For a list of interface design organizations, see Design Organizations. If you're creating a multimedia application, also check Multimedia and Design Organizations in the Resources section of Chapter 9.

- *Put a want-ad online.* If you have access to the Internet, CompuServe, America Online, or another online service or bulletin board, put a request or job advertisement on the online design lists and news groups. See Online Design Resources.

- *Call the designers of the interfaces you admire.* To find an application's designer, look for a design credit in the "about this program" menu item (usually but not always on the Help menu). Also look in books and magazines that cover interface design. See Design Books and Periodicals.

- *Contact schools with interface design programs.* The University of Maryland's Human-Computer Interaction Laboratory (described in Chapter 9) and Carnegie Mellon's Department of Design, for example, connect students with commercial clients who need imaginative interface design solutions (Boyarski and Buchanan, 1994, pp. 25–35). Apple Computer sponsors an Interface Design Project at a number of colleges and universities (Garrison, et al., 1994, pp. 62–69).

## DIALOG BOXES

"Many of the detailed functions that must be dealt with by a user do not occur frequently enough to warrant a dedicated space in the application window. They would be confusing if they were that persistent."

Shiz Kobara on the important and often misunderstood role of dialog boxes in graphical user interfaces (Kobara, 1991, p. 219).

A dialog box is a secondary window used to hold settings, messages, and infrequently used functions or information. Its design is simple (see Parts of a Dialog Box), but its uses are many (see Types of Dialog Boxes).

Dialog boxes can be accessed from menus or pushbuttons (menu options and pushbuttons marked with ellipses generally lead to dialog boxes).

Most development kits include a handful of predefined dialog boxes. For example, the Motif toolkit supplies five types of dialog boxes: command, file selection, message, prompt, and selection. The message dialog box itself has five supplied subtypes: error, information, question, working, and warning (OSF, 1993, pp. 9–23). Apple includes a standard file dialog box (it lets users select files) and a "save changes" alert box (Apple, 1992, pp. 200–201).

## Parts of a Dialog Box

The parts of a dialog box (see Figure 1.20) are:

- *Box frame*, which defines the box's boundaries and separates each box from the other boxes and windows that it may overlap. Modeless dialog boxes have complete frames with title bars; modal boxes often have thin borders and no title bars. For more on modes, see Types of Dialog Boxes.

- *Body*, which contains messages or various controls, such as lists and buttons.

- *Title bar*, which is used primarily as a drag point. Titles may or may not be required, depending on the platform and the use to which the dialog box will be put. See Dialog Box Titles.

- *Control menu or close button.* OS/2 and Microsoft put a control menu at the upper-left corner of the dialog box. Macintosh and NeXTStep put a close button there instead.

- *Disposition pushbuttons.* See Dialog Box Disposition Buttons.

Unlike primary windows, dialog boxes *do not* contain:

- Minimize, maximize/restore buttons, or resizing options. *Note:* Standard NeXTStep dialog boxes can contain miniaturize buttons and resizing bars, but it's rare that either would be needed (NeXT, 1992, p. 78). OS/2 dialog boxes can be resized, but resizing is not a requirement (IBM, 1992, p. 434).

- Menu bar

- Status, message, or information bar

- Scroll bars: See Sizing Dialog Boxes

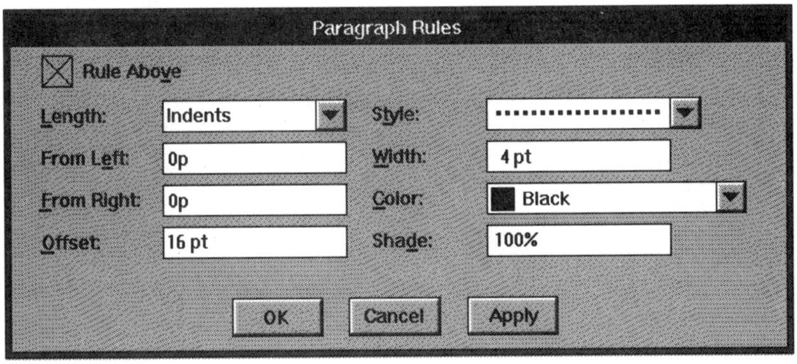

**Figure 1.20  Generic dialog box**

## Types of Dialog Boxes

A dialog box is defined by its mode, a state in which only certain actions are available to the user. Here are some typical modal situations.

- While using the spelling checker, the user discovers that he or she needs to add some text. This is done without closing the spell-checker box.

- When the user is in drawing mode, he or she can use only drawing tools.

- When an error message appears, the user cannot change the item that needs to be fixed without closing the error dialog box. As soon as he or she closes it, the message and its instructions disappear.

- To generate a book file, the user needs to type a list of chapter names into a separate file. To find the file names, he or she looks in the application's *File Open* dialog box. However, because the *File Open* box is modal, the user cannot copy the names from the *File Open* box into the book file, nor can he or she type them while the *File Open* box is on the screen.

The first case is an example of a modeless interaction. The second case is a legitimate use of a mode. The last two cases are exasperating and, therefore, may be illegitimate uses of modes.

Because of the strong possibility of frustration, all of the platform guidelines suggest that you limit modes to these types of situations:

- When the mode is long-term—word processing rather than drawing, for example. (In effect, every type of application is a mode.)

- When the mode matches a real-life situation. For example, picking tools from a drawing palette resembles picking up real pencils, pens, and brushes—you can only use one at a time.

- When the mode is "spring-loaded"—in other words, when the user has to hold down the mouse button or a key to maintain the mode. Scrolling with the mouse or holding down the [Shift] key for extended selection operations are spring-loaded operations.

- When the application displays an alert message to prevent the user from making a mistake or when the system displays a message to warn the user of a problem or change in state—"The network is being shut down in 2 minutes. Please save your work and exit now" (Apple, 1992, pp. 12–13).

Dialog boxes have various default modes, depending on their functions. Table 1.1 compares and contrasts them.

## Designing Dialog Boxes

To design dialog boxes correctly, you have to:

- Pick the right title—see Dialog Box Titles
- Match disposition buttons to the box's function—see Dialog Box Disposition Buttons
- Make the box the right size—see Sizing Dialog Boxes
- Place them in the right places on the desktop—see Dialog Box Locations

### Dialog Box Titles

In general, a dialog box title should match the label of the menu option or pushbutton from which it was accessed (minus the ellipsis). Requirements for additional information vary from platform to platform.

*Macintosh:* Modeless dialog boxes have titles and close buttons at the top. Movable modal dialog boxes have titles but no close buttons. Modal dialog boxes (including message boxes) have no title bars, but titles may appear in the box itself.

Note that a Macintosh dialog box controls the menus at the top of the screen—options may be grayed out, depending on the context and the modality (Apple, 1992, pp. 181–191).

**Table 1.1  Dialog Box Modes**

| Type | Use and Behavior | Examples |
|---|---|---|
| Modeless | The most common. Useful for making multiple setting and style changes. | Toolbars and palettes; find-and-replace panels. |
| Movable (or application) modal | Useful for requesting input; for doing short, simple tasks; and for actions that are done infrequently. Lets the user switch to and work in another application. The user can move the box so that it doesn't obscure the area where he or she is working. | Box used to change a password; box used to do page setup; style changes that are applied by closing the box; notification that an operation is running in background. |
| System modal, alert modal | The user can work only inside the dialog box. He or she must respond to the dialog box before doing anything in any application. | System warning message; alert box. |
| Semimodal (Windows only) | The user can do certain operations outside the dialog box as a way of responding to the dialog. | In a spreadsheet, the user might specify ranges by selecting cells with the mouse as well as with controls inside the dialog box (Microsoft, 1992, p. 127). |

*Microsoft Windows:* A movable dialog box has a title, plus a control menu with only move and close commands. A dialog box that cannot be moved has no title bar. However, unmovable dialog boxes are used only rarely, generally for system messages (Microsoft, 1992, p. 125).

Message dialog boxes always have titles, and their titles contain the name of the application generating the message or, in the case of networking or multitasking environments, the source of the message plus the word "Message" (Microsoft, 1992, p. 128).

*Motif:* The title in a dialog box should indicate the purpose of the box (OSF, 1993, pp. 7–8).

*NeXTStep:* Most NeXTStep dialog boxes (called "panels") follow the window conventions—a title in the title bar, a close button at the upper left, a resize bar at the bottom (if useful), and a miniaturize button at the upper right (if appropriate). Attention panels, however, do not have titles and the user closes them using a close pushbutton at the bottom rather than the standard close button in the title bar. Attention panels are strictly modal—they disable the rest of the application until the user selects a disposition button (NeXT, 1992, pp. 76–78).

*OS/2:* Titles vary according to function (IBM, 1992, pp. 510–511).

- The title of a *message* dialog box should be `Object name - action or situation`. For example, `Drive A: - Format Diskette`.

- The title of a *progress indicator* dialog box should be `Object name - action Progress`. For example, `Chapter.doc - Printing`.

- The title of a *help* dialog box should be `Object name - Help`. For example, P10Font List - Help.

- For all other dialog boxes, the title should be `Object name - Purpose`. For example, `Chapter.doc - Find/Replace`.

### Dialog Box Disposition Buttons

A "disposition button" is a pushbutton that acts on the entire window or dialog box (unlike command buttons that act on only a section of the window). You need at least one disposition button per box. This button must close the box but may also have another function; for example, when the user presses an OK button in a message box, he or she both acknowledges the message and closes the box.

Table 1.2 contains some typical disposition buttons and their behaviors. However, keep in mind that:

- An unmodified "Cancel" button is ambiguous. Cancel can be taken to mean "Cancel this operation" or "Cancel [close] this box." If the desired disposition is "Close this box," use Close. If the disposition is "Cancel this operation," add the name of the operation: "Cancel calculation."

- Give the user an easy way to get rid of his or her changes and go back to the default values—for example, include a "Reset" or "Defaults" button that not only empties the fields but fills in the default values.

- Make sure that there is help for every dialog box, especially the error message boxes. Error messages often require more complete explana-

**Table 1.2  Disposition Buttons in Dialog Boxes**

| Name | Behavior | Close Dialog Box? |
|---|---|---|
| Apply | Accept the user's entries. | No |
| Calculate (Compute) | Calculate the requested values. | No |
| Cancel [operation] | Cancel the current operation. | Yes |
| Clear | Empty out all user entries as well as any changes made by the system in response to the user entries. May be the same as Reset (see below). | No |
| Close | Close the dialog box and, if necessary, save or reset the settings in anticipation of the next use of the window. | Yes |
| Help | Help for the entire dialog box. (Button required only in applications for which there is no other way to get help. Motif applications often require help buttons.) | No |
| No | A negative response to a yes/no question. Use with Yes button. | Yes |
| OK | Acknowledge a message; accept entries and settings. | Yes |
| Pause | Suspend an operation temporarily without ending it. See Resume. | No |
| Reset | Remove any changes and return all fields to their default values. | No |
| Resume | Continues a paused operation. | No |
| Retry | Let the user try the operation again—for example, when the paper runs out during a print job or the network fails. | If the problem is resolved, yes. |

*(continued)*

**Table 1.2** *(Continued)*

| *Name* | *Behavior* | *Close Dialog Box?* |
|---|---|---|
| Run | Start a batch or background operation. | Replace with a "wait" pointer or other progress indicator. |
| Search | Start a search operation. | Replace with a "wait" pointer or other progress indicator. |
| Stop [operation] | Stops the current operation at the next possible breakpoint. | Yes |
| Yes | A positive response to a yes/no question. Use with No button. | Yes |

tions than you can offer in the small space of the dialog box (see Chapter 5 for more information).

- Use "Yes" and "No" only when they are unambiguous answers to unambiguous questions. For example, the answer to the ambiguous prompt "Do you want to exit BoschDraw without saving CIRCLE?" is "Yes, I want to exit BoschDraw, but no, I don't want to save CIRCLE!"
    The unambiguous version would actually be two prompts:
    —CIRCLE is not yet saved. Do you want to save it? with buttons Yes, No, and Cancel Exit.
    —Do you want to exit from BoschDraw? with buttons Yes, No.

### Sizing Dialog Boxes

To prevent users from mistaking dialog boxes for application windows, make them smaller than application windows. However, what if your dialog box contains so many items that it ends up larger than its application window?

IBM offers two suggestions:

*Use notebooks.* When there are too many components to fit into one dialog box—for example, clip-art illustrations—put them in a notebook or catalog object (IBM, 1992, p. 363). Users can then page through the screens to find the items they want. (See Figure 1.21.)

Whatever you do, don't link box after box of components with pushbuttons (see Figure 1.22).

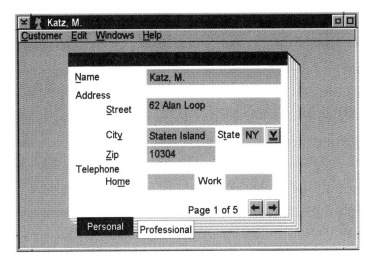

**Figure 1.21 A sample notebook object, in this case used for an online address book**

Notebook objects are supplied with OS/2 development kits and may become part of Motif 3.0. Even if you're not using OS/2 or Motif, check your development kit—any object that uses a paging metaphor will do.

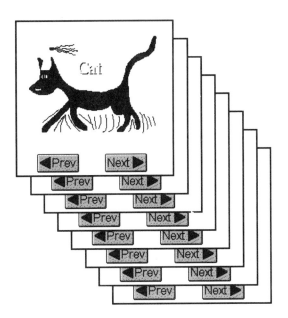

**Figure 1.22 The wrong way to link components**

*Never use scroll bars for dialog boxes:* Don't make the box big enough to hold all of the items, then shrink it and add scroll bars. Instead, add dialog boxes to the dialog boxes: "If the initial size is not large enough to display all components, place less frequently used components out of view" (IBM, 1992, p. 490).

However, layering dialog boxes can violate one of the most important GUI rules: Thou shalt not require more than three levels for a selection (see Chapter 3 for more information on levels). Sidestepping this rule, Microsoft suggests creating an "unfolding" dialog box—accessed with an "unfold" pushbutton (Microsoft, 1992, p. 126):

```
More >>
```

When the user selects this button, the current dialog box gets larger (although still not as large as an application window) and contains both the original and the additional, advanced options. *Note:* The IBM guidelines frown upon unfolding boxes.

However, the best solution to an oversized box is to remove some of its contents.

- Is all of this information needed? Is any of it repeated somewhere else? If yes, remove it so that it only appears once in the application.

- Can labels and messages be shortened without changing their meanings?

- Is all of this information related? For example, a dialog box that is supposed to contain printer options probably shouldn't also contain mail-merge options.


## Dialog Box Locations

When a user opens a dialog box:

- Keep it on top of its parent window. Don't let it slide underneath the window from which it came.

- Position the box where it will get the user's attention without getting in his or her way. For example, put a help window next to the item from which it was requested, not on top of it (if you can, that is—Windows 3.x help always appears in a separate window on the right side of the desktop).

- Position the box near the point at which the user's attention is most likely focused. For example, place the box near the pointer or cursor (IBM, 1992, p. 497).

- Give each dialog box its own unique location rather than letting one fall on top of the next. A stepped alignment scheme is good (Kobara, 1991, pp. 220–221).

- If a dialog box relates to the entire system, center it on the screen. If it relates to a particular document or application object, center it on that application's window (Apple, 1992, pp. 150–151).

- Don't let users move dialog boxes or windows to positions from which they cannot reposition them without resorting to the keyboard or arcane system commands. In other words, don't let the user move the title bar under the top edge of the desktop or the primary window—if the user can't get to the title bar, he or she can't grab the window and move it again (Apple, 1992, p. 155).

## MOVING FROM CHARACTER-BASED SCREENS TO WINDOWS

If you are thinking of transforming your character-based applications into window-based applications, keep in mind that there are significant visual-design differences, not just technological differences, between the two application styles.

### Too Much Furniture in the Windows

In some industries, many standard character-based applications display real-time data in half a dozen or more windows at a time (see Figure 1.23). Financial applications, for example, have always displayed charts, stock quotes, and tickers in windows. To open, close, move, and scroll through these windows, analysts use the arrow keys or type one- or two-letter commands.

Switching from character-based to GUI-based windows should be a simple one-for-one operation. However, GUIs, by default, add scroll bars to windows whenever the content is bigger than the display area. When there are only one or two windows on the display, the standard scroll bars aren't too intrusive, but when an analyst fills the window with 12 charts and quote

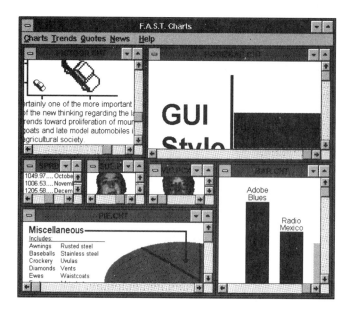

**Figure 1.23  Too much window furniture**

sheets, the most obvious items on the screen become the scroll bars and title bars.

The solution is to modify your development system's default window objects. Use thinner window frames, a smaller title bar (or no title bar), turn off the automatic horizontal scroll bar, and replace the vertical scroll bar with an unobtrusive slider. Also, keep the keyboard-based commands: Commodity traders (for instance) are more likely to use mice as neckties than as pointing devices.

## Tiling versus Cascading

"Tiling the windows" means putting windows next to one another. "Cascading the windows" means layering and overlapping windows. You can choose either method as your application's default style (although users can override it using their environment's windowing options). However, keep in mind that:

- *Tiled windows* seem to be better for single-task activities—tasks requiring little window manipulation can be done faster on tiled windows. Novice users also do better with tiled windows—no matter what the task is.

- *Cascaded windows* seem to be better for situations that require switching between tasks—provided that the users know how to manipulate windows. Although multitasking is quicker with multiple windows, the advantage comes only after the users gain some experience (Galitz, 1989, p. 100).

How many windows should you have open at one time? The active working set seldom exceeds seven. One study found that experienced users have 3.7 windows open at a time (Galitz, 1989, p. 100).

## Alignment May Become Harder to Do

On character-based screens, lining up the edges of labels and fields was easy—you typed monospaced characters on the 26 lines provided, then added or subtracted a few spaces between fields until everything lined up.

GUI screens, however, have no built-in horizontal or vertical alignment points. Trying to align a label to a field by eye is difficult, time-consuming, and inexact. If your company is developing a screen painter or a GUI development system, remember to include a snap-to-grid or select-and-align function (as IBM does in the OS/2 development kit). *Note:* If you add snap-to-grid, make sure that the developer can change the graininess of the grid (a good range is from 1 pixel to about 10 pixels).

## "How Much Room Do I Have?"

On character-based screens, users could tell how much room they had for entries—even without special cues such as overwritable periods (FIRST.....)—because the typeface they used was monospaced. One character filled one space.

Windowing systems, however, use proportional typefaces by default—for example, Arial on Microsoft Windows or Chicago on Macintosh screens. A user can easily bump into the real end of the field before he or she reaches the visual end. In Figure 1.24, the first version of the field uses Arial, a proportional face; the second uses Courier New, a monospaced face. Note the difference in number of characters.

There are a number of possible solutions: Use monospaced typefaces for data entry; add the number of characters to the label as onscreen help; or make the field look shorter than it is so that users stop typing before they fill it up (more useful for user-defined names, which can be any size, than for

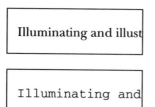

**Figure 1.24  Proportional fonts versus monospaced fonts**

real names or addresses). The best idea, however, is to run usability tests on every solution you can think of—then go with the one that seems to work best.

## REFERENCES

Apple Computer, Inc. *Macintosh Human Interface Guidelines*. Reading, MA: Addison-Wesley, 1992.

Blocksma, Mary. *Reading the Numbers*. New York: Penguin Books, 1989.

Boyarski, Daniel, and Richard Buchanan. "Computers and Communication Design: Exploring the Rhetoric of HCI." *interactions*, April 1994, vol. 1, no. 2, pp. 25–35.

Galitz, Wilbert O. *Handbook of Screen Format Design*, 3d ed. Wellesley, MA: QED Information Sciences, 1989.

————. *It's Time to Clean Your Windows: Designing GUIs That Work*. New York: John Wiley & Sons, 1994.

Garrison, Anne, S. Joy Mountford, and Greg Thomas. "Designing Computers with People in Mind." *interactions*, April 1994, vol. 1, no. 2, pp. 60–69.

Hurlburt, Allen. *The Grid*. New York: Van Nostrand Reinhold, 1978.

IBM. *Object-Oriented Interface Design: IBM Common User Access Guidelines*. Carmel, IN: IBM/Que, 1992.

Kobara, Shiz. *Visual Design with OSF/Motif.* Reading, MA: Hewlett Packard/Addison-Wesley, 1991.

Lewis, Clayton, and John Reiman. *Task-Centered User Interface Design: A Practical Introduction*, P.O. Box 1543, Boulder, CO 80306; available via anonymous ftp from ftp.cs.colorado.edu (referencing Judith Reitman Olson and Gary M. Olson, "The Growth of Cognitive Modeling in Human-Computer Interaction since GOMS." *Human-Computer Interaction*, vol. 5, 1990, pp. 221–265).

Mandel, Theo. *The GUI-OOUI War: Windows versus OS/2*. New York: Van Nostrand Reinhold, 1994.

Marcus, Aaron. *Graphic Design for Electronic Documents and User Interfaces*. Reading, MA: ACM Press/Addison-Wesley, 1992.

Microsoft Corporation. *The Windows Interface: An Application Design Guide*. Redmond, WA: Microsoft Press, 1992.

NeXT Publications. *NeXTStep User Interface Guidelines* (for NeXTStep Release 3). Reading, MA: Addison-Wesley, 1992.

Open Software Foundation. *OSF/Motif Style Guide*. Revision 1.2 (for OSF/Motif Release 1.2). Englewood Cliffs, NJ: Prentice Hall, 1993.

Romano, Frank J. *The TypEncyclopedia: A User's Guide to Better Typography*. New York: R. R. Bowker, 1984.

Schneiderman, Ben. *Designing the User Interface*, 2d ed. Reading, MA: Addison-Wesley, 1992.

## RESOURCES

## Abbreviation Dictionaries

Following are listings of some abbreviation dictionaries.

### *Business*

McGraw-Hill has three abbreviation dictionaries, all compiled by J. M. Rosenberg:

- *McGraw-Hill Dictionary of Business Acronyms, Initials, and Abbreviations*
- *McGraw-Hill Dictionary of Information Technology and Computer Acronyms, Initials, and Abbreviations*
- *McGraw-Hill Dictionary of Wall Street Acronyms, Initials, and Abbreviations*

McGraw-Hill Bookstores, 1221 Avenue of the Americas, New York, NY 10020; 212-512-4100; fax: 212-512-4105. On CompuServe, use GO MH.

### General

CRC Press offers the *Abbreviations Dictionary*, compiled by Ralph De Sola. The eighth edition contains 265,000 definitions in areas ranging from computer jargon, earthquake data, and English grammar and usage, to medical terminology, wedding anniversaries, and zip codes. The 1,328-page book costs $69.95; outside the United States $84.00. Contact CRC Press, Inc., 2000 Corporate Boulevard, NW, Boca Raton, FL 33431; 800-272-7737 or 407-994-0555.

### Medical Codes

The American Medical Association offers CPT codes ("Current Procedural Terminology") and ICD codes ("International Classification of Diseases") on paper and on disk. CPT codes are used to report physician procedures and services to government and private insurance programs. ICD codes describe the disease for which the physician treated the patient. For a catalog of CPT and ICD code books, call 800-621-8335.

### Other Industries

*Desk & Derrick Standard Oil Abbreviator*, 3d ed., by the Desk & Derrick Club, PennWell Books, 1986, 320 pages, 10,500 abbreviations and definitions, $24.95 United States and Canada, $34.75 elsewhere. Contact PennWell Books, P.O. Box 21288, Tulsa, OK 74121; voice: 800-752-9764, 918-831-9421; fax: 918-831-9555; telex: 211012.

## Design Books and Periodicals

These books and magazines offer inspiration and the names of good designers:

*CD-ROM Today: The Leading Guide to PC and Mac Multimedia.* Published bimonthly by GP Publications, Inc., 23-00 Route 208, Fair Lawn, NJ 07410; 201-703-9505. Comes with a CD-ROM sampler.

*I.D.: The International Design Magazine,* 440 Park Avenue South, 14th Floor, New York, NY 10016; voice: 212-447-1400; fax: 212-447-5231. Contains all kinds of international, industrial, and interface design information.

*interactions: New Visions of Human-Computer Interaction,* ACM, 1515 Broadway, New York, NY 10036; voice: 212-869-7440; fax: 212-869-0481; e-mail: interactions@acm.org. A new magazine with lots of screen shots and good ideas.

*New Media.* Published monthly by HyperMedia Communications Inc. (HCI), 901 Mariner's Island Boulevard, Suite 365, San Mateo, CA 94404; 415-573-5170. One of the oldest (four years) and best controlled-circulation multimedia magazines.

*Understanding Hypermedia: From Multimedia to Virtual Reality,* Bob Cotton and Richard Oliver, Phaidon Press Ltd., 140 Kensington Church Street, London, W8 4BN, England, 1993. In the United States, look for it in art bookstores such as the Rizzoli International shops. The book contains many design ideas, both good and bad (unintentionally, one presumes). Well worth $25, nevertheless.

## Design Organizations

Following is a short list of organizations devoted to the graphic side of GUI design (for human factors and usability organizations, see Resources in Chapter 3).

To find out how to add artificial intelligence to your interfaces, join the *American Association for Artificial Intelligence.* The AAAI is "a nonprofit scientific society devoted to the promotion and advancement of artificial intelligence—what constitutes intelligent thought and behavior and how it can be exhibited in computers. Membership is open to anyone with an interest in AI research and development." Contact AAAI Membership, 445 Burgess Drive, Menlo Park, CA 94025; voice: 415-328-3123; e-mail: membership@aaai.org.

The *Association for Software Design* is "a nonprofit organization dedicated to elevating the status of software design as a profession." The organization is "seeking individuals who share our belief that the quality of software and the health of the computer industry depend on recognizing software design as a distinct discipline within the computer science family." If that describes you, contact the Association for Software Design at 2120 Bonar Street, Berkeley, CA 94702; voice: 800-743-9415; e-mail: asd-members@pcd.stanford.edu.

In Australia, contact the *Communication Research Institute of Australia,* P.O. Box 8, Hackett ACT 2602, Australia; fax: +61-62-475-056. Among their many projects are form and interface design.

In Great Britain, contact the *Information Design Association,* P.O. Box 439, Gerrards Cross, Buckinghamshire SL9 9HD, England; phone/fax: 753-892-278.

The *International Visual Literacy Association,* an affiliate of the Association for Educational Communication and Technology, recently celebrated its 25th anniversary. IVLA also sponsors a quarterly newsletter and the *Journal of Visual Literacy.* Educators might be interested in *Visual Literacy in the Digital Age: Selected Readings from the 25th Annual Conference of the International Visual Literacy Association,* edited by Darrell G. Beauchamp, Robert A. Braden, and Judy Clark Baca, 1994. For more information about IVLA, contact Alice D. Walker, Faculty Developer, Educational Technologies, Virginia Tech, Blacksburg, VA 24061-0232; voice: 703-231-8992; fax: 703-231-5922; e-mail: Alice.Walker@vt.edu.

The Università di Bari and ACM SIGCHI cosponsor an annual *Advanced Visual Interfaces* international workshop. "The aim is to bring together experts in different areas of computer science who have a common interest in the design and management of visual interfaces." Topics include cognitive science and metaphor analysis, visual languages and visual database systems, graphical and pictorial communication tools, adaptive interfaces, multimedia environments, and technological developments. For more information, contact Tiziana Catarci, Università di Roma "La Sapienza," Dipartimento di Informatica e Sistemistica, Via Salaria, 113-00198, Rome, Italy; voice: +39-6-49918331; fax: +39-6-49918331; e-mail: catarci@infokit.dis.uniroma1.it or tic@cs.brown.edu.

## Designing for and with Users

Barfield, Lon. *The User Interface: Concepts and Design.* Reading, MA: Addison-Wesley, 1993. A charming book written as a textbook for or an introduction to the field of user interface design.

Bass, Len, and Joëlle Coutaz. *Developing Software for the User Interface.* SEI Series in Software Engineering. Reading, MA: Addison-Wesley, 1991. Explains the concepts underlying the architecture of user interfaces and compares the tools and models available on various windowing systems. Read this book before designing an interface generator.

Brooks, Frederick P. Jr. *The Mythical Man Month: Essays on Software Engineering.* Reading, MA: Addison-Wesley, 1982. How long it takes to write a program, and why it takes so long.

DeGrace, Peter, and Leslie Hulet Stahl, *Wicked Problems, Righteous Solutions.* Yourdon Press Computing Series. Englewood Cliffs, NJ: Prentice Hall, 1990. Explains, among other things, why a "simple" change may not be so simple. Give this book to your end-users.

DeMarco, Tom, and Timothy Lister. *Peopleware: Productive Projects and Teams.* New York: Dorset House, 1987. How to create usable intellectual and physical environments for programmers and technical writers.

Eason, Ken. *Information Technology and Organizational Change.* New York: Taylor & Francis, 1988. How to do joint application design—really. All the pitfalls and how not to fall into them.

Freedman, Daniel P., and Gerald M. Weinberg. *Handbook of Walkthroughs, Inspections, and Technical Reviews: Evaluating Programs, Projects, and Products.* 3d ed. New York: Dorset House, 1990.

Garson, Barbara. *The Electronic Sweatshop: How Computers Are Transforming the Office of the Future into the Factory of the Past.* New York: Penguin Books, 1988. Shows what we, in the computer industry, have done to innocent people and some ways of making the situation better if we refuse to continue along the same paths.

Gause, Donald C., and Gerald M. Weinberg. *Exploring Requirements: Quality before Design.* New York: Dorset House, 1989. How to listen—half workbook, half inspiration.

Glass, Robert L. *Software Conflict: Essays on the Art and Science of Software Engineering.* Yourdon Press Computing Series. Englewood Cliffs, NJ: Prentice Hall, 1991. Includes essays on predicting the future, marketing, the failure of academia and business computer folk to talk to one another, research, and an excellent article by guest artist Nicholas Zvegintzov on the *real* secrets of consulting (see Weinberg).

Grady, Robert B., and Deborah L. Caswell. *Software Metrics: Establishing a Company-Wide Program.* Englewood Cliffs, NJ: Prentice Hall, 1987. A clearly written, slender book about Hewlett-Packard Company's software measurement program.

Hix, Deborah, and H. Rex Hartson. *Developing User Interfaces: Ensuring Usability Through Product and Process.* New York: John Wiley & Sons, 1993. Highly recommended. Describes and explains their process for creating usable interfaces.

Norman, Donald. *The Design of Everyday Things.* Garden City, NJ: Doubleday, 1990. A classic. Explains exactly why you can't open doors, find light switches, or program VCRs.

Weinberg, Gerald M. *The Secrets of Consulting: A Guide to Giving and Getting Advice Successfully.* New York: Dorset House, 1985. For in-house experts as well as outside contractors and consultants. More useful than any 20 how-to-negotiate-anything books.

## General Sources of Information

Following are some general research books:

Robert I., Berkman. *Find It Fast: How to Uncover Expert Information on Any Subject.* New York: Harper and Row, 1990.

Harris, Sherwood (editor). *The New York Public Library Book of How and Where to Look It Up.* New York: Prentice Hall, 1991. Includes online databases as well as paper-based libraries, collections, and other information.

Lesko, Matthew. *Information U.S.A.* rev. ed. New York: Viking Penguin, Inc., 1983.

Makower, Joel, and Alan Green. *Instant Information.* New York: Prentice Hall Press, 1987.

## Official Interface Guidelines

The following books are the platforms' official guides to user interface design.

### *IBM OS/2*

IBM Corporation, *Object-Oriented Interface Design: IBM Common User Access Guidelines.* Carmel, IN: Que Corporation, 1992; 708 pp., $29.95 U.S., $37.95 Canada, £27.45 U.K. Contains the OS/2 and CUA style guidelines. The book also explains and demonstrates the differences between object-oriented and application-oriented interface design, making it very useful for Windows and Motif programming shops whose platforms are about to change from application-oriented designs to object-oriented ones.

## Macintosh

Apple Computer, Inc. *Macintosh Human Interface Guidelines.* Reading, MA: Addison-Wesley, 1992; 384 pp., $29.95 U.S., $38.95 Canada. Even if you aren't writing Macintosh programs, get this book. It covers everything from the true size of a letter (remember the diacritical marks) and how to display colored flags in black and white (the book shows approved substitutions), to the 80 percent solution (if the program's design meets the needs of 80 percent of the users, it's probably good enough and you should stop adding features).

## Microsoft Windows

Microsoft Corporation. *The Windows Interface: An Application Design Guide.* Redmond, WA: Microsoft Press, 1992; 228 pp. and two 3.5" diskettes, $39.95 U.S., $54.95 Canada, £29.95 U.K. *The Windows Interface* comes in two versions—one with diskettes and the other without. The diskettes contain information not in the book—for example, the recommended sizes for icons and buttons—plus a DLL file containing ready-to-use cursors and toolbar buttons.

## NeXTStep

NeXT Publications. *NeXTStep User Interface Guidelines* (for NeXTStep Release 3). Reading, MA: Addison-Wesley, 1992; 184 pp. Most of the guidelines are divided into two parts: Part 1 describes the built-in functionality, and part 2 tells you what you have to do to stay within the guidelines. Programming notes are scattered throughout the book.

## Open Look

Sun Microsystems, Inc. *Open Look: Graphical User Interface Application Style Guidelines.* Reading, MA: Addison-Wesley, 1990; 388 pp. Starts with a set of checklists that help narrow your design decisions. Ends with an appendix on how to write about Open Look (trademark issues and so on). Although Open Look is no longer officially supported, many of the style recommendations are still valid.

### OSF/Motif

Open Software Foundation. *OSF/Motif Style Guide,* Revision 1.2 (for OSF/Motif Release 1.2). Englewood Cliffs: NJ, Prentice Hall, 1993; approx. 404 pp., $27.75 U.S. The Bible for Motif developers.

### PenPoint

GO Corporation. *PenPoint User Interface Design Reference.* Reading, MA: Addison-Wesley, 1992; 310 pp. The book to have if you're writing for the PenPoint operating system. *Note: The Windows Interface* also has a chapter on pen interfaces.

## Online Design Resources

Here are two Internet lists devoted to interface design:

*Information Graphics:* Send a message to listserv@ubvm.bitnet; in the body of the message, type *subscribe ingrafx **your full name**.*

*Visual Design List:* Send a message to *listserv@vtvm1.bitnet*; in the body of the message, type *subscribe visual-l **your full name**.*

For usability and human-factors information, try these lists:

*Organizational Design and Management Technical Group* of the Human Factors and Ergonomics Society: Send a message to *listserv@vtvm1.bitnet*; in the body of the message, type *subscribe orgdes-l **your full name**.*

Computer Systems Technical Group of the Human Factors and Ergonomics Society: Send a message to *listserv@vtvm1.bitnet*; in the body of the message, type *subscribe cstg-l **your full name**.*

# 2

---

# Icons, Buttons, Pointers, and Cursors

---

This chapter describes the little pictures that are part of every graphical user interface:

- Icons, which both identify programs and objects and allow users to access them. See Icons below.
- Buttons, which let users select tools, settings, and processes. See Buttons.
- Pointers and cursors, which indicate mouse movement and, in some cases, the type of activity possible at a particular location. See Pointers and Cursors.

## ICONS

The Icon is that which participates in the nature of the original.

Rev. John Walstead (ret.), Christ Church, Staten Island, New York.

There are two types of pictures in graphical user interfaces: the pictures that appear on icons and the pictures that appear on toolbar and palette buttons.

- Icons represent either system resources (the Macintosh "wastebasket" icon, for example) or applications. Application icons, in turn, represent your company. Think of them as part of your corporate identification system—in other words, your icon is, or should be, a software version of your corporate logo. (In fact, if your icon is better than your logo, you might want to change the logo.) For more on icon design, see How to Design Icons.

- Toolbar buttons represent tools or settings. Although they can be as stylish as your application icons, utility is the primary concern—"Is the meaning of this button obvious and unmistakable?" For more on button design, see How to Design Toolbar Buttons.

## Types of Icons

There are many types of icons:

- Full-size main icons, which are used to start up the applications or select the objects that they represent.

- Mega-icons, which may fill the entire screen and have a number of embedded hot zones (active areas—see Anatomy of an Icon—Hot Zones for details). They are often used in multimedia programs.

- Ear-cons (sound icons) and mi-cons (movement icons) for specialized applications. For example, a recently installed stock-market system uses a "disappearing" icon to visually confirm that an icon has been touched. The icon, brightly colored and with a thick border, zooms from about three-quarters of an inch to nothing in half a second. This type of icon is appropriate for any noisy environment.[1]

- Just-for-looks icons (also called "pictograms"). For example, the icons in the "About . . ." boxes in many GUI programs are pictograms. Note, however, that these icons sometimes dance and do other tricks when you click on them—you should always check.

Each main icon has more than one version:

- Minimized ("iconized") versions of the primary or secondary application window (see Chapter 1 for more on secondary application windows). These icons can, but don't have to, look the same as the desktop-based icon. In fact, developers sometimes create sets of "minimized" icons from which users can choose their favorites.

---

[1] For details, contact CGC Ltd., 6 Fieldcrest Road, Westport, CT 06880.

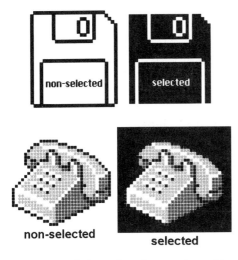

non-selected          selected

**Figure 2.1  Selected and nonselected icons for Macintosh and IBM systems**

- In Macintosh and IBM CUA systems, smaller versions of the icons. These versions are used in lists and, on IBM systems, in the title bar of the window containing its object. Users can manipulate the small icons the same way as they manipulate the full-size icon—they can drag the small icon of a document onto the printer icon, for example, to print it.

- Selected and unselected (or default) versions (see Figure 2.1). In Macintosh systems, for example, when an icon has been selected, its colors shift to a darker shade. In Microsoft Windows, the area around the icon changes color.

Note that two-part programs may require two main icons. For example, many application generators have a creation part that developers use to create screens and processing code for, say, medical office billing systems or truck inventory databases and a run-time part containing programs that use the developers' screens and code. The run-time part may be sold separately to end users. Whenever a program has two (or more) independent pieces, it makes sense to have more than one program icon.

### Standard Sizes

For IBM, Macintosh, and Windows icons, there are two standard sizes: 16 pixels square, and 32 pixels square (see Figure 2.2). Icons can be as small or as large as the target video board allows. However, unless your application

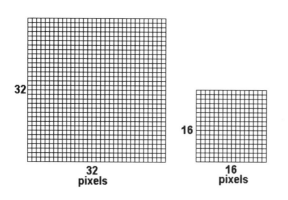

**Figure 2.2  Pixel grids for icons**

requires special hardware and high-resolution displays, design for your market's installed base—for Windows users, this is usually standard VGA, 640 × 480 pixels, and 16 colors or grayscales.[2]

*Note:* Motif icons come in only one size and shape. The image can be either text or a bit map. Every icon has a label, which should be the same text as the title of the corresponding window or an abbreviated version of it (OSF, 1993, p 7-15).

### Helpful Size Hints

William Horton in *The Icon Book* offers many useful suggestions, including this one: "Design is easier if the grid has an odd number of pixels along each side. This is because an odd number provides a center pixel around which to focus the design" (Horton, 1994, p. 162).

Finding the correct size for an icon also depends on the hardware (see Table 2.1). Icons selected with a mouse or trackball should be at least 20 pixels square, touch-screen icons should be about 40 pixels square, and icons selected with a stylus or pen can be 15 pixels square (Horton, 1994, p. 208).

### Anatomy of an Icon—Hot Zones

Hot zones and hotspots go together like fingers and buttons—buttons and icons wouldn't be very useful if you couldn't press them. Every icon (and

---

[2] Not all users have color monitors—keep those laptop computer users in mind when you design your icons and buttons.

**Table 2.1  Recommended Icon Sizes by Platform**

| Platform | Small Size (h×w) | Large Size | Hot Zones | Notes |
|---|---|---|---|---|
| Apple | 16×16 pixels | 32×32 pixels | entire icon | If you don't provide small versions of your icons, the system automatically makes them for you. Icon groups come in three color versions: 1-bit, 4-bit, and 8-bit. There are also icon masks, blacked-out versions of each icon. |
| IBM | 16×16 pixels | 32×32 pixels | entire icon | Icons should not be smaller than 16×16 pixels for visual clarity. Icons can be as large as your screen allows. |
| Microsoft Windows | 16×16 pixels | 32×32 pixels | entire icon | When icons are used as button labels, there must be an "up" and "down" version of each. |
| PenPoint | 18×26 pixels total; 16×12 for body of icon | 34×44 pixels total; 30×30 for body | bottom left corner | PenPoint-compatible displays can be as small as 320×200 pixels. Users can switch between large and small formats. (GO Corporation, 1992, p. 217) |

button) must have a hot zone, the part of the icon that makes something happen when you touch it with the mouse pointer. Every pointer must have a hotspot, the part of the pointer that acts as the finger.

In Figure 2.3, most of the icon—22×22 pixels—is a hot zone, but the hot zone can just as easily cover the entire icon. In fact, the default hot zone *is* the entire icon in most icon-building programs.

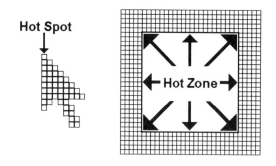

**Figure 2.3  Hot zones and hotspots**

In contrast, the pointer's hotspot is usually very small. In Figure 2.3, although the arrow pointer is made up of 49 individual pixels, only the topmost pixel (the point of the arrow) is the hotspot. For more information, see Hotspots.

## *The 3-D Effect*

Motif and NeXTStep interface objects look three-dimensional, with engraved and beveled edges. IBM CUA and Microsoft Windows 3.x interface objects use what could be called two-and-a-half dimensions. On the IBM systems, although the individual icons and buttons are flat, they float above the desktop surface and project shadows. On Windows systems, buttons have a bit of a bevel and seem to move up and down when pressed, but most of the other elements are flat. Macintosh systems, on the other hand, are unabashedly two-dimensional.

Shiz Kobara explains why the Open Software Foundation developed three-dimensional interface objects for Motif:

"The goal of our . . . GUI was to emulate as much as possible, by visual and behavioral design, the appearance and actions of the real physical world. With the availability of sophisticated color systems, such as we had at [Hewlett-Packard], the opportunity to explore a sophisticated design approach for this new interface became obvious. The design evolved into a scheme in which anything that was part of the system interface would be visually three-dimensional and anything into which the user would type or draw would be visually two-dimensional in a recessed area" (Kobara, 1991, pp. 3–4).

UNIX applications are usually run on workstations with high-resolution monitors and extensive screen processing resources. Macintosh applications, on the other hand, are often not:

> "Three-dimensional effects in icons are difficult to achieve in the Macintosh interface because they require shading and more angled lines. A large percentage of users have black and white monitors and thus complex shading may not display very well on their screens" (Apple Computer, 1992, p. 231).

The Macintosh guidelines also suggest that you use straight lines and 45-degree angles—curves and angles of other degrees don't work well on low-resolution screens because the edges become jagged.

Despite the differences in resolution and style, however, all of the platforms use the same shadowing convention: The virtual light source is at the upper left, so the shadows are always at the lower right.


## How to Design Icons

A successful icon:

- Looks different from all other unrelated icons on the desktop.
- Gives the users some idea of what it does or represents. For example, a word processing program's icon might include a pen, an accounting program might show a ledger, and so on.
- Is recognizable when it is no larger than 16 pixels square.
- Looks as good in black and white as it does in color.

In addition to these constraints, designing icons is a difficult creative process, not unlike painting, composing music, or designing computer programs. To do it well, you need the eye of an artist, the understanding of a psychologist, the practical sense of a human factors engineer, the analysis skills of a technical writer, the expertise of a programmer, the soul of an advertising executive, and the business acumen of an end user.

You may have some of these characteristics but probably not all of them. Then how do you get what you need? Easy—collect one of each and set up a few brainstorming sessions.

Brainstorming and facilitating techniques are outside the scope of this book, but many of the books listed in Designing for and with Users in the

Resources section of Chapter 1 contain descriptions and case studies. Or, find the person in your office with a business administration, marketing, or psychology degree—facilitating and brainstorming are standard parts of these courses of study.

### Recommendations for Designing Icons

You've got your brainstorming group together, so you're ready to begin designing icons. How do you start? The following recommendations will help you translate your ideas into icons.

*At the beginning, don't get too high-tech.* Start designing on paper, not on the computer. Give everyone on the design team a pile of graph (quadrille) paper and a thick marker. Mark off a 32 by 32-box square, and ask everyone to sketch his or her ideas in the large square. Don't worry about exact numbers of pixels at this point—that comes later when you actually draw the icons with an icon editor.

*Show the subject.* This is probably the most direct way of communicating an idea. For example, to represent the idea of printing a file, make an icon of a printer; to delete a file, show a garbage can or wastebasket.

*Use a metaphor.* If you can't show the object itself, try to use an analogy or a metaphor. For instance, say that you need an icon for a maintenance program. To condense a complex idea into a simple image, use a picture of a maintenance tool—a wrench, for example (see Figure 2.4).

*Reuse existing symbols.* Many industries have their own iconographies—electricians have symbols for transistors and electrical lines, telecommunications workers have symbols for central offices and the public network (a cloud), network engineers have symbols for nodes, WANs, LANs, and so on. In the

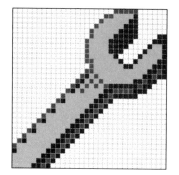

**Figure 2.4  Possible maintenance icon**

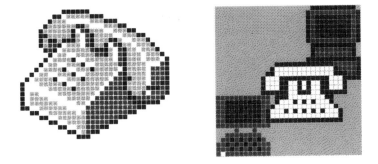

**Figure 2.5  A good design, and a too fancy design**

United States, the American National Standards Institute publishes and/or redistributes national and international standards, including symbol sets. The symbol sets include everything from agricultural equipment and aircraft systems to electrical and mechanical systems to warning signs. For more information, see Resources.

*At the end, simplify the design.* Once you have an icon or set of icons that everyone likes, simplify it. See how many elements (colors, lines, shapes) you can remove without "breaking" the icon. (See Figure 2.5.)

## How to Design Toolbar Buttons

A toolbar is a row of pushbuttons just below the menu bar or a vertical row of buttons on the left or right side of the main application window. (See Figures 2.6 and 2.7.)

Toolbars contain mouse shortcuts for some of the menu options. The shortcuts usually offer only the default version of the option—for example, the Microsoft Word "print" button prints all pages, period. They may also contain graphic tools—in CorelDraw!, for example, the toolbar contains zooming and panning tools and the fill options palette.

Toolbar button labels are usually graphics, not text, which is what makes designing them so interesting (or difficult, depending on your point of

**Figure 2.6  There must be a thread running through all of a toolbar's buttons**

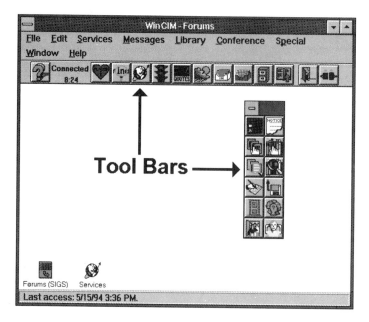

**Figure 2.7  Tool bars and control panels. (Screen shot copyrighted by and used with permission of CompuServe, Inc.)**

view). When you're designing the pictures for toolbar buttons, you can simplify the process by following these recommendations:

- *Give the buttons an intellectual theme.* For example, for a recipe program, "sort" could be represented by a sieve; for a banking program, it could be represented by a coin dispenser.

  For models of good thematic design, look at the symbol sets developed for the Olympic Games and the symbols developed by Xerox Corporation for copier and office equipment.[3]

- *Give the buttons a visual theme*—for example, use only geometric shapes or only rounded shapes, or use a common color palette. Macintosh buttons use similar colors by default, since only 34 colors of the entire 256-color palette are available in ResEdit. Microsoft Windows 3.x provides only 16 colors. For more information, see Chapter 8.

- *Use old-fashioned images.* Note that traditional, simpler, images sometimes work better than new ones. For example, a skeleton key is often

---

[3] Thanks to Ruediger W. Knodt at Xerox Corporation for bringing the Olympics symbols to our attention.

used to represent "key" facts in multimedia presentations. In the United States, the most common image used for electronic mail is the rural mailbox, which is seldom seen in the cities where most users live (Horton, 1994, pp. 46–47).

- *Turn verbs into nouns.* It is much easier to represent an object (a noun) than it is to represent an action (a verb) through pictures. For instance, rather than trying to represent the *action* of printing a document, it is much easier to show the *printer.*

For more sources of design ideas, see Resources.

## BUTTONS

GUI development kits include these types of buttons:

- Pushbuttons, which let users take actions.

- Radio buttons, used for mutually exclusive choices. See Radio Buttons.

- Checkbuttons, usually used for settings. See Checkbuttons.

- Sliders and spin buttons, which let users select points on ranges or select from lists. See Sliders and Spin Buttons.

Note that platform development kits include all of these types of buttons. You shouldn't have to create your own. However, you do have to select the right type of button for the task, write understandable labels for them, and—in the case of disposition pushbuttons—select a default button.

### Pushbuttons

A pushbutton usually resembles an actual button. Pushbuttons are used for designating, confirming, or canceling an action and are therefore also known as "action" and "command" buttons.

Pushbuttons often open dialog boxes; in Motif systems, they can also be used to let users select from a list of choices.

A subcategory of pushbutton is the disposition pushbutton. Disposition buttons act on the entire window or dialog box and are therefore arranged along the bottom of the window or box. For more information on disposition buttons, see Chapter 1.

**Text labels**                     **Symbolic labels**

**Figure 2.8  Pushbutton labels. The button labeled "Save" is the default button**

### Labels

The pushbutton's label must unambiguously identify its use. Since pushbuttons lead to actions, their labels are usually verbs, either text (`Save, Print, Cancel Printing`) or symbolic (for example, VCR controls representing `Rewind, Pause, Forward`). (See Figure 2.8.)

The labels of pushbuttons that bring up dialog boxes have ellipses at the ends: `Print...`

Note that when labels are translated from English into another language, text labels will become longer and the buttons will become too small (unless you build in dynamic resizing). For more information, see Chapter 6.

### Default Pushbuttons

Almost every window or dialog box has a "default" disposition pushbutton. (The ones that don't have a default push button are ones on which any default would be dangerous—for example, a message box that asks the user to confirm a deletion.) The default is indicated by an extra border around the button. Pressing [Enter] activates it. (See Figure 2.9.)

## Radio Buttons

Radio buttons (also called "option buttons") are used for mutually exclusive choices. In any set of radio buttons, only one can be pushed in (like the buttons on car radios).

*Note:* If you are changing a character-based interface to a windows-based interface, keep in mind that you can change many yes/no prompts to radio buttons. For example, "Do you want to save this database as run-time only?" can become two radio buttons, "Creation/Run-time" and "Run-time Only," in a settings dialog box.

Radio buttons are round or diamond-shaped buttons. When a radio button is selected (on), it usually has a black area at the center of the button. In the IBM, NeXTStep, and Motif versions, the button itself appears to be depressed because the shading of the beveled edges shifts. (See Figure 2.10.)

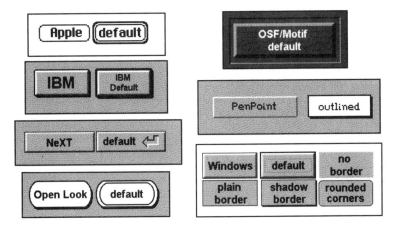

**Figure 2.9  Standard and default pushbuttons**

## Radio Button Labels

Radio buttons have two labels: a label for the overall set of buttons (for example, Sort by) and labels for the individual buttons (Name, Type, Date). Note that you document radio buttons in the online help or paper documentation as a set, comparing and contrasting the choices.

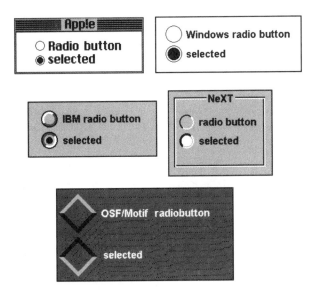

**Figure 2.10  Radio buttons in their "on" and "off" states**

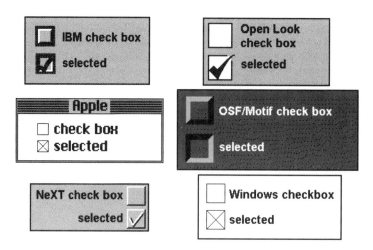

**Figure 2.11  Checkbuttons**

## Checkbuttons

Checkbuttons or boxes are used for multiple, not mutually exclusive choices. For example, you would use check buttons when users could mark text as bold, underlined, *and* italicized. Checkbuttons usually appear in dialog boxes, but they can also be menu choices (see Chapter 3).

Checkbuttons are usually small squares with clear or unmarked center panels. When they are checked (on), a checkmark or an "X" appears in the center of the square. (See Figure 2.11.)

### Checkbutton Labels

Checkbuttons, like radio buttons, have two labels: a label for the overall set of buttons (for example, Style); and labels for the individual buttons (Bold, Italic, Underlined). Note that you document checkbuttons in the online help or paper documentation as a set, comparing and contrasting the choices.

## Sliders and Spin Buttons

Slider buttons are used to represent a value on a scale. Make sure that you represent the scale, either with a set of markers or with a percentage or numerical field.

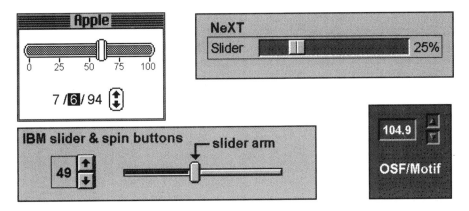

**Figure 2.12  Sliders and spin buttons**

Slider buttons can be horizontal or vertical, with a slider arm or a grabbable or view-only scroll box.

The slider arm can be replaced with spin buttons, which are small squares with up and down or left and right arrows (see Figure 2.12). Use spin buttons to display long lists of choices that increase or decrease in constant units.

## POINTERS AND CURSORS

There are two types of cursors, text and selection:

- Text cursors mark the insertion point—the point where you last made an entry and where you will make your next entry.

- Selection cursors are dotted outline boxes around selected objects.

There are many types of pointers, however. Pointers are those little pictures that cruise freely around the screen as you move the mouse. In fact, a pointer can be considered to be an icon for the mouse movement.

### Hotspots

Pointers have two components: a visual representation (arrow, question mark, and so on) and a hotspot. The hotspot is an area inside the pointer that marks the exact location on the desktop that will be affected by the user's next mouse action (Microsoft, 1992, p. 10).

If you design your own pointers, place the hotspot in one of these two locations:

- At the upper lefthand corner of the image
- Where the user would typically expect it—for example, the hotspot for a cross-hair pointer is logically at the intersection of the two lines (IBM, 1992, p. 378).

Note that "wait" and "do not" pointers have hotspots, but these hotspots do not have any effect on the screen elements.

## Types of Pointers

Different pointers indicate different possibilities—pointers change to show that the user's options have changed. For instance, the standard arrow pointer changes to an I-beam whenever the user moves the mouse into a text area.

Table 2.2 lists most of the standard pointers, plus brief descriptions of their uses and hotspot locations. Note that many of these pointers are supplied with development kits and do not have to be created from scratch. If, however, you find that you have to define your own cursors or pointers, see Designing Pointers and Cursors.

**Table 2.2  Pointer and Cursor Types**

| Platform | Pointer/ Cursor | Type | Description | Hotspot Location |
|---|---|---|---|---|
| **Cursor** | | | | |
| All platforms | 🖗 | Selection cursor. | Used to indicate that an object has been selected. | Not applicable. |
| All platforms | I | Text cursor. | Used to indicate insertion point. | Not applicable. |
| **Text Pointers** | | | | |
| IBM CUA, Macintosh, Motif, Windows 3.x, PenPoint | I | Text pointer (also called "I beam"). | Used to manipulate text. | On vertical bar, about one-third up from the bottom. |

**Table 2.2** *(Continued)*

| Platform | Pointer/ Cursor | Type | Description | Hotspot Location |
|---|---|---|---|---|
| **Cursor** *(continued)* | | | | + |
| NeXTStep | | | | |
| **Select and Manipulate** | | | | |
| IBM CUA, Macintosh, Motif, Open Look | | The default pointer. | Used to select objects and choices. Also used while manipulating objects. | At the point of the arrow or pen. |
| Windows 3.x | | | | |
| PenPoint | | | | |
| Open Look | | Hotspot indicator. | Used to help users select small or narrow objects. The default cursor changes into this "hotspot" indicator when the pointer's hotspot is near the hot zone of a small or narrow object. | At the point of the arrow. |
| Windows 3.x | | Extended selection pointer. | Selects lines, rows, cells. | At the point of the arrow. |
| Windows 3.x | | Column selection pointer. | Selects column. | At the point of the arrow. |

**Table 2.2**  *(Continued)*

| Platform | Pointer/ Cursor | Type | Description | Hotspot Location |
|---|---|---|---|---|
| Macintosh, Motif | | Cross-hairs. | Used to make fine position selections while manipulating graphics. | At the intersection of the lines. |
| Macintosh | | Field selector. | Used to select fields in an array. | Center of cross. |
| **Copy** | | | | |
| IBM CUA | | Copy-object pointer. | Indicates that the result of the oper-ation is a copy. | At the point of the arrow. |
| Open Look | | | | |
| Open Look | | Copy-text pointer. | Indicates that the result of the oper-ation is a copy. | At the point of the arrow. |
| **Move and Resize** | | | | |
| Motif, Windows 3.x | | Move pointer. | Indicates that the selected object is being moved or, for Motif systems, a resize operation before the resize direction has been determined (OSF, 1992, pp. 9–89). | At the center. |
| Open Look | | Move pointer. | Used as a move pointer for objects on desktop. | At the point of the arrow. |

**Table 2.2** (*Continued*)

| Platform | Pointer/ Cursor | Type | Description | Hotspot Location |
|---|---|---|---|---|
| Windows 3.x | | Direction keys move pointer. | Indicates that direction keys (up and down arrows, for example) will move or resize the window. | At the center. |
| Open Look | | Move-text pointer | Used as a move pointer for sections of text. | At the point of the arrow. |
| Motif | | Resize pointers. | Indicate positions and directions for area resize. | At the line or corner to which the arrow points. |
| Windows 3.x | | Vertical and horizontal movement pointers. | Indicates constrained vertical and horizontal movement for selected object (no diagonals). | At the center of the bars. |
| Windows 3.x | | Resize column and row pointers. | Used to indicate that a column or row can be resized. | At the point of the intersection. |
| Windows 3.x | | Resize pointers. | Indicates that the window or dialog box border can be resized in the direction indicated by the pointer's image—vertically, horizontally, or diagonally to the left or right. | At the center of the bars. |

**Table 2.2**  *(Continued)*

| Platform | Pointer/ Cursor | Type | Description | Hotspot Location |
|----------|--------|------|-------------|------------------|
| **Do Not/Cannot** | | | | |
| IBM CUA | | Do not pointer | Indicates that the target object is not a valid target for this operation. | For the IBM pointer, at the point of the arrow (IBM, 1992, p. 380). For the Motif pointer, at the center of the symbol (OSF, 1993, p. 9-90). |
| Motif | | | | |
| Windows 3.x | | No-drop cursor.* | Dropping is not allowed at this location. | At center of symbol (Microsoft, 1992, 39). |
| **Help** | | | | |
| Motif | | Help pointer. | Indicates available context-sensitive help. | For the first two, at the tip of the arrow. For the Open Look version, centered in the bulb of the question mark. |
| Windows 3.x | | | | |
| Open Look | | | | |

**Table 2.2**  *(Continued)*

| Platform | Pointer/ Cursor | Type | Description | Hotspot Location |
|---|---|---|---|---|
| **Other** | | | | |
| Windows 3.x | | Zoom pointer. | Magnifies area of the window. | At center of the magnifying glass. |
| Windows 3.x | | Split pointers. | First pointer splits window horizontally. Second pointer splits window vertically. | At the center, where the lines would intersect across the empty area. |
| Motif | | Out of range. | User has moved pointer outside the application area. | At the intersection of the lines. |
| Open Look | | Panning pointer. | Used to scroll contents of a window without using a scroll bar. | At the point of the arrow. |
| Motif | | Menu pointer. | Indicates pending menu action. | At the point of the arrow. |

*The "do not" symbol is a red circle with a slash going from the top left to the bottom right. If you draw the slash from the top right to the bottom left, the meaning changes to "end of" (IBM, 1991, p. 13).

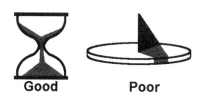

**Good            Poor**

Figure 2.13  A good "wait" pointer and a not-so-good one

## Designing Pointers and Cursors

Here are four design recommendations for pointers and cursors:

1. The shape of the pointer should give some hint as to its purpose (much the same way an icon does).

2. The shape should be easy to see and recognize (see Figure 2.13). Users may be unable to understand the pointer if the image is too small and the details are too fine or if the image is not familiar enough.

3. Avoid visual clutter. A pointer is a small element on a large screen. If you cram too much detail into a tiny space, the users won't be able to figure out what they are looking at. A watch is fine for a wait pointer, but if you include a sweep second hand, day and date function, and a moon-phase indicator, there is probably too much clutter for a successful pointer. (See Figure 2.14.)

4. The hotspot should "feel" obvious. Put the hotspot at the tip of an arrow, not at the blunt end. Put the hotspot on the vertical member of an I-beam cursor, not off to one side or at the bottom or top.

## Warping the Pointer: Arguments for and Against

"Warping the pointer" means to automatically change the location of the pointer based on some system action. For example, Windows 3.x programs usually move the pointer into a newly opened dialog box.

**Good            Poor**

Figure 2.14  Clutter in a pointer

The Motif guidelines argue against this behavior: "Warping the pointer is confusing to users and reduces their sense of control. Also, warping the pointer can cause problems for users of absolute location pointed devices (such as graphics tablets). Graphics tablets map pointer device locations to absolute screen locations; so, if the pointer is warped, the pointer loses synchronization with the pointing device, making some screen locations impossible to reach" (OSF, 1993, pp. 2–10).

Reducing users' control of their systems is something to be avoided. On the other hand, having the pointer jump into the current dialog box can be a timesaver for users who prefer to avoid the mouse (touch typists, for example). The key is to ask your users which they prefer—demonstrate warped and unwarped pointers, then let the users try them and select the interaction they like better.

## REFERENCES

Apple Computer, Inc. *Macintosh Human Interface Guidelines.* Reading, MA: Addison-Wesley, 1992.

Galitz, Wilbert O. *User-Interface Screen Design.* Boston, MA: QED Publishing Group, 1993.

GO Corporation. *PenPoint User Interface Design Reference.* Reading, MA: Addison-Wesley, 1992.

Horton, William. *The Icon Book.* New York: John Wiley & Sons, 1994.

IBM Corporation. *Icon Reference Book,* 1991, pub. no. SC34-4348-00. Contact IBM Publications at 800-879-2755.

———. *Object-Oriented Interface Design: IBM Common User Access Guidelines.* Carmel, IN: IBM/Que, 1992.

Kobara, Shiz. *Visual Design with OSF/Motif.* Reading, MA: Addison-Wesley, 1991.

Microsoft Corporation. *The Windows Interface: An Application Design Guide.* Redmond, WA: Microsoft Press, 1992.

NeXT Publications. *NeXTStep User Interface Guidelines* (for NeXTStep Release 3). Reading, MA: Addison-Wesley, 1992.

Open Software Foundation. *OSF/Motif Style Guide,* Revision 1.2 (for OSF/Motif Release 1.2). Englewood Cliffs, NJ: Prentice Hall, 1993.

Sun Microsystems, Inc. *Open Look: Graphical User Interface Application Style Guidelines.* Reading, MA: Addison-Wesley, 1990.

## RESOURCES

The books listed in the following subsections can help you design icons and buttons.

### Books of Symbols and Pictures

For national and international symbol sets, contact the *American National Standards Institute,* 11 West 42nd Street, New York, NY 10036; voice: 212-642-4900; fax: 212-302-1286.

Modley, Rudolf, and William R. Myers. *Handbook of Pictorial Symbols: 3250 Examples from International Sources.* New York: Dover Publications, 1976.

### Graphic Design

When looking for these books in your library or bookstore, keep in mind that any book on corporate identification, business-card design, logo design, or highway signs and billboards (simplify, simplify, simplify!) will contain good icon-design advice.

Bertin, Jacques. *Semiology of Graphics.* Green Bay, WI: University of Wisconsin, 1983. Long out of print, but the best (and fattest) reference to symbols and symbology systems available. Sometimes available in libraries.

Holmes, Nigel, and Rose DeNeve. *Designing Pictorial Symbols.* New York: Watson-Guptil Publications, 1990. Dozens of problem-solving examples.

Kince, Eli. *Visual Puns in Design: The Pun Used as a Communications Tool.* New York: Watson-Guptil Publications, 1982. Great source of ideas.

Miller, J. Abbott. *Signs and Spaces.* Rockport/Allworth Editions, 1994, distributed in the United States and Canada by North Light Books, Cincinnati, OH.

Murphy, John, and Michael Rowe. *How to Design Trademarks & Logos.* Cincinnati, Ohio: North Light Books, 1988. Step by step instructions.

PIE Books. *Business Card Graphics.* Vol. 2, *An International Collection of Outstanding Personal and Corporate Business Cards.* 1992. PIE Books, 407 4-14-6, Komagome, Toshima-ku, Tokyo 170, Japan; 03-3949-5010; fax: 03-3949-5650. Available in art stores and bookstores with large art and design sections.

Silver, Linda (editor). *Print's Best Letterheads & Business Cards: Winning Designs from Print Magazine's National Competition.* New York: RC Publications, Inc., 1990.

## Programming Concerns

Horton, William. *The Icon Book.* New York: John Wiley & Sons, Inc., 1994. Buy this book—it's full of ideas and information, it includes a case study, and it comes with a diskette containing over 500 icons (copyrighted, however—you can't use them in your own program without permission). Contact the publisher at 605 3rd Avenue, New York, NY 10158-0012.

IBM Corporation. *Icon Reference Book,* 1991, Pub. no. SC34-4348-00. Contact IBM Publications at 800-879-2755. Catalog of IBM product icons (*Standard Icons, Banking, Book Manager, NetView,* and so on). Contains good icon design advice in the first four chapters.

# 3

# Menus

The Scottish philosopher Sir William Hamilton (1788–1856) wrote: "If you throw a handful of marbles on the floor, you will find it difficult to view at once more than six, or seven at most, without confusion." This was confirmed by the English economist William Stanley Jevons (1835–82) by throwing beans into a box and estimating their number. He found that he never made a mistake with three or four, was sometimes wrong when there were five, was right about half the time with ten beans, and was usually wrong with fifteen. These experiments are cited by the American psychologist George Miller, the author of the famous paper, "The Magic Number Seven, Plus or Minus Two" (1956). Miller found that more items can be remembered when they are coded, or "chunked" (Gregory, 1987, p. 148).

Menus are about memory—unburdening it, that is. Menus, unlike command-line commands, take advantage of our ability to recognize things more readily than we can remember them. Instead of trying to remember program names and parameters, menu users merely look at a list and pick the option they want.

Ten or so years ago, most menus were one or two vertical columns of options. Some, in a style made famous by Lotus 1-2-3, were done as lists across the top of the screen. However, although these menus were better than command-line interfaces for most end users, there were still problems. For example, some systems had menus that went on for pages and branched off in many directions. On the Lotus-type menus, selecting certain options meant that the current menu was completely replaced with a submenu. If you weren't paying attention, you might suddenly find yourself lost. In other words, if the menu's structure were not clear, either method could lead to confusion. In GUIs, on the other hand, the structure is completely visible.

- The menu bars on GUI menus provide better navigational cues, since the sections of the program are laid out in the menu titles.

- GUI menus are chunked by design. If you simply follow the development platform specifications, the options tend to fall into understandable categories.

However, developers must be alert to these problems:

*Even GUI menus can become too deeply nested.* Or, to put it more accurately, functionality can become too hidden. See Depth and Breadth in this chapter.

*Menus slow down expert users.* Many expert users would rather type a command and a parameter on the command line than plod through one menu after another. See Accommodating Expert Users in this chapter.

## WHEN TO USE MENUS

The Motif guidelines are explicit: "Because menus are readily available and quickly accessed and dismissed, they (rather than dialog boxes) should be used for components that are frequently used. The time delays of bringing up a DialogBox for frequently used components can greatly reduce user productivity. Because menus are easy to browse through, they should also be used for components commonly accessed by most users" (OSF, 1993, pp. 6-6–6-7).

However, since menus are only displayed while the user makes a selection, they can't be used to make several selections at the same time (unless you use the "tear-off" option—see Accommodating Expert Users). Also, menus are usually modal, meaning that the user can't interact with any other part of the program while a menu is open. If the user wants to make more than one selection at a time or use more than one function at a time, he or she has to use control panels or toolbars instead.

## TYPES OF MENUS

The types of menus are:

*Control:* The menus that control the operations of the windows themselves. In Microsoft Windows and Motif, they are indicated by a space bar or hyphen at the window's upper-left corner. These menus should contain only window operations (open, close, minimize, move, and so on). (See Figure 3.1.)

*Pop-up:* "Secret" expert menus that appear when you click the designated mouse button (usually the right) on an active area in an application window or on the desktop itself. Pop-up menus contain often-used commands and shortcuts. See Pop-Up Menus for details.

*Pull-down:* What most people think of when they think of menus. These are the menus that appear when you select a menu title from the menu bar at the top of an application window. Also called "drop-down" menus.

*Submenus* are attached to pull-down menus. Also called "cascades" in Microsoft and Motif systems and "hierarchical menus" in Macintosh and NeXTStep systems.

Other, less-common, types of menus include:

*Option buttons,* which are lists of options accessed from buttons. However, the problems of organization and unambiguous labeling of individual items are the same as for pull-down and pop-up menus.

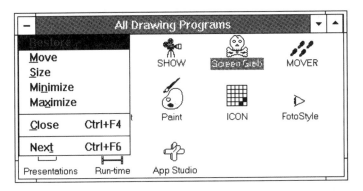

**Figure 3.1  A typical Windows 3.1 control menu**

*Tear-off or "tacked" menus*, which let users keep the menus open and continuously available. Functionally, they are more like control panels or toolbars than menus. Motif, NeXTStep, and the now defunct Open Look environments allow tear-offs. If used too often, they can clutter the desktop.

## HOW TO DESIGN MENUS

To design menus well, you need to:

- Restrict menu depth to three levels (or less). See Depth and Breadth.

- Group options into menus logically and, on individual menus, arrange the options in a logical order. See Order of Menu Items.

- Use the right kind of word for every type of menu option. See Defining Sensible Titles and Labels.

- Be consistent across menus. See Proofreading: Cross-Menu Consistency.

- Let users bypass the menus. See Accommodating Expert Users.

### Depth and Breadth

Menu search is a problem because target items are, in a sense, hidden under successive layers of vague clues. Consequently, the user has to spend a lot of time peeking under the shells to find the pea. Large memory demands are placed on the user to remember where things are buried in the menu structure. Breadth, however, allows the system to lay the cards on the table, so to speak (Kent Norman, *The Psychology of Menu Selection*, 1991, p. 223).

In 1982, J. W. Tombaugh and S. A. McEwen found that when users were searching for information, they were both very likely to choose menu items that didn't lead to the desired information and, on a high proportion of searches, tended to give up without locating it (Norman, 1991, p. 204). In reaction to this sorry state of affairs, researchers asked this question: Does the depth to which menus are nested affect users' ability to use a program? The answer was yes, it does.

A study by Kiger (described in Norman, 1991, p. 203) found that a menu hierarchy (or tree) with no more than two levels and no more than eight items on each submenu (called $8^2$) was rated highest for speed, accuracy,

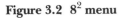

Figure 3.2  $8^2$ menu

and subject preference (see Figure 3.2). A four-level menu with three items per submenu ($4^3$) was the next best style. A deep, narrow tree of six levels with two items on each (called $2^6$) was the slowest, least accurate, and least preferred version (see Figure 3.3). Other studies confirmed that a low number of levels (two to three) and an intermediate level of choices (four to eight) resulted in faster, more accurate performance (Norman, 1991, p. 13).

Nevertheless, the issue may not be so simple. "For lists of linearly organized arrays, such as numbers, alphabetized lists, letters of the alphabet, and months of the year, one should increase breadth to the maximum practical level," says Norman. In other words, users can easily find a month or a font size in an ordered list. Distributing months across winter, spring, summer,

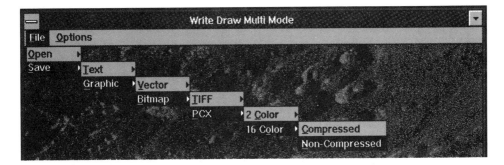

Figure 3.3  $2^6$ menu

and fall submenus, just to fulfill the depth rule, would irritate users very much.

However, Norman goes on to say, "It may very well be that the depth versus breadth tradeoff issue is really misplaced and that the transcending issue is that of effectively revealing menu organization to users, while reducing the number of frames and responses required to locate target items" (Norman, 1991, p. 213).

In other words, offer as many pull-down menus at the top and as many items at the bottom of each pull-down or submenu as possible. A wide number of the choices at the top help the user guess where he or she might find an item. Once the user knows he or she is on the right track, more choices at the bottom is better—now the user can just scan the list to find the one he or she wants. See Alphabetical versus Categorical Order for help in organizing the bottom-level choices.

### How to Violate the Depth Rule without Even Trying

The development guidelines all recommend that menus have no more than two levels. But the depth problem has not necessarily been resolved. Although the menus may be done correctly, functionality may be hidden three, four, or more levels deep on panels and dialog boxes.

For example, Microsoft Word for Windows lets you print gray scales as line art (black and white only) on LaserJet Series II printers. But to set this up, you must:

1. Open the *File* menu.
2. Select *Print Setup*.
3. Select the *Setup* button on the *Print Setup* panel.
4. Select the *Options* button on the H-P LaserJet II panel.
5. Click on the *Line Art* radio button.

Only a few people, relatively speaking, are going to want to use this feature, which is probably why it is hidden deep in the bowels of the program. Nevertheless, five levels down violates the depth rule. The real question is, Why not add another menu of, say, printer options and settings? Another option is to collapse two of the dialog boxes into one. Size is not a problem: The advantage of a graphical user interface is that a dialog box can be *any* size, including the size sufficient to the task. (For more on designing dialog boxes, see Chapter 1.)

## Order of Menu Items

Eight ways of organizing options are described below (Norman, 1991, pp. 133–134). The various styles are not mutually exclusive—you may use all of them in a single application.

*Alphabetic:* Use when the items can be meaningfully alphabetized and scanned. A list of typefaces, for example, is a good candidate for alphabetization—although "serif," "sans serif," and "headline" are all good categories, print designers look for typefaces by name, not category. Also use alphabetical order when no other type of organization springs to mind. See the discussion in Alphabetical versus Categorical Order.

*Chronological:* Use for items that are most effectively organized by date or time. You can sort by age—e-mail messages from newest to oldest, articles in a news service from oldest to newest—or in standard cognitive order—January through December.

*Frequency of use:* Use only when you truly know which items are used frequently and which are not. Some frequency candidates are obvious—for example, in word processing programs, you always have to open a document. Others require user testing before you can define frequency. Test before you code the menu. A fast and easy method is the paper and pencil simulation (see Exercise: Paper and Pencil Simulation in the Testing on Users subsection). If you create a prototype, you can observe users directly or capture keystrokes in a transaction log.

However, keep in mind that usage frequencies often change as users become more expert or as their work roles change. Changing menus dynamically is not the solution, either, as we will discuss shortly.

*Numeric:* Use for items that are associated with numbers—for example, baud rates, type sizes, numbers of copies, and so on.

*Random:* Not recommended, although random order (or what appears to be random to an uninitiated observer) is sometimes unavoidable. For example, windowing environments drop icons more or less at random on the desktop. However, only new users have to spend time hunting for programs. Frequent users soon learn the spatial locations of the various items.

*Semantic similarity:* You can order items in terms of some semantic dimension, such as impact, reversibility, potency, and so on. Items that are most similar are next to each other on the list. For example, you can organize emphasis styles by impact: *Normal, Underlined, Italic, Bold*.

*Sequential processing:* You can list items according to their inferred order in a process or according to a cognitive ordering of items. These options are in process order: *Open Picture, Modify Picture, Save Picture, Close Picture*. These options are ordered cognitively, from large to small: *Galaxy, Cluster, Star, Planet, Moon*.

*Standard or custom:* The platform guidelines suggest certain menu options in certain orders. Although all of these suggestions may not be suitable for your application, use them when you can. Standardization reduces the number of decisions (and arguments) during development and helps users cross program boundaries more easily. See Following the Specifications for details.

### Alphabetical versus Categorical Order

The list of organization types (with the exception of random) falls into two parts—alphabetic, numeric, and chronological orders versus frequency, sequence, and semantic orders. If we call the division "alphabetical versus categorical," can we find any advantage of one over the other?

It seems that when users are looking for an *exact word or label,* alphabetical order is fastest. For example, if you ask a test subject to find "Shiitake mushrooms," he or she will find it quickly on an alphabetized list of foods (see Figure 3.4)

However, when users are looking for an *answer to a question* (or a command leading to a particular outcome), categorical order was fastest, followed by alphabetical order, and then random order (Norman, 1991, pp. 135–137). If you ask a test subject to find "mushrooms, Japanese," he or she will find "Shiitake mushrooms" faster on a categorical menu or set of menus (see Figure 3.5).[1]

---

[1] In libraries, categorical searches often make more sense than alphabetical searches do. As many U.S. public and university libraries are abandoning their paper card catalogs for online search programs, library users are finding that online subject searches are virtually impossible "Card catalogs have the sense not to shuffle together alphabetically the myriad subheadings for 'labor' in the medical sense and 'labor' in the A.F.L.-C.I.O. sense; the online catalogs I've seen don't. Card catalogs don't lump subheadings for traffic control in Alexandria, Virginia, together with ones for the lost library at Alexandria, Egypt, either" (Baker, 1994, pp. 64–86).

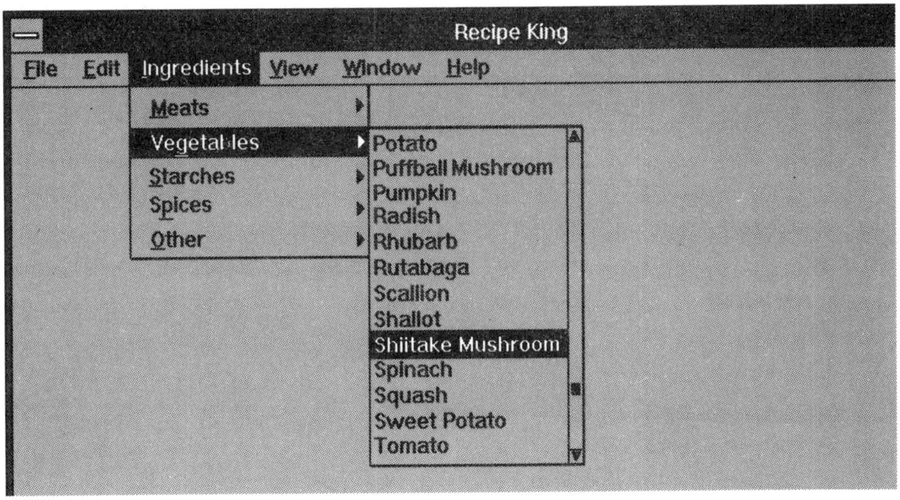

**Figure 3.4  Searching an alphabetized list**

## Other Issues

*Breaking up long lists:* All of the platform guidelines suggest organizing categorical items into logical groups, then separating the groups into sets of no more than four or five items each, following the chunking rule (see Figure

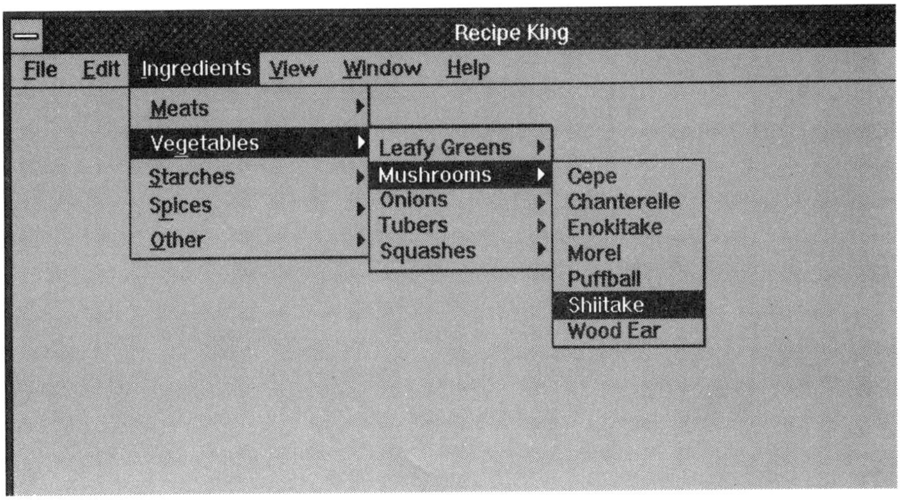

**Figure 3.5  Searching a categorized list**

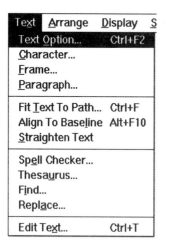

**Figure 3.6  Breaking long lists into shorter lists**

3.6). Separate the groups with lines (each environment provides some sort of separator line).

Recommendations for lines:

- Don't use a line as a first or last component on the menu.

- Make sure that there are at least two options in each group (in other words, don't put lines above and below a single option).

- Use lines to separate lists of checkbuttons or radio buttons from the rest of the menu options.

- Don't separate groups with subtitles (by using dimmed items, for example)—people might mistake them for commands (Apple Computer, 1992, p. 63).

*Dangerous options:* Options like *Quit, Exit, Close Connection,* and *Delete All,* even when easily reversible, should never be default choices and should never be first on pull-down menus. First items may be, by default, the "default" option—if you open the menu and press [Enter], you may automatically select the first option.

*Sorting order for long lists:* When you have a long list of items, such as type sizes, sort it up and down, not side to side.

*International sorting schemes:* Your alphabetical lists may stop being alphabetical as soon as you localize your software—not just because the words change, but also because sort orders, especially for accented letters, vary dramatically between one language and another. Also, ideographic languages such as Chinese don't have alphabetical orders (they don't have alphabets). If your software will be sold internationally, don't depend heavily on alphabetical order. For more information on localization, see Chapter 6.

## DEFINING SENSIBLE TITLES AND LABELS

The menu bar is the area across the top of the application window that contains the titles of pull-down menus. (Note that NeXTStep has a vertical main menu and, therefore, no menu bar.) Each operating-system developer has a recommended line-up of menus, as shown in Table 3.1.

### Menu Bar Titles

There is really only one rule for creating menu bar titles: Menu bar names (the titles of the pull-down menus, in other words) must be no more than one word. The reason for the one-word specification is that the titles aren't visually separated. Until you actually select a menu title, you can't see the edges of the underlying widget. Therefore, a title of two words looks like two menus.

**Table 3.1  Recommendations for Top-Level Menus**

| *Environment* | *Recommended or Required Menus* | | | | | | | | |
|---|---|---|---|---|---|---|---|---|---|
| Apple Macintosh (Apple, 1992, p. 52) | File | Edit | Application-specific (for localized applications add Keyboard menu) | | | | | Help (icon) | Your appli-cation icon |
| IBM OS/2 (IBM, 1992, p. 334) | File | Selected | Edit | View | Options: application-specific | | | Windows | Help |
| Microsoft Windows (Microsoft, 1992, p. 88) | File | Edit | Application-specific | | | | | | Help |
| NeXTStep (NeXT, 1992, p. 111) | Info | Docu-ment | Edit | Format | Windows | Print | Services | Hide | Quit |
| Motif (OSF, 1993, pp. 6-15–6-17) | File | Selected | Edit | View | Options: application-specific | | | | Help |
| PenPoint (GO, 1992, pp. 56) | Docu-ment | Edit | Options | (Many standard functions are handled as icons on the bottom or right edge of the application windows). | | | | | |

*Note:* There is an unapproved but visually palatable alternative to the one-word style: Use an underbar to "attach" two words—for example, *Manage_Books.*

Note that the platform guidelines recommend—sometimes insist—on specific sets of top-level menus. However, some applications don't need every menu. The rules are:

- Provide the recommended menus, in the order shown, if your application provides any of the choices listed in their pull-down menus. NeXTStep advises against one-item menus, however, and suggests adding single items to the next most logical top-level menu (NeXT, 1992, p. 106).

- If your application contains options that don't fit on any of the standard menus, add application-specific, top-level menus in front of the Help menu.

- Help is the last (or, on the Macintosh, next to last) item on every menu bar.

For the list of recommended top-level menus, see Table 3.1.

### Variations and Exceptions

For applications without user-definable files—for example, a game, a collection of financial calculators, a set of telecommunications analyses—the *File, Edit, Format,* and other menus may be meaningless. In these cases, the rule of thumb seems to be, "Put the list of the most important options in the first position." If the application is a set of calculators, then the first title is *Calculators,* and the pull-down options are the names of the calculators.

Most of the environments have window control menus (indicated with a spacebar or hyphen icon). However, Apple has its environment-control "Apple" menu as the leftmost item on the menu bar. The Apple icon brings up the list of all items that users put in their *Apple Menu Items* folder—usually cross-application tools, such as alarm clocks, network access, and games (Apple, 1992, p. 98).

NeXTStep has a vertical main menu with *Help* on the *Info* menu and *Quit* at the bottom of the main menu instead of on a *File* menu. The *Windows* menu on the NeXTStep main menu contains window-management commands, which would appear in command menus in other environments.

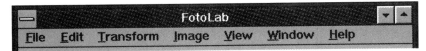

**Figure 3.7 Spacing on menu bars**

Instead of one top-level menu bar, OS/2 has two bars on each window—the top bar contains the system menu and window-sizing buttons, and the second bar contains a standard set of menus.

## Menu Bar Layout

If your development environment doesn't do the spacing for you automatically, then use three spaces between titles. Leave one space in front of the first title and at least one space behind the last title. (See Figure 3.7.)

## Elements of Pull-Down Menus

Pull-down menus contain options of various types (listed below) plus type indicators and keyboard shortcuts. Indicators are described in Indicating Option Types. Keyboard shortcuts are described in Keyboard Shortcuts: Mnemonics and Accelerators.

The main types of options are:

*Action:* A command; an option that does something without asking for additional user input. *Save* is a common action.

*Dialog box or panel:* Use a dialog box to ask for confirmation—"Do you really want to quit?"—or for more information. Save-as options, for example, usually ask for new file names, format types, and so on. Panels, usually collections of attributes, are ends in themselves—color palettes and printer set-up panels are examples.

*Settings or toggles:* You can put individual settings and toggled features on menus instead of making the user open a panel and set the option there. See Creating a Toggled Option for more information.

*Submenu:* A second or third level on a pulldown menu. For example, a *Fonts* option on a *Format* menu might lead to a submenu of typefaces and sizes. Submenus are also referred to as "cascades" and "hierarchical menus."

Other, less common, types of menu items are:

*Files:* A list of the last four to six files opened, usually accessed from the *File* menu if there is one.

*Graphics:* Pictures of selectable patterns or drawing tools.

*Windows:* A list of all open windows, usually numbered.

## Pull-Down Menu Option Labels

Once you've defined the menu bar, you can define the names of the options on the pull-downs. Here are the main issues.

- Indicating the option type
- Following the specifications for your environment
- Creating unambiguous names

Related issues include: how to define a toggled label and how to capitalize.

### Indicating Option Types

Each of these types of menu options—command, dialog box or panel, setting, and submenu—has its own symbol (provided that you consider null a symbol) (see Table 3.2).

### Following the Specifications

Table 3.3, is a comparison of the File, Edit, View, and Help menus across operating environments.

### Creating Unambiguous Names

Using the standard symbols is necessary but not sufficient, since many users neither know the symbols nor care about them. However, you can reinforce the symbol with the right *type* of word (noun or verb) or phrase. Correct wording helps users know what to expect when they choose a new option.

**Table 3.2  Types of Menu Options**

| Option Type | Symbol | Sample |
|---|---|---|
| Actions (commands) | none | Save All |
| Panels or dialog boxes that sometimes work like actions | none* | Tools |
| Dialog boxes (requests for more input) | 3 dots immediately after option name (don't use ellipsis character) | Save As... |
| Settings (checkbuttons) | pushed-in button, checkmarks | √ Align Left |
| Submenus (cascades) | right-pointing triangle, flush right | Print ▶ |
| Indicator for applications running in background (Macintosh only) | diamond (can also use alert box and sound) | ◆ PrintMonitor |
| Indicator of mixed case or partial setting—for example, part of the text is italic, part is roman. | dash on Macintosh, grayed or blanked sample on Windows 3.1 | Style — Plain Text ⌘T — Bold ⌘B  *Italic* ⌘I — Underline ⌘U  Outline |

*Don't use the ellipsis when the option brings up a warning panel or when the option might or might not lead to a dialog. New users sometimes open all of the dialog boxes and panels by selecting the options with ellipses. You don't want them to use options that might log them out, erase their data, or worse (Microsoft, 1992, p. 81; NeXT Computer, 1992, p. 108)

**Table 3.3  Common Pull-Down Menus**

| | *File* | *Edit* | *View* | *Help* |
|---|---|---|---|---|
| **Apple Macintosh,** pp. 98–127 | New   ⌘N<br>Open   ⌘O<br>Close   ⌘W<br>Save   ⌘S<br>Save As...<br>Revert<br>Page Setup...<br>Print...   ⌘P<br>Quit   ⌘Q | Undo/Redo Item   ⌘Z<br>Cut   ⌘X<br>Copy   ⌘C<br>Paste   ⌘V<br>Clear<br>Show/Hide Clipboard | | About Balloon Help<br>Show Balloons<br>Finder Shortcuts<br>*Your Application* Help |
| **IBM OS/2,** pp. 270–271, 280–281, 296–297, 437–438, 492–493 | *Application-oriented:*<br>New<br>Open<br>Save<br>Save as<br>Print<br>*Object-oriented*<br>*(title should be*<br>*name of object—*<br>*for example,*<br>*"Worksheet"):*<br>Open as object<br>Open as settings<br>Print<br>*add options here* | Undo   Alt+Backspace<br>Redo   Shift+Alt+Backspace<br>Cut   Shift+Delete<br>Copy   Ctrl+Insert<br>Create   Alt+Insert<br>Paste   Shift+Insert<br>Delete   Delete<br>Find...<br>Select all   Ctrl+/<br>Deselect all   Ctrl+\ | Types of views<br>Sort<br>Include<br>Refresh → On/Off<br>Refresh now   F5 | Help index<br>General help<br>Using help<br>*Additional help*<br>Tutorial *(optional)*<br>Product information |
| **Microsoft Windows,** pp. 91–96 | New *or* New...<br>Open...<br>Save<br>Save As...<br>Print *or* Print...<br>Print Setup...<br>Exit<br>*Most recently used list* | Undo   Ctrl+Z<br>Repeat Action (optional)<br>Cut   Ctrl+X<br>Copy   Ctrl+C<br>Paste   Ctrl+V<br>Paste Link<br>Links<br>Find<br>Replace | | Contents<br>Search for Help On...<br>Tutorial *(optional)*<br>How to Use Help<br>About *Your*<br>*Application...* |
| **NeXTStep,** pp. 111–132 | *Document (not Files)*<br>Open...   o<br>New   n<br>Save   s<br>Save As...   S<br>Save All<br>Revert to Saved<br>Close | Cut   x<br>Copy   c<br>Paste   v<br>Paste As<br>Link<br>Delete<br>Undo   z<br>*add options here*<br>Find<br>Spelling...<br>Check Spelling   ;<br>Select All   a | | *Info (not Help)*<br>Info Panel...<br>*add options here*<br>Show Menus<br>Preferences...<br>Help...   ? |

**Table 3.3** *(Continued)*

| | *File* | *Edit* | | *View* | *Help* |
|---|---|---|---|---|---|
| **Motif** (OSF, 1993, pp. 6-16–6-26) | New<br>Open<br>Save<br>Save As<br>Print<br>Close (for applications with multiple, independent primary windows)<br>Exit | Undo<br>Cut<br>Copy<br>Paste<br>Clear<br>Delete | Alt+Backspace<br>Shift+Delete<br>Ctrl+Ins<br>Shift+Ins | Application-specific. "Components in the View menu should not actually change the data" but may change the data's appearance, amount of data shown, or the sort order. | Context-Sensitive Help Shift+Help*<br>Overview<br>Index<br>Keyboard<br>Tutorial<br>Using Help<br>Product Information |
| **PenPoint** (GO Corp., pp. 55–67) | *Document, not File:*<br>Checkpoint<br>Revert<br>Print...<br>Print Setup...<br>Send<br>About... | Undo<br>Select All<br>Move...<br>Copy...<br>Delete<br>Find...<br>Spell... | | *Options, not View:*<br>Controls *(for document controls like rulers)*<br>Access *(deletable or not, access speed, etc.)*<br>Comments *(author, title)* | *Accessed from icon or Quick Help sheet:*<br>Using Help<br>PenPoint<br>Applications *(yours)*<br>Index *as tab option* |

*OSF/Motif has two help models. The second is easier to understand, so we chose to reproduce it rather than the earlier model.

Here are some helpful hints.

*Take advantage of the menus' titles.* If you can create phrases or sentences by putting the title and options together, your menus will probably be readily understood. (But still test—see Testing on Users.) For example, on an *Insert* menu, you might have Insert *Picture*, Insert *Box*, Insert *Text*. Or you can use a verb and an adverb—the options on a *Sort* menu might be *Alphabetically, Numerically, In Reverse Order.* The resulting sentences would be *Sort Alphabetically, Sort Numerically,* and *Sort In Reverse Order* (NeXT, 1993, pp. 130–131).

*Use parallel construction.* Here are nonparallel labels: *Print, Execute a Program, Disk Eject.* Here are parallel labels: *Print a File, Execute a Program, Eject a Disk.* The nonparallel version isn't terribly wrong, but it gives a bad impression—it looks as if the developer just threw the menu together and didn't take the time to neaten it up (Norman, 1991, p. 142).

*Don't be too consistent.* A large publishing firm had just suffered the delivery of an expensive accounting system from a large and famous auditing firm.

On the main menu were "Name Maintenance," "Title Maintenance," "Account Maintenance," and so on. The woman who demonstrated the system to us said, exasperated, "These don't lead to maintenance! Most of the submenus let you add, inquire, *and* maintain. And some of them only let you search." The consistency in the text hid major (and legitimate) differences between modules. The neatness was confusing because the system itself wasn't.

*If the label contains a phrase, put the key word first.* The key word is usually a verb—in other words, the command itself. *Open File* is quicker to grasp than *File Open; Show Ruler* is quicker than *Turn Ruler On* (Norman, 1991, p. 142). (See Table 3.4.)

*Don't repeat the menu title in the menu options.* For example, on a *Report* menu, you don't need to say *Format Report, Generate Report, Print Report,* and so on. *Format, Generate,* and *Print* are enough.

*Don't abbreviate or truncate menu labels.* The reasons are:

- Some users won't recognize the abbreviation. Or they may recognize it, but assign the wrong meaning. For example, on Wall Street, the abbreviation "MTG" means "mortgage," not "meeting." "Tick" cannot be truncated and used to stand for "ticker" because "tick" is a word with its own meaning ("the smallest unit used in trading a stock or a bond").

- Some abbreviations don't translate, even from one form of English to another. For example, a menu option called "EZ Add" reads nicely as "Easy Add" in the United States, but as "Ee-ZED Add" in Great Britain.

GUIs are expandable. You don't *have* to abbreviate.

### Creating a Toggled Option

Use a toggled menu option when the user can logically select one of two states *and* it is too much trouble to open a panel. There are three styles.

1. A single option with an indicator in front of its label when it is active: Bold or Italic. Use this style when a *setting* is either on or off (Apple, 1992, pp. 76–77).

2. Two options with an indicator in front of the active item:

   ■ Show Grid
   ☐ Hide Grid

**Table 3.4  Matching Word Types to Option Types**

| | |
|---|---|
| **Actions** | Use verbs (*Save, Copy*) or verb phrases (*Find File*). The commands should fit into a sentence like "Save my file" or "Copy the data" (Apple Computer, 1992, p. 58). |
| **Dialog Boxes** | If the purpose of the option is an action, and a dialog box exists only to set parameters for the action (for example, *Save As* or *Find*), follow the Actions rule—use a verb or verb phrase.<br>    If the purpose of the option is to bring up a dialog box, then name the option after the dialog box—for example, *Spelling* to bring up the spelling panel (NeXT Computer, 1992, p. 108). |
| **Submenus** | If a submenu brings up a menu of actions, use the target of the actions as the label of the submenu. For example, a text-editing submenu might be called *Document* and the submenu options might be *Open, New*, and *Save*. The options can then be read as *Open Document, New Document, Save Document* (NeXT Computer, 1992, p. 109). |
| **Settings** | Use an adjective or adjectival phrase—for example, *Bold, Italic, Underlined*. The action is implied. Setting labels should fit into a sentence such as "Change this text to bold" (Apple Computer, 1992, p. 58). |

Use this style to indicate a change in *state* or the presence or absence of a *feature*, such as a grid or ruler. The two-button style has the advantage of requiring no interpretation—the feature or state is either on or off.

Especially use this option when the choices are not clearly opposites (GO Corporation, 1992, p. 198):

■ Use White Background
□ Use Gray Background

3.  A single option whose label changes to reflect its state:

Show Grid  →  Hide Grid

or that uses a toggle button to reflect a change in state:

□ Show Grid  →  ■ Show Grid

The advantage of the third style is that it takes up only one line on the menu rather than two. The disadvantage is that it is ambiguous and confusing. For example, does *Use Ruler* mean that the ruler is on and selecting the option turns it off, or does it mean that this command turns on the ruler?

☐ Use Ruler   →   ■ Use Ruler

or:

Use Ruler   →   Don't Use Ruler

The user won't know what to expect until he or she tries the option.
   Here is another potentially confusing option:

Full Duplex   →   ■ Full Duplex

Is the opposite "Empty Duplex"? Help users develop their software vocabularies by giving them either:

Full Duplex   →   Half Duplex

or, better yet:

☐ Full Duplex
■ Half Duplex

   In short, reduce ambiguity by using checkmarks only with individual settings (*Bold, Italic,* and so on), never with toggled features (Apple, 1992, pp. 76–77; Microsoft, 1992, p. 83).
   *Multiple choice versus mutually exclusive.* Toggled settings can be equivalent to checkbuttons (multiple choice) or radio buttons (only one choice). Differentiate the two types by using two different symbols—circles for radio button/independent options, squares or checkmarks for checkbutton/interdependent options (Microsoft, 1992, pp. 82–83).

### Capitalizing Labels

You can use either of two methods, provided that you use the chosen method consistently. However, the headline style is more common. Only the IBM OS/2 guidelines show sentence-style labels.

- *Sentence style:* Capitalize only the first letter of each label (unless a proper noun—a product name or person's name—appears in the label)—for example, *Save as.*

- *Headline style:* Capitalize every word in the label except articles (a, an, the), coordinating conjunctions (and, but, or, for, nor), and prepositions (at, by, in, to, from, with), unless they are the first or last words in the label (Chicago, 1993, pp. 282–283)—for example, *Save As*.

Here are the rules for capitalizing hyphenated (compound) words in headline style.

- The first part of a compound word is always capitalized.

- The second (or third or fourth) part is capitalized unless it is an article, a preposition, or a coordinating conjunction—for example, *Run-in Text*. There is one exception: If the compound comes at the end of the label, its final section is always capitalized, no matter what part of speech it is: *Text Run-In*.

- If the compound word is actually a prefix plus a word, the second (or subsequent) part is never capitalized: *Re-save, Re-map* (Chicago, 1993, p. 283).

## Pull-Down Menu Layout

To design pull-down menus correctly (see Figure 3.8):

- Make sure that the width of the menu is the width of the longest *label* on the menu, not the *title* of the menu (titles are usually very short).

- Leave three spaces in front of all menu labels. The first space separates the label from the left edge of the menu; the second contains checkmarks, checkbuttons, or radio buttons when needed; and the third separates the occasional checkmark or button from the label itself.

- Remember to designate a mnemonic or ⌘ shortcut for each option. Except on Macintosh systems, mnemonics are underlined. See Keyboard shortcuts: Mnemonics and Accelerators for more information.

- Accelerator key names (function keys or combinations of [Alt], [Ctrl], or [Shift] and function keys) are flush left on the first *tab* after the name of the longest option label. Don't use spaces to align accelerators—spacing is irregular in proportional typefaces (Microsoft, 1992, p. 87).

- For accelerators, use the key name as it is printed on its key cap—for example, use "Ctrl," not ^. Unfortunately, keyboards vary. For example,

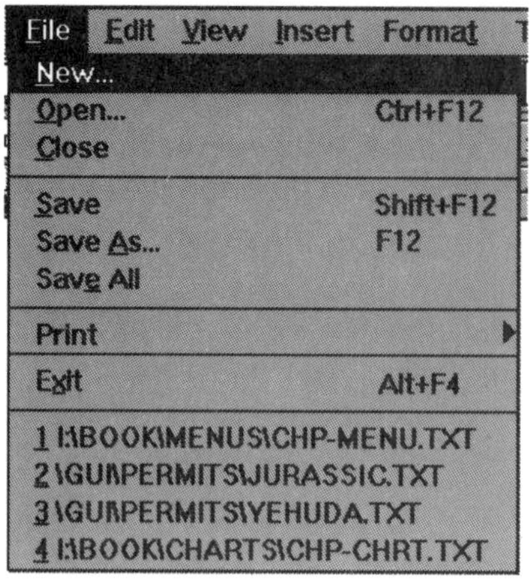

**Figure 3.8  Correct pull-down menu design**

some keyboards say "Del," others say "Delete," and some say both. Keyboards attached to UNIX workstations often have both [Return] and [Enter] keys, which sometimes do different things and sometimes don't. If this variability causes a problem, find the most standard and/or the newest computer in the office and use that one as your model.

- The ellipsis indicator (for panels or dialog boxes) follows the label. Do not add spaces between the label and the ellipsis. Also, don't add spaces between the periods in the ellipsis (this is often done in typesetting).

- The triangle indicator (for submenus) is always flush right. Leave one space between the triangle and the right edge of the menu.

- Don't show a submenu immediately—incorporate a brief pause. This pause keeps the submenu from flashing open and closed when a user runs the cursor over the submenu option (Microsoft, 1992, p. 86).

- Use reverse video to indicate that an option is selected.

- Note that users learn the positions of items on menus very quickly, sometimes within one session. Although individual items may not always be accessible, their positions should remain constant—in other words, graying them out is better than deleting them and closing up the list. Maintain absolute positions, not just relative positions (Norman, 1991, pp. 140, 169–170).

- When your system has a variety of security levels, remove *unavailable* options from menus. In other words, if a user doesn't have access to particular options, don't show them on his or her copy of the menu.

(For some people, a grayed-out "Top Secret Files" option is a challenge, not a restriction.)

*Note:* Your development environment probably takes care of many of these design issues for you.

## Avoiding Problems

Here are some suggested solutions for problems that don't fall into any of the standard categories.

### Singular versus Plural

Default to the singular unless the word you need for the label is a plural—for example, "Graphics" or "Telecommunications."

### Put Menu Labels in Resource Files

Use resource files for ease of translating and for ease of rewriting. If you have to change each menu label individually, you won't change any of them—it's far too much work. For more information about creating easily localized interfaces, see Chapter 6.

### Virtues of Uniqueness

The style guidelines agree: Do not repeat options on top-level menus. If you want to give users more than one way to access a particular function, create pop-up menus, toolbars, or control panels.

In a system with only one menu bar and one set of menus, this is a reasonable rule. However, many applications have more than one menu bar (for the "Create" part of the application and the "Runtime" part, say); pop-up menus also contain duplicated options (see Pop-Up Menus). In cases such as these, use the same labels for the same functions. For example, the printing option should be called "Print" and should use the same mnemonic no matter where it appears.

## Proofreading: Cross-Menu Consistency

Make sure that menus are consistent. Menus will be consistent if the original design specifications (*what* design specifications?) show the menu options in the right, usability tested order, since it is unlikely that a programmer (you or someone else) will rearrange them while actually coding the menu.

However, it is easy enough, during one of the interstices of the programming day (while the network is down or the designers are off arguing about something), to check the menus against one another. If you make a printout of each one as you finish it, you won't need access to the computer.

Also, the technical writers may be willing to add this task to one of their checklists. Eliminating inconsistency on a dozen menus, say, can add a few hours to a writer's schedule. Documenting the inconsistencies, on the other hand, can add *days*—ergo, justification for asking for a writer's help.

## Testing on Users

Usability testing doesn't always require software prototypes, video recordings, one-way mirrors, and other expensive procedures and equipment— "low-fidelity" prototypes of construction paper, 3M Post-It notes, and index

---

**Exercise**: Paper and Pencil Simulation

**Purpose**: To evaluate the intuitiveness and ease of locating menu options.

**Directions**: Names of menus appear above the questions. For the tasks listed in the questions, please write the name of the menu on which you think you might find the option for that task. Guessing is both permitted and expected.

**File**   **Edit**   **Print**   **Format**   **Attach**   **Book**   **Help**

1. Create labels by doing a mail merge. _____

2. Include a video clip in the document. _____

3. Create a new chapter in a book. _____

4. Create a new book. _____

5. Create a chapter template. _____

6. Copy a paragraph of text. _____

---

**Figure 3.9  Paper and pencil simulation**

cards may be more effective during the early stages (Rettig, 1994, pp. 21–27; Spool, 1994, p. 25; Nielsen, 1994, p. 29). In fact, if you consistently test parts of the interface while developing the specifications or prototypes, full-scale testing of the final product should simply confirm that you made the right decisions.

For example, you can easily test menu options with a simple paper and pencil quiz. If your test subjects don't make the right connections, then you know you have more work to do on the design (see Figure 3.9).

## KEYBOARD SHORTCUTS: MNEMONICS AND ACCELERATORS

Keyboard shortcuts are divided into mnemonics and accelerators.

### Mnemonics

Mnemonics in the traditional sense are memory hooks, such as "Every Good Boy Does Fine" (the notes on the musical staff), and rhymes, such as "Red skies at morning, sailors take warning; red skies at night, sailors delight" (for predicting the next day's weather).[2]

Software mnemonics, however, are not related to memory systems at all. (Menus are designed to reduce memorization, not enhance it.) A mnemonic in the software sense is a single-character, programmer-defined keyboard shortcut, which must be visible before you can invoke it. (Accelerators don't have to be visible.)

There is room, however, for some real mnemonics if anyone cares to try. Complicated software operations that are done infrequently—mail merge, for example, or creating a book from a set of chapter files—are good candidates for mnemonic memory aids. So are hazardous and emergency operations—shutting down a power plant, say, or using a complicated software-controlled medical device—that require operators to do things in a particular order. (These kinds of mnemonics may not be in the provenance of menu designers but rather of the writers who create the online help, printed documentation, training materials, and tutorials.)

---

[2] Mnemonics have rhythm and very often rhyme. This is not accidental—it's done by design. "Eenie, meenie, miney, moe, catch a tiger by the foot . . ." That doesn't rhyme: You have to catch him by the toe! Rhyme and rhythm brought Homer through dark ages and made Shakespeare more memorable than these dull pages.

Whether or not software uses *real* mnemonics, keyboard shortcuts do take advantage of human memory, albeit a different sort. Learning to type (and learning such other physical operations as riding a bicycle and driving a car) creates a body memory. This kinesthetic memory is the reason that touch-typists dislike interfaces where too much functionality is tied to the mouse—you can't memorize the mouse's location the way you can memorize keyboard positions. Keys are always in the same place. The mouse pointer rarely is.

### Rules for Defining Mnemonics

The platform guidelines say that mnemonics (or the equivalent)[3] are required for all options except submenus and, in fact, some mnemonics are defined for you in the operating-system specifications—see Table 3.3 for details.

However, because of the chunking rule (you can remember only five items at a time, plus or minus two), defining more than seven mnemonics is overkill. Concentrate your intellectual efforts on the seven most-used menu options, as identified during usability testing. You might also let users redefine the mnemonics to suit themselves—for example, typists who memorized the old WordStar keys might want to redefine your keys to match.

The rules for defining mnemonics (see Table 3.5) are (IBM, 1992, pp. 344–349; Microsoft, 1992, pp. 79–80; Motif, 1993, pp. 5-3–5-4):

- Mnemonics are single characters.

- The program accepting the mnemonic must be case-insensitive (except in NeXTStep).

- When focus is on the menu or menu bar, the user just presses the mnemonic. If focus is anywhere else, he or she must press the special key plus the mnemonic (OSF, 1993, pp. 5-3–5-4).

- The label must contain the character to be used as the mnemonic, *unless* there are no characters in the label (pictures can be used as labels) or the labels will change (on lists of open windows, for example). In either of these situations, number the labels and use the numbers as the mnemonics.

---

[3] Macintosh menus don't have mnemonics per se. The Macintosh keyboard shortcuts require that the user press the [Command] key plus a letter that is often, but not always, one of the letters in the label.

- As long as the label does contain characters, the mnemonic character must be underlined (except in language environments in which underlining is unavailable).

- For all systems except Motif: When a mnemonic is not part of the label but instead is a number or other code, put the number or code flush left in front of the label (at the fourth space) and underline it. Do not include parentheses or periods. For Motif, put a letter mnemonic in parentheses *after* the label (OSF, 1993, p. 5-3). Numbers go in front of the label.

- Don't use the same letter more than once on any individual pull-down menu. You can, however, use the same letter again on a submenu.

- You can also use the same letter more than once on *different* pull-down menus. In other words, you can use F for *File* on one menu and F for *Film Stars* on another. (The items are differentiated from one another by the titles of the menus themselves—say, [Alt]-[F] for *File* menu plus [F] for *File* versus [Alt]-[T] for *Talent* plus [F] for *Film Stars*.)

- All duplicate menu items should use the same mnemonic. For example, if *Save* shows up on two menus, both *Saves* should use the same mnemonic.

**Table 3.5  Decision Table: Mnemonics**

**Default:** Use the first letter in the word or phrase.

| If | Then |
|---|---|
| That letter is already used. | Use the first consonant or the most interesting consonant. |

| If | Then |
|---|---|
| The first consonant is already used. | Use any letter. |

| If | Then |
|---|---|
| The label contains no letters or the letters will change. | Use numbers in front of the label. Start with 1 and end with 9. |

| If | Then |
|---|---|
| The label uses a nonroman writing scheme (Kanji, for example) but a roman keyboard. | Prefix the label with a Roman letter and use that letter as the mnemonic (see Chapter 6 for more on international input methods). |

## Accelerators

Accelerators are function keys, [Ctrl] key or ⌘ key sequences, or keys marked with a function name (for example, "Help" or "Cut"). Accelerator keys are always available—unlike mnemonics, they don't have to be visible to be usable.

Operating-system developers reserve certain key combinations for system-wide accelerators—[Ctrl]-[C], for example, means "copy" in nearly every environment (when it doesn't mean "Cancel," of course). Users automatically have access to the system accelerators unless your program prevents it. Defining new accelerators is encouraged but not required. See Table 3.6 for the reserved accelerator keys.

### Rules for Defining Accelerators

The rules for accelerators are simple.

- Don't use the accelerators that are already defined in the environment for application-specific operations. In other words, don't use [F1] or the [Help] key to open the tutorial. See Table 3.6 for details.

- On option labels, use a plus sign (+) between the key names to indicate that a user must press two or more keys at once—for example, use *Alt+F4*, not *Alt-F4*.

- Remember that function key shortcuts are easier to localize than modifier plus letter shortcuts. Since no name or letter is associated with a key, no translation is required (Microsoft, 1992, p. 87).

*Note:* The IBM guidelines say, "Use the Alt key only to provide access to mnemonics," then list a number of nonmnemonic uses for the [Alt] key (IBM, p. 315). However, that stricture seems to be a "guideline" rather than a "requirement." Just something else to keep in mind.

Table 3.6 contains the most common keyboard accelerators in IBM's OS/2, Motif, and Windows 3.1. Both Macintosh and NeXTStep use *Command*+letter or character shortcuts (refer to Table 3.3). PenPoint doesn't have keyboard accelerators, only pen-based gestures—see GO Corporation reference for details.

For details about additional accelerators, refer to the guidelines for your current environment (IBM, pp. 316–322; Microsoft, pp. 16–17; OSF, pp. 2-3, 6-23).

**Table 3.6  Defined Function Key Accelerators**

| Function Key | Environment | Unmodified | Shift | Ctrl | Alt |
|---|---|---|---|---|---|
| **F1** | IBM OS/2, Motif, Windows 3.1 | Help | Context-sensitive help | | |
| **F2** | IBM OS/2 | General help, in open Help window | Tutorial, in open Help window | | |
| **F3** | Motif | | | | Move window to bottom of stack |
| **F4** | IBM OS/2, Windows 3.1 | | | Close document window | Close application window |
| | Motif | | | | Close application window |
| **F5** | IBM OS/2, Motif | Refresh | | | Restore window |
| | Windows 3.1 | | | Restore window | |
| **F6** | IBM OS/2, Windows 3.1 | Move clockwise to next pane of open window | Move counter-clockwise to next pane of open window | | |
| | Windows 3.1 | | | Move to next document window, put current window on bottom of stack (Shift reverses action) | Move to application's next open non-document window |
| | Motif | | | | Move through secondary application windows (Shift reverses action). |
| **F7** | IBM OS/2, Motif | | | | Move window. |
| | Windows 3.1 | | Move window | | |
| **F8** | Windows 3.1 | Toggle extended selection mode, if available | Toggle add-to-selection mode, if available | | |

*(continued)*

**Table 3.6**  *(Continued)*

| Function Key | Environment | Unmodified | Shift | Ctrl | Alt |
|---|---|---|---|---|---|
| **F8** *(continued)* | IBM OS/2 | Toggle extended selection mode, if available | | | Size window |
| | Motif | | | | Size window |
| **F9** | IBM OS/2 | Keys help, in open Help window | | | Minimize or hide window |
| | Motif | | | | Minimize or hide window |
| **F10** | IBM OS/2, Motif, Windows 3.1 | Toggle menu bar activation | | | Maximize |
| | IBM OS/2, Motif | Display pop-up menu | | | |
| **F11** | IBM OS/2 | Help index in open Help window | | | |
| **F12** | | | | | |

Following are the defined control key accelerators (see Table 3.7). Note that OS/2 uses the old Windows 3.0 key sequences and that Macintosh systems use the ⌘ button instead of [Ctrl] or [Alt].

## ACCOMMODATING EXPERT USERS

*In answer to the question, Does Windows itself contribute to your productivity?*—There's no question about it. If you only use a piece of software once a month, you are an amateur with it, no matter how sophisticated you are. Having this ability to have the software really give you good hints, allowing you to pick it up fresh after dropping it for a few weeks, makes all the difference.

Of course, the downside of that is that I've yet to see any Windows-based package that has learned to stay out of your way once you know what you're doing!

P. J. Plauger, interviewed in *C Development Productivity Research: Six C Authorities and 500 Programmers on Tools, Technologies, and Techniques What Works?* from Rational Systems, Inc.[4]

---

[4] Rational Systems, Inc., 220 North Main Street, Natick, MA 01760; voice: 508-653-6006.

**Table 3.7 Control Key Accelerators**

| Key | Environment | Meaning |
|---|---|---|
| **Ctrl+Z** | Apple, Motif, Windows 3.1 | Undo |
| **Alt+Backspace** | IBM OS/2, alternate for Motif, supported but not recommended for Windows 3.1 | Undo |
| **Ctrl+X** | Apple, Motif, Windows 3.1 | Cut |
| **Shift+Delete** | IBM OS/2, alternate for Motif, supported but not recommended for Windows 3.1 | Cut |
| **Ctrl+C** | Apple, Motif, Windows 3.1 | Copy |
|  | At operating-system level, for communications software, etc. | Break, cancel |
| **Ctrl+Insert** | IBM OS/2, alternate for Motif, supported but not recommended for Windows 3.1 | Copy |
| **Ctrl+V** | Apple, Motif, Windows 3.1 | Paste |
| **Shift+Insert** | IBM OS/2, alternate for Motif, supported but not recommended for Windows 3.1 | Paste |

**Application and Environment Level**

| Key | Environment | Meaning |
|---|---|---|
| **Alt+Esc** | Windows 3.1, OS/2 | Moves top application to bottom of stack |
| **Alt+Shift+Esc** | Windows 3.1, OS/2 | Moves bottom application to top of stack |
| **Alt+Tab** | Motif, Windows 3.1, OS/2 | Shuffles one step from front to back through stack of application windows |
| **Alt+Spacebar** | Motif, Windows 3.1, OS/2 | Opens window's Control menu |
| **Ctrl+Esc** | Windows 3.1, OS/2 | Opens dialog box that let's users switch to any other open application |

Once experienced software users have learned a program, they start looking for the shortcuts. Don't disappoint them. Some of your options are:

- expert activation
- pop-up menus
- multiple-select options, such as tear-off or posted menus
- command-line interfaces

IBM also suggests letting users switch between novice and expert menus and letting them turn certain displays on or off (IBM, 1992, pp. 28–29). Applications can certainly let expert users change the default toolbars, menu items, and so on.

If you define expert modes, make sure that all of the expert functions are available somewhere in the visible menus, buttons, and panels. Since pop-up menus and other shortcuts are designed to be hidden, users may never notice the expert functions and, therefore, never graduate from novice mode. (It doesn't matter that your program comes with training—turnover in some industries runs to 50 percent within six months, 100 percent in a year. Special credit for the answer to this word problem: How many officially trained users will be left by the time *you've* left for another job?)

## Expert Activation

"Expert activation" means "if you double-click here, something extra happens." As the Motif guidelines put it, "the expert action should include the regular action of the component in a more global manner." For example, if pressing an "erase" button turns on the eraser tool, double-clicking it turns on the eraser *and* erases the selected text (OSF, 1993, p. 5-6). In many word processing programs, clicking on a word puts the cursor in the word; double-clicking *selects* the word.

## Pop-Up Menus

Pop-up menus appear when the user moves the cursor over a hotspot (defined by the developer) *and* presses a mouse button (usually the right button). Although a cursor change can be used to indicate that a pop-up exists, the development guidelines are silent about whether an indicator is required or not.

Rules for pop-up menus vary among platforms. Following are the areas of agreement and disagreement.

*Note:* What the Apple Computer guidelines call "pop-ups" are called "option menus" or "option buttons" in the Motif and Windows environments. See Chapter 2 for more on buttons.

*Accelerators and mnemonics:* If the development environment doesn't offer keyboard access for pop-ups, there are neither mnemonics nor accelerators. In environments with keyboard access, the guidelines suggest that you use the same accelerators and mnemonics on a pop-up menu as you use in the top-level pull-down menus.

*Recommended options:* The IBM OS/2 guidelines suggest three groups of items on a typical pop-up: *Help* and *Open* as the first group, clipboard choices as the second group, and application-specific choices as the third group. The third group can also contain choices such as *Undo*, *Print*, and *Clear* (IBM, 1992, pp. 192–193).

Motif recommends that you put options such as *Properties* (set properties), *Cut, Copy, Paste, Undo, Select All,* and *Deselect All* on your pop-ups (OSF, 1993, pp. 6-27–6-30).

The Windows guidelines have no recommended list of options, although *Undo* and *Properties* options are mentioned as typical (Microsoft, 1992, p. 77).

*Submenus:* The Windows guidelines say that one level of submenus is acceptable, but two or more are not (Microsoft, 1992, p. 77).

*Titles:* The Motif guidelines call for a title placed at the top of the menu and separated from the menu elements by a standard separator (OSF, 1993, p. 6-41). The Windows 3.1 guidelines, on the other hand, say that a pop-up menu doesn't have a title (Microsoft, 1992, pp. 76, 79).

## Multiple-Select Options

GUI menus generally disappear as soon as the user selects an option or clicks outside the menu. However, sometimes menus are more useful if they stick around.

The Macintosh, Motif, NeXT, and Open Look environments have methods for turning menus into temporary panels, called "tear-off" menus or "pushpin" menus—when you push the pin in, the menu stays posted (Sun Microsystems, 1990, pp. 287–289). Tear-off menus typically contain tools, patterns, colors, and other items that users select repeatedly.

Advantages of tear-offs over permanent toolbars and control panels are:

- *Relative impermanence* (as well as relative permanence vis-à-vis menus)—you post them when you want them posted and remove them when you don't.

- *No real estate:* Since you don't have to reserve space for a permanent palette, you can create a larger workspace. (The tear-off panel floats on top of the graphic or document wherever the user drops it.)

On Macintosh systems, a user can detach a tear-off menu from the menu bar by putting the cursor on the menu's title, pressing the mouse button, then dragging the menu three pixels away from the menu bar (Apple, 1992, pp. 92–95). There is nothing to indicate whether a menu can be torn off or not.

In NeXTSTEP systems, users can detach *any* submenu from its supermenu (its parent) by simply dragging it away. "As a sign of its independence, it gets, for the first time, its own close button," the guidelines say. "The idea is for users to bring up a submenu, then tear it off and move it to a desired location if they want it to stay on-screen" (NeXT, 1992, p. 103).

In Motif systems, the tear-off point is a button that looks like a dashed line: – – – – – – – –. This button appears on the menu itself, just above the part of the menu that can be torn off. The user can post the menu where it is, just below the menu bar, or drag the menu to another spot on the window (OSF, 1993, pp. 9-126–9-127).

The Microsoft Windows guidelines say nothing about tear-offs or other menu panel hybrids, but clever developers can create them nevertheless. For example, CorelDRAW! and its sister programs[5] offer "Roll-Up™" menus (see Figure 3.10). To use one, you simply select a panel option from a menu. The panel has an arrow button in the upper righthand corner. If you select it, the panel "rolls up" into its title bar, which you can then move anywhere on the window. What's more, the roll-ups persist even after you end the session.

## Command Lines

It is supposedly retrograde to have a command line. However, some programs with new GUIs (askSam, Excel, Xywrite) have included command lines. Why?

---

[5] Corel Corporation, 1600 Carling Avenue, Ottawa, Ontario, Canada K1Z 8R7; voice: 613-728-3733; fax: 613-761-9176.

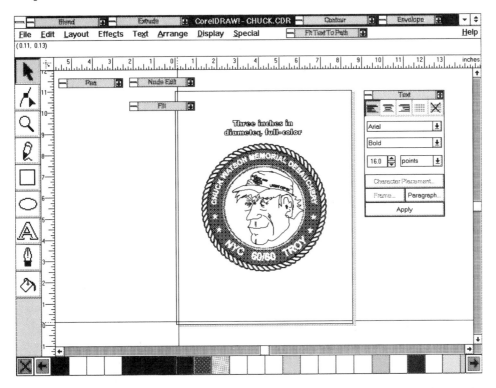

**Figure 3.10 CorelDRAW! Roll-Up (CorelDRAW screen shot reprinted with permission from Corel Corporation. CorelDRAW and Roll-Up are trademarks of Corel Corporation.)**

"It's obvious why *we* did it," said Phil Schnyder, president of askSam Systems (askSam is a text database program).[6] "In askSam, you can search for any word by pressing one key to get into the command line, typing the word, and pressing [Enter]. I've tried other databases—you can put information in theirs just as quickly as ours, but to get it out, you had to go through too many dialog boxes." (See Figure 3.11.)

In short, consider including (or retaining) a command line when:

- The user has to type an entry anyway. Typing the entry on a command line is much faster than accessing the menu, opening a panel, typing the entry, then pressing OK or some other button.

---

[6] askSam Systems, Inc., P.O. Box 1428, Perry, FL 32347; voice: 800-800-1997 or 904-584-6590; fax: 904-584-7481. askSam for Windows is available in English, German, and Italian.

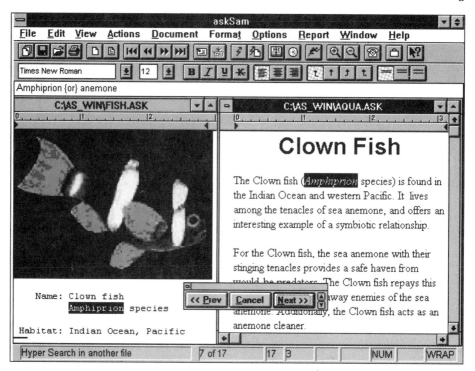

**Figure 3.11  askSam command line**

- Many of your customers are familiar with the old command-line version of the program. Including a command line may help ease them into the new GUI version (OSF, 1993, p. 6-14).[7]

- The GUI adds too much overhead or is too restrictive for expert users. For example, people who normally use SQL to access databases are not going to be happy with canned data views and queries that require lots of mouse and button activity.

Keep in mind, however, that menus give new users an intellectual advantage. Test subjects who are taught to use the menus first, commands second, "fared better in their overall knowledge of the functionality of the system. Subjects in the command language condition learned only a limited number

---

[7] However, we asked Schnyder if askSam's long-time DOS users still used the command line to start programs or access commands. "Not really," he said. "You get tired of typing in the commands. It's easier to use the menus than the command line for the programs."

of task-specific functions" (Norman, 1991, pp. 317–318). In other words, although a command line is a good tool, use it in addition to–not as a replacement for–menu access.

### Where to Put a Command Line

The Motif guidelines suggest putting the command line at the bottom of the window or, if the window also has a message area, just above the message area (OSF, 1993, pp. 6-12–6-13). Windows 3.1 systems often have "Run" command lines on File menus.

## VARIATIONS

This part of the chapter describes some less common menus.

## Audio Menus

Audio menus are usually associated with phone systems, but software designers are beginning to create virtual phones on the desktop. In fact, Microsoft released a Windows Telephony Software Development Toolkit (TAPI SDK) in November 1993 (D'Hooge, 1994, pp. 19–23). See Voice Messaging and Telecommunications for details.

Keep in mind that audio menus, prompts, icons, and other aural widgets are available for blind and partially sighted users, as well as for other users whose eyes must be elsewhere than on a video screen. See Resources at the end of this chapter for more information.

### Voice Messaging Systems

One familiar type of audio menu is the type associated with voice-messaging systems—"Sally Biggles isn't here right now. To leave a message, record after the tone." As might be expected, the International Standards Organization has been developing a standard set of menus for these systems (ISO, 1993, pp. 19–30). See Figures 3.12 and 3.13 and Table 3.8.

*Note:* In Table 3.8, keys are defined as "Mandatory" or "Optional" and "Reserved" or "Not Reserved." All mandatory keys are reserved. Optional keys can be reserved or not reserved. "Reserved" means that even if you don't use them in your application, you can't assign them other functions.

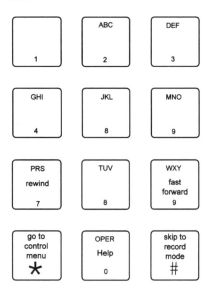

**Figure 3.12  Answer mode key assignments**

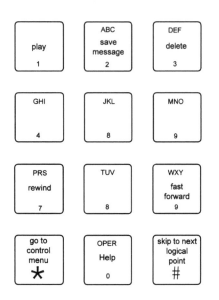

**Figure 3.13  Listen mode key assignments**

**Table 3.8  ISO Voice Messaging Menu Specifications**

**Control Menu**

| 7 | Go to top-level menu of current application | Optional but reserved |
|---|---|---|
| 8 | Select language | Optional but reserved |
| 9 | Disconnect | Mandatory and reserved |
| * | Cancel, back up | Optional but reserved |
| 0 | Help or operator | Mandatory and reserved |
| # | Return to prior context | Mandatory and reserved |

**Call-Answering Menu**

| 7 | Rewind greeting | Optional, not reserved |
|---|---|---|
| 9 | Fast-forward greeting | Optional, not reserved |
| * | Go back to control menu | Mandatory and reserved |
| 0 | Help or operator | Mandatory and reserved |
| # | Skip to next mode, stop greeting | Mandatory and reserved |

**Record Mode Menu**

| * | Go back to control menu | Mandatory and reserved |
|---|---|---|
| 0 | Help or operator | Optional but reserved |
| # | Stop recording | Mandatory and reserved |

**Voice Mail Main Menu**

| 1 | Listen to messages | Mandatory and reserved |
|---|---|---|
| 2 | Create or send messages | Optional, not reserved |
| * | Go back to control menu | Mandatory and reserved |

**Listen Mode Menu**

| 1 | Play messages | Optional and reserved |
|---|---|---|
| 2 | Save message | Optional and reserved |
| 3 | Delete message | Optional and reserved |
| 7 | Rewind message | Optional, not reserved |
| 9 | Fast-forward message | Optional, not reserved |
| * | Go back to control menu | Mandatory and reserved |
| 0 | Help or operator | Mandatory and reserved |
| # | Skip to next mode | Mandatory and reserved |

*(continued)*

**Table 3.8**  *(Continued)*

**Send Messages Menu**

| 1 | Play back message | Mandatory and reserved |
|---|---|---|
| 2 | Save message | Optional, not reserved |
| 3 | Delete message | Optional and reserved |
| 4 | Send message | Optional and reserved |
| * | Go back to control menu | Mandatory and reserved |
| 0 | Help or operator | Mandatory and reserved |
| # | Skip to next mode | Mandatory and reserved |

### Automated Attendants and Information Services

Other common types of phone systems are automated telephone information services, such as the U.S. Postal Services Postal Answer Line, and automated attendant systems used by many U.S. businesses: "Thank you for calling Acme Software. For customer service, press 1. For programming tips, press 2" and so on. Menus for these types of systems are similar to those of the voice-messaging systems except that they are much less constrained. There are, nevertheless, some rules for creating audio menus.

*Use delimiters:* Use the # symbol to delimit data entry when the entry may have an indeterminate endpoint—for example, when the system is asking for a check number or personal identification number. (A time-out can also be used as a delimiter.)

   If the data entry has a known endpoint (when the caller enters a Social Security number, for example), don't ask for the # delimiter. However, don't penalize a caller for pressing # when he or she doesn't have to.

*Allow interrupts:* Let the caller end or interrupt the current activity and skip to the next activity by pressing # or the number of an item on the next menu (allow type-ahead, in other words).

*Be sensitive to callers lacking high-tech vocabularies:* When you write your messages, keep in mind that some customers won't know the name of the # key. Also, the name changes from country to country. In the United States and Canada, it is usually called "pound," but it may also be called "hash" or "sharp" (the musical sharp). In Sweden, it is called "brädstapel," meaning "pile of sticks" (ISO, 1993, p. 40).

Another problem is that although anyone who uses a computer is comfortable with the idea of "entering" a number, the millions of people who don't use computers won't know what you are talking about (Gardner-Bonneau, 1992, p. 223).

Note that there is consensus on the name of the * key—it's called the "star" key (Schumacher, 1992, p. 1053).

*Keep menus short:* Since sound does not persist, audio menus are constrained by short-term memory. (You can't go backwards on an audio menu unless you repeat the recording.) For this reason, menus should contain no more than four items at a time.

*Keep options short:* State options in language short enough to suit expert users but clear enough for novice users. Finding the right mix requires usability testing.

*Use "goal-action" format for messages:* Put the goal first and the action second. In other words, say, "To forward a call, press 6," not "Press 6 to forward a call." The caller is listening intently for the thing he or she wants to do, not for the meaning of a particular button (Schumacher, 1992, p. 1053).

*Take advantage of existing spatial expectations:* Internationally, audio equipment uses left for backward (reverse, rewind) and right for forward (play, fast forward). The ISO specifications suggest matching this style by using keys on the left side for regressive steps (previous, back, slower) and keys on the right side for progressive steps (next, forward, faster). Note, however (as the ISO specifications do), that in China and the Middle East, movements from right to left are progressive, not regressive (ISO, 1993, p. 43).

## Multimedia Menus

If you need information about the Okefenokee Swamp, why not look for it on a map? If you need to set the time, why not use a clock?

Kent Norman says that nonlinear menus (menus that aren't lists, in other words) have two advantages. The first advantage is that visual recognition and spatial memory are powerful tools for locating items. Graphical representations, such as maps, color wheels, and the periodic table of the elements, are already well tested and well understood in the noncomputer world, so you might as well use them in the computerized version.

The second advantage is that nonlinear menus (especially round ones) can speed up selection time by reducing mouse travel (Norman, 1991, pp.

309–310). Selecting a color from a color wheel, for example, can be a tiny movement from the center point to the desired color.

On multimedia systems, the main menu may be a picture that is a collection of "hotspots" (also called "anchors" or "triggers")—when you touch a point on the picture, you go to a section of an online book (hypertext), a photo, an audio clip, or a video clip. For example, Figure 3.14 shows the opening window for a CD-ROM book about the restoration of the Statue of Liberty. When the standard arrow cursor moves over a hotspot, the cursor changes shape and an outline appears. If the user clicks anywhere inside the outline, he or she goes to the part of the book containing information about that part of the restoration.

When the trigger is part of the visual object, you normally have to indicate that it's a trigger. One possibility is to distinguish the triggers visually from

**Figure 3.14  Statue of Liberty mega-icon or picture menu**

the rest of the drawing. For example, you can use a deeper shade of the drawing's main color to indicate the trigger. Or you might render trigger-able mechanical parts in three dimensions, leaving the untriggered parts of the drawing in two dimensions. Or you can put dashed lines around trigger areas, as in Figure 3.14.

Another common method of indicating triggers is to change the cursor shape. For example, you can change the cursor from an arrow to an ear to indicate "audio output here" or a video camera shape to indicate "video here" (IBM, 1992, pp. 16–17).

In games and educational programs, however, there may be no trigger indicator—the user must find the triggers by exploring. For example, in Brøderbund's *Arthur's Teacher Trouble* and *Grandma and Me*, many items in each panel are "live." When you click the cursor on a starfish in *Grandma and Me*, the starfish jumps up and leads nearby shells in calisthenics. In *Arthur's Teacher Trouble*, when you click on the science lab's door, a green puddle leaks out from underneath the door, goes "Bloop, bloop," and then goes back inside. There are no predefined paths, nothing is highlighted; everything is a surprise—a perfect learning tool.[8]

## REFERENCES

Apple Computer, Inc. *Macintosh Human Interface Guidelines*, Reading, MA: Addison-Wesley, 1992.

Baker, Nicholson, "Annals of Scholarship: Discards" *New Yorker*, April 4, 1994, pp. 64–86.

*Chicago Manual of Style, The*. Chicago: University of Chicago Press, 1993.

Gardner-Bonneau, Daryle Jean. "Human Factors Problems in Interactive Voice Response (IVR): Do We Need a Guideline/Standard?" *Proceedings of the Human Factors Society Thirty-Sixth Annual Meeting*, 1992.

D'Hooge, Herman. "The Windows Telephony SDK." *Computer Telephony*, January/February 1994.

GO Corporation. *PenPoint User Interface Design Reference*. Reading, MA: Addison-Wesley, 1992.

---

[8] Brøderbund, 500 Redwood Boulevard, Novato, CA 94948-6121.

Gregory, Richard L. (editor). *The Oxford Companion to the Mind.* Oxford and New York: Oxford University Press, 1987.

Halstead-Nussloch, Richard. "The Design of Phone-Based Interfaces for Consumers." *CHI'89 Proceedings,* May 1989, pp. 347–352.

IBM Corporation. *Object-Oriented Interface Design: IBM Common User Access Guidelines.* Carmel, IN: IBM/Que, 1992.

International Standards Organization. *User Interface to Telephone-based Services: Voice Messaging Applications.* Pub. no. ISO/IEC JTC1/SC18/WG9 N1219, working draft of March 19, 1993.

Microsoft Corporation. *The Windows Interface: An Application Design Guide,* Redmond, WA: Microsoft Press, 1992.

NeXT Publications. *NeXTStep User Interface Guidelines.* (for NeXTStep Release 3). Reading, MA: Addison-Wesley, 1992.

Nielsen, Jakob. "UPA93: Usability Professionals Association Annual Meeting 21–23 July 1993, Redmond, WA USA." *SIGCHI Bulletin,* April 1994, pp. 29–32. (Describes a variety of faster and cheaper usability tests. Also mentions that VHS tapes of 18 talks at the conference are available.)

Norman, Kent L. *The Psychology of Menu Selection.* Norwood, NJ: Ablex Publishing Corporation, 1991.

Open Software Foundation. *OSF/Motif Style Guide,* Revision 1.2 (for Motif Release 1.2). Englewood Cliffs, NJ: Prentice-Hall, 1993.

Rettig, Marc. "Prototyping for Tiny Fingers." *Communications of the ACM,* April 1994, pp. 21–27.

Schneiderman, Ben. *Designing the User Interface,* 2d ed. Reading, MA: Addison-Wesley, 1992.

Schumacher, Robert M. Jr. "Phone-Based Interfaces: Research and Guidelines." *Proceedings of the Human Factors Society Thirty-Sixth Annual Meeting,* 1992, pp. 1051–1055.

Spool, Jared M. "Low-Fidelity Prototypes: Getting Input into the Design." *Interchange Technical Writing Conference Proceedings,* April 4–5, 1994, pp. 25–27. (Contact: STC, Boston Chapter, P.O. Box 670, Canton, MA 02021.)

Sun Microsystems, Inc. *Open Look: Graphical User Interface Application Style Guidelines.* Reading, MA: Addison-Wesley, 1990.

## RESOURCES

### Adaptive Technologies, Audio

For information about audio technologies for computer hardware and software, contact the National Technology Center, American Foundation for the Blind, 15 West 16th Street, New York, NY 10011; 212-620-2080; fax: 212-620-2137.

The Trace Research and Development Center at the University of Wisconsin offers software, telephone communication devices, and computer-access software. Contact: Trace R&D Center, University of Wisconsin-Madison, S-151 Waisman Center, 1500 Highland Avenue, Madison, WI 53705; 608-263-2309; TDD: 608-263-5408.

Librarians and teachers will find Ruth A. Velleman's *Meeting the Needs of People with Disabilities: A Guide for Librarians, Educators, and Other Service Professionals* useful (1990). The book is available from The Oryx Press, 4041 North Central Avenue, Suite 700, Phoenix, AZ 85012-3397.

### Memory Systems

Information about memory systems and mnemonics is readily available. Community colleges and adult education schools often offer classes entitled, "Enhance Your Memory" and "How to Remember Names and Faces." Memory systems are easy to learn (which is exactly the point, of course) and shouldn't require much time or effort. Developing catchy, easy to remember mnemonics for customers, however, may be a little more difficult.

### Recommended Books

Lewis, David, and James Greene. *Thinking Better.* New York: Rawson, Wade Publishers, 1982. (This book tells you how to do better on IQ tests, too.)

Minninger, Joan. *Total Recall: How to Boost Your Memory Power.* Emmaus, PA: Rodale Press, 1984.

## Voice Messaging and Telecommunications

The Telephony Application Programming Interface Software Development Toolkit (TAPI SDK) is available from these sources:

- On CompuServe, download TAPI10.ZIP from the WINEXT forum.
- From the Microsoft Download Service BBS (206-936-6735), download TAPISDK.EXE, a self-extracting archive file.
- From the Internet, download TAPI10.ZIP via remote ftp at ftp.microsoft.com in /softlib/mslfiles or \devtools\tapi.

For more information, contact Microsoft: via voice at 206-936-1144, via fax at 206-936-7329 (address the fax to "Windows Telephony Coordinator"), or via e-mail to telephon@microsoft.com.

The Human Factors and Ergonomics Society has a Communications Technical Group, which consists of approximately 350 people working in telecommunications firms, universities, consulting firms, and manufacturers. For more information, contact the Human Factors and Ergonomics Society, P.O. Box 1369, Santa Monica, CA 90406-1369; voice: 310-394-1811; fax: 310-394-2410.

Two controlled-circulation periodicals from the same publisher contain information about voice messaging.

- *Computer Telephony,* which started publishing in 1994, describes the world of phone/computer hybrids—phone and fax boards in computers, computerized voice-processing applications, speech recognition and text to speech applications, voice processing standards, and so on.
- *Teleconnect,* which publishes articles on automated attendants, call- and voice-processing systems, telephony applications, and hardware of all kinds.

Contact *Teleconnect* and *Computer Telephony* at 12 West 21st Street, New York, NY 10010; voice: 212-691-8215; fax: 212-691-1191; MCI Mail 101-5032 (for publisher Harry Newton).

## Usability and Human Factors

### Organizations

The Human Factors and Ergonomics Society, P.O. Box 1369, Santa Monica, CA 90406-1369; voice: 310-394-1811; fax: 310-394-2410. (See also the publications list below.)

SIGCHI (Special Interest Group, Computer-Human Interaction) of the Association for Computing Machinery (ACM), 1515 Broadway, 17th Floor, New York, NY 10036-5701; voice: 212-626-0500; fax: 212-944-1318; Internet: acmhelp@acm.org. (See also the publications list below.)

## Publications

Publications of the Association for Computer Machinery (ACM) include:

*interactions,* a new publication with a how-to flavor. It includes interviews with interface designers and thinkers, as well as interesting interface design case studies.

*SIGCHI Bulletin,* a quarterly with research papers from the human factors field.

*Transactions on Computer-Human Interaction,* which contains in-depth papers on major issues from a computer science, rather than the psychological, point of view.

Contact ACM, 1515 Broadway, 17th Floor, New York, NY 10036-5701; voice: 212-626-0500; fax: 212-944-1318.

Publications of the Human Factors and Ergonomics Society include:

*Human Factors,* which contains papers on basic and applied human factors research, theoretical approaches to human factors, and review articles.

*Ergonomics in Design,* which contains articles, case studies, anecdotes, debates, and commentary on the importance of ergonomic design and implementation.

Contact The Human Factors and Ergonomics Society, P.O. Box 1369, Santa Monica, CA 90406-1369; voice: 310-394-1811; fax: 310-394-2410.

*International Journal of Human-Computer Interaction* has a broad perspective, covering issues like occupational stress and other management factors related to computer use. The journal is published by Ablex Publishing Corp., Norwood, NJ 07648; 201-767-8450; fax: 201-767-6717.

## Recommended Books

Dumas, Joseph, and Janice Redish. *A Practical Guide to Usability Testing.* Norwood, NJ: Ablex Publishing Corporation, 1993.

Hix, Deborah, and H. Rex Hartson. *Developing User Interfaces: Ensuring Usability through Product and Process,* New York: John Wiley & Sons, 1993.

Lindgaard, G. *Usability Testing and System Evaluation.* London and New York: Chapman & Hall, 1994.

Nielsen Jakob, and Robert Mack. *Usability Inspection Methods.* New York, NY: John Wiley & Sons, 1994.

Nielsen, Jakob. *Usability Engineering,* Boston, MA: AP Professional, 1993.

Rubin, Jeffrey. *Handbook of Usability Testing,* New York, NY: John Wiley & Sons, 1994.

## Testing Software

The University of Maryland's Office of Technology Liaison offers the Questionnaire for User Interface Satisfaction (QUIS) developed by Ben Schneiderman and Kent Norman. The test lets you easily and reliably quantify interface problems and successes. A typical QUIS question is, "Was the highlighting on the screen helpful?" The person taking the test then circles a number from 1 to 9, with 1 being "not at all helpful" and 9 being "very helpful."

Each license includes Windows, Macintosh, and paper versions. Commercial licenses are $750 and nonprofit or academic licenses are $200; site licenses and network licenses can be negotiated as well. For more information, contact Carolyn Garrett, Licensing Manager, Information Sciences, Office of Technology Liaison, 4312 Knox Road, University of Maryland, College Park, MD 20742; voice: 301-405-4209; Internet: CG54@umail.umd.edu.

# PART II

## TEXT

# 4

# Messages

"Keep it simple. The more you say, the less people remember."

Chinese fortune cookie,
Staten Island, New York,
November 30, 1993

Messages fall into four categories—"you might want to know this" (status), "you need to know this" (alert), "you better do something about this" (error), and "hey, STOP!" (hazard). The types of messages normally used in GUIs are status, alert, and error messages. However, hazard messages are also becoming important, as embedded software begins to control mechanical and electronic equipment.

Instructions for creating each type of message appear in this chapter. Also included is information on constructing warning sounds and programming strategies for messages.

## STATUS MESSAGES

Status messages are a running commentary on an application's activity. For example, as a program loads, the status message might be "Loading database . . . ." As the program searches, the message might be "Searching for matches . . . ." Once the program has results, the message might be "Found: 22 records."

Status messages are used to indicate both progress toward a goal and the accomplishment of that goal. "Acknowledgment" status messages are especially important if the process is not visible to the user (it's running in the background) or if it takes so long that the user might have turned away from her computer before the operation was finished (see Unavoidable Delays).

Depending on the application and the length of time needed for the operation, you might want to let users add a beep or a flashing light to the acknowledgment messages. If background processes have indeterminate endpoints (compiling a program, for example), you might want to send the acknowledgment messages to the users' electronic mailboxes instead of popping them onto the screen. Usability testing should be able to tell you which options to offer.

## Unavoidable Delays

Slow response time has been the focus of intense research as well as serious user frustration. Although people can adapt to working with slower response times, they are generally dissatisfied with rates longer than two seconds (Schneiderman, 1992, p. 288).

The problem is that you can hold information in short-term memory for no more than 10 to 15 seconds at a time. As response time increases beyond 10 to 15 seconds, continuity of thought becomes increasingly difficult to maintain, possibly because the sequence of actions in short-term memory is disrupted and must be reloaded (Galitz, 1994, p. 432).

However, expected response times differ by the type of task.

- Typing, cursor motion, or mouse selection: 50–150 milliseconds
- Simple frequent tasks: less than 1 second
- Common tasks: 1–4 seconds
- Complex tasks: 8–12 seconds.

But once users know what to expect for particular tasks, *variability* in response times can also create anxiety and dissatisfaction. Variability can occur in either direction: A response that is suddenly too fast causes as much anxiety as one that is too slow (Galitz, 1994, p. 432). The anxiety comes from uncertainty—"Did the process I asked for work?" or "Why is this taking so long? Did I break something?"

As well as providing feedback, therefore, status messages help mitigate the effects of too long or too short response times. Users tolerate delays when they know how long the process will take and that the process is, indeed, still continuing. They will tolerate too fast responses if an acknowledgment message shows that their request was actually acted upon.

### Add a Cancel Option

If a particular process takes a very long time (30 seconds to minutes), always include a cancel option. People sometimes change their minds; they often pick the wrong things by mistake. Forcing a user to wait 10 minutes before he or she can get the machine back is very rude. Therefore, either accept a key-based interrupt—[Esc] or [Ctrl]+[Break], for example—or display a status message with a prominent "Cancel this Operation" button.

## How to Write Status Messages

In general, use standard punctuation and syntax—put periods at the ends of sentences, use colons to indicate "as follows," and so on. For example:

```
Found: 23 out of 88 records.
```

To indicate time passing, use an ellipsis (three periods) at the end of the word or phrase:

```
Searching...
```

Unlike other types of messages, status messages do not require user interaction.

You can also use progress indicators in the status area. See Progress Indicators for more information.

## Progress Indicators

Progress indicators and "waiting" pointers are status-message subtypes used to indicate, and psychologically mitigate, time delays. Whenever a process takes more than a second, show a wait pointer, as illustrated in Figure 4.1.

Wait pointers are good from one to five seconds. After five seconds, however, users think that the system is hung and will try to cancel the operation. Therefore, if the process normally takes more than five seconds, add a progress indicator. The types of progress indicator are: elapsed time message, percent complete message, and progress indicator bar (Galitz, 1994, pp. 433–434).

**Figure 4.1 "Wait" pointers**

## Elapsed Time Message

When the user needs to know exactly how long a process will take ("Do I have time for a cup of coffee?"), use the elapsed time message. For example:

```
Expected backup time: 20:10 minutes
Elapsed time: 08:48 minutes
```

Or:

```
Time remaining: 11 minutes
```

## Percent Complete Message

If other methods of showing progress are too slow, too memory-intensive, or too complicated for a particular application, use a simple percent complete message, updated every few seconds. For example:

```
20% complete
```

## Progress Indicator Bar

A progress indicator bar is a long rectangular bar (horizontal or vertical) that starts out empty but is filled as the operation proceeds. (See Figure 4.2.)

Amount completed

| | | | | | | | | | | | | | | | | | | | | | | | | | | | | | | | | | | | | | | |
0%        25%        50%        75%      100%

**Figure 4.2 Progress indicator bar**

Fill a horizontal bar with a color or shade of gray from left to right. Fill a vertical bar from bottom to top (like a thermometer or like pouring water in a glass).

---

## ALERT MESSAGES

An alert (also called "note," "prompt," "attention panel" in NeXTStep, or simply "message") conveys information and asks for a response. Display an alert:

- To report on the current state of the system. For example, "Memory is running low. Please close some windows."

- To let the user back out of an irreversible action (this kind of message is known as a "chicken switch"). For example, "About to replace all file names with FILE000.000. This action cannot be undone. Continue?"

Alerts may or may not stop the user from doing other work before the message is cleared. In other words, they may or may not be modal. See Types of Dialog Boxes in Chapter 1 for details.

### How to Write Alert Messages

Suggestions for writing alert messages, in priority order, are:

*Use the goal-action format for messages:* Put the problem or goal first and the action to be taken second. In other words, write "This directory, FILEDIR, does not exist. Do you want to create it?" rather than "Do you want to create FILEDIR? It does not exist."

*Start where the user is:* End where the user wants to be. For example, write "This record is filled. Do you want to go on to the next record?"

*Use chronological order:* If the user has to do first one thing, then another, then write the message that way. For example, write "Please enter the zip code, then press OK to continue." If, instead, you write "Press OK after you enter the zip code," a significant number of users will immediately press OK.

*Avoid negatives in prompts:* Native English speakers find sentences like this difficult to understand (nonnative speakers find them impossible):

```
Are you sure that you don't want to save the file?
```

How are you supposed to answer this? By reversing the sense: Yes, I don't want to save the file. No, I do want to save the file. The correct version is:

```
Do you want to discard the file?
```

### Possible Responses

Questions or prompts require Yes, No, and Cancel buttons. Information messages require OK or Continue buttons. The IBM CUA guidelines suggest including a help button as well (IBM, 1992, p. 338).

Remove the message automatically whenever your application can determine that the error has been corrected. For example, if the printer sent an "out of paper" message to your application but now sends a notice that the paper tray has been refilled, remove the alert message. Don't wait for the user to do it (IBM, 1992, p. 206).

### Titles

For titles, use:

- An alert icon and no title, as in Macintosh systems (Apple Computer, 1992, p. 195)
- A nonthreatening term, such as "Information," "Prompt," or "Question" (OSF, 1993, pp. 9-58, 9-97, 9-101).

You can also:

- Use the program name as the title, especially in multitasking environments. If the message comes from a system or network process, add the word "Message" to the name of the network or system product. Users are often unaware of the background processes, so a message from the network might come as quite a surprise. Feel free to use a longer title to explain why the message appeared (Microsoft, 1992, p. 128).
- Use the problem description as the title (for example, "Printer Out of Paper") and the suggested response as the body of the message (IBM, 1992, p. 206).

### Icons

The suggested icon for a prompt or question is a question mark. Except for the Macintosh and Motif systems, the suggested icon for an information-only

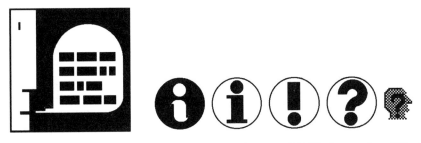

**Figure 4.3  Alert message icons: Macintosh note; IBM information; Windows information, warning, and question; Motif question**

message is the lowercase letter i. Macintosh and Motif systems use "talking head" icons (Apple Computer, 1993, p. 195). (See Figure 4.3.)

## Margins

A ragged right margin is usually better than a justified margin because it looks more interesting and because it doesn't require hyphenation. In addition, justification often leaves large white spaces between words or letters, interrupting eye movement.

## Shortening Text

Messages should be no longer than two or three lines of 40 to 60 characters each (five to eight words). If they are any longer, you tend to lose your place as your eyes move from one side of the line to the other.

Writing short is harder than writing long (because it requires more revision), but it gets easier with practice. All professional writers know how to write to fit the space available—if you ever wondered how magazine articles fill their pages so neatly, the answer is that the editors rewrite them to fit. If, however, you don't yet have a professional technical writer on staff, refer to Table 4.1.

**Suggestions:**

- Read Table 4.1 quickly now, then refer to it later if you get stuck.

- Use a global search and replace to change the words and phrases in the first column to the words and phrases in the second.

- Memorize *The Elements of Style,* which writers usually call "Strunk and White." Strunk & White is a mere 85 pages long (and the pages are only

4 ¼" by 7"), making it a masterpiece of succinctness and an exemplar of its own recommendations.

• Get a reference copy of the well-respected (and nearly as small) *Guide to Managerial Communication*.

See References for the full citations.

**Table 4.1  How to Shorten Text** (*Note:* **The offending words are underlined**).

| Original | Shorter (and Better) | Why |
|---|---|---|
| If you want to change the organization of the list... | To change the organization of the list... | "You" is implied. |
| Select the Search button [or pushbutton] | Select Search. | "Button" and other object names can usually be implied from the context. If not, include the object name. |
| Use this window to search... | Use to search... | "Window" or other object can be implied. |
| Select the type of messages you want to appear... | Select the type of messages you want to display... Select the type of messages to be displayed... | If read quickly, "you want to appear" is ambiguous. Do *you* intend to appear? No— messages either appear or are displayed. |
| Are not allowed to be used... | Cannot be used... | Much shorter. |
| Are required to... | Must... | Shorter and simpler. |
| Allows you to... | Lets you... | Shorter and simpler. |
| This window allows you to... | Use to.... | Shorter. Also, the window can't do anything. You do things with the window. |
| The selected color is displayed in the color field... | The selected color appears in the color field... | Shorter. |

**Table 4.1** *(Continued)*

| Original | Shorter (and Better) | Why |
|---|---|---|
| To make modifications... or To make changes... | To change... | Shorter. |
| Utilize | Use | Shorter. "Utilize" is also usually incorrect (look at the dictionary definitions). |
| In order to | To | Eliminates redundancy. |
| Already existing | Existing | Eliminates redundancy. |
| To save a new file, enter a new name | To save a new file, enter a name. | Eliminates redundancy. |
| The Option Buttons let you select chart types. | The option buttons [or options] let you select chart types. | Unnecessary capitals. Capital letters are bigger than lowercase, so they take up more room in a dialog box.<br>*Note:* The Motif 1.2 guidelines capitalize all widget names, for example, "Dialog Box." If you're writing specifications for people familiar with these guidelines, you might want to use the same style. However, note that the Motif 2.0 guidelines use standard capitalization. |
| The memo template must be selected. | You must select the memo template. Select the memo template. | Unnecessary passive voice.<br>*Note:* To catch incidents of passive voice, do a global search on forms of the verb "to be"—*is, should be, will be, was, were. Then look for the past tense—usually "-ed."* |

### Bad Breaks

If a message doesn't fit on one line, split it or rewrite it in such a way that each line can be read as its own sentence or phrase (which is how headlines are written):

```
Clinton Confronted
By Some Governors
On Economic Plan
```

Otherwise, you can end up with some very odd statements:

```
Marinated & Grilled Whole Baby
Chicken Served with Herbed Butter
```

(From a menu at an upscale New York pub.) Bad breaks can be especially troublesome when writing messages for embedded-system LCD panels (common on copiers and vending machines). Each message on a well-designed LCD panel must be a self-explanatory word or phrase. See Hazard Messages for other bad breaks.

## ERROR MESSAGES

Error messages fall into two categories: user and system errors.

- A user (or "program") error appears when the program detects a slip or a mistake (see Slips versus Mistakes). The user must respond, either by acknowledging the message—"Sorry, but there are no reports available for this module. Select OK to continue"—or by correcting the error— "Sorry, but you must enter a dollar amount in this field. Select OK, then enter a dollar amount."

- A system error appears when something is wrong with the hardware or software system. For example, "There is no disk in drive B. Insert a disk, and then try again." These errors are usually defined by the platform developers and cannot be changed or expanded upon by your program. However, you can add more detailed explanations to your own online help and printed documentation.

Most error messages are modal. See in Chapter 1 for details.

### Slips versus Mistakes

User errors fall into two categories: "slips" and "mistakes" (Norman, 1988, p. 106).

A slip is the result of automatic behavior gone awry—either a simple error like pressing [Ctrl] instead of [Shift] or an interference error like picking "add index entry" instead of "add bookmark" because you were thinking you ought to do some indexing next. Slips are usually simple and easily corrected. A "slip" error message is easy to write as well—for example, "You must select a line style before selecting *Close.*"

A mistake, on the other hand, is the result of forming the wrong model or goal, then acting on it. The user may find it difficult or even impossible to detect the mistake—after all, the action is appropriate for the goal. He or she simply doesn't know that the wrong goal was selected.

Anticipating mistakes is far more difficult than anticipating slips. However, there are ways to do it.

- One of the most effective ways is to run user testing and watch closely for nonsensical requests or actions. (Actually, they may seem nonsensical to *you*, the designer. They do make sense to the test subject—because he or she has a different model in mind.)

- Another way is to eliminate ambiguity from your design. For this, see *Exploring Requirements: Quality before Design* by Donald C. Gause and Gerald M. Weinberg.

For the theoretical underpinning of error analysis, see Donald Norman's *The Psychology of Everyday Things*, which provides an excellent comparison and analysis of the two types of errors.

*A caveat:* In certain fields, such as financial analysis and astronomy, trying the illogical or unanticipated is standard operating procedure. Experienced developers take a "hands-off" approach in systems directed to these users. In other words, rather than preventing users from making certain intellectual mistakes, these developers give them enough rope to hang themselves—or go rappelling.

An ideal error message for the financially sophisticated audience might look like this: "A negative yield for this bond is unlikely. Continue?"

## How to Write Error Messages

Error messages are difficult to write well, not because the writing is hard but because the precise language programmers use to describe problems to other programmers is impenetrable to end users. For example, the messages "Invalid handle" or "Get is not allowed on attribute when 'Sec.Seg' is NULL_Seg" are clear within the context of a development system (the users are other programmers). However, they wouldn't make sense to a financial analyst.

Before an end-user application can be released, therefore, at least some of the problem descriptions must be rewritten into jargon-free (and dismayingly vague) error messages. If that weren't bad enough, writing error messages is usually a last-minute chore and never gets the tender loving care it requires.

Professional technical writers, however, are often willing to take over this job. Rewriting error messages in the program is far less work than trying to explain them later in the documentation. Technical writers are also adept at translating jargon into terms that end users are comfortable with.

### Text of Error Messages

The suggestions for writing error messages is the same as for writing alert messages, with a few additional suggestions.

*What it is and what to do about it:* Write two-part error messages: "Here's the problem. To solve it, do this." If you only describe the problem, the user won't know how to solve it. If you only present the solution, the user can't avoid making the same mistake later.

*Be polite:* Since the computer does not have an ego, an excellent design approach is to let it assume the blame for all misunderstandings (Galitz, 1993, p. 106).

Avoid the words "error," "illegal," "failure," and so on, since they focus attention on the person rather than on the problem. For example, instead of writing "Numbers are illegal in this field," write "Enter the names of months—for example, *January.*" Simply offering the correct format also lets you avoid pointing out the error.

A useful writing strategy is to start each message with, "Sorry, but . . ." Besides fulfilling the politeness requirement, this phrase puts you in the correct frame of mind (humble).[1] An example: "Sorry, but the selected service is unable to carry phone traffic from this location. Please select a different service. Press any key to continue."

---

[1] This strategy was brought to an art form by Bob Wimpfheimer in the telecommunications analysis system *NODE/1.* NODE/1 is available from Comware Systems, 370 Lexington Avenue, New York, NY 10017; 212-686-5558.

### Possible Responses

There are at least four possible responses, described in order of complexity:

- *Explain this:* Make sure that all error message dialog boxes contain a Help button. If the reason for the error message is not *immediately* obvious (i.e., it was a mistake), the user needs good help. For assistance writing error message help, see Three-Part Help Strategy.

- *Acknowledgment:* If the only possible response to the error is simple acknowledgment, then use an OK button.

- *Retry or cancel:* Offer "retry" and "cancel" options when the user has to fix a system or application problem before work can continue. If the problem can be fixed quickly, a Retry button lets the user fix it, then continue working. If the problem requires too much work or someone else's time (most users depend on system administrators to take care of network problems), Cancel lets the user go on to something else while the problem gets resolved.

- *Fix it now:* If the user has forgotten to enter a file name, path, or other required data, you can put an entry area into the dialog box itself. Once the user enters the required information and selects the OK button, the procedure can continue (IBM, 1992, p. 91). Or, if the user has typed the entry incorrectly, the dialog box might present a list of likely options and let the user pick one.

These types of responses bypass short-term memory failures—the user doesn't have to cancel the message, then try to remember which field or situation caused the problem. It's also more polite—if the program knows what the problem is, why doesn't it just fix it (with confirmation, of course)?

### Titles

Some of the possibilities for titles are:

- Use a "halt" icon and no title, as per Macintosh error boxes (Apple Computer, 1992, pp. 310–311).

- If you differentiate between types of messages, use the word "Error" or "Warning" in the title of the dialog box (OSF, 1993, pp. 9-33, 9-134).

- Use the program name as the title, especially when the message is generated from a program running in the background (Microsoft, 1992, p. 128).

- Use the problem description as the title and the suggested response as the body of the message (IBM, 1992, pp. 206, 339).

## Icons

The icon for a program error message is an exclamation point. The icon for a system error or for a potentially destructive action is a stop sign (Windows), a "don't" sign (Motif), or a "halt" picture—hand, palm towards the user (Macintosh). (See Figure 4.4.) *Note:* An open hand is an offensive gesture in some cultures, warns Apple Computer: "Make sure you replace it with a more appropriate stop icon when you localize your application" (Apple Computer, 1993, p. 196).

## Three-Part Help Strategy

Over the years, IBM has developed an excellent three-part software diagnostic style based on its hardware diagnostic method. The three parts are:

1. **XXXNNN:** A three-digit product code, an error message number, then the message itself.

2. **Explanation:** The most likely explanation of the problem, followed by the next most likely explanation, and so on through all possible explanations. (The hardware diagnostics include actual "likelihood" percentages based on the service representatives' experiences in the field.)

3. **User response:** Suggested actions or user responses, again ranked by likelihood.

The error message and ID number, plus the most likely explanation and suggested action, should all appear in the error message dialog box. However, since you can fit only about three lines of text in the typical message box, the additional explanations and details should go into the online help or printed documentation.

**Figure 4.4 Error message icons**

There are two reasons to show error message numbers or identifiers. The first is that if the system gets completely fouled up, the number may be the only information that appears on the screen. As long as the documentation lists the numbers with the messages, users will at least be able to find the message by number.

The second reason has to do with internationalization. If your application will be internationalized, the numbers help translators track messages and panels throughout the translation process. The messages for an application are often translated a year or two earlier than the online or print documentation. Once the documentation is ready to be translated, the translators can simply copy the original translation of the message into the documentation, provided that they can tell which message is which—ergo, the message numbers (IBM, 1991, pp. 2–5).

## HAZARD MESSAGES

Hazard messages are rarely used in PC-based software, since PC software does not, as a rule, involve life-threatening procedures. However, as software embedded in mechanical devices becomes more and more common, hazard warnings may begin to appear in LCD message panels or on labels attached to the equipment's control panels.[2] Also, depending on the industry and the application, multimedia training programs may have to include standardized hazard warnings. Whether the instructions appear in a repair manual or on a monitor on the shop floor, the requirement to warn, and the legal liabilities, remain the same (Coonrod, 1993, p. 3).

### ANSI Safety Standards

The American National Standards Institute, under the direction of the U.S. National Safety Council, published four standards for creating safety signs and labels in 1991 (for ordering information, see Resources). Standards

---

[2] For hazard horror stories from a wide range of industries, see *The Day the Phones Stopped: How People Get Hurt When Computers Go Wrong* by Leonard Lee. One of the most chilling is that of the Therac-25 radiation therapy linear accelerator. If the technician running the machine switched from x-ray mode to treatment mode too quickly, a bug in the embedded software caused the machine to send out a high-intensity beam of radiation that essentially cooked whatever was in its path.

Z535.2 and Z535.4 describe a three-level hazard-alert system using these "signal" words:

DANGER indicates an imminently hazardous situation which, if not avoided, *will* result in <u>death or serious injury</u>.

WARNING indicates a potentially hazardous situation which, if not avoided, *could* result in <u>death or serious injury</u>.

CAUTION indicates a hazardous situation which, if not avoided, *may* result in <u>minor or moderate injury</u>.[3]

The differences between the levels are indicated with *italics*, the similarities with underlines.

There are also two other less-serious categories: NOTICE is used for hazards that may result in property damage only. IMPORTANT designates an operating tip or maintenance suggestion.

Each hazard type also has its own color scheme (Kemnitz, 1991, p. 72):

Danger          Black lettering on red background
Warning         Black lettering on orange background
Caution         Black lettering on yellow background

NOTICE and IMPORTANT messages or signs often appear in white lettering on a blue background.

### Hazard Message Elements

Figure 4.5 illustrates a hazard message. ANSI specifies seven elements for each hazard sign:

1. The hazard alert symbol: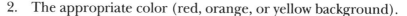
2. The appropriate color (red, orange, or yellow background).
3. A pictograph that shows the effect of the hazard.

---

[3] U.S. military specifications, or MILSPECS, define a WARNING as "a procedure which, if not performed correctly, could result in injury or death," and define a CAUTION as "a procedure which, if not performed correctly, could result in damage or destruction of equipment, or a long-term health hazard." There is no parallel for the ANSI DANGER. The MILSPEC NOTICE is the same as its CAUTION but without the long-term health hazard. The ANSI IMPORTANT is the equivalent of the MILSPEC NOTE, which means "essential operating information" (d'Albenas, 1992, pp. 4–5).

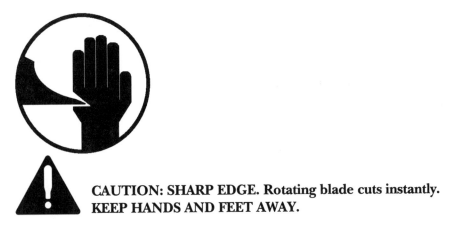

CAUTION: SHARP EDGE. Rotating blade cuts instantly. KEEP HANDS AND FEET AWAY.

**Figure 4.5  Hazard message**

4. The signal word (DANGER, WARNING, CAUTION, NOTICE, IM-PORTANT). Note the use of all uppercase letters—SHOUTING is useful in hazard messages.

5. After the signal word, the type of hazard followed by text describing the hazard. For example, "DANGER: POISONOUS GAS."

6. The consequences of ignoring the hazard. For example, "Can cause immediate unconsciousness and death."

7. A description of how to avoid the hazard. For example, "PUT ON RESPIRATOR BEFORE OPENING CONTAINER."

## How to Write Hazard Messages

Elements 4 to 7 comprise the hazard message itself:

- Signal word
- Type of hazard
- Consequences of ignoring the hazard
- Avoiding the hazard

### Signal Word

The signal words are DANGER (death or serious injury will occur), WARN-ING (death or serious injury may occur), CAUTION (minor or moderate injury may occur), and NOTICE (damage to property may occur).

Use IMPORTANT for operating or maintenance instructions or additional information.

### Type of Hazard

The rules for writing hazard identifiers (one or two words) and descriptions are (Kemnitz, 1991, p. 71):

- Be forceful. If the hazard can cause death, say so.

- For the hazard identifiers, don't use articles (*a, the*), pronouns (*it*), or forms of the verb "to be." For example, "DANGER: THIS GAS IS POISONOUS" isn't direct enough. It should be "DANGER: POISONOUS GAS."

- Keep the message clear: Describe only one hazard at a time.

    The only exception to this rule is when more than one hazardous situation exists, but all hazards can be avoided at the same time. For example, hazard signs on gasoline pumps indicate an explosion hazard and warn drivers not to smoke while refueling.

    On multiple hazard messages, put the most important, most likely, or most dangerous hazard first.

Keep in mind that injuries (amputated fingers) are separate from hazards (for example, moving parts). Injuries are always described in the consequences section, not in the hazard section.

### Consequences of Ignoring the Hazard

The pictograph is probably the most important part of the consequences section. It should show the result of ignoring the hazard, not how to avoid it. (See Figure 4.6.)

The consequences text should reinforce the pictograph, rather than the other way around. For example: The statement "CAUTION: ACID may burn clothing or skin" simply reinforces the graphic.

As well as adding a second channel (the visual) to the hazard message for readers, pictographs also allow nonreaders to recognize and avoid the hazard.

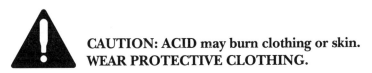

CAUTION: ACID may burn clothing or skin.
WEAR PROTECTIVE CLOTHING.

**Figure 4.6 Caution sign for acid**

### Avoiding the Hazard

Suggestions for writing the avoidance part of the message are (Kemnitz, 1991, p. 71):

- Be as forceful as possible. Use all uppercase, use the words DO NOT, and use as few words as possible.

- Use chronological or step-by-step order. Bad version: OPEN CONTAINER AFTER PUTTING ON GOGGLES. Corrected version: PUT ON GOGGLES BEFORE OPENING CONTAINER.

- Watch for contradictory instructions. For example, putting a "DO NOT REMOVE" sign on a circular saw blade guard is nonsensical if the guard must be removed for routine maintenance. A better instruction would be "USE GUARD WHEN RUNNING SAW."

- Watch for bad line breaks. The user must be able to read each instruction as a unit. Bad version:

```
PULL SECOND RIP
CORD IF MAIN
PARACHUTE FAILS
```

Corrected version:

```
PULL SECOND RIP CORD
IF MAIN PARACHUTE FAILS.
```

Real example off the back of a fungicide bottle:

**Physician**: Emergency information—call 1-800-555-2000. **ENVIRON-MENTAL HAZARDS:** This product is toxic to fish and other aquatic

*Note:* If you don't understand these bad-break examples, you may be reading the text word by word instead of in chunks, like many readers do. Try glancing at the entire block of text or reading it while holding the book at arm's length.

## WARNING SOUNDS

"We have a very delicate internal mechanism for locating sounds. It depends on the minute differences in the way our two ears hear the onset of the sound. The mechanism works wonderfully for the sound of a twig snapping, but it's quite useless for continuous sounds, without clear beginnings. That's the reason a lot of people just sort of freeze when they're driving in traffic and they hear a siren—they can't figure out where the damn thing is coming from."

From an interview with Max Neuhaus, a sound environment artist, in the *New Yorker* (Tomkins, 1988, p. 119).

Warning sounds are occasionally used in personal computer software, but they are more common in dedicated software systems, such as automatic teller machines or network monitoring systems. If you need to construct a warning sound, keep in mind that a good one is made of four cumulative parts (Edworthy, 1991, p. 206):

- *Loudness level,* rising or falling. The loudness level, or amplitude, must be chosen for the specific acoustic environment and noise spectrum of the area in which the warning will be heard.

- *Starting block:* A small pulse of sound, 100 to 300 milliseconds long, that starts the warning. The starting block should come up to full amplitude quickly, then drop off quickly. Its harmonic content is a fundamental frequency plus several harmonics.

- *Burst of sound:* A repetition of the pulse at different pitches and loudnesses and with different time intervals between each repetition. The burst of sound lasts about two seconds and is similar to a rhythmic, atonal melody.

- *Complete warning:* A burst repeated once or twice, followed by a period of silence. The complete warning is then repeated, more or less insistently, depending on the situation.

You can make an acoustic warning sound more or less urgent by manipulating the four building blocks. Details follow.


## Loudness Level

Changing the loudness level obviously changes the urgency level (usually by sending people scampering for the OFF button). However, changing the onset and offset characteristics can be effective as well.

A slow onset envelope (a packet of sound in which the loudness builds slowly) is more urgent than a slow offset envelope, probably because a slow onset sounds like an approaching object while a slow offset sounds like an object that is moving away. (Think of the whistle of a train coming toward you, then passing you.)


## Starting Pulse

Higher frequencies sound more urgent than lower frequencies. Changes in the frequency also lead to changes in the sense of urgency.

A regular harmonic series is one in which all the harmonics are exact integer multiples of the fundamental frequency. A 10 percent irregular harmonic series is one in which the even harmonics are 10 percent higher than their integer values, giving the pulse a harsh timbre.

The more unpredictable the series, the more urgent the pulse is perceived to be, with a random series being seen as the most urgent. A 10 percent irregularity is next most urgent, followed by a 50 percent irregularity (the 50 percent irregularity creates a new harmonic equidistant between two regular ones). A 100 percent regular harmonic series sound the least urgent.


## Burst of Sound

The burst of sound is affected by speed, rhythm, pitch range, and pitch contour. Speed and changes in speed had the largest effects on perceived urgency. When the interpulse time (from pulse start to start) was shortened

**Table 4.2  Effects of Parameters on Perceived Urgency**

| Parameter | Effect |
| --- | --- |
| Speed | Fast speeds are more urgent than slow speeds. |
| Speed change | Speeding up is more urgent than holding the speed steady, which is more urgent than slowing it down. |
| Rhythm | A regular rhythm is more urgent than a syncopated rhythm. |
| Interpulse intervals | Warnings with no silences between pulses are the most urgent; warnings with short silences between pulses are more urgent than ones with long silences. |
| Number of repeated pulses in the same burst | Four repeats are more urgent than two or one. |
| Pitch range | A large change in the pitch range is more urgent than a small change. However, a small change is more urgent than a moderate change, probably because "a small pitch range necessitates the introduction of small, chromatic (semitone) pitch changes, which introduces an element of atonality into the burst" (Edworthy, 1991, p. 226). |
| Pitch contour | A random contour is more urgent than a down/up contour. |
| Musical structure | Atonal melodies are more urgent than unresolved melodies, which are more urgent than resolved melodies. |

from the start to the end of the burst, the sound was heard as urgent. When the interpulse time was lengthened from start to end, the sound was heard as not urgent. Other factors are summarized in Table 4.2 (Edworthy, 1991, p. 226; Haas, 1992, p. 251).

## Complete Warning

To construct an urgent warning, use these parameters (Edworthy, 1991, p. 227):

- The pulse has a high fundamental frequency, an inharmonic series, no delayed harmonics, and a standard or slow loudness-onset envelope.

- The burst built from this pulse has a fast speed, a regular rhythm, a large pitch range, a random pitch contour, and an atonal pitch pattern.

To construct a low-urgency warning, use these parameters:

- The pulse has a low fundamental frequency, regular harmonics, delayed harmonics, and a slow offset amplitude envelope.
- The burst has a slow speed, an irregular rhythm, an up/down pitch contour, and a resolved musical structure.

Intermediate values yield intermediate urgencies.

## PROGRAMMING STRATEGIES FOR MESSAGES

Put all messages in resource files. Don't embed text in the dialog boxes themselves. The reason for resource files is that they make changing text relatively easy. But why would you change text? There are at least three reasons.

- *Changes in corporate terminology:* The name of the software will probably change between alpha and release, approved names of objects may change, even the company name may change.
- *Corrections:* Usability tests often lead to changes in terminology. Changing embedded text requires opening every affected file, finding the text, changing it, recompiling, retesting—in other words, time and money. If the text is in resource files, however, human factors personnel, technical writers, and entry-level programmers can change it without inadvertently damaging underlying code.
- *Internationalization and localization:* As soon as you translate an interface in which all text is embedded, you have two versions of the program to support—one of them in a language you may not know.

For more on translation and the use of resource files, see Chapter 6.

## REFERENCES

Apple Computer. *Macintosh Human Interface Guidelines.* Reading, MA: Addison-Wesley, 1992.

Coonrod, Kathryn. "Why Should Technical Communicators Care about Product Liability?" *Intercom* (Society for Technical Communication), February 1993, pp. 3–5.

d'Albenas, Ken. "But Doctor, the Manual Only Said Caution, Not Warning!" *Intercom* (Society for Technical Communication), October 1992, pp. 3–5.

Edworthy, Judy, Sarah Loxley, and Ian Dennis. "Improving Auditory Warning Design: Relationship between Warning Sound Parameters and Perceived Urgency." *Human Factors,* 1991, pp. 205–231.

Galitz, Wilbert O. *User-Interface Screen Design.* Wellesley, MA: QED Information Sciences, 1993.

———. *It's Time to Clean Your Windows: Designing GUIs That Work,* New York: John Wiley & Sons, 1994.

Gause, Donald C., and Gerald M. Weinberg. *Exploring Requirements: Quality before Design,* New York: Dorset House, 1989.

Haas, E. C. "A Pilot Study on the Perceived Urgency of Multitone and Frequency-Modulated Warning Signals." *Proceedings of the Human Factors Society Thirty-Sixth Annual Meeting,* 1992, pp. 248–252.

IBM Corporation. *Object-Oriented Interface Design: IBM Common User Access Guidelines.* Carmel, IN: IBM/Que, 1992.

Kemnitz, Charles. "How to Write Effective Error Messages." *Technical Communication,* 1st Quarter 1991, pp. 68–73.

Lee, Leonard. *The Day the Phones Stopped: How People Get Hurt When Computers Go Wrong.* New York: Primus/Donald I. Fine, 1992.

Microsoft Corporation. *The Windows Interface: An Application Design Guide.* Redmond, WA: Microsoft Press, 1992.

Munter, Mary. *Guide to Managerial Communication.* 3d ed., Englewood Cliffs, NJ: Prentice Hall, 1982.

Norman, Donald A. *The Psychology of Everyday Things.* New York: Basic Books, 1988. Also published as *The Design of Everyday Things.*

Open Software Foundation. *OSF/Motif Style Guide,* Revision 1.2 (for Motif Release 1.2). Englewood Cliffs, NJ, Prentice Hall, 1993.

Schneiderman, Ben. *Designing the User Interface,* 2d ed. Reading MA: Addison-Wesley, 1992.

Strunk, William Jr., and E. B. White. *The Elements of Style*, 3d ed., New York: Macmillan, 1979.

Tomkins, Calvin "Onward and Upward with the Arts: Hear." *New Yorker*, October 24, 1988, pp. 110–120.

## RESOURCES

## Hazard Signs

The American National Standards Institute publications on hazard and safety signs are:

- *Safety Color Code*, ANSI Z535.1-1991 ($35.00)
- *Environmental and Facility Safety Signs*, ANSI Z535.2-1991 ($35.00)
- *Criteria for Safety Symbols*, ANSI Z535.3-1991 ($35.00)
- *Product Safety Signs and Labels*, ANSI Z535.4-1991 ($35.00).

For more information or to order these publications, contact American National Standards Institute, Attn.: Customer Service, 11 West 42nd Street, New York, NY 10036; voice: 212-642-4900; fax: 212-302-1286.

# 5

# Online Help

Tim suddenly found himself lost in a tangled series of monitor control screens, as he tried to get back to the main screen. Also, he was certain that help commands had been built into the system, but he couldn't find them either, and Lex was jumping up and down and shouting in his ear, making him nervous.

"Will you shut up? I'm trying to get help." He pushed TEMPLATE-MAIN. The screen filled with a complicated diagram, with interconnecting boxes and arrows.

No good. No good.

"What's that?" Lex said. "Why aren't you turning on the power, Timmy?"

He ignored her. Maybe help on this system was called "info." He pushed INFO.

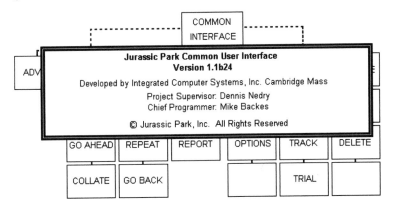

"Tim-ee," Lex wailed, but he had already pushed FIND. He got another useless window. He pushed GO BACK.

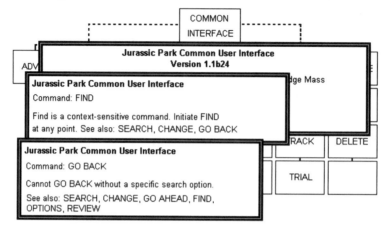

On the radio, he heard Muldoon say, "How's it coming, Tim?" He didn't bother to answer. Frantic, he pushed buttons one after another.

Suddenly, without warning, the main screen was back.

From *Jurassic Park* by Michael Crichton (1990, pp. 345–346).[1]

## ONLINE HELP, DEFINED

Online help has multiple layers. First of all, there are two types of online help: context-sensitive and reference.

Context-sensitive help generally contains the "need to know" information—what this is, how it works, how to change it. Context-sensitive help appears when you ask for help on a particular screen object. Macintosh "balloon" help is one of the better-known types. Reference help (or reference *book* help) generally contains the "nice to know" information—which formula is being used, how this procedure is affected by government regulations, what this word means. (See Figure 5.1.)

There are three layers of context-sensitive help:

1.  Object—what is this?
2.  Procedure—how does it work?
3.  Overview—how does this relate to everything else?

---

[1] Copyright © 1990 by Michael Crichton. Reprinted by permission of Alfred A. Knopf, Inc.

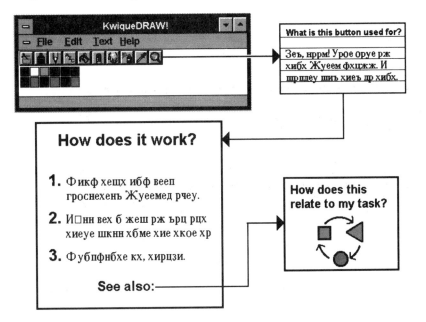

**Figure 5.1 From button (object help) to window (procedure help) to application (overview)**

There are also two types of reference help.

1.  Glossary definitions or footnotes, which are one- or two-line explanations of terms and concepts.

2.  Reference books, which can be anything from specifications and system administration guides to actual reference books (dictionaries and encyclopedias, for example).

The final layer is the programming layer. Context-sensitive help is tied to screen objects by actual object IDs (sometimes called "resource IDs" or "context IDs"). The help developer embeds the object ID in the help text, and the compiler program indexes the two sets of IDs against each other. When the user asks for help on the object, the display program captures the object ID, looks it up in the help file, and displays the help text containing that ID.

The help text itself can be cross-linked with internal "hypertext" IDs. When a user clicks on a glossary item or a cross-reference, the help system uses the hypertext ID to go to the linked text. For more information, see Programming Issues later in this chapter.

## WHAT TO PUT IN ONLINE HELP

A mature and complete online help system includes:

1. Context-sensitive help for objects on the application window. In Macintosh systems, "balloon help" is context-sensitive help (Apple Computer, 1992, pp. 314–315).

2. Task-oriented quick reference to the important procedures. "Task orientation" means describing an operation or object in terms of a user's task rather than the software's design. In a task-oriented help system, a user reads a procedure for doing a mail merge rather than being forced to figure it out from help entries on "merge" and "macros." Two subtypes of task-oriented help are online tutorials and interactive assistants (see Demonstrate Instead of Describe).

3. Detailed reference to all menu options, commands, and objects in the software application (the same as most standard paper documentation). The detailed reference books can also include design specifications, release notes, internal memos, customer-service guides, and system-administrator guides (with access restricted by user or site ID, perhaps).

4. Detailed reference to related business information, either written in-house or licensed from the original authors.

Options 1 and 2 contain the "need to know" information. Options 3 and 4 contain the "nice to know" information. They may require mass storage facilities, such as a CD player or a few megabytes of space on a network server.

### Where to Start

If your application is new, start with options 1 and 2—especially option 2, task-oriented help. However, much software development actually entails rewriting old applications for new platforms. If this is the case, you already have a set of paper documents—a detailed reference guide and a quick reference guide, perhaps—that fulfill the requirements for option 3 (with a few changes, of course, to match the new platform).

Users expect GUI applications to have online help. Rather than disappoint them, use what you already have for release 1 of the application. If the current documentation is machine-readable, then add a few top-level links between the text and the program and compile it as an online help file. The results will be far from ideal, since the structures of books and help text are very different (see Horton, 1990, pp. 15–30; Boggan, 1993, pp. 35–36). However, by release 2, you'll have added task-oriented help and, by release 3, object help.

## WHAT NOT TO PUT IN ONLINE HELP

Put online the things that you do online. Put on paper the things that you do offline.

For example, you can't put installation instructions online, since the instructions haven't been installed yet.

On the other hand, most accountants would rather learn about the latest tax accounting practices from a book than from the computer screen.

In fact, putting all of the software-related information online and the business-related information offline solves two problems.

- Keeping the online help up to date is easier, since the help can be maintained and distributed with the software. Also, there are no printing costs or delays while the print shop fits your project into their schedule.

- With the changeable software information online, the technical writers may have more time to put real-world business information in the paper documentation. Instead of describing how to use the software to pick a tax strategy, for example, the documentation can describe tax strategies in detail, putting the software instructions in the online help or in notes in the paper documentation.

## DESIGNING CONTEXT-SENSITIVE HELP

"I like this context-sensitive help. You poke at the screen and this cloud of information appears in front of you."

Dimitri Rotov, documentation manager, BFR Systems, New Jersey.[2]

There are two types of context-sensitive help: Window or top-level help and object-level help (help for the smaller objects). The window-level help can itself be divided into two types: description and procedure (see Window-

---

[2] BFR Systems, 31 Clyde Road, Somerset, NJ 08873; 908-873-1200.

Level Help for details). Object-level help is generally just description—"this is what this button does and this is where you go." See Object-Level Help later in this chapter.

Object-level help should be short—ideally, no more than what would fit on a 3" by 5" index card. Window-level help usually has to be longer, but even the longest pieces of help text should contain no more than 125 to 250 words (a quarter to a half piece of paper).

Because of the limited space, you have to structure the text carefully.

- Put the need-to-know information at the top of the help panel. (If you slowly build up to the important ideas, they'll probably end up below the bottom of the help frame.) Address either or both of software's two domains: business and computer. For help deciding what to put in the window-level text, see Table 5.1.

- Use titles to help readers orient themselves. Use subtitles to break up the text, making it easier to scan.

- Use numbered steps, bullets, and tabbed or indented text—but one level only, please. Too many tabs in help text leads to broken lines and text running off the bottom of the help panel.

## Titles for Help Panels

To help users orient themselves, make sure every panel has a title. A title should be composed of the object's label, if you're writing object help, or a descriptive label, if you're writing reference help.

*Abbreviated or truncated names:* Abbreviations can be ambiguous. If the object's label contains abbreviations or truncated words, spell out them out. For example, if a field is labeled "Stud Addr," use "Student Address" as the help title.

*Object names:* Append the object type to the title if two or more objects on the window have the same or similar names. For example, a direct-mail tracking window might have a client *column* and a client *field*. In this case, the titles would be "Client Column" and "Client Field."

There is, of course, a problem when the object has no name. You can describe nameless objects in either of two ways: by position ("the list on the left side of the panel") or by usage ("the list containing charts"). The best solution, however, is to change the interface itself and give the object a label.

## Window-Level Help

If you have limited resources, spending time on top-level help is more effective than documenting each individual object on the window. Users can usually puzzle out the meaning of individual objects if they understand the whole.

Help for a window or panel consists of two parts: a description of the window and procedures for using the window. You don't always have to write procedural help, but you must write a description.

### Descriptions

Here are recommendations for description sections.

- Describe what the user can do with the window. For example, does this window help users run their businesses or do particular types of spectral analyses?

- When a window offers users more than one option, list the options and prioritize them.

**Table 5.1 Decision Diagram for Window Help**

| Is the window hard to use mechanically? | | | |
|---|---|---|---|
| **Yes** | | **No** | |
| Concentrate on the hardware or software aspects. | | Concentrate on the business aspects. | |
| **Is the design bad?** | | **Are the business aspects hard to understand?** | |
| **Yes** | **No** | **Yes** | **No** |
| Redesign the window. | If the window is unavoidably complicated, include a procedure section. | • Concentrate on the business purpose of the window and its benefit to the user.<br>• For technical information and jargon, use glossary references and hypertext links.<br>• Direct users to printed documentation and to commercially available reference books or texts. | • Concentrate on the computer or software aspects.<br>• Offer expert-level shortcuts and hints on working faster. |

- State overall restrictions in the top-level help. For example: "You can enter no more than three dependents on this screen."

- Describe the object's initial state in the top-level help—what fields are filled in, what the default sort is, what the default parameters are.

- List required fields or actions.

- Talk about only those objects that appear on the current window. Refer readers to other windows or to a program map or overview using "see also" hypertext links.

- Include troubleshooting information—for example, "Why does each letter appear twice when I use my modem?"

## Procedures and Instructions

The traditional procedure section is a set of step-by-step instructions. Procedures can also be tutorials, computer-based training (CBT), interactive assistants, and video and animation instructions. For more on CBT, see Resources. For more on interactive or multimedia procedures, see Demonstrate Instead of Describe.

General recommendations for procedure sections include the following.

- Use a task orientation, not a program orientation. Program-oriented help would explain how to use the *Format Picture* command. Task-oriented help, on the other hand, would describe two or three ways to box a graphic (drawing a box around it with the box tool, putting the graphic in a frame and adding a border to the frame, putting a black box under the graphic, and so on). Plus, it might describe two or three ways to resize a graphic—a different interpretation of "formatting" but valid nevertheless.

- Provide easily scannable one-line introductions to step-by-step instructions. Readers read the instructions faster and make fewer mistakes if you tell them what they are about to do (Spyridakis, 1992, p. 208).

- Use no more than seven steps (because of the chunking rule—you can remember only five things, plus or minus two, at a time). If the instructions seem to require more steps, break the procedure into two or more parts or redesign the window or procedure to simplify it.

- Whenever there is more than one step in a step-by-step instruction, number the steps. If there is only one, don't number it.

Following are some recommendations that require more explanation.

## Avoid the Future Tense

There is no future tense in step-by-step instructions. The reason is that the user is right in the middle of the operation you describe—in the midst of the present tense, in other words.

Incorrect:

```
1. You will select OK.
```

Correct:

```
1. Select OK.
```

This rule is self-evident, once you've heard it. But sometimes, despite your best intentions, "will" creeps into instructions. The reason it happens is that while you're writing it, the instruction *will* be followed at some point in the future.

If you make this mistake often, add a global search for "will" to your list of finishing steps.

## What Comes First?

Whenever the user has to make a decision before doing something else, say so immediately. For example, this instruction creates more questions than it answers:

```
To add customers, select Customer from the File menu. To
add locations, select Location from the File menu.
```

Is the user supposed to add both customers and locations at the same time? Or one after the other? *Must* customers and locations be added?

End the confusion by adding a leading sentence:

```
At this point, you can add either customers or locations.
To add customers, select Customer from the File menu. To
add locations, select Location from the File menu.
```

Also, whenever you suggest a particular action, first say why you're suggesting it. For example, this sentence is reversed:

```
If a document is locked, you must unlock it before you
can open it.
```

A better version is:

```
Before you can open a locked document, you must unlock it.
```

It's better because a user who wants to cancel a window now knows this sentence is for him or her. On the other hand, does the user know the window is locked? More likely, he or she just spent a minute or two trying, unsuccessfully, to close the window. The best version is probably:

```
If you can't open a document, it may be locked. Unlock it
by selecting the "lock" button at the upper righthand
corner.
```

Make sure that you immediately let the user know that he or she is *not* supposed to do something. For example, this instruction is potentially dangerous:

```
Select the Exit button. Warning: If you haven't saved
your changes, they will be lost when you select Exit.
```

By the time the user gets to the warning, it may be too late. The instruction should read:

```
You can either save your changes, then exit, or exit
without saving the changes.
Save the changes by selecting the Save button, then exit
using the Exit button.
Cancel your changes by selecting Exit only.
```

### Give Each Step Its Own Sentence

The easiest way to avoid ambiguous instructions is to make sure that every step is its own sentence. For example, this is an ambiguous instruction:

```
Use this button to confirm your selection, then return to
the main window.
```

It is ambiguous because it can be interpreted in more than one way:

```
Use this button. Then do some other thing to return to
the main window.
```

Or:

```
Use this button. Using the button returns you to the main
window.
```

Or even:

```
Use this button. When you press the Return button, you'll
end up at the main window.
```

Depending on what you meant, you could rewrite it as:

```
When you press this button, you both confirm your
selection and return to the main window.
```

Or:

```
Use this button to confirm your selection. Then select OK
to return to the main window.
```

### Demonstrate instead of Describe

Rather than describing what something looks like or how it works, show it. Use illustrations to help explain difficult ideas, use schematics and diagrams for overviews and use screen shots to isolate parts of the window you're describing. Use interactive assistants to walk users through difficult procedures. Use video and animation clips to demonstrate activities. Following are some ideas and examples.

Isolate parts of windows by including a picture of the part you're documenting. For example, instead of trying to describe the control menu's button, just show it (see Figure 5.2).

Some help systems let you create hotspots and hypertext links right on the picture itself. Before you add pictures, however, pick a picture format that doesn't require a lot of space. Clipboard files are often small, as are vector formats like CGM. Also, monochrome or grayscale versions of color pictures are smaller than the color versions but often just as useful. Find the best format by experimenting with the graphic options available on your system.

Don't overuse pictures, though. If the window is in front of the user, he or she doesn't need another copy of it in the help window.

**Figure 5.2  Control-menu button**

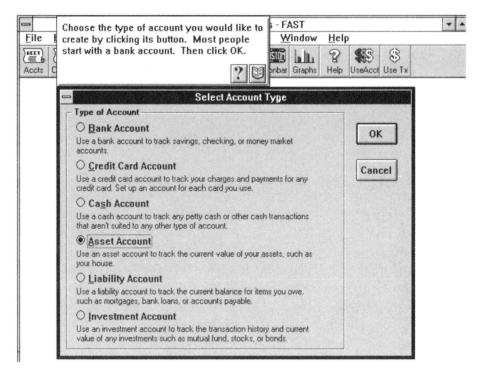

**Figure 5.3  A QCard in Quicken 2 for Windows (at top)**

*Replace tutorials and procedures with "interactive assistants."* Interactive assistants or wizards take users through a procedure step by step. Unlike tutorials using "canned" information ("how to set up Acme Corporation's checking account"), the assistants help users do real work. In Quicken 2 for Windows,[3] for example, "Qcards" help boxes and a getting started script take new users through the steps required to set up an account. (See Figure 5.3.).

*Include multimedia in help.* A video clip in an online car-repair manual will show a mechanic how to replace a part far quicker than any written instructions could.

*Illustrate procedures cartoon-style.* If your company is developing online help for international audiences, you may be able to avoid translation costs if you illustrate each step in a procedure with a screen snippet. Users whose English (or other language) is imperfect will be able to follow the instructions by looking at the pictures. (See Figure 5.4.)

---

[3] Intuit, P.O. Box 3014, Menlo Park, CA 94026; 415-322-0573.

1. Select the Help menu:

2. Select *BoschDraw Tutorial*:

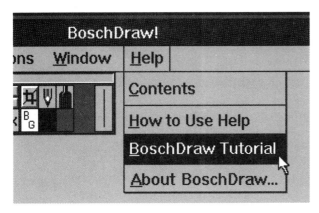

3. Select *Click here to start*:

**Figure 5.4  Cartoon-style procedure**

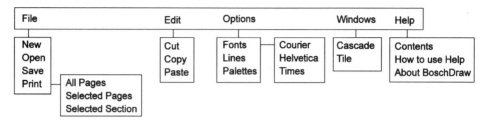

**Figure 5.5  A menu map**

*Include a menu map.* A menu or program map is a diagram of the entire menu system laid out on screen or on paper. For overviews, a menu map is better than the menus themselves, since you can see all of the menu options and all submenus side by side. In the live program, you can open only one menu and one submenu at a time. (See Figure 5.5.)

## Object-Level Help

If you offer object-level help, provide help for every individual object except:

- Radio buttons, which are mutually exclusive options. It is better to contrast and compare them as a set.
- Related checkbuttons—for example, bold, italic, underlined. Describe them as a set.
- Screen furniture like lines and separators that have no meaning. If the user asks for context-sensitive help on furniture, display the window or parent-object help.

Two other general recommendations are:

- State restrictions and data format requirements (dates must be in YY/MM/DD format, for example).
- If the software doesn't allow users to reset defaults easily, describe the object's initial state and/or default state or content.

For object-specific recommendations, see Table 5.2.

### Menu Help

Good menu help is important if users are to have a sense of the application as a whole. A 1985 experiment on help for menus found that the group of subjects that received information about upcoming selections had signifi-

**Table 5.2  Quick Reference Guide to Objects**

| Object | Function | Type of Help |
|---|---|---|
| **Windows and subwindows (see also Window-Level Help)** | | |
| Main window | The application itself; a calculator, worksheet, text-entry area, and so on. | Write top-level help describing the business purpose, how to use it step by step, and how parts of the window interact with other main windows. |
| Message dialog box | A box containing a request for more information, a warning, a reminder, or an error message. | Explain purpose of the question, warning, or error message. |
| Dialog box | A collection of buttons, input fields, parameters, and so on, in one window. Dialog boxes do not have menu bars. | Write top-level help describing how to use the items in the dialog box and how parts of the dialog box interact. |
| **Menu components (see also Menu help)** | | |
| Menu bar | Contains the titles of the pull-down menus. | Do not document the bar, only the pull-down menus themselves. |
| Menu title | The label on menu bars and option menus for pull-down menus. | Give the title, then describe the kinds of options that appear on the pull-down menu (Apple Computer, 1992, p. 320). |
| Menu options | The choices—actions, dialog boxes, panels, settings. | Describe the purpose of each option (Apple Computer, 1992, p. 320). |
| **Buttons and components** | | |
| Checkbutton | Used to select any number of options or states from the group shown. | Document as a member of a set of buttons, if appropriate. Explain business purpose of the choice. |
| Option menu | Menu on a button that lets users choose one characteristic of an item. | Describe the purpose of the entire menu. Optional: Describe each option on the menu. |

*(continued)*

**Table 5.2** *(Continued)*

| Object | Function | Type of Help |
|---|---|---|
| Pushbutton | Used as a window disposition control (OK, Cancel) or to make a dialog box appear. | Describe the purpose of the button in one or two lines. If the button brings up another window, mention the window's name. |
| Radio button | Used to switch between options or states. | Document as a member of a set of related buttons. If possible, write different help for selected, unselected, and unavailable buttons. Selected: "Aligns items on the left. This button is selected." Unselected: "To align items on the left, select this button." Unavailable: "Aligns items on the left. Not available because no items are selected." (Apple Computer, 1992, p. 321). |
| Tools on palettes or control panels | Used to act upon or change the selected item. Button shortcuts for often-used options. | Name the tool, which may help explain what it's used for. The name will allow users to search for more information in the reference help. Describe one or two ways to use it (Apple Computer, 1992, p. 323). |
| **Boxes and lists** | | |
| Multiple-selection list | A list from which a user can select more than one item at a time. | Describe the purpose of the items on the list. Include information on how to select more than one item at a time. |
| Single-selection list | A list with mutually exclusive items. User can select only one item at a time. | Describe the purpose of the items on the list. |

*(continued)*

**Table 5.2** *(Continued)*

| Object | Function | Type of Help |
|---|---|---|
| Scrolled box, list box | Used for lists. Can have scroll bars on the side or bottom, or both, to let users see and move through the entire list. If the list is too short to require scroll bars, the bars disappear. | Describe the purpose of the box.<br>*Note:* If the contents of the scrolled list are abbreviated or ambiguous, the list should have its own help. |
| Simple box, frame | On application windows, used to visually organize a group of fields. | If the simple box has an etched-in edge and a title, write "section" help. |
| **Fields, entry areas** | | |
| Input field (text field) | Accepts user input. | List the types of entries that are accepted—dates in YY/MM/DD format, decimal numbers, only uppercase text, and so on. |
| Multiple-line input field | Lets users enter notes or memos. | Describe how to enter, delete, and save text. Address privacy issues. |
| Output field | Contains the results of a selection, calculation, or other operation. Cannot be changed from the keyboard. | If the field contains abbreviations, create a definition table on which users can look up meanings of the abbreviations.<br>For calculations, list the inputs to the field and the meaning of the result. Link to formulas. |
| **Other** | | |
| Chart or graph | Shows relationships among parameters, sets of data, and so on. | Explain mechanics of setting up the graph correctly—for example, "Use segmented bars to show how parts add up to a whole." Explain the key: "The right-pointing bars represent closing prices." |

*(continued)*

**Table 5.2**  *(Continued)*

| Object | Function | Type of Help |
| --- | --- | --- |
| Label | A title for a field, box, window. Also a usage hint that appears on the screen itself. | Link titles to help for the boxes or windows within which they reside.<br>    For usage hints, add more detail to the hint. |
| Table | Used for lists of data or results. | Document each column. Make sure that units of measurement are clear. |

cantly fewer errors than the groups that did not. They also found what they were looking for more quickly. Interestingly, the experimenters also tested whether providing a list of *previous* selections (showing you where you had come from) was helpful. They found that it wasn't—the list slowed the subjects down significantly, perhaps because it meant more reading (Norman, 1991, p. 186).

There are at least two suitable types of help for menus. The first is to give users longer definitions than are possible in one-word menu titles (see Chapter 3 for information on menu titles). Some environments let you describe menus and buttons in a status bar—when the user runs the mouse over the menu or button, a short description of it appears in the status area.

The second type of help for menus is a look-ahead feature that lets users see the structure of individual menus or all of the menus together. Many hardcopy quick reference guides now contain a menu map—a picture of the tree structure. You should be able to add such a graphic to the help files easily.

## DESIGNING REFERENCE HELP

Reference help differs from object help in that it contains background information (tax laws affecting your income tax filing, for example) or overview information (how the software modules relate to one another). Users access reference help either directly, from the help system's menu or table of contents, or indirectly, through hypertext links in the context-sensitive help.

Users need reference help when:

1.  They are trying to orient themselves in the system. They need pictures and narratives that show them where they are in the work flow, as well as how to get from one place to another in the system.

2.  A task is first computerized or a new version is released. Users need to see what the program does and doesn't do for them. For example, they need to know if the program makes decisions for them, and, if it does, whether it uses the same numbers and assumptions that they would.

3.  They are inexperienced with either the business or the software aspects. Users may need explanations of business concepts or information about how the interface works.

    Keep in mind that a user can be a novice one month and an expert a month later and also that a user can be an expert bookkeeper but an amateur accountant. Insisting that "no user will need information that simple!" or "that complex!" is a mistake.

*Note:* Paper documentation is organized differently from online help, so it isn't usually very helpful to people trying to find out what some object is or how to use it. The only advantage of putting books online is that most help systems let users do full-text searches.

## Volume Problem

If you do put a number of books online, you may discover that the help menu or table of contents has become unwieldy—200 to 1,000 separate topics, say, in five or ten different books.

The solution is to chunk the items into groups of about eight options at a time. Use your platform's menu-creation system to define the levels (see Chapter 3 for more information). Also, some help systems let you expand and contract headings on the contents windows. (See Figures 5.6 and 5.7.)

The key, as in any menu system, is to give users a sense of where they are and what they will find. If they can orient themselves in your system, the number of items and levels becomes irrelevant.

## Designing Quick Reference Guides

Expert technical writers advise that if you can't do the complete help system, then at least do a task-oriented, quick-reference guide online. Note that

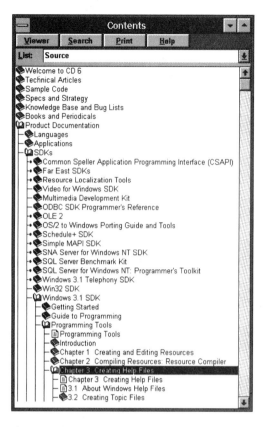

**Figure 5.6  Expanded listing**

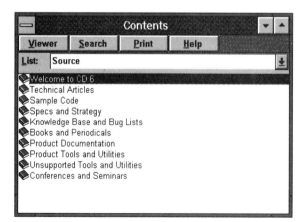

**Figure 5.7  Contracted listing, Microsoft Developers Development Library contents**

there is an easy way to create a quick-reference guide—ask your clients for their crib sheets.

This approach is well documented in the technical communication literature. For example, when Muriel Zimmerman looked for professional writers and writing at her clients' firms, "I couldn't find what I was looking for, because what I was looking for was everywhere." Users often write and maintain their own documentation, Zimmerman said, and these crib sheets were "the real successes in documentation" (Zimmerman, 1988, pp. 279–288)

At an IBM shop, user testing indicated that end users wanted a card that covered the most frequently used Office Vision/MVS (OV/MVS) tasks. "Because such a card was unavailable for the first two releases of OV/MVS," said Suzanne Ryan, "many office administrators created their own cards . . . I collected samples of the cards the office administrators wrote to determine which tasks customers felt were the most frequently used and what format the office administrators used for their cards" (Ryan, 1993, p. 99).

## HYPERTEXT AND CROSS-REFERENCING

When users need overviews, glossary definitions, or background information, give it to them with hypertext. "Hypertext" is a catch-all phrase meaning "a nonsequential retrieval of a document's text. The reader is free to pursue associative trails through the document by means of predefined or user-created links" (Pfaffenberger, 1992, p. 305).

Early hypertext systems tended to leave users in hyperspace, which provoked a flurry of articles and books explaining how *not* to do hypertext. As a result, links in business-oriented online documents are now mostly predefined. (Links in more artistic endeavors, on the other hand, are often user-defined and open-ended.)

This section describes the two types of hypertext links, plus hints on the most effective ways to use hypertext in business systems.

### Types of Links

There are two kinds of hypertext links:

1. Glossary links (also called "footnotes" in OS/2 systems), used for quick definitions. Glossary links generally appear in small boxes near or on top of the main help window.

   Glossary links are indicated with reversed type, a broken underline, a color change, a change in the cursor when it moves on top of it, or some combination of all four.

2. Cross-reference links, used primarily for reference. When the user selects a cross-reference link, the cross-reference text replaces the current text in the display panel.

   Cross-reference links are also indicated with reversed type, an underline, a color change, a cursor change, or some combination of all four.

*Note:* If you can select the indicators yourself, select more than one indicator per type of link. For example, use two different colors plus two different types of underlines, or italic type in one color and bold type in another. Color is a good secondary cue, but often fails as a primary cue. See Chapter 8, Color and Pattern, for more on color.

General usage guidelines follow.

## Glossary Links

Glossary links tie terms on the help panel to corresponding definitions in the glossary file. Use glossary links to define all business and computer terms that might be unfamiliar to your users.

Also use your glossary entries to answer these types of questions:

- Is a familiar term used differently from the way many users would?

- Is an unfamiliar term actually the same as another term some users already know?

- What is the relationship between this concept or item and other concepts and items in the system?

If you decide that a term must be defined, make sure that you add a glossary link to each panel in which the term appears. Within a panel, however, link it once, not every time it appears.

### Avoid Embedded Definitions

Do not define terms in the body of the help text for these reasons:

- *Maintenance:* Definitions will change when the program changes or when someone finds a better source on which to base a definition. It is much easier to correct a definition in one place, the glossary file, instead of in many places in many files. The definitions will then be updated automatically whenever the glossary item is updated.

- *Gets in the way for expert users:* Many users will know what the defined term means, and the rest will find out as soon as they read the definition for the first time. Putting the definition into a link instead of in the text keeps the definition out of the way, so to speak, for the expert users but still provides access for the users who need it.

- *Uses up valuable screen real estate:* Help panels have limited amounts of space. Definitions may push more important text below the bottom of the frame.

- *May require clauses, which are hard on the reader:* Research indicates that online help readers have trouble with sentences divided into two parts by clauses (Spyridakis, 1992, pp. 206–207). They cannot easily pick up the sense of a sentence again on the far side of the clause. In other words, if you embed a definition in a sentence—with dashes, for instance (or parenthetically)—you interrupt the reader's train of thought.

## Cross-Reference Links

Cross-reference links are used for detailed information that is too complicated or too long to put in the current help panel. For example:

- In "see also" sections, to link to information in online reference books
- To link from top-level overviews to nice-to-know business information
- To link to instructions for program-wide operations (how to use help, how to select items from lists, how to enter horizon dates, and so on)
- For examples. If possible, let users cut and paste the example text into the running application.
- To link from overviews to details about using sections of the window

Cross-reference links are not generated automatically—the help developer must define them.

Note that free-form word search, history, bookmark, and sticky notes let users create their own cross-references in effect. If you have a way to log help usage, watch for repeated searches. If many users look for the same item, add a cross-reference link to relevant points in the help files.

### Lost in Hyperspace

To prevent users from getting lost in the hypertext system, separate the cross-reference links from the body of the help text. For example, this kind of embedded link might cause trouble:

```
Select a color for the panel, then press OK.
```

When links are embedded in the text, users may feel they must jump immediately to the new help section. But by doing so, they may miss important information below the jump point, as well as forget where, exactly, they came from (especially if the help system returns them to the top of the panel rather than to the jump point). Also, a user might click on the link expecting a glossary definition—imagine his or her surprise when the whole help panel changes instead.

Two ways of separating the links are:

- Put them at the bottom of the help panels in a "see also" list. For example (the underline indicates a link):

```
See also:
Choosing Appropriate Colors
Choosing Sounds
```

*Note:* To simplify user access, alphabetize see-also lists. Also make sure that the title of the link is the same as the title of the help panel.

- Put the links in parentheses after the related information. For example:

```
Select a color for the panel (see Choosing
Appropriate Colors), then press OK.
```

By using parentheses, you indicate that the information is "nice to know," rather than "need to know."

## PROGRAMMING ISSUES

Creating online help requires:

- A text editor
- A help compiler
- A display system
- For context-sensitive help, the application software's object IDs

The text editor can be:

- A word processor or desktop publisher, such as Word for Windows, Framemaker 4, or Interleaf

- An old-fashioned ASCII editor such as vi or edlin

- A help authoring tool that overlays a word processor–for example, RoboHelp or Doc-to-Help on Windows 3.x systems

- A hypertext program such as Hyperties or HyperCard

- An SGML editor, such as Arbortext (used if the compiler requires SGML input)

The compiler program turns the text files into read-only files that are accessible from your application's help menu (or, less commonly, stand-alone text files accessible from the desktop).

The compiler can be part of the development system—for example, Microsoft's WinHelp system or the IBM OS/2 IPFC compiler. Or, it can be part of the editor—Framemaker 4, for example, lets you turn text files into online help documents by saving the original files in view-only mode. (Creating links to screen objects, however, requires more work.)

The compiler can also be a separate program. Electronic Book Technology's DynaText program indexes the text against the program, then sets up display panels for the online help.

To be accessible from your application, the help file needs only to be in a recognizable format. For context-sensitive help, however, the compiler must be able to match software object IDs to IDs embedded in the text file.

The help writers embed the object IDs in the text files, either by typing them in or by using tools. For example, some platforms let you capture IDs in a transaction log file ("tail -f logfile" works well in UNIX systems). You can also set up a system for reading IDs from the code itself, then writing the IDs to a text file.

Display systems can be included with your development platform, or they can be separate run-time modules with their own licenses and fees. Framemaker, for example, offers Frame Viewer display modules—rather than pay full fees for copies of Framemaker 4, end users pay a smaller fee for the display modules.

At run-time, the display system watches for help requests. When the user presses the help key on a particular object ([Shift]+[F1], usually, for context-sensitive help), the display system tries to match the object ID with the section of help text containing that ID. If it can make the match, it displays help for that object. If it can't, it defaults to higher-level help or to the help system's table of contents.

## Object-Oriented Programming and Help IDs

Object-oriented programming styles have a profound effect on help development. Following are some of the issues.

### Inheriting Help

In object-oriented development environments, objects can have one or two roles: as "parents" and as "children." Parent objects can be children of other parents; children can be parents of other children.

This terminology is a quick way to describe how the activity of one object might affect others related to it. For example, an application window is usually the parent of its dialog boxes and panels. When the user closes the application window, this action also closes its dialog boxes and panels as well, since the children "inherit" the states of their parents.

Inheritance and parent-child relationships have this important effect on context-sensitive help: If you don't write help for the child objects, the help system usually defaults to the help for the child's parent. Therefore, when you're short of time, write the top-level help first—window overview, task-oriented procedure, and so on. Even if you don't finish help for each individual object on the window, the top-level help still appears. If you write only button help, on the other hand, the user will get no help on the window as a whole.

### Reusing Object IDs

Another object-oriented programming concept is the reusability of objects. Instead of recoding an object each time it appears, the developer accesses a single copy each time he or she needs it in an application. For example, in many systems, even though OK and Cancel buttons show up in dozens of places, there is only one OK button ID and only one Cancel button ID.

This means that the writer can write only one piece of help for each reused button. In other words, if the OK button is reused, its help has to be the same no matter where it appears.

Reusable objects are often fine with reusable help. Certain objects act the same no matter where they appear in the application and, therefore, truly require only one piece of help text. Other objects, however, may be used completely differently depending on the context. In these cases, the object's reusability is a liability as far as the help goes.

For example, say that a window can be used in one context to calculate mortgage interest expense and in another context to calculate credit-card interest expense. The inputs for each are different—for example, mortgages run to the hundreds of thousands of dollars, while credit cards are tens of thousands or less. You have two poor choices when you're writing two-context help: Either specific "if context A, then do this" help: "Enter up to $5 million if you're using the mortgage application but only up to $10,000 if you're using the credit-card analyzer" or generic help: "Enter a number of dollars in the field and press [Return]."

A programming solution that may or may not be possible in your environment is to add a context marker—in other words, a prefix or suffix that differentiates the two help contexts without disabling the object's reusability. For example, if the generic window ID is "calculator," the mortgage version of the ID could be "mort-calculator" and the credit-card version could be "ccard-calculator."

## Indefinite IDs

When object IDs are based on a context that contains no intellectual information, you have another kind of problem.

Say that your application has a table with columns whose contents can be changed at will. The user can create a table with columns like *Dollars Received, Dollars Spent, Cost of Money, Exchange Rates*, and dozens of other categories. In this situation, there are two ways to define the column IDs: by data type or by column position.

- If the table is data-oriented, each type of data has its own column and its own object ID (for example, *dollarsreceived*). You can easily write help for the contents of each column.

- If, however, the table is column-oriented, each column can access any type of data. Since its ID is not tied to the information, you cannot write help for the contents of the column. Or you can write help for column 1, but it would have to be a long list of the various data types. The help for column 2 would be the same, as would column 3, and so on.

Another no-context area is the single dialog box with variable error or warning messages.

Aside from creating information-oriented objects, we know of no programming solutions. The best you can do, helpwise, is explain how to use the table features, then point users to your online glossary for descriptions of the types of data.

## Defining Help System Specifications

If you are defining a help system from scratch, remember to:

- Select an editor that is easy to use and that is tool-rich (spell checkers, thesauruses, grammar checkers, and so on). Well-known word processors and desktop publishing systems have the advantage here.

- Select a compiler that generates useful error messages. There is nothing more frustrating than a file that won't compile—except for a compiler that won't say why.

- Select a display system that lets users do full-text searches. At a minimum, users should be able to access a table of contents and an index—make sure that the system you select generates them automatically.

*Note:* Make sure that the object-oriented help text can be searched from the reference help system. Sometimes you need to look up a button or option that doesn't appear on the current window—there's nothing more frustrating than being unable to find something you *know* is in the system somewhere.

## WRITING ONLINE HELP: A SHORT STYLE GUIDE

This section might be said to contain too little grammar advice for most technical writers and too much for most programmers. However, we err by design.

- *From the writer's point of view:* There is as yet no software-related style guide comparable to the *Chicago Manual of Style* or to industry-specific guidelines such as the ones published by the Council of Biology Editors and the American Medical Association. As a start towards filling the gap, this section contains software-specific guidelines that you won't find in other, more traditional sources.

- *From the programmer's point of view:* English has all the earmarks of a game: arbitrary rules; a dependence on historical precedent; apprentice, journeyman, and master levels; and, most important, memorization of enormous amounts of information and exceptions. Unlike most games, however, "losing" English has actual consequences. If you don't play well, your peers decide that you're uneducated and your customers decide that you're sloppy. One of the purposes of this section, then, is to show inexperienced writers how to write master-level online help. It describes routes around the problem areas and hints for making even a rushed and hurried job look professional.

## Examples

Most help speaks directly to the reader—to the second-person "you," in other words. However, sometimes you need to compare and contrast two or more uses of the program or module. To do this, you need case studies and examples. Following are a few professional writing tricks for making your case studies memorable as well as exemplary.

### Names

When writing examples, you usually need names. Taking names at random from the phone book is not a good idea, since you can be sued by the people whose names you've used (if they ever find out). One solution to the name problem comes from the advertising field. Agencies will either borrow the names of their employees or pay one person for the use of his or her name. Then, if a second Joan Doe comes around to complain, the agency can explain that they used the first Joan Doe's name, not *her* name.

Another solution, once you've used the names of all of your coworkers, friends, relatives, and pets, is to use the names of historical figures—not well-known historical figures but people who were important in the field for which your software is written.

To find these names, search the indexes of history and trivia books for topics having to do with your field, then look for the names of people associated with that topic. (Biographical dictionaries could be another source, but since they're usually organized alphabetically, you can't easily find people in your field unless you already know their names.)

If you're in the telecommunications field, for example, you could look up communications, hearing, telephones, etc., and find:

- Almon Stroger, an Indiana undertaker who, in 1889, patented the automatic switch that led to direct-dial telephones.
- Emma Nutt, the first female switchboard operator. She started on September 1, 1878, and worked for Bell Systems for 37 years.
- Robert W. Devonshire, the first Bell Systems employee, hired as the bookkeeper in Boston on August 10, 1877. (Bell and Watson were both owners, not employees.)

*Note:* You might want to link to footnotes or glossary items that explain who each person is.

See the Resources section for a short list of history and trivia books.

## Phone Numbers

When you need to include a phone number in an example, follow the lead of TV shows and use *555* as the exchange.[4] For example, "If your number was 212-555-1234, you would enter it in the field like this . . . ."

Phone companies (at least in the U.S. and Canada) reserve numbers in the 555 exchange for their own purposes or as nonworking numbers.

## Sexism and Other -isms

*He or she?* Use both genders (and as many kinds of people as possible) in your help and training documents, not just because it's politically correct but because your examples will seem less generic.

Writers have developed a variety of methods for making text gender-neutral. One of the most effective is to simply switch between genders as you write the examples: "Mary Patel uses the Quick and Easy version to set up the account." Then, later, "Eric Jones uses the memo module to add customized messages to his bills."

You can also replace the singular with the plural: Instead of "The programmer . . . he," you can write, "The programmers . . . they." Don't write sentences such as "The user can reset the colors at their own discretion,"

---

[4] There are people who have so little else to do that they will call the numbers they see on TV. Therefore, producers never use real numbers.

however common this style may be. Most readers will see it as a mistake (a disagreement of number) rather than a solution to the gender-sensitivity problem.

*Salesman, saleswoman, sales representative?* Use the gender-neutral term unless your example talks about a particular person of a particular gender. For help with terminology, get a copy of *The Dictionary of Bias-Free Usage* (see Resources for details).

## Grammar, Spelling

The topics in this section address common grammatical and spelling difficulties that you are most likely to encounter in online help writing.

### Abbreviations

If a word is abbreviated on the screen, spell it out in the title of the help panel. Abbreviations can be confusing, especially if the user isn't clear about the context. For example, "Sec" can mean "Security," "Sector," "Second," "Secretary," or "Section."

In the help text, avoid abbreviations—an abbreviation the user doesn't know will stop him or her dead. Also, it's hard to tell which abbreviations are unfamiliar—many people don't know that "w/" or "wf." mean "with," for example, or what the difference is between "i.e." and "e.g." ("in other words" versus "for example").

*Note:* Many style guides eschew "etc." in user documentation. Experience with online help suggests that since "etc." is both easily read and compact, it should be acceptable in online help.

### Capitalization

*Acronyms:* Some acronyms—*radar, snafu, fubar*—have become words. Acronyms that haven't, however, should be written in all caps, no periods. For example, the acronym for Committee on Uniform Security Identification Procedures should appear as CUSIP.

If you aren't sure whether a term is an acronym, look it up in an abbreviations dictionary (see Resources in Chapter 1 for some of the better-known dictionaries).

*All-uppercase:* All-uppercase text causes problems. First of all, uppercase letters take up more room than lowercase letters. A title that breaks into two

LOW PRICED DEVICE RESTS IBM DISPLAYS

Publisher to drop copy protection

**Figure 5.8  Uppercase versus lowercase text**

lines when it is all uppercase will often fit on a single line when it is in upper- and lowercase.

Second, all uppercase is hard for nonprogrammers to read.[5] Reading studies indicate that:

- People get their cues from the tops of letters
- Capital letters give them fewer cues than lowercase letters

In Figure 5.8, see which of the two samples you can read more easily.

*Electronic mail:* e-mail system operators (sysops) often warn their subscribers not to use all uppercase because it looks like shouting.

*Proper names:* In English, capitalize only proper names, not names in general (the rules in other languages are very different—see Chapter 6 for more information). To find out if a name is a proper name, do these two tests.

*Test #1: Uniqueness.* Use of plurals and the indefinite article (*a*) indicate that the word in question is not a proper noun and therefore should not be capitalized. For example: "a section of text" or "a line drawing."

*Test #2: What does the program say?* Check the title. For example, if the window's title is simply "Files," the correct capitalization is "Files list," not "Files List."

*Titles of glossary entries:* Use initial uppercase for glossary titles only in the glossary, not when the words are embedded in the help text.

*UNIX beware!* Note that the convention on UNIX operating systems is that string comparisons are case-sensitive. If you're writing help for a UNIX application or an application that runs on more than one platform, don't change the case of a file name or command without checking for case sensitivity first. In other words, try the file name or command in the new case and see if it still works.

---

[5] Developers who've been writing in all uppercase for many years read uppercase as easily as most people read mixed-case text.

## Colons and Semicolons

*Colons:* A colon is two dots, one on top of the other. Use colons to introduce lists of definitions, actions, or bulleted items. For example:

```
Use the search function to:

Quickly locate a file.

See multiple views of the same file.

And so on.
```

*Semicolons:* A semicolon, a dot above a comma, is used as a "half stop"—more than a comma, less than a period. However, don't use semicolons in help text because they are easy to miss. Instead, replace the semicolon with a period and start a new sentence. For example, this sentence:

```
Switch product types; for example, from "Chrysler parts"
to "Volvo parts."
```

should be changed to:

```
Switch product types. For example, switch from "Chrysler
parts" to "Volvo parts."
```

*Periods, when to use:* In short, use a period whenever you end a sentence. In a step-by-step list of instructions, each instruction is a complete sentence. Therefore, all steps must end with periods. For example:

```
You can:

Address the message to a specific user-support
representative.

Send log files. The log files contain information that
the representative can use to debug your problem.
```

If the items are not complete sentences, end the entire list with a period. For example:

```
You can find information:

By searching for a word or phrase

By selecting from a list of topics

By selecting from a list of applications

By selecting from a table of contents.
```

There are three reasons for this rule: One, it gives the reader closure; he or she knows that this is indeed the end of the list. Second, it can be argued that conceptually the entire list is a sentence, and, because it is a sentence, it takes a period at the end. Third, this is standard IBM style—in other words, since it is fairly common, it will look correct to many readers (but not to all).

## Negative Contractions

*Note:* Contractions of "not" (for example, "It isn't" for "It is not") can cause problems because fast readers or readers for whom English is a second language may miss the apostrophe and even the contraction itself. Also, contractions are seen as informal and casual. For example, "Don't put your installation diskette on top of the telephone" does not impart a sense of seriousness to the reader. "Do not put your installation diskette . . ." is better. "*Do not,* "Do not," or "Do NOT" are better still.[6]

Some technical style guides frown upon contractions because of their informality. But why should technical writing be formal? If you're sure that the contraction can have no adverse effects, feel free to use it.

*It's versus its: It's* stands in for "it is." *Its* means "belonging to *it.*" Both words ought to be spelled the same way, but they're not. If you're uncertain about which one to use, do what the professionals do. Ask: "Can I replace *it-s* with *it is?*" If yes, then it's *it's.*

## Hyphens and Dashes

*Avoiding confusion:* Use hyphens between prefixes and words whenever you can read the same word or phrase two different ways. For example, is this statement about a vacation spot for software or a reorganization?

```
To resort a file...
```

Add a hyphen:

```
To re-sort a file...
```

---

[6] Underlining words sets them off from the rest of the text better than either bolding or italicizing them. Be careful, though: In online help, underlines often indicate links. In Microsoft Windows Help, unbroken underlines indicate cross-reference links, and broken underlines indicate glossary links. (If your help files will ever be distributed on paper, keep in mind that typesetters and professional desktop publishers automatically change underlined text to italic.)

*Combined modifiers:* Use a hyphen when you use two terms as one modifier. For example:

```
The X-axis location is the upper lefthand corner of the
box.
```

Here, the "X" and "axis" together modify "location," and the hyphen reinforces the connection between the two terms. No hyphen is necessary when "X" modifies "axis," however.

```
The X axis runs from left to right.
```

However, you never need a hyphen after an "-ly" construction, since the -ly means that what follows is the modified word. For example, in this statement, no hyphen is needed between *relatively* and *slow*.

```
The operation is relatively slow.
```

*Two-part words:* Compound words are hyphenated:

- When they are first coined
- If the two words together scan badly without the hyphen.

However, when the coinage is no longer new and if the compound word can be understood without its hyphen, "The progress of each two-part word is toward the single word" (Follett, 1966, p. 428)

The word "online/on-line" is a good test case. It is no longer a new word, and it scans better without the hyphen. And, in fact, movement is toward "online." Recent books about online text, such as *Writing Better Computer Documentation: From Paper to Online* (Brockmann, 1990) or *Designing and Writing Online Documentation* (Horton, 1990), do not hyphenate the word.

If you're unsure about a word, check it in a spelling and hyphenation dictionary. These are small books (usually 3" by 5" or so) that contain just words, no definitions. Each listing shows the correct spelling, the syllable breaks and stresses, and whether the word contains a hyphen or not. The variants are included as well. For example:

```
cross'-re•fer, -ferred', -fer'ring
cross'-ref'er•ence
```

Keep in mind, however, that dictionaries are more conservative than the language as a whole. A fast growth field like information science leaves dictionary publishers far behind.

*Dashes:* Use a long dash (called "em" dash since it is the width of an M) to set off examples or important information at the end of a sentence. For example:

```
Enter two or three securities--no more than one in the
buy column and two in the sell column.
```

*Note:* If an em dash is not available in the editing program, use two hyphens and *no* spaces before or after.

However, avoid dashed clauses in help text (see Clauses, Eliminating, for more on clauses). Instead, rewrite a dashed clause as a separate sentence. For example, "The standard colors—red, green, blue, and yellow—appear on the table" should be rewritten as "Standard colors appear on the table. The standard colors are red, green, blue, and yellow."

## May or Can?

"May" implies either a possibility or a need to get permission; "can" indicates ability. Don't use *may* when you mean *can* because you leave the sentence open to interpretation.

For example, "You may print reports after generating them," leaves these questions in the reader's mind: "Can they be printed or not? Do I have to get permission—a license agreement?—before I print them?"

A more correct statement would be, "You can print reports after generating them."

## Numbers

*1000, 1,000, or $1,000?* If the number to be input or displayed is actually "1000" (or some other number), use "1000" in the help text.

However, when you're not showing an actual input or output, add commas—for example, 1,000, 1,000,000. The commas make large numbers easier to read. Also add a dollar sign if the number is actually a dollar amount.

*Note:* The names of large numbers and the type of decimal point and thousands separators differ from language to language. See Chapter 6 for more information.

*To spell out or not:* Do not write out a number if it is:

● An actual number—for example, "The correct PSI is 100."

● A number containing a fraction or decimal—for example, "The price is $89.50."

For situations in which you mention a number of items, however, write out the number. For example, "The six files on the menu are the six files saved most recently." Up to a point, that is. The Associated Press and *New York Times* style books tell writers to spell out numbers between zero and nine but switch to numerals at 10. *The Chicago Manual of Style,* on the other hand, suggests spelling numbers between zero and ninety-nine, then switching to numerals at 100.

We recommend following the Associated Press and *New York Times* guidelines, which are oriented toward news writing, rather than *The Chicago Manual of Style*, which is oriented to academic writing.

Nevertheless, keep in mind that it is easier for readers to understand "2 million" than "2,000,000" or even "two million."

*Number as first word in a sentence:* Spell out a number if it's the first word in the sentence. For example, write:

```
Twenty percent of the students failed.
```

Not:

```
20 percent of the students failed.
```

*Percent versus percentage:* If you're referring to a particular number, use percent—"3 percent." Otherwise, use percentage—"the total percentage of college students."

### Parallel Construction

Make liberal use of parallel construction because it quickly tells readers that the items or concepts are related.

For example, this construction fails to indicate the difference between replacing individual characters and replacing parts of words.

```
Use ? to stand in for individual characters. The asterisk
can be used to replace parts of words.
```

Notice how the relationship appears when you recast the sentences into the parallel form:

```
Use ? to stand in for individual characters. Use * to
stand in for parts of words.
```

### Plurals

Don't use parentheses, s, close parentheses—(s)—to stand in for "singular or plural"—for example, *item(s)*. The construction attracts attention to itself unnecessarily and is hard to read. An alternative is: "Select one or more items."

### That or Which?

A clause introduced with "that" is a restrictive clause. In other words, the sentence describes a particular set of things.

```
The six files that appear on the File menu are the six
files used most recently.
```

Out of all possible files, you're speaking only of the six that appear on the menu.

A clause introduced with "which," on the other hand, is a nonrestrictive clause.

```
The six files, which appear on the File menu, are the six
files used most recently.
```

In this case, you're talking about six files that just happen to appear on the menu.

Note that "that" clauses never use commas. The absence of commas means, "this part of the sentence you cannot do without." "Which" clauses do use commas, meaning that "you can skip this bit if you want."

If you have trouble telling the difference, try these tests.

*Test #1:* Read the sentence to yourself and listen for a pause. If there is one, the clause uses "which." If not, it uses "that."

*Test #2:* Try adding a comma before "that" or "which." If the comma seems natural in front of a "that," the "that" should be a "which."

*Test #3:* Try reading the sentence without the clause. If the sentence still makes sense without it, use "which." If not, use "that."

Also, consider whether you need a clause at all. See Clauses, Eliminating.

## Terminology

Following are a handful of standard English terms that are known to cause trouble for inexperienced writers, plus a handful of computer terms that cause trouble for inexperienced software users.

## And versus Or (Boolean Logic and English)

If you ask your human assistant for the "New Jersey and California customers," he or she will bring you all of the New Jersey and California customer files. If, however, you ask the software for "New Jersey and California customers," you'll get only the customers who have offices in both states. To get both sets, you have to ask for "New Jersey *or* California customers."

The difference between the natural language and the Boolean terms is very confusing to inexperienced users until you explain it. Once explained, most users understand the difference and can use the selection logic correctly. To eliminate difficulty, therefore, explain the difference with an example or two.

## Data

*Data* is the plural of *datum*. A sentence like "The data is fine" is therefore incorrect. It should be "The data are fine." If you don't like the sound of "data are," do what professional writers do—change *data* to *information*: "The information is fine."

## Database, Data Base

The *Penguin Dictionary of Information Technology and Computer Science* and the *Oxford Dictionary of Computing* both say "database." The computer dictionaries are more current for computer terms than *Webster's Ninth New Collegiate Dictionary*, which shows "data base.".

## Default

In common language, "default" means "fail to pay obligations, go bankrupt." This is not what it means in the computer world: "the option selected automatically when the user doesn't select an option." Write a glossary definition for "default," then link to it whenever necessary.

## Dictionaries

*Everyday terms:* Pick one dictionary and stick with it. *Webster's Ninth New Collegiate Dictionary* is a good standard dictionary because it has the virtue of being prescriptive (it tells you what the rules are) rather than descriptive (it tells you what people actually do).

*Business terms:* Find out what dictionary or source book the in-house subject matter experts and your customers use. (If your subject matter expert says he or she doesn't use dictionaries, ask which dictionaries he or she wrote, cowrote, or edited. If the answer is "none," then mention that you will need his or her phone number, e-mail address, and beeper number, since you expect to need his or her help while you're writing.)

*Computer terms:* There is no definitive dictionary for computer terms. However, *Computer User's Dictionary* from Que Corporation is good for end-user definitions and *The Penguin Dictionary of Computers* and the *Oxford Dictionary of Computing* are good for technical terms. There is also *The New Hacker's Dictionary,* which is good for etymologies. See Resources for more information.

## Electronic Mail

The currently acceptable contraction of "electronic mail" seems to be "e-mail." However, "email" is catching up. See Two-Part Words in the Hyphens and Dashes subsection for more information.

## File Name, Filename?

Use *file name.* However, you might want to avoid the use of "file name" by using the name of the type of file. For example, although saved templates are files, it is simpler to call them "templates."

## However

"However" is not a conjunction. In other words, a sentence that uses *however* to glue together two thoughts is incorrect.

```
Historical information is available for many of the
bonds, however in some cases it does not go back to the
issue date.
```

The corrected version is:

```
Historical information is available for many of the
bonds. However, in some cases, the information does not
go back to the issue date.
```

### Keys on the Keyboard

Surround the key name with brackets: [Return] or [F6]. (Brackets are used because they are a visual reminder of the edges of the keys.) Do not use angle brackets—<N>—because they take up too much space.

Match the text printed on the keyboard: Use [Back Space], not [Backspace].

If there are important functional differences between keys on the number keypad and those on the main keyboard, or between [Delete] and [Back Space], or [Return] and [Enter], say so.

Call the space bar the "space bar." Don't use brackets and initial capitals because: (a) there is no label and (b) because it is a generic term. As you wouldn't normally write "pick up the Hammer," you also wouldn't write "press the Space Bar."

### Login, Log In, Log On

Use *login* for the name of the ID (noun). Use *log in* or *log on* for the process of logging in or on (verb). Examples: "Your login is used to log onto the system." "Log in using your login."

### Real Time, Real-Time?

*Real-time* is used as a modifier: "The real-time version of the program . . ." *Real time* is used as a modifier+noun: "The program works in real time."

### Start versus Run

Start an application, not run, invoke, or launch. However, run is permissible if the application is a batch program.

### Use or Utilize?

"Utilize" refers to using a tool or process, invented to do one thing, for something unrelated to its original purpose. It is not a synonym for "use." For example, you can utilize a shoe to pound in a nail, but you'd better use a hammer when you put together a roof.

### Wildcard

A useful but sometimes unfamiliar computer term. When writing help, create a "wildcard" glossary item and link to it whenever it appears in the help text.

## Style

Style issues are more open to argument and interpretation than, say, spelling. The style recommendations in this section are, nevertheless, based on research and experience with the peculiarities of writing for online.

### Clauses, Eliminating

> *Reading what you wrote:* Read your work out loud to locate problems. If you run out of breath, the sentence is too long.
>
> Robert Kanigel, writer and editor, Baltimore, MD (Parker, 1990, p. 113).

Avoid embedded clauses in sentences. Embedded clauses appear between commas and often after the relative pronouns "who," "which," and "that." Researchers have found that any embedded clause places extra demands on short-term memory (Spyridakis, 1992, p. 206). When writers reduce the number of clauses or shorten the clauses, readers process the text more accurately and retain more information.

For example, this sentence contains three major clauses, one embedded inside another.

```
The first coupon factor, FCF, is a fraction that, when
multiplied by the normal coupon payment, gives the actual
first coupon payment paid per $100 on the bond.
```

You can usually eliminate clauses by creating separate sentences. The same sentence could be rewritten as these two sentences.

```
The first coupon factor is a fraction of the bond's face
amount. When you multiply the normal coupon payment by
the first coupon factor, you get the actual amount of the
first coupon payment.
```

Although the two-sentence version is not as brief as the one-sentence version, it is easier to understand even when you have no idea what *coupons,* *factors,* and *bonds* are.

## Controlled English

Help text must be as unambiguous as possible. One way to keep help text unambiguous is to restrict your vocabulary—in other words, use the same word over and over again rather than a synonym.

If you don't reuse terms, readers are sometimes left wondering if you're still talking about the same thing or have gone onto something new. For example, a reader will probably have a few questions after reading a statement like this:

```
To find zero-coupon CMO classes, search for "Accrual" in
the Tranche field.
```

Some of the questions might be:

- "Are find and search the same process?"

- "If I'm looking for zero-coupon CMOs, why should I search for accrual?" (Answer: Because at least one category of zero-coupon CMO tranches accrue principal over time, and that category is the only one currently in the database.)

- "Are accrual bonds the only type of zero-coupon classes in the program?" (This question suggests that the writer's scope may be too narrow, not too broad.)

- "Why should I look for a class in the tranche field?" ("Class" and "tranche" are synonymous. The writer should pick one of the two synonyms and stick with it.)

A better way to write the help would be:

```
The only zero-coupon CMO tranches in the database are
accrual tranches. Search for them by typing "accrual" in
the Tranche field and pressing [Enter].
```

*Translations:* A restricted vocabulary also simplifies translations into other languages. In fact, many multinational industries have developed controlled English vocabularies and style sheets to facilitate translation. Fields that are by nature international (air and sea transportation, for example) also have developed controlled or simplified English dictionaries. For more information, see Controlled English in the Resources section.

### Dates and Times

*AM, A.M. or a.m.?* *The Chicago Manual of Style* says that American style is A.M. in small caps. British style is a.m. or p.m., "an alternative that is acceptable here also" (Chicago, 1994, p. 469). Small caps aren't always available online, however, and since lowercase is generally more readable than uppercase (see Capitalization), a.m. and p.m. may be the best choice.

*Noon and midnight:* Noon is not 12 p.m. and midnight is not 12 a.m. Noon is 12 noon, midnight is 12 midnight. Developers would often rather not use *midnight* and *noon* because they don't fit into fields as nicely as *a.m.* and *p.m.* However, "12 p.m." is ambiguous—if you don't believe this, ask any four people in a room what 12 p.m. means. *Solutions:* Display the time in 24-hour format or make the display field wider.

### Humor

I remember presenting at one of IBM's "100 Percenters" conferences in Britain and being very struck with a few of the American executives who arrived. They were not in tune with the audience. They were quite uncomfortable with the fact that I was making this audience laugh. Well, I can tell you, it was the most intelligent audience I've ever played in front of. They were so fast that you could make the subtlest joke and they would get it in a flash . . . . That was the level at which you communicated with these very, very smart people.

John Cleese in an interview with *Training* magazine (Filipczak 1993, p. 40).

Many technical style guides suggest that you avoid humor—it's hard to do without offending someone, jokes don't translate well, and so on. However, as John Cleese has been pointing out in interviews and by example, in the training films he has done for Video Arts, humor helps establish rapport, relaxes the atmosphere, and produces a greater flexibility of mind in those who laugh.

You can safely include humor in online help:

- By using situational humor—in other words, by picking a situation that everyone in the software's business domain would think was funny. For example, the title of one Video Arts training video is "Who Sold You This, Then?" Its target audience, repair and service personnel, start laughing as soon as they hear the title.

- By telling stories on yourself, your program, or your company. (However, since none of these three parties usually star in online help, this suggestion has limited use.)

As for bona fide jokes ("A funny thing happened on the way to the office . . ."), avoid them—they really don't translate well from one language to another.

## Lists

There are two types of lists: bulleted lists and numbered lists. Use *bulleted lists* whenever:

- You are writing about more than two or three items.

- A sentence or paragraph has become long and unwieldy because it contains a number of items. Break it into a bulleted list.

Use *numbered lists* for either of two purposes:

1.  For the steps, whenever you have a procedure with more than one step.

2.  Whenever you mention a particular number of items (like "either of two purposes").

*Putting lists in order:* When you create a bulleted list, give a thought to organization.

- Is the user going to use it to look up a word or abbreviation? Then use alphabetical order.

- Is the user going to look up a number? Then use numerical order.

- Is the list a collection of thoughts? Then use any logical order.

## Personalizing Programs

Personalizing a program is saying things such as "Recipe King does this," as if the program acts on its own volition, or "the file's ID appears on the panel," as if the file owns its ID.[7]

Style guides frown on personalizing objects and, in fact, some corporate style guides forbid constructions that use the company name informally—

---

[7] This construction is called the *genitive* and does not denote ownership or possession. For example, in the phrase "my mother," the genitive "my" doesn't mean that I own my mother. Nor is personification implied in "tomorrow's breakfast." More information is available in any style guide or grammar book and in most dictionaries.

for example, "Acme's car-replacement policy" is not allowed but "The Acme car-replacement policy" is fine.

However, writing these sentences correctly is often cumbersome:

- "Recipe King is designed to do this" (instead of "Recipe King does this").

- "The ID of the file appears on the panel" (instead of "the file's ID appears on the panel").

As long as you don't violate corporate policy, we suggest that you personalize programs for brevity's sake. Just keep in mind that some people think that personalizing computers and programs is a bad idea.

## Tone

Be professional, not friendly. For example, telling users to select their "favorite" template is inappropriate since users are unlikely to feel any favoritism towards a software file. A more appropriate (and useful) statement would be, "Select the template designed for use with this memo."

## Units of Measurement

Help the user out: What kind of unit does the field accept? What does the table show? Basis points? Standard deviations? Numbers of millions of dollars, in what format—"2" or "2,000,000" or "$2000000"? Percentages? Does "1.0" mean 1 percent or 100 percent?

Showing the units of measurement is one of the most effective ways to make software easy to use and understand. However, putting them on the screen itself is much better than putting them in the help text.

## Voice (Who Did This?)

The "passive voice" is a sentence construction in which the subject is acted upon. A passive sentence is created by adding the past participle of a verb (underlined in the examples) to a form of the verb *to be.* "It *is* creat<u>ed</u>," for example, or "The string *is* call<u>ed</u> (*was* call<u>ed</u>, *has been* call<u>ed</u>, *may be* call<u>ed</u>, *will be* call<u>ed</u>)." In the active voice, the subject is the actor: "The subroutine calls the string."

Many style guides disapprove of the passive voice. The reasons include:

- Many readers, especially those for whom English is a second language, find passive voice hard to understand.

- Some languages do not have passive constructions, making translations difficult.

- Passive constructions are usually longer, thereby slowing down most readers.

- Since the actor is unnamed, no one (or no thing) takes responsibility for the action. For example, notice the difference between "The files got erased somehow" and "I erased the files somehow." When you know that Jane User erased the files, you can prevent further erasures. If no one admits responsibility, troubleshooting takes much longer.

For all of these reasons, don't use passive voice in instructions. When you write instructions, you must tell the reader what he or she must do. If you say, "The F1 key should be pressed," it's not clear who should press it. On the other hand, if you say, "Press F1," the reader immediately knows that you're talking to him or her. *Note:* You can check for the passive voice mechanically by searching for the words "be" and "is," then looking for "ed" endings.

However, passive voice can be useful in other situations. For example, you can use passive voice to indicate an action done by an unknown agent, especially if an active-voice rewrite would impart the wrong idea.

For example, say that the user opens a window, and it contains information from a previous session, another user, or the system administrator. The following statement would be either false or incomplete:

```
...the data you entered earlier.
```

A better version would be:

```
...the data that were entered earlier.
```

Other situations in which passive voice is appropriate are:

- When unidentified or unidentifiable parties do something: "The mail sent to you by other users appears in the mailbox."

- When problems occur: "The news feed is down" or "If the server is down, no information appears."

- When the actor is either unknown or the computer system itself: "Permission is denied" or "When the recipient is added to the system, your mail will be delivered."

## REFERENCES

Apple Computer, Inc. *Macintosh Human Interface Guidelines.* Reading, MA: Addison-Wesley, 1992.

Boggan, Scott, David Farkas, and Joe Welinske. *Developing Online Help for Windows.* Carmel, IN: Sams Publishing, 1993.

Brockmann, R. John. *Writing Better Computer User Documentation: From Paper to Hypertext.* New York: John Wiley & Sons, 1990.

*Chicago Manual of Style, The,* 14th ed. Chicago, IL: University of Chicago Press, 1993.

Crichton, Michael. *Jurassic Park.* New York: Alfred Knopf, 1990.

Filipczak, Bob. "An Interview with John Cleese" *Training,* November 1993, pp. 37–41.

Follett, Wilson. *Modern American Usage,* edited and completed by Jacques Barzun. New York: Avenel Books, 1966.

Horton, William K. *Designing and Writing Online Documentation,* New York: John Wiley & Sons, 1990.

Norman, Kent L. *The Psychology of Menu Selection.* Norwood, NJ: Ablex Publishing Corporation, 1991.

Parker, Tom. *Never Trust a Calm Dog and Other Rules of Thumb,* New York: HarperPerennial, 1990.

Pfaffenberger, Bryan. *Que's Computer User's Dictionary,* 3d ed. Carmel, IN: Que Corporation, 1992.

Ryan, Suzanne. "Cinderella's SlipperDoes It Fit Americans and Europeans?" *Proceedings of the Fortieth Annual Conference of the Society for Technical Communication Conference,* 1993.

Spyridakis, J. H., and M. J. Wenger. "Writing for Human Performance: Relating Reading Research to Document Design," *Technical Communication*, 2d Quarter 1992, pp. 202–215.

Zimmerman, Muriel. "Are Writers Obsolete in the Computer Industry?" In *Text, ConText, and HyperText*, edited by Edward Barrett. Cambridge, MA: MIT Press, 1988.

---

## RESOURCES

---

## Controlled English

The Aerospace Industries Association of America offers their controlled-English dictionary for aviation and space-related terminology, *A Guide for the Preparation of Aircraft Maintenance Documentation in the International Aerospace Maintenance Language*. Send a $50 U.S. check or money order to: Erin Moore, Aerospace Industries Association of America, 1250 I Street NW, Suite 1100, Washington, DC 20005. For overseas rates or other information, call 202-371-8435.

### Articles

Calistro, Ralph F. "Simplified English Roundup: Fait Accompli or Impossible Dream?" *Proceedings of the Society for Technical Communication Annual Conference*, 1993. A good list of references, plus the important question: Does rewriting text into simplified English change what the original author meant to say? Some anecdotal data say that it may.

Elliot, Keith H. "A Layered Approach to Translating Online Documentation." *Proceedings of the Society for Technical Communication Annual Conference*, 1993. The author describes SAP AG's four-level online help system–interface itself (fields, menus, messages), objects (field help, menu help, message help, and glossary), task, and reference. Then he describes a method, based on marketing analysis, for deciding how many of these layers to translate when you can't afford to translate all of them. Also includes some interesting problems that this approach can cause. See also Ladd's companion piece in this list.

Gustafson, Gayle. "Controlled English for International Audiences." *Proceedings of the First Annual AT&T Customer Documentation Symposium,* AT&T Bell Laboratories, Holmdel, NJ, October 19, 1988, pp. 91–101. An excellent roundup of controlled English activity in multinational organizations.

Hudson, Dave. "Authoring for Electronic Delivery." *Proceedings of the Society for Technical Communication Annual Conference,* 1993. A description of the Caterpillar, Inc., online help system, which is ISO compliant.

Humphreys, R. Lee. "From Blazonry to PoliceSpeak." *English Today,* vol. 7, no. 3, July 1991, pp. 37-39. An article about the simplified English used to communicate in the Chunnel as well as heraldic symbols defined during the Middle Ages.

Ladd, Dennis D. "SAP*help*: A Multilingual Authoring Tool." *Proceedings of the Society for Technical Communication Annual Conference,* 1993. SAP AG, a German software house, supports 12 languages fully or partially (that is, interface only). Although SAP*help* is a proprietary system for translating online help concurrently and semimechanically, the ideas presented are portable to other systems. See also Elliot's companion piece in this list.

Phillips, Wanda Jane. "Controlling Terminology for Translation." *Proceedings of the Thirty-Eighth International Technical Communication Conference,* 1991. Uses RightWriter to scan all documents for commonly used words and create a controlled-English dictionary for both software and documentation. Her organization translates English into French, Spanish, Chinese, Arabic, and Thai: "The Thai character set," she writes, "uses the same ASCII values that we were using to draw lines around menus."

Velte, Charles E. "Is Bad Breadth Preventing Effective Translation of Your Text?" *Proceedings of the Thirty-Seventh International Technical Communication Conference,* 1990. Includes an eye-opening list of everyday words with multiple meanings.

### Controlled English Programs

*ClearCheck, Controlled English Authoring and Checking Software,* is available from Carnegie Group, 5 PPG Place, Pittsburgh, PA 15222; voice: 800-284-3424; fax: 412-642-6906. The software is SGML compliant.

# Dictionaries

It helps to have a few dictionaries on hand when creating your own glossary. Keep in mind that you'll need specialized dictionaries as well as the computer and general dictionaries.

### Bias-Free Usage

Maggio, Rosalie. *The Dictionary of Bias-Free Usage*, Phoenix, AZ: Oryx Press, 1991.

### Computer Terminology, End User

Pfaffenberger, Bryan. *Que's Computer User's Dictionary*. 3d ed., Carmel, IN: Que Corporation, 1992.

### Computer Terminology, Technical

Chandor, Anthony *The Penguin Dictionary of Computers*, 3d ed. New York: Viking Penguin, 1983.

Illingworth, Valerie (editor). *Dictionary of Computing*, 3d ed. Oxford and New York: Oxford University Press, 1991.

Raymond, Eric. *The New Hacker's Dictionary*. Cambridge, MA: MIT Press, 1991.

### General

*Webster's Ninth New Collegiate Dictionary*. Springfield, MA: Merriam-Webster, 1991.

# Grammar Help

More than 60 college or university English departments in the United States and Canada offer grammar hotlines. For the list of hotlines, send a stamped, self-addressed #10 envelope to Writing Center/Grammar Hotline, Humanities Division, Tidewater Community College, 1700 College Crescent, Virginia Beach, VA 23456; 804-427-7170.

## Help Systems

Following are a handful of popular help editors and compilers for various platforms. The list is not exhaustive.

### Cross-Platform Editors

*Framemaker 4,* available on more than a dozen platforms and in a variety of natural languages, lets you turn standard paper documents into online hypertext documents. With the addition of Frame Viewer and the Frame Development Kit, you can turn the same documents into context-sensitive online help. For more information, contact Frame Technology Corporation, 1010 Rincon Circle, San Jose, CA 95131; 800-U4-FRAME; e-mail: comment@frame.com.

*Interleaf's World View* lets you distribute view-only documents developed on nearly any platform in nearly any format over a network. Interleaf files can also be turned into context-sensitive online help. For more information, contact Interleaf, Inc., Prospect Place, 9 Hillside Avenue, Waltham, MA 02154; 800-955-LEAF.

### Apple Computer Editors

*HyperCard* is the original Apple hypertext engine, supplied free with all new Macintoshes. HyperCard 2.2, QuickTime, CD, and electronic book development programming environments are available from APDA, Apple Computer, P.O. Box 319, Buffalo, NY 14207-0319.

### IBM OS/2 Programs

The Presentation Manager help development system is called *Information Presentation Facility.* IPFC.EXE compiler and VIEW.EXE viewer are supplied with the OS/2 development toolkit. Writers set up the help text using SGML-like Bookmaster codes, then compile the files with `IPFC /INF`. (The /INF switch creates online files, which require the extension `.INF`.) For details, see the OS/2 development toolkit's *Programming Guide.*

### Microsoft Windows Editors

*Doc-to-Help* lets you create printed documentation, then automatically convert it, with topic, contents, and index links, into online help. Requires Word for Windows. Contact WexTech Systems, 310 Madison Avenue, Suite 905, New York, NY 10017; voice: 212/949-9595.

*ForeHelp* is a WYSIWYG editor (no RTF codes or placeholders in the display) for Windows help files. Contact ForeFront Inc., 5171 Eldorado Springs Drive, Boulder, CO 80303; voice: 800-357-8507 or 303-499-9181; fax: 303-494-5446.

*HelpMagician* lets you add video, audio clips, and animation to hypertext help files, then display the files without Microsoft Viewer. Contact Software Interphase, Inc., 82 Cucumber Hill Road, Foster, RI 02825; voice: 800-542-2742 or 401-397-2340; fax: 401-397-6814.

*RoboHelp* is one of the most popular Windows help editors. Requires Word for Windows. Contact Blue Sky Software Corp., 7486 La Jolla Boulevard., Suite 3, La Jolla, CA 92037; voice: 800-677-4946 or 619-459-6365; fax: 619-459-6366.

The "unsupported" *Windows Help Authoring Utility* has two components—WHAT, the Windows Help Authoring Template, and WHPE, the Windows Help Project Editor. WHAT helps you code the help files, which you create with Word for Windows. WHPE helps you modify project file options such as compression, reporting, file directories, and titles; add object IDs and resize the window positions and sizes; and compile the files. The programs and documentation are available on the Microsoft Developer Network CD (along with many other tools and books) for $199. Contact Microsoft Developer Network CD, One Microsoft Way, Redmond, WA 98052-6399; voice: 800-759-5474 or 402-691-0173; in Europe: 31-10-258-8864.

### UNIX Editors and Compilers

*Arbortext, Inc.*, 1000 Victors Way, Suite 400, Ann Arbor, MI 48108; voice: 313-996-3563; fax: 313-996-3566. Arbortext offers a somewhat WYSIWYG editor that can be used to create online help files in SGML format. Use with Electronic Book Technology's Dynatext display system.

Hewlett-Packard offers *HP Help* for OSF/Motif systems. For a copy of the *HP Help System Developer's Guide* (part number B1171-90055, 1992 edition), contact Hewlett-Packard Company, User Interface Technology Division, 1000 NE Circle Boulevard, Covallis, OR 97330, USA; 800-752-0900 or 503-757-2000.

*HyperHelp* lets you use either Microsoft Windows or UNIX word processing files (RTF format) to create UNIX context-sensitive online help. For details, contact Bristol Technology Inc., 241 Ethan Allen Highway, Ridgefield, CT 06877; voice: 203-438-6969; fax: 203-438-5013; e-mail: amy@bristol.com.

*DynaText* is an online help indexer and viewer that accepts SGML files as input. For more information, contact Electronic Book Technologies, One Richmond Square, Providence, RI 02906; voice: 401-421-9550; fax: 401/421-9551; e-mail: ebt-inc!lrr@uunet.uu.net.

### CompuServe Online Resources

For *OS/2 IPF* help, go to the IBM OS/2 developers' forums: *GO OS2DF1* for development tools and debugging tips or *GO OS2DF2* for network, database, and CD ROM development.

For *Windows help development*, try the Developers Network Forum: *GO MSDN*.

### Internet Online Resources

For cogent information about all aspects of online help writing and development, subscribe to the *Technical Writers List.* Address the message to *LISTSERV@VM1.UCC.OKSTATE.EDU*, then type this as the message: *sub techwr-l firstname lastname*.

*Winhlp-L* is a list server for people creating Windows help. To subscribe, send a message via Internet to *listserv@Admin.HumberC.ON.CA* or via Bitnet to *listserv.Humber.Bitnet*. Type this as the message: *sub winhelp-l firstname lastname*.

## Sources for Names

### History Timetables

For masses of raw data, "timetable" books are good. Here are three typical books.

Grun, Bernard. *The Timetables of History: A Horizontal Linkage of People and Events.* New York: Simon & Schuster, 1982. The categories covered are: History, Politics; Literature, Theater; Religion, Philosophy, Learning; Visual Arts; Music; Science, Technology, Growth; and Daily Life. The chronology starts in 5000 B.C. and ends in 1978 (there may be a later edition available).

Hellemans, Alexander, and Bryan Bunch. *The Timetables of Science: A Chronology of the Most Important People and Events in the History of Science.* New York: Simon and Schuster, 1988. The categories here are: General,

Anthropology/Archeology, Astronomy, Biology, Chemistry, Earth Science, Mathematics, Medicine, Physics, and Technology. The chronology starts in 600 B.C. and ends in 1988.

*The Timetables of Technology, A Record of Our Century's Achievements.* London: Michael Joseph Limited, 1982. The categories are: Communication, Information (and in the later sections, Space Applications); Transport, Warfare (and in the later sections, Space Exploration); Energy and Industry; Medicine and Food Production; and Fringe Benefits ("1924: The self-winding watch is patented"). The chronology starts in 1900 and ends in 1982.

### Trivia Books

Panati, Charles. *Extraordinary Origins of Everyday Things.* New York: Harper & Row, 1987. This is a classic collection of trivia.

Adams, Cecil. *The Straight Dope,* Chicago: Chicago Review Press, 1984, and *More of the Straight Dope,* New York: Ballantine Books, 1988.

These books are compilations of Adams's weekly columns, called "The Straight Dope," which have appeared since 1973 in weekly and college papers around the country. Readers write in with questions, and Adams finds the answers. Sample topics in *More of the Straight Dope:*

- What is the origin of the word "Yankee"? Or, who is Jan Kaas? A derogatory nickname, meaning "John Cheese," bestowed upon the Dutch by the Germans and the Flemish. In the New World, the English applied it to Dutch pirates, and Dutch settlers in New York applied it to English settlers in Connecticut. During the French and Indian Wars, the British general John Wolfe took to calling his New England troops Yankees, and the name stuck (p. 260).

- To whom or what does the "Franco" in "Franco-American" spaghetti refer? Alphonse Biardot, who emigrated from France in 1880 and started the Franco-American Food Company, which was eventually bought out by Campbell Soup (pp. 36–37).

## Words as They're Actually Used: Corpora

*English Today: The International Review of the English Language* has published a series of articles about "electronic language corpora" and their impact on dictionaries, English as a second language (ESL) texts, and linguistic analysis. The developers of an electronic language corpora put as much text as possible into an enormous database (the "corpus"), then create concordances of word usages in context.

The results are surprising. For example, the word "represent" is usually defined in dictionaries as "to exist or act in place of someone or something else." In one of the new corpora, however, linguists discovered this usage: "to amount to or to constitute," as in "This strategy represents the most promising yet suggested." Most dictionaries do not include this frequent usage.

As corpora become more accessible, they may be helpful in developing or checking controlled English glossaries. For more information, we recommend these articles.

Greenbaum, Sidney. "ICE: The International Corpus of English." *English Today,* vol. 7, no. 4, October 1991, ET28, pp. 3–7.

Leech, Geoffrey. "100 Million Words of English," *English Today,* vol. 9, no. 1, January 1993, ET33, pp. 9–15.

Rundell, Michael, and Penny Stock. "The Corpus Revolution," Part 1. *English Today,* vol. 8, no. 2, April 1992, ET30, pp. 9–14.

———. "The Corpus Revolution," Part 2. *English Today,* vol. 8, no. 3, July 1992, ET31, pp. 21–32.

———. "The Corpus Revolution," Part 3. *English Today,* vol. 8, no. 4, October 1992, ET32, pp. 45–51.

Contact: *English Today,* Cambridge University Press, 40 W. 20th Street, New York, NY 10011-4211. Dr. Tom McArthur, Editor, *English Today, 22-23 Ventress Farm Court, Cherry Hinton Road, Cambridge CB1 4HD, Great Britain.*

The SUSANNE Corpus is an annotated sample of about 130,000 words of written American English text, designed to "exemplify a set of annotation standards which attempt to specify an explicit notation for all aspects of the surface and logical grammar of real-life English." Release 3 of the corpus is available via the Internet from the Oxford Text Archive—log in by anonymous ftp to black.ox.ac.uk, move to the directory ota/susanne, and follow the directions in the README file.

# PART III

# DESIGN

# 6

# International Software

This chapter helps you define the scope of an internationalization project. However, it also describes ways to standardize and simplify all interfaces, even ones that may never be translated. The techniques described in Enabling Programs may, in the long run, speed up development, simply because an "internationalized" version of an application easily accommodates naming and terminology changes.

## WHY CONSIDER INTERNATIONAL DEVELOPMENT?

One reason for considering the international market is making money. Another is saving money. A third is expanding into untapped local markets.

### Making Money

In 1989, the international market for information services (non-PC and in-house programming, as well as shrink-wrapped packages) was $36.7 billion. Of this total, 43 percent was U.S. sales, 39 percent was European sales, 9 percent was Japanese sales, and 9 percent was sales in the rest of the world. In 1994, the total worldwide market is expected to double to $80.7 billion (Press, 1993, p. 63).

Keep in mind that U.S. developers are creating most of this software. U.S. information technology companies control 75 percent of the worldwide market in shrink-wrapped software (ITAA. 1992, p. I-13). Canada is a lucrative market—40 percent of the Canadian demand for computer software and services$1.56 billion out of $3.9 billion total—was met by U.S. exports (ITAA, 1992, p. I-16). (However, we have a $2.1 billion trade deficit with Canada in telecommunications equipment—Northern Telecom's SL-1s are very popular systems.)

Although the international marketplace is interesting just because it is huge, savvy software companies have other reasons for marketing overseas.

- Multinational corporations want software that works in all of the countries where they have offices, and will standardize on software packages offering multiple languages.

- U.S. software companies find that they can sell packages at full price overseas, sidestepping the heavy competition and price-cutting rampant in the United States (Cunningham, 1993, p. 30).

- Internationalization leaders can become market leaders. For example, MicroPro International's WordStar was the leading word processor in many nations long after it had lost that position in the United States (Press, 1993, p. 64).

- U.S. companies can also become market leaders by picking under-served but growing markets. South Korea, for example, had 3.1 million PCs and about 1 million installed copies of Windows at the end of 1992 but hardly any Korean-language end-user applications. Microsoft's Korean applications are selling well, but Microsoft alone can't provide all of the specialized software Korea needs, say Microsoft representatives (Microsoft, 1994, p. 1:23). Other markets with growth potential are Turkey, Taiwan, Thailand, People's Republic of China, and the Middle East.

- Certain markets are by their natures international—for example, energy (oil, gasoline), gold, and money are traded internationally. Restricting trading or news-service software to one language restricts the market for that software.

In short, by offering *translated* packages, Microsoft Corporation, IBM, WordPerfect, and Borland International have seen more than 50 percent of their total revenues come from overseas (versus the 28 percent mentioned earlier for the software industry as a whole). At Software Publishing Corporation, international versions now account for almost 40 percent of their annual profits (Russell and Thomson, 1993, p. 69).

## Saving Money

A survey of 50 Fortune 1000 companies in the United States found that 38 percent have decentralized application development and 22 percent are thinking about the idea. Once a company decides to outsource development, it might also decide to look beyond national borders (Press, 1993, p. 64).

Edward Yourdon[1] points out that about a third of all software development and maintenance is now being done overseas. In 1987, overseas development—not counting U.S. multinational offshore subsidiaries, of which there are about a dozen—was worth about $29 billion. These overseas shops, he says, are competing not only on cost, but on quality—the reason he calls one of his latest books *The Decline and Fall of the American Programmer* (Yourdon, 1992, p. 10).

Many of the largest U.S. software firms develop their international versions internationally. Ashton-Tate/Borland, Claris, Lotus, and Microsoft translate and test their European-language software and documentation in Ireland. Lotus and many other firms do their Asian localization in Japan and Taiwan (Press, 1993, pp. 64–65).

The multinationals with offshore programming subsidiaries include IBM, which has in-house software shops in England; Texas Instruments, which has in-house software shops in India; and Andersen Consulting, which does internal development in Manila (Yourdon, 1992, p. 10).

Overseas software houses are also making inroads in U.S. markets. (In fact, the authors would like to apologize right now to our non-U.S. readers for our U.S.-centric approach. We had to pick a spot from which to write the book, though, so we picked here—Staten Island, New York.) There are two Chilean firms with successful products in the U.S. market—Logmeter from Excelsys Engineering, which estimates the expected volume of wood from a

---

[1] Yourdon is famous as the developer of the "Yourdon method" of structured programming and as editor of the newsletter *The American Programmer.* If all the other MIS management books haven't convinced your firm to add professional management, *The Decline and Fall of the American Programmer* might. Overseas software shops, Yourdon says, write better software in less time for less money and will put U.S. programmers out of work unless we learn to manage our resources better.

video picture of logs brought in on a logging truck, and Search City from Ars Innovandi, a world-class text retrieval system (Press, 1993, p. 65). Graphisoft, which markets a popular Macintosh CAD package, is a Hungarian firm. And, of course, one of the most successful PC graphic programs is CorelDRAW!, published by the Canadian firm Corel.

## The International Market At Home

A perhaps unexpected benefit to internationalizing software is that you can serve some of your local markets better.

*Immigration:* Both the United States and Canada have significant numbers of non-English speaking immigrants. According to the U.S. Immigration and Naturalization Service, over 7.3 million people immigrated to the United States from 1980 to 1990, the second largest wave of immigration since the beginning of the century (Hayflich, 1992, p. 75). Any software that is translated into Spanish, for example, can be marketed in the large Latin American communities in Canada and the United States.

*English as a second language:* Any software that uses controlled English will accommodate users for whom English is a second language (see Standardizing the English later in this chapter).

*Limited reading ability:* People who are deaf from birth or who were raised by wolves[2] may have difficulty reading complicated English. For example, students with profound hearing losses may show little growth in reading ability between the ages of 13 and 20 years; only 10 percent of deaf young adults read at or above the eighth-grade level (Crandall, 1985, p. 5).[3] (The Flesch and Gunning Fog reading-difficulty tests use the seventh to eighth grade level as the "standard" reading level.)

---

[2] See Oliver Sacks's *Seeing Voices: A Journey into the World of the Deaf* (New York: HarperCollins, 1990), Susan Schaller's *A Man without Words* (New York: Simon & Schuster, 1991), and Russ Rymer's *Genie: An Abused Child's Flight from Silence* (New York: HarperCollins, 1993). Although the first two books are not primarily about wild children, there are sections describing both the effects of language deprivation at early ages and the converse—the extraordinary three-dimensional reading abilities of American Sign Language users.

[3] Connecting phonemes ("th," "ah," "es") to the written representation of these phonemes ("the," "apple," "Sally") is impossible for profoundly deaf students. That deaf students can read English at all is remarkable.

**Figure 6.1  Some international symbols**

*Can't read this language:* According to the National Adult Literacy Survey of September 1993, about 40 to 44 million adults are nonreaders and another 50 million have limited reading ability. Others read well in their own language but may find themselves in another country where they can't read the language. Both sets of people may, however, be able to puzzle out an interface that uses graphic symbols, pictures, or cartoons. In fact, nonreaders generally understand international symbols ("Ladies Room," "Handicapped Access," "No Smoking," and so on) more quickly than most readers, since they have had more practice puzzling out the meaning of signs and icons (see Figure 6.1). They usually win at games like Pictionary.[4]

Keep in mind, therefore, that although a nonreader will not be using a word processing program, he or she might want to use an automatic teller machine, a foreign-exchange machine, an information kiosk, or a fancy vending machine with an LED and embedded computer.

## Be Prepared

This vast international marketplace is likely to interest your firm's top management, if not the development staff. However, marketing elsewhere will make life miserable for your company's developers, technical writers and artists, and human factors experts unless you plan ahead.

Any company wishing to internationalize must first answer these questions.

- How hard will it be to separate text from program elements, so that text can be translated in bulk rather than icon by icon, menu by menu, and message by message? See Enabling Programs.

---

[4] Personal communication with Jeff Charboneau, assistant director of marketing and communications, Literacy Volunteers of America. See Resources for more information.

- Can your organization make translation cheaper by simplifying and standardizing the text? Can you avoid translation costs by simplifying messages, standardizing labels, and replacing text in the online help or the documentation with pictures? For help simplifying text, see Standardizing the English.

- What will it cost to buy translation services? See Localizing Software (In Other Words, Translating).

## When to Internationalize

Plan to enable your software for multiple languages when:

- The market for your program includes few or no English speakers.

- You want a wide market share.

- You're starting from scratch. (Since you have the opportunity, why not internationalize the software? See Enabling Programs.)

- You are required to translate, by law or by custom.

Legal requirements may be a large stumbling block for organizations without deep pockets or without strategic alliances with the organizations that do. For example, although the majority of Canadians speak English, a significant minority speak French. Therefore, Canada mandates bilingual materials. (However, Canada provides help for organizations translating technical materials—see Resources.) Also, the European Economic Community (EEC) will, at some point, require that the documentation shipped with imported products be written in all of the EEC languages, *whether or not* you intend to sell the product in all of the EEC countries.[5]

## Which Languages to Translate First

The world is divided into three parts, at least from the translator's point of view.

- Europe, where the difficulties include changes in words caused by gender, accented letters, and text expansion

---

[5] Another requirement will be ISO 9000 registration, which is a system of creating and documenting quality assurance procedures. The guideline for software is 9000-3: U.S. $40 from the American National Standards Institute (ANSI), 11 West 42nd Street, New York, NY 10036; 212-642-4900.

- Middle East, where the difficulties include bi-directional text and cursive letters (see Bidirectional Text)

- Far East, where the main difficulty is double-byte character sets (see Double-Byte Characters).

Microsoft translates into German first, because German solves for accents, gender, and expansion issues.

Of all the Middle Eastern languages, Microsoft translates into Arabic first, since once you've localized for Arabic, you've localized for Hebrew as well as for Farsi, Dari Persian, Pashto, and the Indian languages Sindhi and Urdu.

Of the Asian languages, Microsoft translates into Japanese first. Japanese is one of the most difficult Asian languages because of its ten thousand ideograms divided into four different characters sets, specialized methods for entering all these characters, and double-byte character designations (see Double-Byte Characters for more information). Japan is also an enormous market for Microsoft products—more than one million installed copies of Windows, with more than a thousand Windows end-user applications available (Microsoft, 1994, p. 1:22).

### When Not to Internationalize

*On the ubiquitous presence of English in France:* To give one example, which speaks volumes: 77 percent of the databases in France are in English, as against only eight percent in French.

From "550 at Montreal Language Industries Conferences," by Yvan Gelinas, in *Language International*, 3.2, 1991, quoted in *English Today*, vol. 7, no. 3, p. 25.

Do not internationalize:

- When the cost of rewriting or retrofitting the software is prohibitive. Enabling software is a design issue, not something you can add at the end.

- When your audience already reads English.

The current estimate for worldwide speakers of English is 700 million to 2 billion (Tripathi, 1992, p. 8). Although not all of these English speakers are facile readers and writers, many do speak English as their native language or are taught English (either the British or American form) from early ages.

The native-born populations of the United Kingdom, the United States, Canada, Australia, New Zealand, South Africa, and many Caribbean countries (Jamaica, Barbados, Bermuda, Trinidad, Belize) speak English as their first language (McArthur, 1992, pp. 18–21).

English is widespread, although not always primary, in these countries (McArthur, 1992, p. 21):

| Country | Millions of People |
| --- | --- |
| Bangladesh | 107.8 |
| Ghana | 13.8 |
| India | 810.8 |
| Kenya | 22.9 |
| Malaysia | 17.0 |
| Nigeria | 112.3 |
| Pakistan | 109.4 |
| Philippines | 58.7 |
| Singapore | 2.6 |
| Sri Lanka | 16.6 |
| Tanzania | 24.0 |
| Zambia | 7.4 |

Countries with significant numbers of English speakers are (McArthur, 1992, pp. 18–21):

| Country | Millions of People |
| --- | --- |
| China | 1,088.2 |
| Egypt | 50.3 |
| Indonesia | 175.9 |
| Israel | 4.5 |
| Japan | 122.6 |
| Nepal | 18.0 |
| Saudi Arabia | 13.0 |
| South Korea | 42.6 |
| Taiwan | 19.8 |
| USSR | 285.8 |
| Zimbabwe | 8.9 |

English is sometimes used as a *lingua franca* among members of business communities. For example, Japanese scientists and engineers prefer to communicate research findings in English because it offers greater precision (Kohl, 1993, pp. 66–67).

Airplane and ship captains have long used special operational languages to communicate with each other and with land-based traffic control. Most of the terminology is English. (One noteworthy exception is "mayday," or, in the original French, "m'aidez"—"help me!") Police officers on both sides of the Chunnel linking Great Britain with France are now developing PoliceSpeak, a restricted set of terms for handling police actions—again, mostly in English (Humphreys, 1992, p. 37).

The necessity for translation, then, depends on the countries to which you hope to market and the industry for which you're writing the software. If neither the country nor the industry requires translation, then your concerns are simply cultural (Chapter 9 contains information on some unexpected cultural differences).

For detailed information on whether English is acceptable or not, see Chapter 7 in IBM's *National Language Support Reference Manual.* This is a list of countries, their official languages, and substitute languages, if any, tolerated by end users and service or support personnel (National Language Technical Center, 1992, pp. 7-1–7-8). The *Guide to Macintosh Software Localization* contains information on more than 100 countries, regions, and other political divisions. Each entry contains the area's primary language, writing system, and the Macintosh system localized for that writing system (Apple Computer, 1992a, pp. 131–156).

### *Piracy: Another Reason Not to Internationalize?*

Piracy is rampant in certain countries. However, the reasons for piracy and illegal copying vary from country to country (Microsoft, 1994, p. 4:5).

- There are no copyright laws, or the laws aren't enforced. For example, until recently, Russia had no copyright laws.

- Software has always been free, so why do we have to pay for it now? In Japan, for example, where personal computers cost $12,000 to $14,000 until a few years ago, software was simply bundled with the hardware. (The same was true of mainframe software 10 years ago.)

- People don't understand the idea of intellectual property. In Communist countries, where land and many goods are owned in common, the thought of owning an idea is very foreign.

- Copying is easy to do. This is a problem in the United States and other Western nations as well as in the less-developed software markets.

- There are no legitimate distribution channels. If you can't buy the software you need from a local dealer, of course you're going to get it any way you can.

However, don't avoid international markets because there are problems. The problems have solutions (Microsoft, 1994, p. 4:8–9):

- Join organizations such as the Business Software Association, which lobbies the U.S. trade representative, conducts educational programs, and sponsors antipiracy hotlines. BSA will look for your software during raids.

- In tough markets, you might want to use copy protection or special hardware ("dongles" that attach to an I/O port of the computer).

- Promote user registration by offering incentives and customer service only to registered users.

- In countries with no authorized dealers, create some. For example, Microsoft's Russian representative took the original—and successful—tack of searching out the worst offenders, warning them that the copies they were making were illegal, then offering to authorize them as Microsoft's local dealers.

- Control your replication. When copying your diskettes for distribution, use reputable copying companies and count each copy.

- Lobby the U.S. government—the U.S. trade representative, members of Congress, and the Departments of State and Commerce are all interested in international violations of U.S. copyright laws.

## ENABLING PROGRAMS

Software companies with extensive international experience use similar approaches to enabling software (Hemme, 1993, p. 410). The core of each program is stripped of all hard-coded language and country-specific information. What is left is a generalized base product, which makes no assumptions about the customer.

In the meantime, the text and edits (dates, currency, and so on) needed to create a different language version are stored in an independent "national" database. This database can be accessed by the core program using generalized routines (many of which come with the localized versions of the operating systems).

An enabled program has these characteristics.

- Text is isolated from code. See Isolate Text below.

- Text (and objects containing text) is allowed to expand. See Let Text Expand.

- It accommodates different formats for time, money, and other locale-specific information. See Accommodate Different Formats.

- It accommodates other writing styles. See Accommodate Other Writing Systems.

- It does not confuse the internal storage of information with its presentation. See "The Problem Space" in Accommodate Other Writing Systems.

## Isolate Text

The first step in enabling software is separating all culture-sensitive information from the program code. Anything that might have to be translated or changed to suit a country or culture is saved in resource files.

Culture-based information includes:

- Field labels, messages, audio, help text, menu descriptions, and other text

- Presentation control information, such as color, loudness, and window size

- Dates, times, currency, control characters

- Synonym lists for command parsers

### *Put Text in Resource Files*

A "resource file" is a file that can be compiled separately from the executable files. All development environments let you save localization information in resource files.

Microsoft, for example, identifies two types of resource files in their internationalization guidelines: "resource script" file (*.rc*) and "dialog-script" file (*.dlg*). The resource script file contains the application's menus, strings, and messages, while the dialog script file contains all of the dialog box information. "If you do this," the guidelines say, "there will be no need to recompile the executable file for a localized version of your product. Just use the Resource Compiler (*rc.exe*)" (Microsoft, 1993a, pp. 6–12).

The first reason for using resource files is that changing from one language to another becomes almost trivial—you simply point your compiler to, say, the German-language resource files in the GERMAN directory when you want a new German version or to the Thai files in the THAI directory for a new Thai version.

A second reason is that maintaining an application with *embedded* translated text is a logistics problem. Now that the translators have gone home, you have more than one version of the program to support (always a problem) and—what's more—some of them are in languages you don't even know. If adding a menu item to one hard-coded menu is irritating enough, think about adding it to two, three, or more copies of the program.

Another small reason (small because it will only happen once) for separating cultural information into resource files is that if the text is separated from executable code, the translator can't translate the code by mistake. Imagine the effect of changing such words as "IF," "THEN," and "WHILE" to "SI," "ENSUITE," and "TEMPS".

IBM warns, however, that designing national-language (NL) enabled software can be expensive: "There is certainly a cost in education: designers, planners, and programmers must become aware of the principles of NL-enabling and how they relate to the proposed product . . . . In addition, there is a need for extra preparations or hooks built into the code, the need for carefully structured software, and a dialog manager that permits efficient translation" (National Language Technical Center, 1991, p. 1-4).

Retrofitting already-existing software is even worse: For each new language version, the developers have to reopen the code to change formats, sorting routines, and other functions, and the translators have to find the nonexecutable text and translate it. "And what happens when a new release comes out? The retrofits have to be separately reworked, increasing the costs and risk of errors" (National Language Technical Cente, 1991, pp. 1-4–1-5).

Then why enable software? "It is in the implementation phase that the savings are realized. The cost to implement NLS for each additional country can be an order of magnitude less when a product is NL-enabled . . . . Multiply [this savings] by the number of countries in which you intend to market your product, and you will see that the savings far exceed the initial enabling costs" (National Language Technical Center, 1991, p. 1-4).

### Provide Calls and Exits

Removing all text from the code is not enough. Design basic functions in such a way that they can accommodate different sort orders, different rounding algorithms, different writing systems, and so on.

For example, say that a search routine monocases characters to speed up searches. To enable the software, you must separate the routine from the table used to cross-reference upper- and lowercase characters. Then, instead of writing a new copy of the routine with table for each new language, you can simply revise the table, and leave the routine alone (National Language Technical Center, 1991, p. 4-1).

When you separate routines from culture-dependent information, also remember to add the calls and exits needed to access the national-language information. For example, to accommodate non-Western calendars (Chinese, Hebrew, Arabic, Iranian, and so on), don't use a single date routine—instead, write a call to a procedure that changes the era of the date. When the software is used in the U.S., the call simply returns the Gregorian year. In Israel, on the other hand, the same call will access an algorithm that calculates and returns a Jewish-era year (National Language Technical Center, 1991, p. 4-3).

*Note:* You don't have to create these calendars and algorithms from scratch. Most of the operating-system manufacturers supply calendars, algorithms, and other localized information with the local versions of their system software. For example, Apple supplies localized system resource types that format monetary values, times, and short dates; format long dates and specify the calendar system in use; parse tokens in text; modify keyboard layouts, and so on (Apple Computer, 1992a, p. 195). See Resources for more information.

The Motif standard states that "internationalization issues are handled by tools available to programmers on their system. For example, the ANSI C standard (ANSI X3.159-1989) and POSIX 1003.1 have defined internationalization in terms of locale. The locale can then be set as part of the user's environment" (OSF, 1993, p. 8-1).

### Be Careful with Substitutions

*Structure problems:* A common and efficient method for creating customized messages is to embed variables in strings of text. For example, instead of writing, "The hard disk drive has crashed," "The scanner has become disconnected," "The floppy disk drive has crashed," "The hard disk drive has a boot error," and so on, the savvy programmer might write:

```
MSG=The %1 has %2.
```

where the first variable could be "hard disk drive," "scanner," or "floppy disk drive," and the second variable could be "crashed," "become disconnected," or "a boot error."

But this is not an enabled message because the %2 variables are different parts of speech. In English, you can use "has" as:

- An indicator of a not-so-distant past tense
- A past-tense indicator and part of a verb phrase
- Meaning "owns" ("the drive owns or suffers an error")

However, there is no reason to believe that a similar substitution would be possible in any other language.

*Gender problems:* Here is another straightforward string substitution (as long as you stick with English):

```
Your mission is to shoot down this bomber before it
reaches our %t and destroys it. You will start near the
%t. Engage the %b bomber when it approaches.
```

If, however, you were to translate this phrase into a language with different word forms for different genders, you would have to substitute more than locations (%t) and bomber names (%b). As Steve VanDevender says in *The (Much Requested) Translation Manifesto,* "Where in English we have one accusative possessive article 'our,' German has 'unseren' used with masculine nouns, 'unsere' used with feminine nouns, and 'unser' used with neuter nouns [as well as] separate articles used with different grammatical cases— like 'der/die/das' used where we would use 'the' before a subject [and] 'des/der/des' used where we would use 'of the'" (VanDevender, 1993, p. 3).

In the sample above, then, the *our* and each *the* would have to be tested and set to the correct form, or the substitutions would have to include the correct *our* or *the.* Instead of *before it reaches our %t,* the phrase would be *before it reaches %t.* [6]

*Bits and pieces problems:* Don't construct messages from parts of words or phrases. Word order and gender requirements in other languages may make nonsense out of the concatenation (Apple Computer, 1992b, p. 19). For example, concatenating *Mon, Tues, Wednes,* and so on, to *day* works well in English, but not in French—lundi, mardi, mercredi, jeudi, vendredi, samedi, and *dimanche*—or German—Montag, Dienstag, *Mittwoch,* Donnerstag, Freitag, Samstag, and Sonntag (National Language Technical Center, 1991, p. 2–8).

---

[6] Van Devender's manifesto contains many before and after code samples as well as recommendations backed by real-world examples. We highly recommend that you get this article from the Internet: insoft-l/doc/guidelines/manifesto.

*Solutions:* These examples give you an idea of the kinds of problems substitutions can cause if the substitution process is not carefully thought out. However, the examples are not exhaustive. To avoid problems, consult a translator early in the design process—he or she should be able to spot the likely difficulties and help you develop specifications for substitutions.

## Let Text Expand

English is a compact language compared to most others. English speakers coin new words readily, often by shortening old words ("fax" from "facsimile machine," "co-op" from "cooperative apartment"). English speakers also use various types of elisions with impunity, replacing nouns ("Sally") with pronouns ("she") and eliminating words whenever the context makes it possible: "Will Mary rub Sally's head?" "Yes, she will." And there's always apostrophe s for shortening possessives. For example, *Les Enfants du Paradis* could be translated, for a saving of five letters, as *Paradise's Children* instead of *The Children of Paradise.*

**Table 6.1  Translation Expansion Table**

| *Number of Characters in Text (including spaces and punctuation)* | *Additional space required* |
| --- | --- |
| **Field labels, menu options** | |
| up to 10 | 100–200%* |
| 11 to 20 | 80–100% |
| **Messages, on-screen instructions** | |
| 21 to 30 | 60–80% |
| 31 to 50 | 40–60% |
| **Online help, documentation** | |
| 51–70 | 31 to 40% |
| over 70 | 30% |

*Larry Childs, manager of International Products Development Group, Novell, Inc., Provo, Utah, confirms that based on preliminary data, 95 percent of Novell's messages stay within the 100 to 200 percent expansion range for messages between 1 and 40 characters (CompuServe personal message). Novell's messages were translated into French, Spanish, German, and Italian.

Computer jargon is an even more compact form of the language. Many programming terms are difficult to translate, sometimes because they are puns (UNIX, a pun on "eunuchs" and a take-off from "Multics," UNIX's predecessor at Bell Labs) and sometimes because their etymologies are grounded in U.S. or U.K. culture. For example, "booting up" may have come from "pulling yourself up by your bootstraps," which was a political catch-phrase during the 1960s' civil rights movement. Bootstrapping in the computer sense had no political meaning, however. It was just a useful metaphor when it was coined.

Therefore, expect text to expand when translated from English. The minimum expansion level is about 33 percent. But, as Table 6.1 indicates, the shorter the text, the more room you may need (National Language Technical Center, 1991, p. 2-4).

### Screen Objects that Change Size

These objects are affected by translation expansion:

- Entry areas and entry-area labels
- Menu buttons and option labels
- Alert, warning, pop-up, and other message boxes
- Text display areas
- Icon labels
- Audio tracks

### Don't Put Text Inside Icons

Apple Computer strongly suggests that you put words or letters *outside* your icons, not only because text inside the icons can be confusing but because you can't translate the icon without redrawing it (Apple Computer, 1992b, p. 230). You should provide labels with icons, but use the labeling facility built into the icon object. See Chapter 2 for more on icon design.

### Watch the Vertical Letter Size

Another potential pitfall is vertical letter size. In many languages, the accents on uppercase letters rise above the usual ascender line and descenders fall below the usual descender line (see Figure 6.2). Make sure that you leave enough *vertical* room to accommodate non-Roman lettering systems (Apple Computer, 1992b, p. 24).

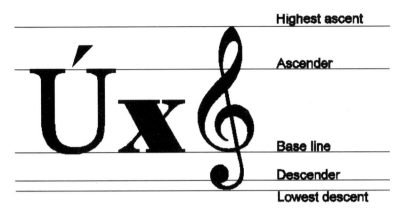

**Figure 6.2 Font boundaries**

## Solution: Dynamic Sizing

When you can, create or use objects that resize themselves dynamically. For objects that cannot be resized automatically, keep their dimension data in a separate resource file. Then the dimensions can be modified as needed without forcing you to recompile the program (VanDevender, 1993, p. 5).

## Audio Tracks and Translation

When you're creating applications with voice tracks:

- Keep the voice track separate from the music and video tracks, since translation can result in segments that are longer or shorter than the original.

- Provide frequent checkpoints (every 20–30 seconds) in long speech segments so that video and speech can be re-synchronized easily after translation.

- End full-motion video segments with a still of the last frame. Make sure that the program waits for the voice track to finish, rather than the video track, before letting the user go on to the next segment. In other words, key trigger fields to the voice track, not to the video track.

- To avoid lip-synch problems, avoid close-ups (National Language Technical Center, 1991, pp. 5-7–5-8).

- When using spoken instead of written messages, make sure that the accent of the speaker you use for the translated text is appropriate for the intended users. For example, using a speaker with a rural accent in messages addressed to urban accountants is probably a mistake (Apple Computer, 1992a, p. 51).

## Accommodate Different Formats

Different cultures have different calendars, different ways of presenting dates and times, different ways of indicating currency, different weights and measures, and different requirements for control characters.

The next few sections contain information about various data formats. However, these tables are designed to show the range of variations rather than every possible format. You might want to consult an experienced translator during the design phase for any exceptions or recent changes to the target-language standards.

### *Calendars*

Some of the calendar systems used in different countries or industries are:

*Civil or Business*

| | |
|---|---|
| **Arabic astronomical lunar calendar** | A lunar calendar beginning on the first day of the month preceding Mohammed's journey from Mecca to Medina (July 16, 622 Gregorian); it measures the Era of the Hegira. |
| **Arabic civil lunar calendar** | A lunar calendar that retains the traditional method of calculating exact lunations for the user's location (Apple Computer, 1992a, p. 226). |
| **Buddhist calendar** | Countries using Buddhist calendars specify their year as the Buddhist era, which varies from country to country, as does the recognized birthdate of the Buddha (National Language Technical Center, 1992, p. 4-1). |
| **Japanese imperial calendar** | The same as the Gregorian calendar except that its year number is based on the year of accession of the current emperor. Since each emperor gives a name to his reign, the dates also include the name of the reign (Apple Computer, 1992a, p. 228). |

*Civil or Business*

**Jewish calendar**

A solar and lunar calendar that measures time from the traditional date of creation, which can be extrapolated to October 6, 3761 B.C. on the Gregorian calendar. A year can be 353 to 355 days long or 383 to 385 days long (Apple Computer, 1992a, p. 227).

**Gregorian calendar**

A solar calendar that measures time since the date accepted as the birth date of Jesus Christ. Used as the civil calendar in English-speaking and western European countries and as a business calendar worldwide.

*Professional*

**Julian day**

Astronomical day count. January 1, 1987, is Julian day 2,446,795.5, for example (National Language Technical Center, 1991, p. 3-2).

**Day number reference**

YYDDD format. January 1, 1995, is 95001 (National Language Technical Center, 1991, p. 3-2).

Many of these calendars, or algorithms that can be used to switch from one to another, are supplied with localized versions of operating-system software. The items listed in Software Development Resources and Books can offer you more information.

## Date Formats

The short-date formats are methods for writing the day, month, and year in numbers. In long-date formats, the date is spelled out—December 5, 1995, for example.

Date formats vary between different calendar systems as well as between countries and regions. Here are some short-date samples:

| *Country* | *Format* | *Sample* |
|---|---|---|
| Bulgaria | yyyy-*mm*-dd (months use roman numerals) | 1995-XII-05 |
| Canada, English | dd/mm/yy | 05/12/95 |

| Country | Format | Sample |
|---------|--------|--------|
| Canada, French | yy-mm-dd | 95-12-05 |
| France | dd/mm/yyyy or dd.mm.yyyy | 05/12/1995 or 05.12.1995 |
| Germany | dd.mm.yyyy | 5.12.1995 |
| Japan, civil | yyyy.mm.dd | 1995.12.05 |
| Japan, imperial | *era* yy *year* mm *month* dd *day* | must be written in Kanji characters |
| United States | mm/dd/yy | 12/05/95 |

## Time

Ways of presenting time of day also vary, although not as often as dates. Here are some samples (National Language Technical Center, 1992, p. 4-9):

| Country | Format | Sample |
|---------|--------|--------|
| Canada, English | hh:mm:ss | 22:49:11 |
| Canada, French | hh *h* mm *min* ss *s* | 22 h 49 min 11 s |
| Sweden | *kl* hh.mm.ss | kl 22.49.11 |
| United States | hh:mm:ss *a.m.* or *p.m.* | 10:49 p.m. or 10:49:11 |

## Money

Currency has these variables:

- The symbol used to indicate the currency—for example, £ for British pound, ¥ for Japanese yen
- Where the symbol appears in the number
- The format of the monetary fields themselves
- How negative numbers are shown (see Mathematical Formats)
- Field sizes

*Formats:* Here are some examples of monetary formats (National Language Technical Center, 1991, p. 3-6).

| Example | Country and Currency Name |
|---------|---------------------------|
| $12,345.67 | U.S. dollar |
| DM12.345,67 | German mark |
| 12 345,67 F | French franc |
| N$ 123,45- | Uruguayan nuevo peso, negative |
| 123$45 | Portuguese escudo |

*Note:* ISO 4217, *Codes for the Representation of Currency and Funds,* is a list of unambiguous, uppercase, three-letter codes for all national currencies. Although many countries use dollars, the ISO codes differentiate among them well: For example, the code for the U.S. dollar is USD, the code for the Canadian dollar is CAD, and the code for the New Zealand dollar is NZD. For lists of international currencies (in a currency commodities application, for example), using these codes may be easier and less ambiguous than trying to use the national symbols.

*Field size:* Although localized operating systems accommodate different currencies, you must remember to leave enough space in your fields. Some currencies use numbers that are up to four digits larger than what you'd need to express the same amount in U.S. dollars. For example, the equivalent of $10,000 is approximately 16,850,000 Italian lira. If the country uses brackets to indicate negative numbers, you must add another two characters, plus up to four more characters for the currency symbol, and two characters for delimiters (National Language Technical Center, 1991, p. 3-6).

### Mathematical Formats

Although mathematics is an international language, it does have dialects. Here are some areas of differences.

*Negative numbers:* You may find a leading hyphen -10, a trailing hyphen 10-, parentheses (10), or square brackets [10] being used to indicate negative numbers. Remember to align numbers correctly:

```
123 456 789
[234 567 890]  ←out of alignment
```

*Names for large numbers:* In the United States, this amount—1,000,000,000—is a billion. In the United Kingdom (and Europe generally), this same amount is called a "thousand million" or a "milliard." A British billion is the same as the U.S. trillion—1,000,000,000,000.

*Separators for decimals and thousands:* Here are some common variations in decimal and thousand separators (National Language Technical Center, 1991, p. 3-6; National Language Technical Center, 1991, pp. 5-3–5-4; Apple Computer, 1992a, p. 200; Microsoft, 1993b, pp. 217–228):

| Convention | Decimal | 4 Digits Plus Decimal | More Than 4 Digits | Used In |
|---|---|---|---|---|
| Comma, period | .123 | 1,234.56 | 12,345,678.90 | U.S., English-speaking Canada |
| Apostrophe, period | .123 | 1'234.56 | 12'345'678.90 | Switzerland |
| Space, period | .123 | 1 234.56 | 12 345 678.90 | Greece |
| Space, comma | 0,123 | 1234,56 | 12 345 678,90 | French-speaking Canada, France, South Africa |
| Period, comma | 0,123 | 1.234,56 | 12.345.678,90 | Poland, Iceland, Brazil |

*Rounding conventions:* Rounding conventions vary not only from one country to another but from one industry to another and sometimes within industries according to convention.

In Switzerland, for example, legislation governs the rounding of monetary values. Instead of rounding up by .01, Swiss francs round up or down by .05. For example (National Language Technical Center, 1992, p. 5-2):

12.325 rounds down to 12.30
12.326 rounds up to 12.35
12.376 rounds up to 12.40.

Another example: In the U.S. bond market, prices of primary-market treasuries ("primary" means sold by the federal government to brokers) are rounded to three decimal places, but secondary-market treasury prices (from brokers to portfolio managers and other buyers) are rounded to six decimal places. Corporate, government agency, and municipal securities are truncated at three decimal places.

## *Weights and Measures*

Most countries use metric systems rather than the imperial system used in the United States and the United Kingdom. Therefore, enabling weights and measures usually means accommodating metric weights, measures, and unit names or symbols. It may, however, include transforming numbers from one system to another in countries such as the United States and Canada that use both metric and imperial measurement systems.

Also, some industries have their own systems. For example, U.S. land surveyors and engineers use an imperial foot divided into 10 rather than 12 segments. Paper manufacturers measure their paper by caliper thickness and weight. Font manufacturers use points, picas, and agates. Jewelers use carats. Some of these systems are local; others, to facilitate trade, are international.

## *Control Characters and Other Special Characters*

U.S. programmers sometimes use graphic characters or characters not often used in English as control characters. However, these characters may either not exist in other languages *or* may be used regularly as normal parts of the language. Following are some of the issues involved in selecting control characters.

*Missing characters:* An application that requires a special character must give the user some way of entering that character. For example, say that an accounting application requires # as the first character of a set of files. If users don't have that character on their keyboards, they can't create new files or, possibly, even write to the old ones (National Language Technical Center, 1991, p. 6-3).

*Often-used characters:* Apostrophes are often used in English-language applications as string delimiters. Where apostrophes used as contraction indicators could be confused with a delimiter, most compilers simply require that you double the apostrophe. For example (National Language Technical Center, 1991, pp. 6-5–6-6):

```
PRINT 'Your fax machine isn''t attached.'
```

However, in the normal run of things, French uses many more apostrophes. When this statement:

```
'The address does not exist.'
```

is translated into French, it becomes:

```
'L'adresse n'existe pas.'
```

Or, in computerese:

```
'L''adresse n''existe pas.'
```

Keeping track of that many apostrophes is likely to be an error-prone process. A better solution would be to let the user define a different character as the delimiter. For example:

```
"L'adresse n'existe pas."
```

Or:

```
/L'adresse C01 n'existe pas./
```

Another related problem is that some languages use the [Alt] or [Option] key to shift between one set of characters and another, whereas in the United States we use [Alt] or [Option] for graphic characters and keyboard shortcuts. This can create a conflict: Your application uses [Alt]-[C] for "cut," but the French keyboard uses it for cedilla. The solution is simply to let users redefine the keyboard shortcuts (or do it for them before releasing the product in that country).

## Accommodate Other Writing Systems

A "writing system" is a method of putting symbols that represent words on paper or some other storage medium. Some of the most widely distributed systems are Roman (English, French, German, and so on), ideographic (Chinese, Korean, Japanese), and bi-directional (Arabic, Hebrew).

- The Roman writing system uses representations of sounds to build words and is always written from left to right, top to bottom.

- Chinese, Korean, and Japanese writing systems use ideograms (pictures representing entire words, although sometimes not the same words from one language to another) and can be written right to left and top to bottom or left to right and top to bottom.

- Lines of Hebrew and Arabic writing run from right to left except for numbers, which run from left to right. Also, Arabic uses a cursive script (letters in individual words touch each other).

Although there are thousands of languages and dialects in the world, and nearly as many writing systems, a study of the Far East and Middle East writing systems presents most of the problems you will have to address. For details, however, consult a translator with experience in the target language.

### The Problem Space

Every character in a software system has at least three versions:

- A presentation version for screens and print-outs
- A method for inputting it from a keyboard, pen-based interface, touch screen, or other device
- An underlying representation of its meaning (the numeric code that exists on the hard-disk drive)

*Presentation:* The roman writing system is a "small" writing system, with a set of letters, symbols, and numbers that is easily accommodated within the 128-character ASCII table (plus extended ASCII sets for certain European languages). Correspondence between the presentation and input versions is nearly one to one.

However, even the unaccented English character set has more than one form—uppercase and lowercase. The two forms "A" and "a" are equivalent, by default, in DOS and Macintosh systems, but UNIX systems sort them in ASCII table order (so that lowercase letters fall 26 positions later than upper-case ones).

*Input methods:* The Japanese writing systems (there are four) contain more than 10,000 individual ideographs, essentially one per word. There simply aren't enough keys to input that number of characters—the input cannot correspond to the presentation (as described in Double-Byte Characters).

*Underlying representation:* Every letter in Arabic, on the other hand, has one input version but up to four presentation versions. The different versions are used to link with adjacent characters and to begin or end words.

Nevertheless, software can "know" the difference between display or input forms and the underlying representation. The key is a standard coding system for computerized information—see Standards: ISO 10646 and Unicode.

Detailed information about sorting orders, code pages, keyboards, and so on, is also available.

- The Apple Computer *Guide to Macintosh Software Localization* and the IBM *National Language Support Reference Manual*, vol. 2, contain sorting orders, code pages, and character sets for Arabic, Hebrew, and most European languages, plus some information about the ideographic Asian languages.

- Lunde's *Understanding Japanese Information Processing* explains the many methods used to sort Japanese ideographs—by the value of the byte used to represent them (like the Roman ASCII sort), by pronunciation, by radical and number of strokes per ideograph, and by combinations of all three (Lunde, 1993, pp. 187–188).

- Microsoft's *International Handbook for Software Design*, currently available as part of the "Microsoft Around the World with Windows Development Seminar," lists sorting orders for code pages 437, 850, 860, 863, and 865 (Microsoft, 1994, pp. 9-2–9-8).

For other information sources, see Software Development Resources and Books.


### Double-Byte Characters

Why do Japanese, Chinese, and Korean writing systems require double-byte (16-bit) characters? The reason isn't that ideographs are fatter or more complicated—it's simply that there are more of them. The standard ASCII table has 128 positions. The nine extended ASCII tables each contain 128 additional positions, which are enough for accents, Cyrillic characters, Greek characters, and so on.

Nevertheless, 256 one-byte characters are not sufficient for languages with more than 10,000 characters. Two bytes, on the other hand, can provide up to 65,536 positions; four bytes can provide millions.

*The underlying representation:* Characters are not simply numbered from 0 to 65,535 (0000 to FFFF in hexadecimal numbers), however. Rather, each country developed basic sets of characters long before computers arrived, and each set must now be encoded into computer-readable form. For example, Japan has four writing systems.

- Roman characters

- Hiragana, which is a cursive Japanese syllabic writing system used for "glue" words such as "and" and "do"; to indicate possessives; and to act as object markers

- Katakana, a square-shaped Japanese syllabary (consonant plus vowel) that is used to write recent words of foreign origin

- Kanji, which are ideographs borrowed from the Chinese over 1,500 years ago

The Japanese Industrial Standards Committee has codified these character sets for the computer industry. Details are available in Ken Lunde's *Understanding Japanese Information Processing* (1993).

*Input:* Since no keyboard has 10,000 keys, Japanese data processing engineers had to develop a method for entering these characters. The method they came up with is called "FEP" (for "front-end processor"). Although there are a variety of FEP methods, the most common accepts entries of one to three characters (sometimes roman letters), displays a set of likely Kanji ideographs, and lets the user select the one he or she wants (similar to spell-checkers that present a list of choices for a misspelled word). That choice is then saved online using its underlying numeric code (Lunde, 1993, p. 102). FEPs are available from Microsoft, Apple Computer, IBM, and other operating-system manufacturers as well as from independent vendors.

Note, however, that pen-based systems are ideal for ideographic input—ideographs are taught stroke by stroke, and pen systems work by capturing strokes. In fact, Japanese schoolchildren are reprimanded if they make the strokes in the wrong order, even if the resulting ideograph looks fine. If your program is written for or accommodates a pen-based operating system, you might want to internationalize the interface for ideographic languages. The Japanese version of GO Corporation's PenPoint operating system comes with a full Japanese environment, including input software, two outline fonts, and Unicode support (Lunde, 1993, p. 203).

*Warning:* For ideographic writing systems, you must let users create new ideographs—in programming terms, your application should not prevent changes to the active code page. New words in English are simply rearrangements of the same 26 letters. In Chinese, however, a new word requires a new character (National Language Technical Center, 1991, p. 7-2).

## Bidirectional Text

Middle Eastern texts present a second set of problems, at least from the European and North American points of view:

- Hebrew and Arabic writing systems are bidirectional—text is entered and displayed from right to left, but numbers (and any roman-alphabet words) are entered and displayed from left to right (Apple Computer, 1992a, pp. 105–107). (See Figure 6.3.) The first page of a Middle East-

## $1000,00—amanaP ,lanac a ,nalp a ,nam A

**Figure 6.3  A sample, done in English, of bidirectional text. Note that the number is (within the context) reversed.**

ern book starts on what would be the last page of a North American book.

- Arabic is cursive, meaning that letters within words must touch. As mentioned earlier, each letter must have four shapes—a starting version, an ending version, and two middle versions.

The implications for software and hardware are intriguing. For example, some printers pause for a microsecond between letters to let the machine cool down a bit. However, in Arabic (and in languages such as the Indian language Devanagari), there are no spaces between letters. To prevent mechanical failure, the printer must be slowed down, preferably automatically. "Enabling the design is done by allowing for more than one print speed, not by actually providing support for any particular font or language" (National Language Technical Center, 1991, p. 5-7).

Another example: Depending on the field type—text or number—the [Tab] key should move the cursor from right to left *or* from left to right (National Language Technical Center, 1991, p. 8-4). You can enable this activity with software or hardwarecheck with the operating-system developers. See Software Development Resources and Books for details.

### Standards: ISO 10646 and Unicode

Two consortiums have developed sets of double-byte characters that are designed to be both all-inclusive and international.

- Like so many other software and hardware breakthroughs, Unicode started at Xerox PARC and was picked up by Apple Computer. Microsoft, Lotus, IBM, Sun, and other manufacturers soon joined the party, creating the Unicode Consortium. Unicode is a 16-bit character encoding system that contains all characters used worldwide.

- The International Standards Organization developed its own character set based on Unicode. The set, described in ISO document 10646, contains both 16-bit (double-byte) and 32-bit (quadruple-byte) representations of characters. (See Figure 6.4.) The 16-bit version accommodates all Chinese, Korean, and Japanese characters if the characters that look alike use the same representation (called the Han unifica-

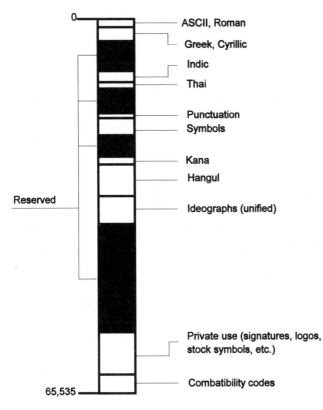

**Figure 6.4  Schematic of the Unicode/ISO 10646 character set**

tion). The 32-bit (four-byte) version, which could provide up to 4.3 million characters, accommodates separate sets of Chinese, Korean, and Japanese characters. (However, there doesn't seem to be much support for the 32-bit version—see Pike and Thompson, 1993, p. 2-3.)

According to Microsoft, ISO Draft Industrial Standard 10646.2 has been merged with Unicode version 1.0 to form Unicode's current version, 1.1 (Microsoft, 1993a, pp. 3–19).

The advantages of Unicode are:

- No shifting between states is required. Earlier solutions required state information—"am I a single-byte character in a double-byte stream or am I half of a double-byte character?"

- Switching from one language's characters to another's within the same text stream is no longer an issue. In Unicode environments, all characters are available at every point.

Many U.S. operating-system developers are incorporating Unicode into their systems. Pike and Thompson used Unicode when they designed Plan 9, Bell Laboratory's new distributed operating system (Pike and Thompson, 1993, pp. 2–3). PenPoint by GO Corporation currently supports the Unicode character set (Lunde, 1993, p. 57). Microsoft is supporting Unicode in the 32-bit API for Windows (Microsoft, 1993a, p. 3–19).

## STANDARDIZING THE ENGLISH

*Shopkeeper:* It's not [dead], it's pining.

*Mr. Praline:* It's not pining, it's passed on. This parrot is no more. It has ceased to be. It's expired and gone to meet its maker. This is a late parrot. It's a stiff. Bereft of life, it rests in peace. If you hadn't nailed it to the perch, it would be pushing up the daisies. It's rung down the curtain and joined the choir invisible. This is an ex-parrot.

From Volume 1 of *The Complete Monty Python's Flying Circus: All The Words* (Chapman et al., 1989, p. 105).[7]

There are two reasons to simplify the English you use in labels, messages, and online help.

- International clients may understand enough English to use the software without translation.
- Simplifying and restricting the language used in your software will make translation relatively easy and inexpensive.

In the 1980s, technical writers in a variety of industries developed methods for writing simplified or "controlled" English. Most of the formal methods have been abandoned (probably because they were too rigid), but the ideas underlying the methodologies still work. Two of the most important are:

- Develop a *restricted vocabulary.*
- Use *restricted sentence structures:* noun-verb-object.

*Restrict vocabulary:* Create a word list or dictionary of approved terms and banish all synonyms and alternate meanings from the interface.

---

[7] Reprinted with permission of Python Productions, Ltd., 68A Delancy Street, London, England NW1.

For example, in a telecommunications application, you might restrict the use of the word "switch" to "the apparatus used to move phone calls from one trunk to another." For its other meaning, "to change from one mode or state to another," you would use "toggle" instead. No confusion.

*Restrict sentence structure:* English lets you write sentences many ways. For example, all of these sentences have the same meaning: "The cat sits on the printer." "The cat is sitting on the printer." "On the printer, the cat sits." "On the printer sits the cat." "The printer is being sat on by the cat."

English composition teachers have many reasons for encouraging students to use a variety of structures: Different sentence lengths make the text look more interesting. You can create different rhythms by selecting different structures. Different word orders let you stress different items. For example, since the last position in a sentence is the strongest, you can change the focus from "printer" to "cat" by rearranging "The cat sits on the printer" to "On the printer, the cat sits."

In other languages, however, word order affects the meaning, not just the stress. A translator (or a reader for whom English is a second language) might assume, on first glance, that each of the sentences in the Monty Python sketch means something different. If you want to be understood, therefore, you must forgo the variations and stick with "The parrot is dead."

Simplified messages may seem boring and childish to native English readers. However, when the user is desperate to know why his or her system is dumping core files all over the hard disk drive, these same messages will become very interesting.

Professional technical writers are familiar with these ideas and techniques. In fact, your company's writers may have already created a dictionary that the programmers can use, too. They can certainly help you rewrite messages for simplicity. For more information about writing messages, see Chapter 4. For more on controlling English text, see Chapter 5.

## LOCALIZING SOFTWARE (IN OTHER WORDS, TRANSLATING)

"In Hebrew, unlike English or German or even the Latinate Romance languages, there aren't complex tense and mood structures, all of the structures I had so much trouble learning in school, such as the future present, the future past, the pluperfect. Structures such as 'I should have been' or 'What will you have done tomorrow?' In Hebrew, and in Arabic, most tenses revolve around the present— you can change easily from present tense to past tense or from present tense to future tense. There seems at times almost to be no difference and, as often happens in the Biblical texts, the future tense is used to describe something that happened in the past."

From The Art of Poetry interview with Yehuda Amichai, *The Paris Review* (Joseph, 1992, pp. 237–238)[8]

Current operating systems let developers and users switch from American English keyboards and alphabets to dozens of other keyboards and alphabets. However, switching keyboards does not automatically translate your English text into a new language. Life is more difficult than that.

Although computerized translation programs are available (see Resources), the results, unless the input is very simple or controlled (like part names and prices in a catalog), can often be ludicrous. For example, when a computer translated this sentence, "Daddy is hairy, like a monkey," into Japanese, then back into English, the result was "Our long-tressed sire is fond of an ape."[9]

Machine translation programs can quickly translate large bodies of text, but the results must be read and corrected—"postedited." Postediting effort is reduced if the text is also "preedited" to increase clarity and reduce ambiguity. Texts using controlled English need less pre- and postediting.

## Hiring Translators

To stand the handle, pull it straightly (from the view point where you face the rear panel), turn it to the downward and push it into the groove vertically.

From the *Toshiba T3100 Portable Personal Computers Maintenance Manual,* first edition (dated 5/19/86), p. 5-3.

When hiring a translation firm, ask these questions:

1. *Is the translator's native language the target language?* Translators generally do better when translating *into,* rather than from, their native

---

[8] Reprinted by permission of *The Paris Review*, 45-39 171 Place, Flushing, NY 11358.

[9] This may be an apocryphal story, says Richard Weltz, editor of *Spectrum Newsletter.* Spectrum ran a contest, asking readers to send in sentences to run through their computer translation program. The funniest results were to be published in the next issue, but no one sent in any samples. Oh well.

   Spectrum, however, is an excellent source of other types of translation foibles. A subscription is $11 a year. Send your check to Spectrum Multilanguage Communications, 225 West 39th Street, New York, NY 10018; 212-391-3940, fax 212-921-5246.

language. In other words, to translate Japanese text into English, hire a native speaker of English as the translator.

2. *Does the firm have experience in your subject area?* For example, a firm that does excellent psychology textbook translations may not be able to translate a telecommunications package—not sensibly, anyway.

3. *Does the firm have experience with software?* Dr. Albert Bork, chairman of the American Translators Association's dictionary committee, says that in Latin America, the gender of the word used to translate "computer" varies between countries. Only a translator experienced with software, the target language, and the target country will know which gender to use, he says.

## The Translation Process

Translating software messages and labels, online help, and documentation includes the following.

*Step 1: Develop a glossary:* You must, with the translation firm, develop a bilingual glossary of the terms your firm uses to describe both your product and the domain. Since different firms use different terms for the same function, the translators need to know which English terms you use and, sometimes, exactly what you mean by them. For example, some Wall Street firms call the parts of CMOs (which are bonds created from large numbers of home mortgages) "classes," a word with many meanings, most of them better known than the financial meaning. Other firms call them "tranches," which, although obscure as an English word, is unambiguous in English. (It may be ambiguous in French, however, where it means *slice, slab,* or *block of shares.* A block of shares is similar, but not the same as an English tranche.)

If you've already created an in-house dictionary or word list, as described above, the translators will take five to ten days to create the bilingual version (Hussey and Homnack, 1990, pp. RT-44–47).

Before moving to step 2, send the glossary to one of your foreign distributors or to some other knowledgeable native speaker and ask him or her to review, modify, and approve it. Ask the reviewer to make sure that the translated terms are up to date but not slangy (unless that's your corporate culture).

Pick someone with a stake in the project—in other words, someone who will meet your schedule—since you'll need his or her help throughout the translation process.

*Step 2: Translate the interface:* Microsoft, IBM, and Apple Computer strongly suggest that you segregate the program's messages, labels, field names, prompts, help screens, menus, and edits (how time, dates, and currencies are to be handled) in resource files. Once you've done so, you can simply hand the translators a set of diskettes containing the English text and a working copy of the program.

These resource files should be "live," so that the translators can enter the translations, run the translated text with the current program, proofread it, fix it, retest it, and so on, until all parties are satisfied. *Note:* The resource files may have to be compiled, either by your firm or by the translators, before they can be used. In any case, schedule plenty of interaction between the translation firm and your firm during the process. If the translators are involved from the start of the project and can talk to your engineers regularly, the end product is more likely to be of high quality, on schedule, and within the stated price quote (Rosseel and Roll, 1990, pp. RT-99–102).

If, however, you cannot put the text in resource files, you will have to deliver print-outs of all screens to the translators (and hope that you got everything—remember the copyright and disclaimer). Once the translation is done, keep in mind that you will also have to enter the translated messages and labels into the program yourself (leading to typographical errors and other mistakes).

*Note:* Giving the user documentation to the translators as a source for the messages and labels is useful but not sufficient, since technical writers do not include every prompt, screen, and message in books for end users. (Interface specifications, however, may be useful if they have been kept up to date.)

Again, send the translated software to the reviewer for modifications and approval.

*Step 3: Translate the help and the documentation:* With the glossary and screens done, translating the online help and other documentation should be relatively easy. An experienced translator can translate about 10 pages of text a day.

Ask for a 10-page sample before the translation starts in earnest, however, to check for style and sensitivity to your corporate needs. It is very important to send this sample to the native speaker for review. Different cultures expect very different tones and writing styles in their documentation (Van Nuys-Brown, 1990, pp. RT-48–50):

- Germans expect historical background and in-depth explanations (Nash, 1990, pp. ET-188–190). German writers often begin their books, articles, and reports with extensive histories or overviews of the topic being discussed. "A manual for a computerized accounting system, for example, not only describes the operations of the system and details how to use it, but also presents the reasoning behind many of the system's operations . . . . The Germans explicitly state known tradeoffs or problems as they delve into a topic" (Hein, 1991, pp. 125–127).

- Arabic readers expect language that, to American eyes, seems ornate and flowery—even in technical materials (Nash, 1990, pp. ET-188–190).

- Japanese readers expect to be drawn into the text gradually, by being introduced to the parts one at a time before encountering the whole. The direct "Do this, press that" style of American writing is not Japanese style, at least not in Japanese—it *is* accepted, however, in English-language technical and scientific writing. Japanese readers are also very sophisticated readers of pictures, charts, and graphics (Kohl et al, 1993, pp. 63–73). Japanese manuals often incorporate comic-book styles and characters (Lombard, 1992, pp. 689–691).

Printed documentation will also have to be formatted for print. However, keep in mind that many high-end word processing and desktop publishing programs have international versions—contact the manufacturers for details (Gable, 1992, p. 30). The text of the translated guides will probably be longer than the English version (see Let Text Expand).

*Step 4: Analyze the results:* If the authors of the articles referenced here are to be believed, no one gets a translation project right the first time. The organizations that succeed the second time, however, have postproject analyses in common. For example, Software Publishing Corporation found that they shouldn't organize a guide alphabetically. A guide for a graphics package worked well domestically, but the translators had to rearrange the text completely for each translated version (Russell and Thomson, 1993, p. 71).

## Costs

In 1990, American Translators International, Inc., quoted these rates (Hussey and Homnack, 1990, p. RT-46):

- Glossary compilation, translator training, software translation, and formatting—$40 to $60 an hour.

- Documentation—billed on a per-word basis, ranging between $50 to $150 per page.

Translating in the target country often results in better quality than using translators living in the United States (Florsheim, 1989, pp. MG-132–134). However, keep in mind that costs are affected by the target country's cost of living (Burnette, 1992, pp. 438–442) and by foreign exchange rates.

## REFERENCES

Apple Computer. *Guide to Macintosh Software Localization.* Reading, MA: Addison-Wesley, 1992.

———. *Macintosh Human Interface Guidelines.* Reading, MA: Addison-Wesley, 1992.

Burnette, Monica. "Managing English-to-Japanese Translation Projects." *Technical Communication,* 3d Quarter, 1992.

Calistro, Ralph F. "People and Machines: An Experience in Machine-Aided Translation." *Proceedings of the Thirty-Eighth International Technical Communication Conference,* 1991.

Chapman, Graham, et al. *The Complete Monty Python's Flying Circus: All The Words.* vol. 1, New York: Pantheon Books, 1989.

Crandall, Kathleen Eilers. "Writing for Adult English Language Learners." *IEEE Transactions on Professional Communication,* vol. PC 28, no. 4, December 1985, pp. 3–10.

Cunningham, Cara A. "Software Profits Speak Many Languages." *Computerworld,* October 4, 1993, p. 30.

Fowler, Susan. "Banking on a New Interface." *I.D.,* September/October 1993, pp. 70–72.

Gable, Gene. "From Arabic to Urdu." *Publish,* December 1992. AT&T tackles the last barrier to global publishing using an army of translators and new technology.

Hayflich, P. Faith, and Anne E. Lomperis. "Why Don't They Speak English?" *Training,* October 1992.

Hein, Robert G. "Culture and Communication." *Technical Communication,* 1st Quarter, 1991.

Hemme, Hartmut. "Multi-Language Working in a UNIX Environment: The Concept of Internationalization." *Proceedings of the Society for Technical Communication Annual Conference,* 1993.

Hinson, Don. "Simplified English—Is It Really Simple?" *Proceedings of the Thirty-Eighth International Technical Communication Conference,* 1991.

Humphreys, R. Lee. "From Blazonry to PoliceSpeak." *English Today,* July, 1991, pp. 37–39.

Hussey, Tim, and Mark Homnack, "Foreign Language Software Localization," *Proceedings of the Thirty-Seventh International Technical Communication Conference,* 1990. This paper is written by the president and translation manager of ATI, P.O. Box X, Stanford, CA 94309; 415-323-2244; fax: 415-323-3233.

Information Technology Association of America (ITAA). *The U.S. Information Technology Industry Profile 1992.* ITAA Press, 1650 Bluegrass Lakes Parkway, Alpharetta, GA 30201-7714. *Note:* ITAA used to be ADAPSO. Contact ITAA at 1616 N. Fort Myer Drive, Suite 1300, Arlington, VA 22209-3106; 703-522-5055; fax: 703-525-2279.

Joseph, Lawrence. *Paris Review,* vol. 34, no. 122, Spring 1993, pp. 212–251.

Kohl, John R., Rebecca O. Barclay, Thomas E. Pinelli, Michael L. Keene, and John M. Kennedy. "The Impact of Language and Culture on Technical Communication in Japan." *Technical Communication,* 1st Quarter 1993.

Lombard, Catherine "Let's Get Visual: Revelations after Six Days with Japanese Customers." *Technical Communication,* 4th Quarter 1992.

Lunde, Ken. *Understanding Japanese Information Processing,* Sebastopol, CA: O'Reilly and Associates, 1993.

McArthur, Tom. "Models of English." *English Today,* vol. 8, no. 4, October 1992, pp. 12–21.

Microsoft Corporation. *International Handbook for Software Design.* Redmond, WA: Microsoft Corp., 1993.

———. *Microsoft around the World with Windows Development Seminar Presentation Book.* Redmond, WA: Microsoft Corp., 1994. Overheads from the seminar.

Nash, Gail. "Cross-Cultural Communication and Technical Communication." *Proceedings of the Thirty-Seventh International Technical Communication Conference,* 1990.

National Language Technical Center. *National Language Design Guide: Designing Enabled Products.* vol. 1. 1991. IBM Canada Ltd., National Language Technical Center, Dept. 979, 895 Don Mills Road, North York, Ontario, Canada M3C 1W3.

———. *National Language Support Reference Manual,* vol. 2. 1992. IBM Canada Ltd., National Language Technical Center, Dept. 979, 895 Don Mills Road, North York, Ontario, Canada M3C 1W3.

Open Software Foundation. *OSF/Motif Style Guide,* Rev. 1.2. Englewood Cliffs, NJ: Prentice-Hall, 1993.

Pike, Rob and Ken Thompson. *Hello World.* Internet, pub/lists/insoft-l/doc/unicode/hello.world.

Press, Larry. "Software Export from Developing Nations." *Computer,* vol. 26, no. 12, December 1993.

Rosseel, Peter, and Mary K. Roll. "Cross-Cultural Technical Translations: From an Isolated Translator to a Business Communicator." *Proceedings of the Thirty-Seventh International Technical Communication Conference,* 1990.

Russell, Anne, and Monet Thomson. "Planning for Translation: What We've Learned the Hard Way." *Proceedings of the Society for Technical Communication Annual Conference,* 1993.

Tripathi, P. D. "English: 'The Chosen Tongue'." *English Today,* vol. 8, no. 4, October 1992, pp. 3–11.

VanDevender, Steve. *The (Much Requested) Translation Manifesto.* April 22, 1993. Available from *insoft-l/doc/guidelines/manifesto;* Internet.

Van Nuys-Brown, Sally. "Spanning the Pacific Gap: Working with a Japanese Company to Produce Product Documentation." *Proceedings of the Thirty-Seventh International Technical Communication Conference,* 1990.

Yourdon, Edward *The Decline and Fall of the American Programmer.* Englewood Cliffs, NJ: Yourdon Press/PTR Prentice Hall, 1992.

# RESOURCES

## Adaptive Technology

### Nonreaders

For more information about nonreaders, contact the national office of the Literacy Volunteers of America at 315-445-8000. There are over 450 affiliates throughout the country—check your phone book for a local affiliate..

### Deafness and Difficulty with Hearing

The CPB/WGBH National Center for Accessible Media offers *Guidelines for Producing Accessible Multimedia for Deaf and Hard-of-Hearing Students.* Sections of the book are: "Access to the Audio" (provide captions), "Access to the Language" (provide a sign language version), "Access to the Text" (provide pictorial glossary, text at multiple reading levels, and ways to find more information), and "Access to Enhanced Teaching and Learning Tools." Contact CPB/WGBH National Center for Accessible Media, WGBH Educational Foundation, 125 Western Avenue, Boston, MA 02134; 617-492-9258 (voice and TTY).

## Dictionaries and Other Resources

For a book dedicated to all aspects of internationalization: *Software Internationalization and Localization: An Introduction,* by Emmanuel Uren, Robert Howard, and Tiziana Perinotti. New York: Van Nostrand Reinhold, 1993.

### Cross-Cultural Guides

The current business classic is *Do's and Taboos Around the World,* 2d ed., edited by Roger E. Axtell. The book was "compiled by The Parker Pen Company, with offices in 154 countries." Presumably, then, they know what they're talking about. Available at most bookstores or from The Benjamin Company, John Wiley & Sons, One Westchester Plaza, Elmsford, NY 10523.

## Chinese Technical Information

For help with Chinese localization, contact the Chinese Language Computer Society. Membership includes its quarterly journal, *Computer Processing of Chinese and Oriental Languages.* Write to: Professor Yaohan Chu, CLCS Membership Chairman, Dept. of Computer Science, University of Maryland, College Park, MD 20742; voice: 301-405-2719; fax: 301-405-6707. Internet address: ychu@cs.umd.edu.

An often-recommended book is *An Introduction to Chinese, Japanese, and Korean Computing* by Jack Huang and Timothy Huang (World Scientific Computing, 1989).

## French-Canadian Technical Information

If you want to sell software in Canada, you must do two versions: one English and the other French. However, the Translation Bureau of the Department of the Secretary of State of Canada helps out by publishing English-French technical terminology books.

Some recent titles are *The Combinatory Vocabulary of CAD/CAM in Mechanical Engineering* (cat. no. S52-2/219-1993; $15.95 Canadian, $20.75 U.S.), *Desktop Publishing* (cat. no. S52-3/28-1989; $8.95 Canadian, $11.65 U.S.), *Artificial Intelligence Vocabulary* (cat. no. S52-2/184; $38.95 Canadian, $50.65 U.S.), and *Security Equipment Glossary* (cat. no. S52-3/26-1993; $16.95 Canadian, $22.05 U.S.).

For the list of publications or to order:

In the United States, contact International Specialized Book Services, Inc., 5602 NE Hassalo Street, Portland, OR 97213; 800-944-6190, 503-287-3093. Fax: 503-280-8832.

In Canada, contact Canada Communication Group—Publishing, Ottawa, Canada, K1A 0S9; 819-956-4802; fax: 819-994-1498.

In France, Germany, Italy, and Belgium, contact Abbey Bookshop, 29, rue de la Parcheminerie, 75005 Paris, France; Paris 46.33.16.24; fax: 46.33.03.33.

In all other countries, contact Books Express, P.O. Box 10, Saffron Walden, Essex, CB11 4EW, Great Britain; 0799 513726; fax: 0799 25047.

### *Japanese Technical Information*

O'Reilly & Associates, Inc., offers *Understanding Japanese Information Processing* by Ken Lunde (435 pages, 1993). Chapters include: Overview of Japanese information processing, writing systems, character set standards, encoding methods, input, output (including different kinds of fonts), information processing techniques, text processing tools, using Japanese e-mail and news, and a set of 15 appendices, including a glossary.

O'Reilly & Associates also offer translations of some of their titles in Japanese (for example, *Using UUCP and Usenet* and *Practical C Programming*) and German (*Programming perl*). For more information, subscribe to the Internet list *listproc@online.ora.com* by typing *subscribe ora-news **your name your company***. Or contact O'Reilly & Associates, Inc., 103A Morris Street, Sebastopol, CA 95472; 800-998-9938 or 707-829-0515.

For a bibliography of Japanese high-technology information produced in Japan but available in English, see *Japan's High Technology: An Annotated Guide to English-Language Information Sources* from Oryx Press. Contact: Oryx Press, 4041 North Central #700, Phoenix, AZ 85012; 602-265-2651; fax: 602-265-6250.

For technical or specialized dictionaries in Japanese or English and Japanese, contact the Kinokuniya Bookstore closest to you. The bookstores offer a dictionary catalog entitled "Books on Japanese Language." The 37 titles listed under "Dictionaries for Special Subjects" include *Current English Financial Terms, Dictionary of Technical Terms* (1,253 pages, in Japanese, English, and Spanish), *Inter Press Dictionary of Biology and Medical Science, Inter Press Dictionary of of New Business and Science, Inter Press Dictionary of Science and Engineering,* three different glossaries of computer and data processing terms, and glossaries of scientific terms ranging from agriculture to zoology that were compiled by the Ministry of Education of Japan.

Contact:

New York Kinokuniya Bookstore, 10 West 49th Street, New York, NY 10020; 212-765-1461. fax: 212-541-9335.

San Francisco Kinokuniya Bookstore, 1581 Webster Street, San Francisco, CA 94115; 415-567-7625; fax: 415-567-4109.

Los Angeles Kinokuniya Bookstore, 123 Onizuka Street, Suite 205, Los Angeles, CA 90012-3815; 213-687-4480; fax: 213-621-4456.

### Latin-American Technical Information

*Graphically Speaking* by Mark Beach (published 1992) is an excellent English/Spanish printing, publishing, and design dictionary. Available from North Light Books, 1507 Dana Avenue, Cincinnati, OH 45207.

*English/Spanish Glossary of the Petroleum Industry*, 2d ed., PennWell Books, 1982, 378 pages, 15,000 technical terms, $39.95 U.S. and Canada, $55.75 elsewhere. For PennWell's Energy Catalog, call 800-752-9764 or 918-831-9421; fax: 918-831-9555; telex: 211012. Write to PennWell Books, P.O. Box 21288, Tulsa, OK 74121.

Imported Books offers dictionaries, audio cassettes, maps, and grammars in many European, African, and Asian languages, but their interest is clearly the Americas. For example, they offer dictionaries in Ch'ol, Cocama, Comanche, and many other native American, Peruvian, and Mexican languages. Also available: Creole-Spanish dictionary, many Spanish dictionaries, and many Portuguese dictionaries. For a catalog, contact Imported Books, P.O. Box 4414, Dallas, TX, 75208; 214-941-6497. Street address: 2025 West Clarendon Street.

### Technical Dictionaries, All Languages

The Internet contains lists of bookstores, arranged by location, which may help you find foreign-language bookstores near you. For the list of New York City bookstores, for example, do an anonymous ftp to rtfm.mit.edu under /pub/usenet/news/answers/books/stores/north-american/nyc.Z. Or send e-mail to mail-server@rtfm.mit.edu with "send usenet/news/answers/books/stores/north-american/nyc" in the body of the message.

*Medical Dictionary of the English and German Languages*, 10th ed., by Dr. D. W. Unseld, is available from CRC Press, Inc., 2000 Corporate Boulevard, NW, Boca Raton, FL 33431. "The book will be essential for doctors, dentists, veterinary surgeons, psychologists, pharmacists, biologists, chemists, physicists, translators, and others who must be familiar with medically related terminology in English and German," according to CRC Press. Price for the 700-page dictionary is $69.95 in the United States, $84.00 outside the United States.

French and European Publications, Inc., offers a 178-page catalog of dictionaries covering subjects from architecture, biological sciences, and coins to petroleum, transportation, and zoology. In data processing alone, they offer dictionaries in Arabic, Catalan, Chinese, Czechoslovakian, Dutch, Finnish, French, German, Italian, Japanese, Norwegian, Polish, Portuguese, Russian, Spanish, and Swedish. For a catalog, write to Dept. D, French and

European Publications, Inc., 115 Fifth Avenue, New York, NY 10003; 212-673-7400; fax: 212-475-7658; telex: 125151; cable: Francopub New York.

Translation firms around the world have translated Que Corporation's excellent *Que's Computer User's Dictionary* into various languages. Contact the translators directly.

*Chinese:*

Simon & Schuster Asia
Ms. Jerene Tan
Alexandra Distripark Block 4
#04-31 Pasir Panjang Road
Singapore 0511
Voice: 65-278-9611
Fax: 65-273-4400

*Danish:*

Borgen Forlag
Attn.: Translation Department
P.O. Box 424
Valbygardsvej 33, DK-2500
Copenhagen Valby, Denmark
Voice: 45-31-46-2100
Fax: 45-36-44-1488

*Greek:*

Vasilis Giurdas Publisher
Attn.: Translation Department
4, Sergiou Patriarchou
114 72 Athens, Greece
Voice: 30-1-36-30-219
Fax: 30-1-36-24-947

*Portuguese:*

Editora Campus Ltda.
Attn: Translation Department
Rua Barao Itapagipe 55
CEP 20261
Rio De Janeiro, Brazil
Voice: 55-21-293-6443
Fax: 55-21-293-5683

*Spanish:*

Prentice Hall Hispanoamericans
Attn.: Translation Department
Enrique Jacob G. No. 20
Col El Conde, C.P. 53500
Naucalpan De Juarez
Edo De Mexico
Voice: 52-5-358-8400
Fax: 52-5-576-0613

## Foreign-Language Translation

### Bibliography

Bennett, Winfield Scott. "Machine Translation and Technical Communication." *Proceedings of the Society for Technical Communication Annual Conference*, 1993. Talks about the kinds of ambiguity that bring machine translation systems to their knees. Also describes four strategies that may make machine translation more context-savvy or viable in other ways: "Dialog translation," in which the software prompts the translator for help (like optical character readers); "example translation," in which the software uses large databases of examples for help understanding context; "statistical translation," which uses probability formulas to find bilingual equivalents; "sublanguage translation," in which the translation project is restricted to a particular subject area and set of words (a controlled English glossary, for example).

Burnette, Monica. "Managing English-to-Japanese Translation Projects." *Technical Communication*, 3rd Quarter 1992. Includes sample "Vendor Checklist" and "Request for Information," plus price negotiation hints.

Burns, Ann Lyn, and Kristy Roesner. "Localization Management of a Horizontal Software Product." *Proceedings of the Society for Technical Communication Annual Conference*, 1993. A description of a revised translation process for Hewlett-Packard's NewWave user interface. With the new process, the authors say, Hewlett-Packard released European-French, Canadian-French, and German versions that were half the cost and better quality than the prior two releases. Also, the new releases were finished in two-thirds the time of the earlier releases.

Calistro, Ralph F. "People and Machines: An Experience in Machine-Aided Translation." *Proceedings of the Thirty-Eighth International Technical Communication Conference*, 1991. An interesting French-English machine-aided translation system developed by Bell-Northern Research for Bell Canada and Northern Telecom. The system, half UNIX and half Microsoft Word for the Macintosh, lets the translators retain the formats of the documents. It also looks ondisk for material that has already been translated and uses that material instead of retranslating.

Coward, Nancy Caswell. "Cross-Cultural Communication: Is It Greek to You?" *Technical Communication*, 2nd Quarter 1992, pp. 264–266. Reminds readers that there are legal aspects to translation as well: "Companies that overlook the legal implications of marketing their products overseas may be exposing themselves to the high risk of lawsuits stemming from incidents of product malfunction or misuse." She suggests hiring a lawyer practicing in the target country to review the documentation for compliance with laws and standards and also to develop reusable boiler-plate warnings, warranties, and disclaimers.

Florsheim, Stewart J. "Technical Translation: In the U.S. or the Target Country?" *Proceedings of the Thirty-Sixth International Technical Communication Conference*, 1989. Another case study, this time for translating from English into French, in France, and quickly. They solved their deadline problem by translating only the quick reference guides and the software but not the manuals.

Gallup, Sharlene. "Caterpillar Technical English and Automatic Machine Translation." *Proceedings of the Society for Technical Communication Annual Conference*, 1993. The author describes a machine translation system, currently under development, which she says will deliver text that does not require posttranslation editing. She expects translation processing time to be about 40 pages per hour, at a cost per page of less than $5 (a savings of between $30 and $55 per page).

Hinson, Don. "Simplified English—Is It Really Simple?" *Proceedings of the Thirty-Eighth International Technical Communication Conference*, 1991. Critique of the movement towards controlled English from a linguistic point of view.

Kohl, John R., Rebecca O. Barclay, Thomas E. Pinelli, Michael L. Keene, and John M. Kennedy, "The Impact of Language and Culture on Technical

Communication in Japan." *Technical Communication,* 1st Quarter 1993. Excellent article on the differences between Japanese and English languages, grammars, and writing styles. Also full of fascinating bits of information. For example, the authors mention that the Japanese use the Chinese writing system (plus two others), but spoken Japanese is as different from Chinese as it is from English. The language's closest linguistic relative may be Korean, but there are similarities to Mongolian and Turkic languages as well.

Lombard, Catherine. "Let's Get Visual: Revelations after Six Days with Japanese Customers." *Technical Communication,* 4th Quarter 1992. One of the revelations included competitors' manuals that "looked like glossy magazines. They were filled with photographs, color graphics, and artwork not typical of a technical guide. One manual was full of comic-book characters sitting at terminals and pointing to step-by-step instructions. 'Is your session parameter screen big enough?' a bespectacled character asked about database software." Includes a wish-list compiled from conversations with Japanese customers.

Nash, Gail. "Cross-Cultural Communication and Technical Communication." *Proceedings of the Thirty-Seventh International Technical Communication Conference,* 1990. Compares American, German, Arabic, and Japanese notions of personal space and writing styles.

Russell, Anne, and Monet Thomson. "Planning for Translation: What We've Learned the Hard Way." *Proceedings of the Society for Technical Communication Annual Conference,* 1993. Excellent article about the pitfalls of translating software into eight dialects or languages (American, International English, German, French, Spanish, Italian, Dutch, and Swedish). The authors suggest that the developers freeze the user interface as early as possible, preferably just after the alpha version. Otherwise, the translators are left trying to hit a moving target.

Van Nuys-Brown, Sally. "Spanning the Pacific Gap: Working with a Japanese Company to Produce Product Documentation." *Proceedings of the Thirty-Seventh International Technical Communication Conference,* 1990. Good information on how to translate from Japanese to English.

### How to Find a Translator

The American Translators Association publishes an annual *Translators Services Directory,* which lists all accredited translators with their languages and areas of expertise. The directory is available for $50 from the American Translators Association, 1735 Jefferson Davis Highway, Suite 903, Arlington, VA 22202-3413; 703-412-1500. You may be able to find a copy at your public library.

## Machine Translation Programs

Says Andreas Ramos in an Internet message: "It's not just the articles, the tons of information and addresses, nor the ads. *Multilingual Computing* is a platform on which the localizing industry can stay in touch." The magazine also regularly lists machine translation programs. For information about subscribing to *Multilingual Computing,* contact Seth Thomas Schneider; voice: 208-263-8178; fax: 208-263-6310; AppleLink: MULTILINGUAL; CompuServe: 71224,1003.

## Online Information Sources

*CompuServe:* For quick answers to terminology questions, try the Foreign Language Forum (GO FLEFO) on CompuServe. Other CompuServe forums with international members or interests are:

- Section 14, "Language Arts," of the Education Forum (GO EDFORUM)
- IBM European Users Forum (GO IBMEUR)
- Section 14, "Bilingual Tech," of the IBM Special Needs Forum (GO IBMSPECIAL)
- WINEXT Forum (for Windows 3.1): Far East SDK section and Arabic/Hebrew SDK section
- Section 3, "Japanese Win32 Beta," of the MSWIN32 Forum; also Unicode/NLS sections
- Section 12, "International," of the Public Relations and Marketing Forum (GO PRSIG)
- Section 6, "International," of the TAPCIS Forum (GO TAPCIS)
- Section 15, "International," of the Telecommunications Forum (GO TELECO)
- International Entrepreneurs Forum (GO USEN)

*Internet:* To subscribe to an Internet list on which internationalization issues are discussed, mail the message (Press, 1993, p. 64):

```
sub insoft-l your name
```

to:

```
insoft-l-request@cis.vutbr.cs
```

Some of the interesting items you can get from the insoft list (using the "get" command) are:

- Lists of internationalization organizations: *get pub/lists/insoft-l/doc/organizations/organizations*

- *Hello World,* a paper by Rob Pike and Ken Thompson, AT&T Bell Labs, about the new UNIX distributed operating system called Plan 9. Plan 9 is, for the most part, enabled for languages other than English. *Note:* The file is in PostScript, so you'll need a PostScript printer or display program to read it. *get pub/lists/insoft-l/doc/unicode/ hello.world*

- *The (Much Requested) Translation Manifesto* by Steve VanDevender, which describes his team's difficulties with and solutions to the problems of enabling game software: *get pub/lists/insoft-l/doc/guidelines/manifesto*

## International Organizations

As an ISO member, *American National Standards Institute* publishes ISO standards as well as U.S standards. For a catalog of all ANSI publications, contact American National Standards Institute (ANSI), 11 West 42nd Street, New York, NY 10036; 212-642-4900.

For Chinese standards, contact *Chinese Association for Standards,* P.O. Box 820, Beijing, China.

*International Standards Organization* publishes the ISO technical manuals. Contact ISO, 1, rue de Varembe, Case Postale 56, CH-1211, Geneva 20, Switzerland.

*Japanese Standards Association* publishes the technical manuals for the JIS standardized character sets. Contact Japanese Standards Association, 4-1-24 Akasaka, Minato-ku, Tokyo 107, Japan; voice: 03-3224-9366; fax: 03-3224-9365.

The *Society for Technical Communication* has an International Technical Communication Professional Interest Committee as well as chapters in Canada, France, Israel, Japan, Singapore, and Taiwan. For contacts and more information, contact the Society for Technical Communication, 901 North Stuart Street, Suite 904, Arlington, VA 22203-1854; voice: 703-522-4114; fax: 703-522-2075; BBS: 703-522-3299; Internet: stc@tmn.com.

The Unicode standards are available as books:

- *The Unicode Standard: Worldwide Character Encoding*, Version 1.0. vols. 1 and 2. Reading, MA: Addison-Wesley, 1991.

- *The Unicode Standard: Worldwide Character Encoding*, Version 1.0. vol. 2. Reading, MA: Addison-Wesley, 1992.

For other information, contact Unicode, Inc., P.O. Box 700519, San Jose, CA 95170-0519; 415-966-0305. Internet address: *unicode-inc@unicode.org.* Send subscription requests to *unicode-request@unicode.org.*

## Software Development Resources and Books

Apple, Microsoft, and IBM have internationalization guidelines. Oddly, the contents of the various guidelines don't overlap as much as one might expect. Ignore the development environment and get these books for the information.

### Apple Computer

Apple Computer's *Guide to Macintosh Software Localization* (Reading, MA: Addison-Wesley, 1992) covers everything from localization pitfalls in software design to detailed cultural hints. Chapter 14 is a very useful collection of primary and secondary sorting orders for the supported character sets (standard Roman, Croatian, Czech, Danish, Finnish, Greek, Hungarian, Norwegian, Polish, Russian, Spanish, Swedish, and Turkish).

Apple Computer also offers *Localization for Japan* (1992) and various developers' toolkits and resources. For more information, contact APDA, Apple Computer, Inc., P.O. Box 319, Buffalo, NY 14207-0319; voice (U.S.): 800-282-2732; fax: 716-871-6511; voice (Canada): 800-637-0029; telex: 171-576; voice (international): 716-871-6555; AppleLink: APDA; CompuServe: 7666,2405; Internet: APDA@applelink.apple.com; America Online: APDAorder.

### IBM

IBM's *Object-Oriented Interface Design* (Carmel, IN: Que Corp., 1992) contains lists of translated object names for 16 languages (see Microsoft's *The GUI Guide*).

IBM also offers detailed internationalization guidelines.

- *National Language Design Guide: Designing Enabled Products.* vol. 1 (SE09-8001-01)
- *National Language Support Reference Manual.* vol. 2 (SE09-8002-02)
- *Arabic Script Languages.* vol. 3 (SE09-8003-03)
- *Hebrew.* vol. 4 (SE09-8004-04)

(Yes, the books are related even though the titles aren't the same.) Volume 1 contains planning information, IBM's rules and guidelines for designing software that can easily be internationalized ("enabled," in IBM's parlance), and bits of sample code. Volume 2 contains the code pages (tables of characters for each language), sorting orders, and so on, plus toll-free support numbers for designers developing or marketing software overseas. Volume 3 contains general information about Arabic script languages, and Volume 4 contains information about Hebrew.

To order the IBM books, call IBM Publications at 800-879-2755. Credit cards are accepted. Make sure you write down your requisition order number.

## Microsoft

Microsoft's internationalization offerings include a book of translated terminology, internationalization support via the Microsoft Developer Network, and an excellent one-day seminar.

*Books: The GUI Guide: International Terminology for the Windows Interface* from Microsoft Press (Redmond, WA, 1993) contains the names of window objects in Czech, Danish, Dutch, Finnish, French, German, Hungarian, Italian, Norwegian, Polish, Portuguese, Russian, Spanish, and Swedish. The terms are also available on the book's companion diskette. To contact Microsoft Press, call 800/MS-PRESS (United States), 800-667-1115 (Canada), or 615-793-5090.

*Developer network:* Microsoft offers two levels of developer support. With level 1, you get the Microsoft development library, tools, and utilities on a quarterly CD-ROM, plus the *International Handbook for Software Design* and, in the bimonthly *Developer Network News,* a regular column on internationalization. With level 2, you get all of the level 1 information and tools, plus international operating systems, SDK and DDK toolkits, and beta releases. Level 2 also includes support 24 hours a day, 7 days a week. For more information, call 800-759-5474.

*Seminar:* For more information about the one-day Microsoft around the World with Windows Development Seminar, contact the Microsoft Developer Relations Group, Globalization Team, at 206-882-8080; Internet address: global@microsoft.com.

Included with the seminar are:

- *Microsoft around the World with Windows Development Seminar Presentation Book,* which contains copies of the seminar's overheads.

- *International Handbook for Software Design,* which contains background information about adapting software for foreign distribution; technical implementation details; a glossary; and appendices of character sets, keyboards, sorting tables, currency, date, number, and time formats; metric conversion tables; and a list of Microsoft's international subsidiaries.

- The *Microsoft Windows Globalization Resource Kit,* which contains white papers on particular markets, plus a list of outside suppliers and copies of their brochures, data sheets, and marketing materials.

## Pen-Based Systems

GO Corporation offers a version of PenPoint, a pen-input operating system, that is localized for Japan. For more information: GO Corporation, 919 East Hillsdale Boulevard, Suite 400, Foster City, CA 94404; voice: 415-345-7400; fax: 415-345-9833. For Internet access, use *gocustomer@go.com.* In Japan: GO Corporation, 2-7-8 Higashi Gotanda, Shinagawa-ku, Tokyo 141, Japan; voice: 03-5421-1721; fax: 03-5421-1729. For access to an Internet list, send a subscription request to *penpoint-request@netcom.com.*

Microsoft and a number of third-party vendors also offer pen-based interfaces. For pen-based systems in general, access the Pen Technology Forum on CompuServe. For Usenet News users, access the *newsgroup comp.sys.pen.*

## Programs

*GARJAK International, Inc.,* offers these bilingual electronic dictionaries:

- English/Traditional Chinese and English/Simplified Chinese general dictionaries, each containing 135,000 word pairs. These are supplemented with more than 15 specialized dictionaries in business, accounting, electronics, law, and so on.

- English/Korean dictionaries of 95,000 word pairs, plus specialized dictionaries of business, computer, and military terms.
- English/Japanese electronic dictionaries are in development.

For more information, contact: Dr. Gary G. Erickson, GARJAK International, Inc., 5330 Carroll Canyon Road, San Diego, CA 92121; 800-833-7088; CompuServe 70313,2170.

IBM's *Natural Language Processing Service* is a set of linguistic programs that can be used to process natural language text. For example, an editor application might use the spell-checking, hyphenation, and synonym aid functions. An information retrieval application might use the text extraction functions for generating index terms, and the morphology and synonym functions to aid in searches. Machine-assisted translation programs might use all functions in both the source and target languages.

The NLP Service provides an application programming interface for all systems. It is written in C but is callable from languages other than C if the caller can use another language to simulate the C call interface.

Functions include dictionaries (application-supplied and user-amended), text analysis, spell checking and hyphenation, morphology (identify stem, generate inflected forms), synonym aid, and text extraction.

Supported languages include: Afrikaans, Catalan, Dutch (modern and preferred), English (Australian, United Kingdom, United States) Finnish, French (national and Canadian), German (national and Swiss), Greek, Icelandic, Italian, Japanese, Korean, Norwegian (Bokmål and Nynorsk), Portuguese (national and Brazilian), Spanish, and Swedish.

For more information, contact Bruce Carucci, IBM, P.O. Box 60000, Cary, NC 27511; 919-469-7280.


## U.S. Government Publications and Services

*Translated technology:* The Library of Congress National Translation Center is a national clearinghouse for current journal articles, patents, conference papers, standards, and technical reports that were translated into English and deposited in the center by both private and public organizations. These articles are not published elsewhere in English. Natural, physical, medical, and social sciences are covered in the database.

The center will send you copies of translations in their database for $35. You can search for articles online or ask NTC to search for you. Discounts are given to organizations who add translations to the database.

For more information, contact National Translations Center, Library of Congress, Washington, DC 20541; 202-707-0100; fax: 202-707-6147.

*NTIS publications:* The National Technical Information Service (NTIS) of the U.S. Department of Commerce offers these computer-related internationalization publications:

- *Guide to Computer Hardware and Software Markets of Poland,* $125, order no. PB92-120880/CAU

- *Guide to Computer Hardware and Software Markets in Latin America,* $120, order no. PB90-163197/CAU

- *Software Partners (v.1.0J): The Directory of Japanese Software Distributors,* $150, order no. PB93-209369/CAU

- *Software Reuse in Japan,* $325, order no. PB93-170215/CAU

For a copy of the complete NTIS catalog, contact NTIS, 5285 Port Royal Road, Springfield, VA 22161; voice: 703-487-4650; fax: 703-321-8547; international telex: 64617; TDD: 703-487-4639.

NTIS bibliographic information and ordering services are available online through commercial services such as BRS and DIALOG and via Internet at fedworld.gov.

# 7

# Charts and Graphs

If the data show pronounced trends, making an interesting picture, use a graph. If the numbers just sit there, with no exciting trend in evidence, a table should be satisfactory.

Robert A. Day in *How to Write and Publish a Scientific Paper* (1988, p. 56).

*Charts show overviews. For details, use tables.* Some chart programs show underlying numbers or let users access the numbers in some way on the chart itself (see Helping Users Interpret the Numbers). However, if users need to study the data or retrieve specific information, let them switch to tables (Coll et al., 1994, pp. 77–86).

Following are descriptions of the most common types of charts. Note, however, that every industry and intellectual specialty has its own types of charts. For help, use reference books in your area of interest (see *Resources* at the end of this chapter for some of the most popular books).

However, the key to developing a good set of charts or a charting program is to think about your audience. Don't put highly technical charts in a consumer product, because users may not be able to read them correctly (unless your users are Japanese, who are taught how to read and create charts in primary school). On the other hand, don't restrict yourself to pie charts in an economics package—your users will throw the package out or, worse, demand refunds.

**Table 7.1 Types of Charts**

| Chart Name | Uses | Picture | Other Names | Variations |
|---|---|---|---|---|
| **Area** | Shows cumulative totals (numbers or percentages) over time. | | Surface, component part, belt, mountain | |
| **Bar** | Shows observations over time. Data sets must be small. | | Column | Clustered bar, zero-line |
| **Frequency polygon** | Shows frequency distributions (the count for each interval during which data were collected). | | Bell curve | |
| **Histogram** | Shows frequency distributions. | | Step | Pyramid histogram |
| **Line** | Shows trends. | | | High/low/close (in commodities field, also called "bar") |
| **Pie** | Snapshots of proportional relationships. | | Circle, cake, sector | |
| **Scatterplot** | Each data point is the intersection of two variables plotted against the two axes. | | Scattergram, XY scatter | |

**Table 7.1**  *(Continued)*

| Chart Name | Uses | Picture | Other Names | Variations |
|---|---|---|---|---|
| **Segmented bar** | Shows proportional relationships (like pie charts) over time (like bar charts). | 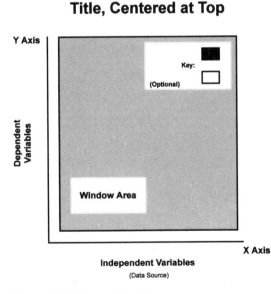 | Stacked bar chart | Paired horizontal bar chart |

*Note:* The terms "chart" and "graph" are essentially interchangeable, although "graph" is more often used to refer to scientific or statistical presentations. We have selected "chart" (somewhat arbitrarily) to refer to all of the two-dimensional picures of data relationships discussed in this section. (See Table 7.1.)

## PARTS OF A CHART

All charts, with the exception of pie charts, have at least two axes, two scales, and a window. (See Figure 7.1.) Charts may also have keys, which explain the symbols, if any, used on the chart. Keys are described later in this chapter.

**Title, Centered at Top**

Y Axis

Key:

(Optional)

Dependent Variables

Window Area

X Axis

Independent Variables

(Data Source)

**Figure 7.1  Parts of a chart**

## Axes

The horizontal axis is called the X, abscissal (Scientific Illustration Committee, 1988, p. 86), or category (McKenzie, 1989, p. 80) axis. The vertical axis is called the Y, ordinal, or value axis. *Note:* If the chart uses three dimensions (as computer-aided design programs like AutoCad do), the third axis is the Z axis. The Z axis points out of the plane of the graph.

*Independent* variables are generally plotted against the X axis, and *dependent* variables against the Y axis.

- Use the X axis to show the time or cause of an event—the independent variable.
- Use the Y axis to show the caused effect—the dependent variable.

For example, if the independent variable is years, and the dependent variable is profits, the chart then shows profits per year.

## Scales

Each axis has a scale—a set of measurement points or markers. The scales are marked with ticks. Put the ticks on the *outside* edge of the axis—otherwise, the ticks may interfere with data that are close to the axis. Make the ticks only as long as necessary and only one or two pixels wide.

### Standard Scaling Practices

*Start with 0,0 at the bottom left corner of the chart,* not the top, and increase numbers, dates, and so on from there.

*By default, start numeric scales at zero.* Users expect zero to be the starting point, *even if* a zero starting point would distort the chart. If you can't use zero as the starting point, flag the new starting point in some way.

There are two situations in which you must violate the zero-starting-point rule.

- *The range of data is nowhere near zero.* For example, the activity on a typical corporate bond chart ranges between $100,000 and $100 million. Starting the chart at zero restricts all of the activity to a narrow band near the top of the chart. Users won't be able to see the details. In these cases, either don't use a zero starting point or let users change the starting point themselves by zooming in on the data, dragging the starting point, or setting a new point.

- *Some of the data points are negative numbers.* In this case, move the zero point toward the center of the chart.

*Mark the scales with tick marks at standard multiples or customary intervals.*

- Use *multiples* of 1, 2, or 5: The numbers themselves and their successive differences should break into units of 1, 2, or 5, or be multiples of 1, 2, or 5 (Murphy, 1991, p. VC-35). Examples:

    —Intervals of 1: *0, 1, 2, 3 . . .*

    —Intervals of 20: *0, 20, 40, 60, 80 . . .*

    —Intervals of 0.5: *0, 0.05, 0.10, 0.15, 0.20 . . .*

    —Bad example: *4, 14, 18, 23, 28, 34, 42 . . .*

- *Customary intervals* include days of the week and months of the year.

Use the axis labels to state the units.

*On scales, put zeros in front of decimal numbers.* For example, use 0.1 rather than .1. Otherwise, the decimal point is too easy to miss.

*Display one scale on each axis.* This is not a hard and fast rule, since some designers do successfully put two different scales on the same chart (see Figure 7.2). However, the reader has to work harder for the same amount of information than if the two sets of information were shown on two separate charts.

## Cats and Mice

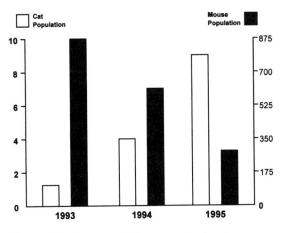

Figure 7.2  A successful two-scale chart

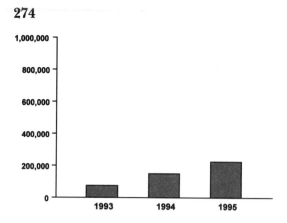

**Figure 7.3  Too much empty space**

## Window

The window is the central area that contains all the data. The charted information should nearly fill the window. In other words, if your largest data point is "1000," but your scale goes up to 1 million, your window is too large (Rabb, 1989, p. 116). (See Figure 7.3.)

## LABELING CHARTS

Charts have these types of labels:

- Title, centered at top (or flush left if it would overlap a key at the right)
- Y-axis label, centered above or left-aligned with the Y-axis scale
- X-axis label, centered below the X-axis scale
- Keys (also called "legends")

Also include information about the source of the data (Marcus, 1992, p. 105). This information can appear in small type below the X-axis label; in a caption, if any; or in online help.

### Recommendations for Chart Labels

*Make labels clear.* Spell out all words. If space is very tight, you can abbreviate, but use only standard abbreviations or symbols (check an abbreviation dictionary).

*Use standard capitalization.* For titles, use initial uppercase. For labels and keys, use either all lowercase or capitalize the first word, then use lowercase for the rest.

*State the units of measurement.* Include the units in the X- and Y-axis labels. For example, if the dependent variables are percentages, include "Percent" or "%" in the Y-axis label.

*Don't stack letters vertically.* When the left margin is too narrow for the Y-axis label, the label should appear above the margin. If you cannot, for some reason, put the label there, don't stack the letters like this:

L
a
b
e
l

Stacking letters may solve the space problem, but it creates a readability problem. Most people read by recognizing the entire shape of the word, not individual letters. When you stack the label, you force the reader to puzzle out the word from the letters. You can, however, turn the label sideways without causing as bad a readability problem. See Figure 7.1.

*Try to avoid keys (legends) when possible.* Instead, put explanations on the bars, lines, or data points themselves. For example, rather than creating a key to explain what a set of colored bars mean, you can label them directly. Add numbers to the data points or on the tops of bars, if possible.

If you do use a key, try to put it inside the window, in a spot where there are no data. If you put it outside the window, the eye is drawn away from the data. Do not box the key, because the box will draw attention to itself.

*If you add explanations to lines, do not curve the lettering to match the slope of the line.* Run the text horizontally. See Figure 7.4.

*Use only one typeface, one font, and one weight.* Too many variations creates confusion. For example, readers might assume that if Helvetica is used for titles and labels, text in Times Roman must not be part of the chart.

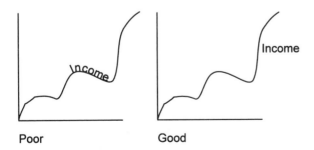

**Figure 7.4  Curved lettering is harder to read than straight lettering**

If you need to emphasize text, use a different type size. For example, use 12-point bold for the title and 10-point bold for the axis labels.

## USING GRIDS ON CHARTS

A grid is an optional visual aid. Use a grid only if users must look up individual points on the chart *and* if you can offer no other quick-reference option, as described in Helping Users Interpret the Numbers.

*If you must use a grid, keep it low-key.* Use thin lines, gray (rather than black) lines, or stippled lines (Tufte, 1983, pp. 112–116). The reason is that dark or thick lines seem to move to the foreground. If both the data and the background information have the same visual weight, readers have trouble picking out the important information. See Figure 7.5.

You can also use colored lines, but pick colors that seem to move into the background. Blues are usually good choices. See Chapter 8 for more on color.

*Put the grid behind the data.* Do not overlay the data with the grid.

## HELPING USERS INTERPRET THE NUMBERS

A computerized chart, unlike a printed chart, can be designed to be manipulated. To help users find out more about the underlying data:

- Display a grid on user request.
- Let the user click on a data point to see the exact values.
- Show the numeric values automatically for each point or bar.
- Let the user zoom in on an area of the chart or change the scales.
- Toggle between the chart and a table.

Poor                              Good

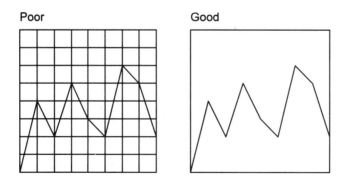

**Figure 7.5  Dark grids overwhelm data**

## AREA CHARTS

Use area charts to show two things at once: how a group of items add up into one whole and what part of the whole each item is.

Area charts look like filled-in line charts. However, they are more like pie charts than line charts because the areas are cumulative. Each area is added to the area below it—each boundary line is determined by the height of the line below it. Since area charts are not often used (or not often used correctly), readers may misread the chart unless you explain how the chart was made.

There are two types: *percentage* and *cumulative total.* To make either type of area chart, you must:

- Decide which data set is least variable. That data set goes on the bottom (see Layout Guidelines).

- Put in the bottom line.

- To each data point on the bottom line, add the next data set's point.

- Continue until all data sets appear on the chart.

This table is a set of fictitious data, in percentages, from an equally fictitious small fruit stand. In Figure 7.6, these data are used to create a percentage chart.

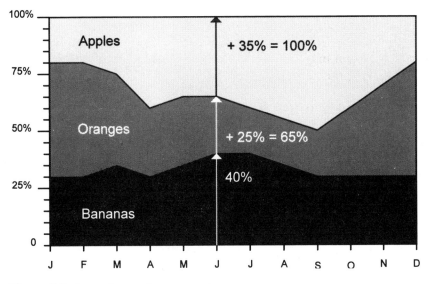

**Figure 7.6  Area chart using percentages**

**Total Fruit**
**in Pounds**

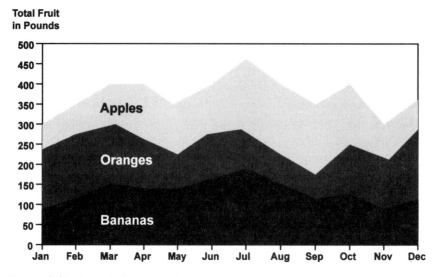

**Figure 7.7  Cumulative area chart**

| Fruit | Jan | Feb | Mar | Apr | May | Jun | Jul | Aug | Sep | Oct | Nov | Dec |
|-------|-----|-----|-----|-----|-----|-----|-----|-----|-----|-----|-----|-----|
| Apples | 20 | 20 | 25 | 35 | 35 | 35 | 40 | 45 | 50 | 40 | 30 | 20 |
| Bananas | 30 | 30 | 35 | 30 | 35 | 40 | 40 | 35 | 30 | 30 | 30 | 30 |
| Oranges | 50 | 50 | 40 | 35 | 30 | 25 | 20 | 20 | 20 | 30 | 40 | 50 |

Note that the percentages add up to 100 percent. One-hundred percent is the top edge of the chart.

In Figure 7.7, the same information, but shown in numbers of pounds this time, is used to create a cumulative total chart.

| Fruit | Jan | Feb | Mar | Apr | May | Jun | Jul | Aug | Sep | Oct | Nov | Dec |
|-------|-----|-----|-----|-----|-----|-----|-----|-----|-----|-----|-----|-----|
| Apples | 60 | 70 | 100 | 140 | 122.5 | 140 | 180 | 180 | 175 | 160 | 90 | 70 |
| Bananas | 90 | 105 | 140 | 120 | 122.5 | 160 | 180 | 140 | 105 | 120 | 90 | 105 |
| Oranges | 150 | 175 | 160 | 140 | 105 | 100 | 90 | 80 | 70 | 120 | 120 | 175 |
| Total pounds: | 300 | 350 | 400 | 400 | 350 | 400 | 450 | 400 | 350 | 400 | 300 | 350 |

## Layout Guidelines

*Put the smoothest area at the bottom.* Irregularities in the bottom curve affect all of the curves above it. If your bottom curve has a big jump, so will all of the curves above it, even though they would otherwise be flat. For example, in Figure 7.8, the drop in orange consumption drags the banana curve down with it, even though banana consumption is stable.

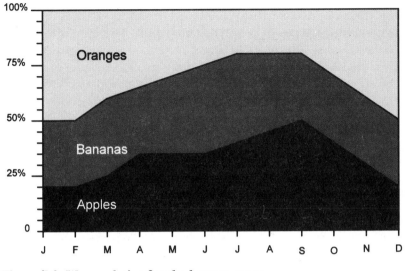

**Figure 7.8 Wrong choice for the bottom curve**

Displaying the least variable area at the bottom minimizes this effect. If, however, the areas cannot logically be rearranged, don't use an area chart. Use a segmented bar chart instead (Galitz, 1993, pp. 418–419).

*Put the widest area at the bottom.* Large areas look like they're supposed to be at the bottom. Narrow areas, on the other hand, look like they've been squashed.

*Put the darkest color or pattern at the bottom.* Dark colors look heavier than light colors.

*Reinforce the data with colors:* If these charts were in color, the apple sections could be in red, the banana sections in yellow, and the orange sections in orange.

## BAR CHARTS

Use bar charts to show a few observations over time—for example, five bars for five years of profits. For dozens of observations, use a line chart instead, since line charts show trends better (Marcus, 1992, p. 102).

## Layout Guidelines

*A bar chart has one axis and a baseline, not two axes.* In other words, bar charts have only one variable—sales levels, market values, numbers of returns audited, and so on. The other ends of the bars are simply labels—years, the names of the companies, types of products, and so on. The baseline doesn't even have to be drawn—the ends of the bars can be used to imply the baseline (Scientific Illustration Committee, 1988, p. 99).

*Bars can be aligned either horizontally or vertically.* Vertical bar charts are sometimes called "column charts."

*Use vertical bars* when the count—number of dollars spent, number of electrons freed, and so on—is more interesting than the time frame (Galitz, 1993, p. 419). (See Figure 7.9.)

*Use horizontal bars* (see Figure 7.10):

- When the labels for each data set are long.

- To highlight the information rather than the count. Since horizontal bar charts are labeled on the left, the reader sees the labels first.

*Bar charts can be used to compare more than one category at a time* (See Figure 7.11).

*Put spaces between the bars.* Bar charts without spaces are histograms, which are used much differently. The spaces should be narrower than the bars—about half the width of the bar is the rule of thumb.

For groups of bars, put spaces between the groups, not between the bars in the group.

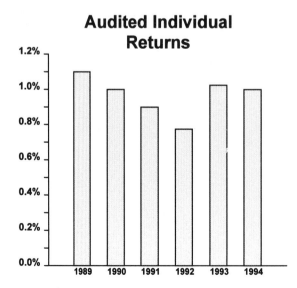

**Figure 7.9 Vertical bar chart**

## Market Value of Companies

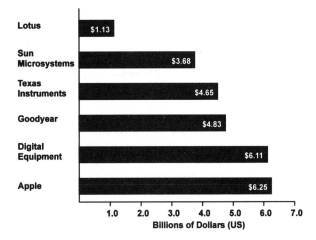

Figure 7.10  Horizontal bar chart

*Select an organizing principle.* Some suggestions are:

- Time—for example, costs between January and December
- Volume—number of barrels shipped; return on investments
- Alphabetical—if users want to look up a particular stock, for example, organize the chart alphabetically

## Who's Buying What

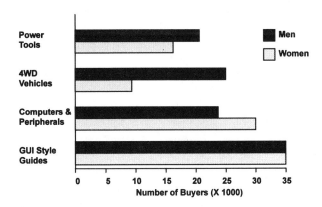

Figure 7.11  Comparing more than one category

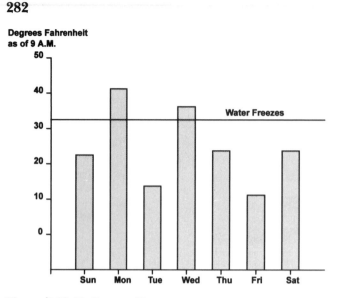

**Figure 7.12  Reference line**

If the bar chart has no other organizing principle, arrange the data so that the lengths of the bars are in ascending or descending order.

*Show comparison data, if necessary.* Put the bar containing an experiment's baseline or control at the far left in vertical charts and at the top in horizontal charts. You can also compare the data to a standard or critical value by adding a reference line. (See Figure 7.12.)

*Show margins of error, if necessary.* Use error bars (also called "deviation bars"). If the bars are dark, use half of the error bar (see Figure 7.13). In the caption, state whether the error bars represent standard deviations, standard errors of the mean, confidence limits, or ranges. Also state the number of observations (Scientific Illustration Committee, 1988, p. 111).

*Indicate statistically important differences* with asterisks above the significant bar or bars (Scientific Illustration Committee, 1988, p. 112).

## Labeling Guidelines

*Label the axis and the bars.* Put a scale and ticks on the axis. Label the bars below (vertical chart) or to the left (horizontal chart) of the baseline.

*For groups of bars,* label the *groups* below or to the left of the baseline. For the bars inside the groups, either:

- Put labels for each type of bar in the chart window, or
- Use shading or pattern plus a key to label the bars.

## Projected Man-Hour Totals

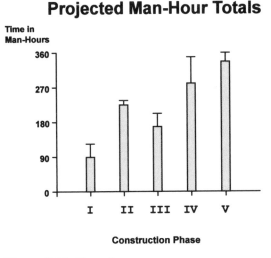

Figure 7.13  Error bars

*If the labels on a horizontal bar chart are short,* left-align them. If the labels are long, right-align them against the edge of the chart.

## Visual Guidelines

*Use one color or pattern for each data set.* For adjacent bars in a data set, use colors or gray patterns with a contrast of at least 30 percent (see Chapter 8).

*To avoid optical illusions when using striped patterns,* select stripes with a 45-degree angle to the baseline. Run all stripes in the same direction (Scientific Illustration Committee, 1988, p. 104). However, avoid stripes altogether if you can—use solid patterns instead. (See Figure 7.14.)

See Chapter 8 for more information.

Figure 7.14  Patterns—stripes versus gray tones
(30 percent difference between tones)

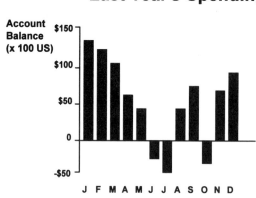

**Figure 7.15  Zero-line bar chart**

*If possible, use a pattern or color that reinforces the data* (Scientific Illustration Committee, 1988, p. 102). For example, on a chart showing the results of a series of pH tests, you could use yellow for acidic pH, light blue for neutral pH, and dark blue for alkaline pH.

## Variations

### Zero-Line Bar Chart

The zero-line bar chart shows negative as well as positive numbers (see Figure 7.15). Move the zero point toward the middle of the scale.

## FREQUENCY POLYGONS AND HISTOGRAMS

Frequency polygons and histograms both show exactly the same information—frequency distributions—except that frequency polygons use a curved line and histograms use bars.

A "frequency distribution" is the number of measurements in each interval, whatever that interval might be. For example, you would use a frequency distribution to show how many times, in a month, that a stock hit a particular price.

To create a frequency distribution:

1.  Choose intervals into which to divide the measurements. The intervals can be arbitrary, but:

- There must be enough of them to show the general distribution clearly. Rule of thumb: 15 to 20 intervals are usually enough.

- All of the intervals should be equally wide.

2. Count the number of observations falling into each interval.

The result is the frequency distribution. You can now show the distribution graphically on either a frequency polygon or a histogram (Morgan and King, 1971, pp. 293–299).

## Frequency Polygons

A frequency polygon is made of points connected by a curved line (see Figure 7.16). To create it, calculate the height of each point, based on the count, then tie the points together with a curved line.

Curved lines summarize the relationships between points. In other words, the curve indicates that if you had simply had the patience to collect thousands of observations, the line would have smoothed out.

## Histograms

Histograms are made of bars that touch (see Figure 7.17). Unlike the bars in bar charts, which are scaled in only one direction (height), the bars in histograms are scaled in two directions (width and height—area, in other words).

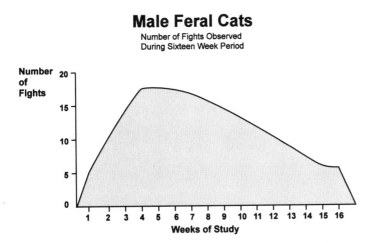

**Figure 7.16  Frequency polygon**

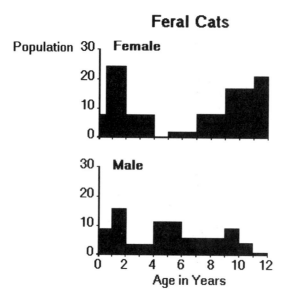

**Figure 7.17  Histogram**

Keep in mind that the heights of the bars represent the count only if the widths of all the bars are equal (Scientific Illustration Committee, 1988, p. 106). If, for some reason, you cannot make the intervals equal (for example, every interval is 5 seconds long except for one that is 8 seconds long), you must adjust the height of each bar so that its overall *area* is correct. However, all but the most sophisticated readers will have difficulty interpreting the chart.

## Variations

### Pyramid Histograms

A common variation of the histogram is the pyramid histogram (see Figure 7.18). It looks like the paired horizontal bar chart, but it is used to compare two closely related frequency distributions, not trends.

The two histograms or polygons are rotated so that the two variable classes are on the vertical axis.

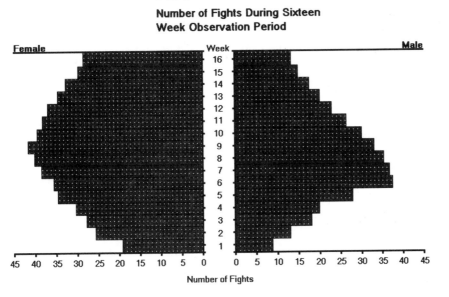

**Figure 7.18  Pyramid histogram**

# LINE CHARTS

Line charts are especially useful for showing changes over time—trends. In contrast, although bar charts show trends, they show only selected points on the line—January, February, and so on. Line charts, on the other hand, can show the movement *between* January and February.

Line charts make it easy to:

- Show long series of data
- Interpolate between points
- Extrapolate beyond known values
- Compare several lines (Marcus, 1992, p. 99).

Line charts can use either straight or curved lines.

- Use straight lines to connect actual data points.

- Use curves to summarize relations between points or to indicate interpolated points.

For example, the U.S. Treasury curve charts used by bond traders contain only nine real prices, since there are only nine Treasury securities—3 month, 6 month, 1 year, 2 year, 5 year, 7 year, 10 year, 20 year, and 30 year. However, the charts are drawn with an unbroken line. The points in between are mathematical interpolations of what the prices of bonds with the intermediate maturities *might* be.

## Layout Guidelines

*Use the Y axis for the variable information, the X axis for the fixed information.* On a chart showing profits over 10 years, for example, the profits are tracked on the Y axis, the years on the X axis (see Figure 7.19).

Figure 7.20 shows what happens if you get the axes backward.

*To compare sets of data, plot them all on one chart, one line per data set.* However, limit the number of lines to four or five. If you need more lines, you actually need more charts. You can break up a too complicated chart two ways:

- By plotting the most important line against every other line, one chart per line

- By plotting the most important line against a small group of the lines (Galitz, 1993, pp. 416–418).

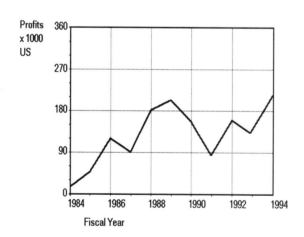

**Ten-Year Profit Margin**

**Figure 7.19  Standard line chart**

## Ten Year Profit Margin

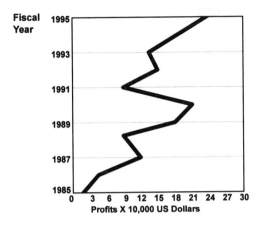

Figure 7.20  Line chart done backwards

*There are no fixed rules for the size of the intervals* on a line chart's axis (unlike histograms or scatterplots). Instead, look at the impression that the line or curve makes. Too steep or too shallow a curve can be misleading. (See Figures 7.21 and 7.22.)

*Label each curve or line,* unless the spacing is too tight. In that case, use a key and differentiate the lines with color or pattern (Galitz, 1993, pp. 416–418).

*Display a reference line if useful.* To compare the current data to a standard index or critical value, add a reference line or curve to the chart.

*Use symbols to separate lines.* If the chart has more than one line, you may want to use symbols for the data points, if any. Symbols should be two to three times wider than the line.

## Visual Guidelines

*If there are several data lines,* use a different color or style (dashed, undashed, and so on) for each line.

*If lines overlap,* watch for problems with the mix of colors or styles.

*Set off the most important line, if any, with the brightest color or heaviest weight line.* However, all of the other lines should have the same brightness or weight as one another. Otherwise, the actual information disappears in the confusion.

*When lines cross,* interrupt (if possible) the background line so that one line clearly passes in front of the other.

Figure 7.21  Too steep . . .

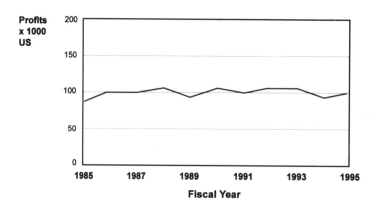

Figure 7.22  And too shallow

*Keep all labels horizontal.* Don't try to match the curve or direction of the line.

## Variations

### Error Bars

Line charts can include error bars (see Figure 7.23).

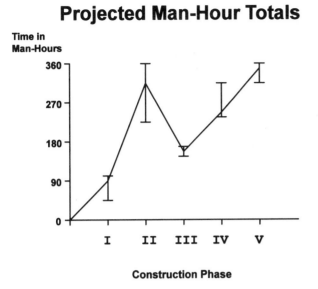

**Projected Man-Hour Totals**

Figure 7.23  Error bars

## Logarithmic Charts

Logarithmic scales are useful when the focus is on the rate of change or when the range is extremely wide—typically, when the change in one variable is geometric or exponential (McKenzie, 1989, p. 86). There are two types: semilogarithmic (called "semi-log"), which uses only one logarithmic scale, and logarithmic (called "log-log"), which has two logarithmic scales.

Since most people are not familar with logarithmic charts and may not notice the different scale immediately, use them with care. Include an explanation if necessary.

*Readers understand logarithmic scales* more easily if the intervals are indicated by tick marks, and the tick mark at the beginning of the cycle is longer than the others, as shown in Figure 7.24 (Scientific Illustration Committee, 1988, p. 91).

## High/Low/Close Charts

High/low/close charts show changes in the prices of stocks, bonds, and other financial products over a particular period of time. (See Figure 7.25.)

Each vertical bar indicates an hour, day, month, or year, depending on the type of analysis desired. The high price is indicated by the top of the

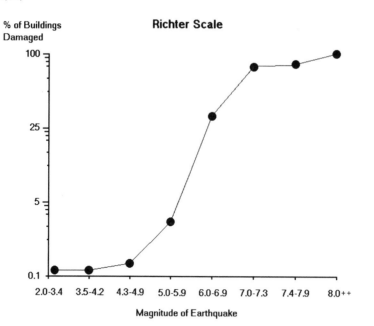

**Figure 7.24  Richter scale, done as semi-log chart**

vertical line, the low by the bottom, and the closing price by a right-pointing mark. Opening prices, if shown, are indicated with left-pointing marks (but opening prices are usually omitted, since this morning's opening price is the

**Figure 7.25  High/low/close chart**

same as yesterday's closing price—in other words, opening prices are redundant).

Although the vertical lines do not touch, the overall impression is of a moving line.

*Note.* In the commodities field, the high/low/close chart is called a "bar chart," and a bar chart is called a "column chart."

## PIE CHARTS

Use pie charts, also called "circle charts," to compare parts to a whole for one point in time.

*Note:* To compare two or more wholes, do not use two or more pie charts next to one another—readers cannot easily compare relative sizes of wedges. Instead, use segmented bar charts or area charts.

Cautions against pie charts:

- Pie charts cannot show totals greater than 100 percent.

- Each pie chart can show only one point in time.

- Estimating the size of angles accurately is harder than estimating the size of lines or bars.

- Pie charts do not show many small percentages well (Galitz, 1993, p. 421).

### Layout Guidelines

*Start at noon.* Put the largest wedge at 12:00 or at a quarter hour and run the rest of the segments clockwise, in order of size (Scientific Illustration Committee, 1988, p. 110).

*Pie charts must add up to 100 percent.* Convert from percentages to degrees by multiplying the percentage by 3.6 (360 degrees divided by 100 percent) (Scientific Illustration Committee, 1988, p. 110).

*Don't use wedges that are too small.* Wedges that are less than 18 degrees, or 5 percent, are too small to label or even see clearly unless the pie chart is shown very large (Marcus, 1992, p. 105). Instead, lump the small pieces into one "other" slice, then list the condensed categories in a caption or note.

*Label each segment.* Don't depend on a color key, since you can't assume that all users will have color monitors (not on their Macintoshs or laptops, in any case). For more on color, see Chapter 8.

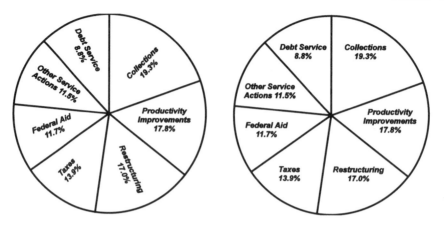

**Figure 7.26  Incorrect versus correct labeling—keep labels horizontal**

*Labels can go inside or out.* If the labels are short and the wedges are large, put the labels inside the wedges. If the labels are long and the wedges are small, put them in a column next to the pie chart or in two columns, one on each side, with leader lines running from each label to its segment (Scientific Illustration Committee, 1988, p. 110). Keep the labels horizontal—don't try to match the angles of the wedges. (See Figure 7.26.)

*Show actual values.* Because estimating the size of angular areas is hard to do, add a quick-reference option. For example, let users click on a wedge to see its percentage or value, or include the numbers in the label.

## Visual Guidelines

*Only use highlighting if the chart seems to require it.* Otherwise, the relative sizes of the wedges themselves are contrast enough.

Highlighting options include (see Figure 7.27):

- Separating one segment from the rest
- Using different colors or patterns

*If you use patterns,* try alternating between a pattern and a solid. Avoid patterns that seem to vibrate or create optical illusions. See Chapter 8.

*Unless distortion really doesn't matter,* do not tilt three-dimensional pies. Small wedges at the front of a tilted chart will look much larger than they should (see Figures 7.28 and 7.29).

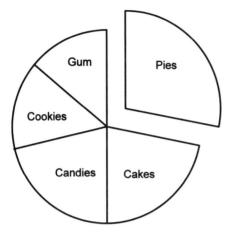

**Figure 7.27  Separating a segment**

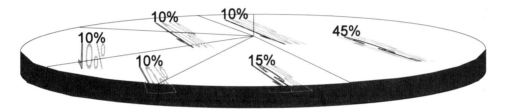

**Figure 7.28  Small wedge looks big because of its position . . .**

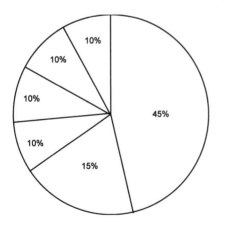

**Figure 7.29  But it's only 15 percent of the whole**

## SCATTERPLOTS

Scatterplots show how two sets of data correlate.

The chart contains *two dependent variables*—one of which is tracked against the Y axis, the other against the X axis. The *independent variable* is the intersection of the two dependent variables and appears on the chart as a point (McKenzie, 1989, p. 88).

### Visual Guidelines

*Make scatterplots square.* To avoid distorting the chart and thereby the data, make the physical spaces between ticks on both axes the same size—if the X-axis ticks are one-quarter inch apart, separate the Y-axis ticks by a quarter inch. See Figure 7.30. (Scientific Illustration Committee, 1988, p. 91).

*If there is more than one set of data on the same chart,* use different symbols for each data set's points.

- For the symbols themselves, use ○, ●, □, ■, △ , and ▲ You can also use ▽ and ◆ (empty or filled in), but these symbols are not as visually distinctive.

- Symbols that differ in color (even if just black versus white) are easiest to distinguish. Comparing circles to triangles is the next easiest. Don't

# Automobile Purchasing Considerations

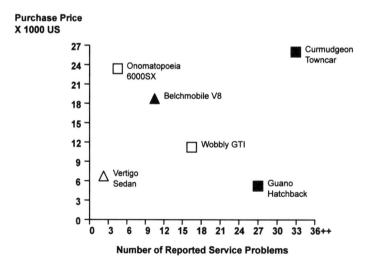

Figure 7.30  Scatterplot

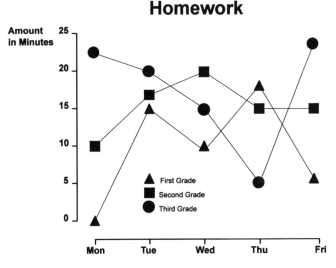

**Figure 7.31  Offset the axes**

put circles next to squares, if possible—they are hard to distinguish in small sizes.

- Color can be used symbolically. For example, O can be used for "no treatment" and ● for "treatment." Or use color plus shape to group the data—O for "before treatment #1," ● for "after treatment #1," △ for "before treatment #2," and ▲ for "after treatment #2." Note, however, that some color combinations cause problems. See Chapter 8 for guidelines.

- All symbols should be (or at least look to be) the same size. (Light-colored symbols often look larger than dark ones.)

- Points that overlap should be drawn overlapping: ◖●

- Points that coincide can be shown using a third symbol that represents all coinciding points (Scientific Illustration Committee, 1988, pp. 95–97). For example, if O is "no treatment" and ■ is "treatment," points where "treatment" and "no treatment" intersect (in other words, the treatment had no effect) could be □.

*Distinguish significant points* from the others by using high intensity, color, or shape—an asterisk, for example (Galitz, 1993, p. 417).

*If you use regression lines or curves,* find the line or curve statistically—don't estimate it. Users expect mathematical accuracy in regression lines and curves. (Regression lines, which are used in statistics, are created by plotting the mean of two sets of related data points. The result is a third line that shows the degree of correlation between the actual data points.)

*Coping with points that are right on the axes.* If, when you plot data points, one or more points fall on the axes themselves, you can set off the axes slightly. See Figure 7.31.

## SEGMENTED BAR CHARTS

Segmented bar charts are a cross between pie charts and bar charts (see Figure 7.32). They not only show parts of a whole, but show changes over time (Scientific Illustration Committee, 1988, pp. 109–110). (A pie chart cannot show change over time.)

### Guidelines

*Note:* For scales, axis, and design information, follow the bar chart guidelines in the Bar Charts section.

*Put the segments in the same order on every bar.*

*Don't put segment labels inside the segments.* (They usually won't fit.) Instead, put the labels to the right of a vertical chart or above a horizontal chart, or

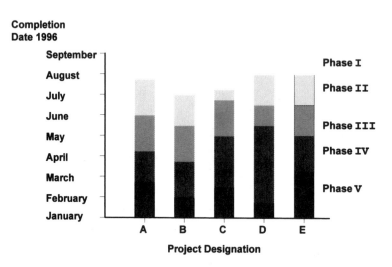

# Construction Schedule

Figure 7.32  **Segmented bar chart, with segment key at right**

use a key. One set of segment labels per chart is enough (Scientific Illustration Committee, 1988, p. 109).

*If possible, put the least variable categories at the bottom and the most variable at the top.* Putting the smoothest categories at the bottom simplifies the comparisons across bars. Putting the most variable categories at the top emphasizes their differences (Galitz, 1993, p. 420).

*Make sure that the segments are visually distinct.* Use the most intense color or pattern for the most important data. For more information, see Chapter 8.

*Limit the number of segments to those that are big enough to be seen and labeled.* Group too-small components into one "Other" segment (Scientific Illustration Committee, 1988, p. 110).

## Variations

### Paired Horizontal Bar Chart

To compare two or more related sets of data, try a *paired horizontal bar chart*, as illustrated in Figure 7.33. The opposition of the two sets of information is the first thing that users notice, instead of the length of the bars.

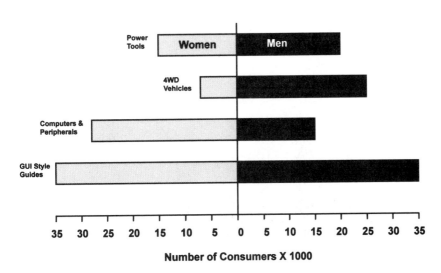

Figure 7.33  Paired horizontal bar chart

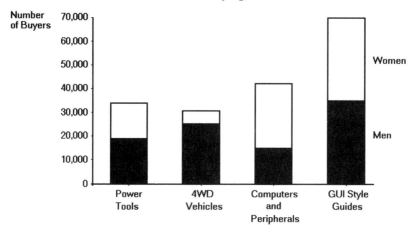

**Figure 7.34 Same chart as Figure 7.33 reformatted as a segmented bar chart**

Zero for both charts appears in the middle and all of the bars meet at zero. The first scale reads to the left of zero, the second to the right. Notice that each two bars add up to one total.

These charts can be reformatted as segmented bar charts (see Figure 7.34), and, in fact, they *are* two-segment segmented bar charts. The difference is that the segments' breakpoints are aligned.

Some of the other names for these charts include "sliding multicomponent bar chart," "population pyramid," and "butterfly chart."

## PROBLEMS

Following are some conundrums you may find yourself in and their solutions.

*Use common units for comparisons.* For example, remember to compensate for inflation—1985 dollars are not as valuable as 1975 dollars. Changes in population size, foreign exchange rates, and the book value of certain assets can also affect your units of measurement (Horton, 1991, p. 77).

*Use all the data (not just the part you like).* (See Figure 7.35.) Deceptive comparisons occur if the chart:

- Compares only a selected range of values
- Compares unequal ranges, spans, or units
- Fails to distinguish between missing or interpolated data and real data (Horton, 1991, p. 78).

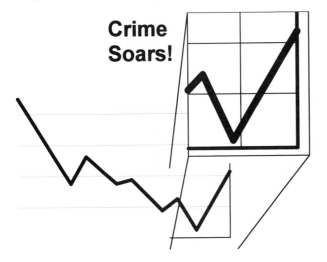

**Crime Soars!**

**Figure 7.35  Crime out of context**

*Watch out for changes in volume.* In a bar chart made of cubes, whose edges represent the value of a variable, tripling the values (height and width) increases the size of the cube 27 times. In Figure 7.36, for instance, bar 2 looks 27 times larger than bar 1, instead of just three times (Horton, 1991, p. 78).

The correct way to show the difference is to multiply only one axis, not all three.

Pictographs (charts in which bars are replaced with or are made up of pictures) are prone to volume exaggeration as well (see Figure 7.37). If you

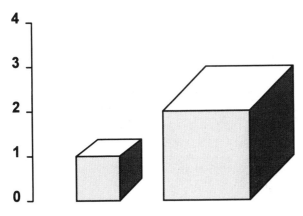

**Figure 7.36  Exaggerated volumes**

**Peanut Exports Double**

**Figure 7.37 An exaggerated pictograph—at a quick glance, exports seem to have quadrupled, not doubled**

double the height of a pictograph, its width and volume double as well. The new pictograph looks four times bigger, not just twice as big (Huff, 1982, pp. 68–69).

## REFERENCES

Coll, Richard A., Joan H. Coll, and Ganesh Thakur. "Graphs and Tables: A Four-Factor Experiment." *Communications of the ACM*, April 1994, pp. 77–85.

Day, Robert A. *How to Write and Publish a Scientific Paper.* 3d ed, Phoenix, AZ: Oryx Press, 1988.

Galitz, Wilbert O. *User-Interface Screen Design.* Boston: QED Publishing Group, 1993.

Horton, William. *Illustrating Computer Documentation.* New York: John Wiley & Sons, Inc., 1991.

Huff, Darrell. *How to Lie with Statistics,* 1954. Reprint. New York: W. W. Norton, 1982.

Marcus, Aaron. *Graphic Design for Electronic Documents and User Interfaces.* Reading, MA: ACM Press/Addison-Wesley, 1992.

McKenzie, Bruce G. *The Hammermill Guide to Desktop Publishing in Business.* Memphis, TN: Hammermill Papers, 1989.

Morgan, Clifford T., and Richard A. King. *Introduction to Psychology.* 4th ed., New York: McGraw-Hill, 1971.

Murphy, Peter, and W. Robert W. Rhiner. "Editing Graphs for Maximum Effect." *Proceedings of the Thirty-Eighth International Technical Communications Conference,* Society for Technical Communication, Alexandria, VA, 1991.

Rabb, Margaret (editor). *The Presentation Design Book,* Chapel Hill, NC: Ventana Press, 1989.

Scientific Illustration Committee of the Council of Biology Editors. *Illustrating Science: Standards for Publication.* Bethseda, MD: Council of Biology Editors, 1988.

Tufte, Edward R. *The Visual Display of Quantitative Information.* Cheshire, CT: Graphics Press, 1983.

————. *Envisioning Information.* Cheshire, CT: Graphics Press, 1990.

## RESOURCES

Following are some books and other resources that may help you in developing your own charts.

### Charts in General

Robertson, Bruce. *How to Draw Charts and Diagrams.* Cincinnati, OH: North Light Books, 1988.

Tufte, Edward R. *The Visual Display of Quantitative Information.* Cheshire, CT: Graphics Press, 1983. The two Tufte books are eye-openers. Dip in when you need to clear your mind—for any reason.

————. *Envisioning Information,* Cheshire, CT: Graphics Press, 1990. Contains some of the same material as *Visual Display* but includes more color examples.

White, Jan V. *Using Charts and Graphs.* New York: R. R. Bowker, 1984. White says in all his books that aesthetics must serve sense, then explains exactly how to do that.

Zelazny, Gene. *Say It with Charts: The Executive's Guide to Successful Presentations in the 1990s,* 2d ed., Homewood, IL: Irwin, 1991. Designed for people doing business presentations, this book explains what all of the major chart types are, how to use the various types correctly, and how to make them easy to read. Zelazny then goes a step further and shows you how to create sophisticated and elegant charts from the basics.

## Science and Medicine

Hensyl, William (editor). *American Medical Association Manual of Style.* 8th ed., Baltimore: Williams & Wilkins, 1989. The few pages of text on charts and illustrations in this guide is about captions and labels. However, in section 2.15, the authors describe the National Auxiliary Publications Service, a repository for "material such as auxiliary tables, graphs and charts, computer print-outs, bibliographies, and complex formulas that are adjuncts to articles published in scholarly or technical journals but that would require too many journal pages to publish in full." For more information, write to ASIS/NAPS, c/o Microfiche Publications, P.O. Box 3513, Grand Central Station, New York, NY 10163-3513.

Scientific Illustration Committee of the Council of Biology Editors. *Illustrating Science: Standards for Publication.* Bethsesda, MD: Council of Biology Editors, 1988. If you are writing software for medical researchers or biologists, you need this book. It contains cogent answers to all questions about scientific illustration.

## Statistics

Freund, John E., and Frank J. Williams. *Dictionary/Outline of Basic Statistics.* Mineola, NY: Dover Books, 1966, $6.95. Dover reprints classic math, engineering, physics, astronomy, biology, and other books. Write for their "Mathematics and Science Catalog" (59065-8) or their complete catalog (59069-0): Dover Publications, Inc., 31 East 2nd Street, Mineola, NY 11501.

Huff, Darrell. *How to Lie with Statistics.* 1954. Reprint. New York: W. W. Norton, 1982. A slender book that's in its fortieth edition—for good reason.

## Finance

Colby, Robert W., and Thomas A. Meyers. *The Encyclopedia of Technical Market Indicators.* Homewood, IL: Irwin, 1988.

Kaufman, P. J. *Commodity Trading Systems and Methods.* New York: John Wiley & Sons, 1978.

# 8

# Color and Pattern

In graphical user interfaces, color and pattern are used:

- *For background objects,* such as the application windows, buttons, panels, and so on
- *For foreground objects,* such as charts and icons

This chapter explains, for both types of objects, why color is important, why it causes problems, how pattern can be used to solve these problems, and what the development-platform style guidelines say about using color.

## WHY USE COLOR?

*Color is more interesting than black and white.* The advertising industry confirms that color is strikingly successful. According to *Starch Tested Copy,* a newsletter published by the market-research firm Starch INRA Hooper, the average one-page full-color ad in a business publication earned "noticed" scores 45 percent higher than the average one-page black and white ad (Sawyer, 1992, p. 4).

*Color can alert users to problems or to changes in system states quickly.* Network troubleshooting software often uses red for overloads and crashes, yellow for problem spots, and green for normal situations. (The hotter, brighter colors are used for the most important information.) A system monitoring pH levels might use yellow for acidic solutions, dark blue for alkaline solutions, and shades of green for the ranges in between.

*Color coding shows relationships quickly.* Assigning "false" colors to particular types of information adds extra dimensions to the underlying picture. Pseudocolors are used to indicate temperatures and types of reflected light (including invisible infrared) in satellite images and weather maps; to indicate hot and cold spots in medical CAT and MRI scans; and to separate layers—plumbing, electrical, indoor surfaces, outdoor surfaces—in architectural drawings (Banks, 1992, p. 144).

However, even in mundane situations, color can be used to link information. For example, accounting systems often show overdrafts and negative amounts in red, making it easy to spot all of the problem points at the same time.

*Color coding shows differences quickly.* In the same way that color-coding helps users see relationships, colors help users separate the unrelated items.

When searching, for example, a user can scan for the hits (the found text) much more quickly if they appear in a different color from the normal text. (Note that you should reverse the video rather than simply add color, both because many users have black and white monitors and because colored text is harder to read than black or white text—see Problem: Color Does *Not* Make Type Stand Out.)

Before you color code your software, note that there are four coding rules (Banks, 1992, pp. 146–147):

- Color coding is useful only if the user knows the code. Red for port (left) and green for starboard (right) will make sense to boat owners and airplane pilots but not to car drivers.

- The advantage of color increases as clutter increases. In an uncluttered display, color adds nothing to performance. In a complicated, high-density display (60 items), however, color can reduce search time by 90 percent.

- Average search time increases linearly as the number of items using the same color increases (by 0.13 seconds per extra three items). In other words, you lose some of your color advantage if too many items have the same color.

- Items that *don't* use the target color have no effect on search time if their color is sufficiently dissimilar from the target color. In other words, since red is very different from yellow, no user will pick a yellow triangle when he or she is looking for a red triangle. However, the user might mistake an orange triangle for a red one since orange and red are too close, especially for red-blind individuals (see Color Confusions).

## WHY USE PATTERN?

"If you generate a cash-flow graph for [security] FH 1080, it is difficult to delineate the PACs. Even worse, when you print it out, it looks like three black cows on a dark night."

Neill Reilly, director of sales, EJV Partners, New York.

Despite color's appeal, color is not enough. In fact, color should be used second, pattern first. There are three reasons for this—all having to do with hardware (human or machine).

- *Black and white printers:* Most users have only black and white printers, since color printers are too slow and too expensive for day to day work. So, say that you design a lovely chart with four or five colored lines. When you print it out, what do you get? A lovely chart with four or five undifferentiated black lines.

- *Monochrome monitors:* Many users buy laptop computers with gray-scale monitors (a quick check of hardware ads in the *New York Times* indicates that colorless laptops are a third to a half less expensive than color laptops). Also, users who work only with black and white text (newsletters, technical manuals, and so on) often stick with monochrome monitors, as do users with visual impairments—see Variations: Visual Impairment.

- *Color blindness,* which is better described as "color confusion" or "color weakness."

## Color Confusions

Approximately 8 percent of all males and 0.5 percent of all females have a color blindness (Hackman, 1992, p. 653).[1] Color blindness or weakness has four basic varieties.

---

[1] Eight percent, or 1 in 12, is a little less than the proportion of members of the AAA among U.S. citizens—1 in 10; more than overall membership in the YMCA—1 in 18 (Krantz, 1992, p. 175); a little less than the number of divorces among couples married 15–19 years—1 in 11 (Krantz, 1992, p. 83); and a little less than the proportion of males who say they are either gay or bisexual—1 in 10 (Krantz, 1992, p. 128).

- Green blindness—individuals confuse greens, yellows, and reds (6.39 percent)
- Red blindness—individuals confuse various shades of red (2.04 percent)
- Blue blindness—individuals confuse blues (0.003 percent)
- Total color blindness, which affects no more than 0.005 percent of both sexes

"Color blindness" is actually a misnomer, since color-blind individuals see all of the colors in the spectrum, not just black and white or shades of grey. Color-blind individuals simply confuse certain colors.[2] For example, a person with a red confusion might label a pale-green item as tan or orange. A person with a green confusion might label dark blue as purple or yellow as bright red (Milhaven, 1989, p. VC16–19).

If you have standard color vision, you can reproduce the effect, although not the actual confusion, by looking around through a pair of deeply saturated colored sunglasses, a colored filter or theater-light gel, or half of a pair of 3-D glasses (close one eye). If you're looking through a red filter, for example, everything red looks white, and everything blue or green looks black. The reason is that only red light can pass through the red filter. Since pure blue and pure green contain no red light, they don't get through the filter: "no light" equals "black."

*Hint:* If you offer 3-D glasses with your software, use red and *blue* instead of red and green. Red and green glasses don't work for people with red or green confusions.

There are at least two theories about what causes color vision and color confusion, both of them having to do with missing color receptors in the eye. One theory suggest that a type of cone is missing. The other suggests that a color chemical or chemical response is missing (Gregory, 1987, pp. 150–154). Whatever the explanation, persons with green confusions say that red and green seem to bleed into one another when these colors are next to one another. Individuals can often differentiate reds and greens when the colors

---

[2] Many "deficiencies" are not actually deficiencies in the Darwinian sense. For example, sickle-cell anemia persists in Africa and the Middle East because persons who carry one sickle-cell gene are protected against malaria; diabetes persists because persons with mild forms are protected against starvation. It may be that color deficiencies persist because color-deficient individuals see better at night or detect motion more readily than color-enhanced individuals.

are separated. Persons with red confusions can often differentiate among shades of red and orange if there is enough light.

Unfortunately, many pieces of software are blind to color blindness. For example, an expensive and sophisticated DOS telecommunications program had bright blue windows crowded with white text and error-message boxes that appeared in the center of the screen but looked no different from any other window on the screen except that they had red borders. Two men who were taking the software's training class were completely befuddled by the program—it kept beeping and then freezing up. Finally, the teacher came over and said, "Oh, you have to clear the error message." "WHAT error message?" they both shouted. The problem was that the red border simply didn't exist for these two color-blind customers. Although they now knew that a beep meant "error message," they could only find it by searching the screen line by line.

Another gotcha: The active window in a Motif-based software program had a red border and the inactive window had a green border.[3] No one realized this could be a problem until the company did some usability tests and one of the subjects was unable to tell which window was active. He had, of course, a red-green confusion. What made the problem worse was that the software's target audience was stockbrokers, who are (still) predominately male.

## UN-DESIGN FOR CLARITY

*Today the competition is at the user interface . . . .* Skillful visual design of computer screens—with care given to color, typography, layout, icons, graphics, and coherency—substantially contributes to quality and usability. Poor screen design can destroy underlying excellence in software and hardware. Graphic design details are not cosmetic matters or decorative touches. In fact, careful attention to visual craft is a distinguishing characteristic of nearly all excellent user interfaces now in the marketplace.

Edward Tufte, in introduction to *Visual Design of the User Interface*, written for IBM (Tufte, 1989, p. 1)

---

[3] Unfortunately, the window-border colors in an X Window systems are not controlled by the application but rather by the X Window Manager. However, system administrators can, for entire sites or for individual users, specify window border colors in a resource file used by *mwm* (Motif Window Manager). Applications can also suggest "hints" to mwm.

**Figure 8.1  1 + 1 = 3**

All of the development-platform guidelines recommend against overusing color. Edward Tufte, in a report he prepared for the IBM Design Program (Tufte, 1989) and in his own books (Tufte, 1983, 1990), points out that less is more.

"In the simplest case, when we draw two black lines on a white surface, a third visual effect results, an active white stripe between the two lines," he writes. "Nearly all the time, such surplus visual activity is disinformation, clutter, noise. This two-step logic—recognition of 1 + 1 = 3 effects and the consideration that such effects clutter information displays—provides a powerful tool for editing and refining user interface designs." (See Figure 8.1.)

Any first version of a window or an icon will contain a lot of noise. But by studiously eliminating extra patterns, using gray instead of black lines, or eliminating lines altogether, you can reduce the noise and bring information forward. (See Figure 8.2.)

## BACKGROUND COLOR AND PATTERN

With the stumbling blocks of black and white printers, monochrome monitors, color-blind users, and the risk of overdesign, how do you pick the right colors?

The answer is that you don't. Don't pick the colors first—pick contrast and pattern first, then pick colors. The next few sections (plus some definitions) explain how.

### Definitions

*Achromatic color:* Black, white, or gray—colors without saturation.

*Chroma:* A synonym for "saturation."

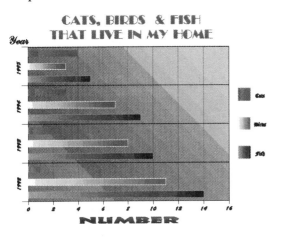

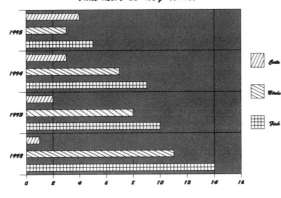

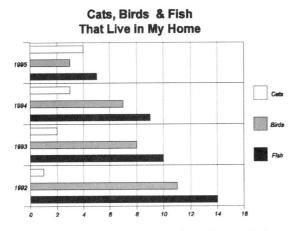

Figure 8.2  Three steps to uncluttering a window

*Complementary colors:* On the standard color wheel, complementary colors lie directly opposite each other. They are called complementary because, between them, they contain all the colors of the spectrum, not because they get along well (see Problem: Complementary Colors Flicker). The standard complementary pairs are: red and blue-green, orange and blue, yellow and blue-violet, chartreuse (yellow-green) and violet, green and red-violet.

*Contrast:* The greater the contrast, the better the visibility. Black on white has the strongest contrast. However, contrasting colors (colors with three hues between them on the color wheel) can cause optical illusions along the edges where they meet. See Problem: Contrasting Colors Create Intense Edges.

Common pairs of contrasting colors are red and green, red and blue, orange and blue-green, yellow and blue, and violet and green.

*Dithering:* Also called "texture mapping." A type of optical illusion. If you put pixels of two or more colors next to one another, the human eye automatically combines them into a third color. If you look closely at color pictures in magazines, you will see that only four colors of dots in various combinations make up the entire full-color picture. The four colors are cyan (light blue), yellow, magenta (pinkish red), and black.

Dithering is also used to simulate gray scale when you only have black and white pixels to work with—see Monochrome Widgets.

*Gray scale:* A system in which all of the hues are replaced with various shades or brightnesses of gray. See Pick Colors with Enough Contrast for reasons why the gray scale is important. Not the same as monochrome.

*HSV:* Hue, saturation, value (in some Macintosh programs, HSL—hue, saturation, lightness). A system available on some palette editors as an alternative to the RGB color-definition system. Matches the widely used Munsell method of color notation. See also *Hue, Saturation,* and *Value* in this list.

*Hue:* What is normally called "color." Hues are designated by such names as red, green, yellow, blue, and so on. Hue is a function of wavelength.

*Monochrome:* Black and white, period. No grays except those created by dithering. However, also used to refer to monitors with one color (usually amber, green, or orange) on a black background (or vice versa).

*RGB:* Red, green, blue. Three wavelengths of light—red, green, and blue—create all of the hues visible to primates such as ourselves.[4] Computer monitors use light, not pigment, to create colors. By adjusting the amounts of red, green, and blue light, you can create any of the dozens to millions of colors available on your or your clients' monitors.

When you paint with light, red, green, and blue together make white. When you paint with pigments, however, red, green, and blue make black (or, actually, a dark muddy brown that is familiar to most of us from grade school). There are other differences as well. Red light and green light make yellow light, whereas red pigment and green pigment make brown pigment (actually, in grade school, any two pigments seemed to make brown).

Hence the "R," "G," and "B" labels on the palette editors in many programs. (Macintosh programs, as usual, spell out the words.) Each of the three scales has 256 points (usually shown as 0 to 255). Winn Rosch explains why there are 256: "The digital to analog converter chip used by the VGA system does more than just convert digital signals to analog. It's actually three DACs in one—one for each color. In addition, it contains the *color look-up table* for the color mapping process which assigns one of the 262,144 colors [2 to the 18th power] possible under the VGA system to each of the 256 values that can be stored in memory in the VGA 320x200 color-graphics mode. The look-up table values are stored in 256 registers inside the DAC chip itself" (Rosch, 1989, p. 318). In other words, whenever you change a red, green, or blue scale, you are changing a value in one of three 256-cell tables.

*Saturation:* Also "purity" or "chroma." The intensity or vividness of a color. Red is more saturated than pink; navy blue is more saturated than sky blue. The more saturated a hue is, the more visible it is at a distance. The less saturated it is, the more difficult it is to see.

*Spectrum:* The band of colors produced when sunlight is passed through a prism—red, orange, yellow, green, blue, indigo, violet. (Just remember Mr. *Roy G Biv.*)

*Value:* Also "lightness." The amount of white or black mixed into the hue. Some hues are inherently lighter or darker than others—yellow, for instance, is very light while violet is very dark.

---

[4] Many insects can see ultraviolet light. Cats must be able to see infrared light, since they unerringly find the warmest spot in any room they enter.

The word "shade" usually describes a darkened hue, produced by removing light (lowering the CYM values). The word "tint" describes a light hue, produced by adding light.

## Start with Black and White

The development platform guidelines recommend that you design the objects in your application in black and white, and then add color. This guarantees, they say, that the icons and windows will work just as well in black and white as in color.

### Variations: Visual Impairment

> The icons on Citibank's Americans with Disabilities Act screens were designed for customers who can see, even if not very well. The screens use only black and white, since these two colors have the most contrast. Using white lettering on a black background, rather than black on white, was an important design decision. "For visually impaired customers," said David Peters, "a white screen with black lettering is like staring into a light bulb—the light overwhelms the image."
>
> David Peters, Two Twelve Associates, quoted in "Banking on a New Interface," *I.D.* magazine (Fowler, 1993, p. 72)[5].

In the United States, of the 1.1 million people who are legally blind, only 220,000 are totally blind, according to the American Foundation for the Blind. The disabilities of the partially sighted range from super-sensitivity to light to extreme near-sightedness or far-sightedness to effects in which the visual field is reduced to a tunnel (no peripheral vision) or a doughnut (no central and no peripheral vision).[6]

Many visually impaired people have taken to computers because they can control the image—for example, by magnifying text on-screen with software and hardware tools (the Americans with Disabilities Act recommended text size is 5/8 inch high)—or can have the computer translate printed text into audible speech.

---

[5] David Peters, Two Twelve Associates, 596 Broadway, Suite 1212, New York, NY 10012-3234; 212-925-6885.

[6] The definition used by the Center for the Partially Sighted is that a partially sighted individual's best corrected visual acuity is no better than 20/70 in either eye, but he or she has more than the mere perception of light.

If you're writing software for visually impaired users, the organizations listed in Resources can help you find usability test labs and test subjects as well as more information. Even if you aren't, however, you may be able to apply some of the solutions developed for partially sighted users in your domain space. For instance, Roger Whitehouse's tactile lettering (Slatin, 1993, pp. 81–82) might well be useful in low-light emergency situations, as would human-factors research into making computer-generated voices and tones more intelligible.

## Pick the Background First

Some designers try very hard to come up with imaginative ideas in an attempt to design attractive furniture for offices. They visualize pitch-black office machines on a bright table or dark furniture neighboring bright walls. Such designers don't care about ergonomic principles or balanced surface luminances.

Etienne Grandjean in *Ergonomics in Computerized Offices* (Grandjean, 1987, p. 46).

There are two types of background:

- The environment of the computer or workstation itself
- The application background—the application window or the video screen

If you know anything about your typical users' workplace, you can easily design your program's backgrounds and foregrounds to accommodate your users' visual situation. If not, you can still pick a range of contrasts that reduce users' discomfort while they're looking at your windows.

## Environmental Contrast

Etienne Grandjean is one of the inventors of ergonomics and human factors. From 1950 to 1983, he was director of the Institute for Hygiene and Work Physiology at the Swiss Federal Institute of Technology in Zurich. From 1961 to 1970, he was general secretary to the International Ergonomics Association.

In *Ergonomics in Computerized Offices*, Grandjean describes the ill effects of high illumination levels on computer users. Although glare, reflections, and deep shadows on the monitor are often extremely irritating, an unrecognized eyestrain culprit, he concludes, is too much contrast between the foreground (computer monitor) and the background (everything else—desktops, walls, curtains, windows, and so on). (See Figure 8.3.)

**Figure 8.3  Why office-mates fight over the light switch**

The human eye adapts so well to shifts in light and dark that we can see nearly as well in moonlight as in the brightest sunlight, even though the illumination level differs by more than 100,000 times. However, dark adaptation takes a relatively long time—25 minutes to reach 80 percent adaptation, an hour for full adaptation. Light adaptation is quicker than darkness adaptation—a reduction in light sensitivity by several powers of 10 in a few tenths of a second. However, light adaptation involves the entire retina. Whenever a bright image falls on any part of the retina, reduced sensitivity to light spreads to all parts of the retina. Since this adaptation includes the fovea, visual acuity for reading or fine details drops (Grandjean, 1987, pp. 23–24).

Since office designers usually recommend lighting levels of over 1,000 lux,[7] luminance readings in typical modern offices can cause severe acuity

---

[7] A lux is one lumen per square meter (Barnhart, 1986, p. 371). A lumen is the "SI unit of luminous flux, equal to the amount of light given out through a solid angle by a source of one candela radiating equally in all directions" (Barnhart, 1986, p. 369). An "SI unit" is any unit of measurement defined in the International System of Units (Barnhart, 1986, p. 600). A "candela" is the SI unit of luminous intensity, equal to 1/60 of the radiating power of 1 square centimeter of a blackbody [a body that absorbs all light] at the temperature at which platinum solidifies (1772° C) (Barnhart, 1986, p. 86).

For those of us with premetric minds, a lux is 0.0929 foot candles (or a foot candle is 10.764 lux). A rough approximation is 1 fc = 10 lux, 1/10 lux = 1 fc.

problems (leading to eyestrain, headaches, squinting, wrinkled brows, and so on). A thousand lux is a lot of light: The range of light in a typical living room is 50 to 200 lux. Bright sunlight is 50,000 to 100,000 lux, and a well-lit street at night is 10 to 20 lux. Reflected light is about 60 percent of the original brightness, so overhead light of 1,000 lux reflected off an office wall could be as much as 600 lux (Millerson, 1991, p. 11).

Research indicates that the ratio in brightness between the video screen and a document from which the user is typing should be no more than 1:10; the ratio between the video screen and the immediate background (walls, desktop, and so on) should be no more than 20:1; and the ratio between the video screen and the entire room should be no more than 40:1. The reality is much different. Researchers who surveyed 109 VDT workstations found a ratio of 1:10 to 1: 81 (average 1:21) between the screen and source documents and a ratio of 1:87 to 1:1450 (average 1:300) between the screen and nearby office windows (Grandjean, 1987, p. 43).[8]

In short, to avoid dazzling and prevent eyestrain (your own or your users), try to keep all surfaces at the same brightness by matching the overall brightness or dimness of your screens to the office environment. If users typically use your software in brightly lit offices or if they type from bright source documents, use light or off-white backgrounds. If your software is used in dim or dark areas (air traffic control towers, for example), use dark backgrounds. If you can't find out what the background will be, you might want to include two wallpapers, one light and one dark, with your program.

---

[8] You can test the visual environment with a camera's light meter. First, hold the shutter speed and film speed steady—you're looking only for changes in the f-stop. Next, point the light meter at the brightest area in the room (probably a window or a light-colored wall) and note the f-stop. Point the meter at the darkest area in the room that is within the user's normal range of peripheral vision (for example, under the desk is dark but not in the normal range). Note that f-stop. Finally, aim the meter at the monitor and note the f-stop. You might want to do the monitor test twice: Check one program with a light background and one with a dark background.

The f-stop series is 1, 1.4, 2, 2.8, 4, 5.6, 11, 16, 22, and 32. (The f-numbers are the result of multiplying the previous number by the square root of 2, which is 1.4, and rounding off the result to the nearest decimal.) Small f-numbers indicate low light (and a wider aperture for the lens). Each successive f-number indicates *double* the amount of light in front of the lens. The differences in light levels, therefore, are f1 = 1, f1.4 = times 2, f2 = times 4, f2.8 = times 8, f4 = times 16, f5.6 = times 32, f11 = times 64, f16 = times 128, f22 = times 256, and f32 = times 512.

So, if the lowest level in the room is f – 1 (times 1) and the highest f – 16 (times 128), the proportional difference in brightness is 1:128.

*Note:* If you design for a dim background, keep in mind that some color-blind users, who have no trouble distinguishing red from green or red from orange in bright light, cannot distinguish between the two colors in dim light (Kunz, 1987, p. 315).

### Variation: Backgrounds and Foregrounds for Presentations

Use dark backgrounds and light foregrounds (text, lines, and so on) for long-distance, low ambient-lighting situations such as slide shows or projected computer presentations. If you're creating a video presentation (live action or cartoon), use colors with low saturation (Marcus, 1992, p. 84). Red, especially, blooms and bleeds all over the pictures in which it appears, especially after you've copied the video tape once or twice.

Use light backgrounds and dark foregrounds for situations with high ambient light—for example, when you're using an overhead projector (Marcus, 1992, p. 84).

### Onscreen Contrast

A human eye can be divided into two parts: a pupil, cornea, and lens for focusing light and a retina for gathering light. (See Figure 8.4.) The retina itself has these parts:

*Rods:* Visual cells embedded in the retina that are sensitive to light and dark, not to color. There are about 130 million per eye.

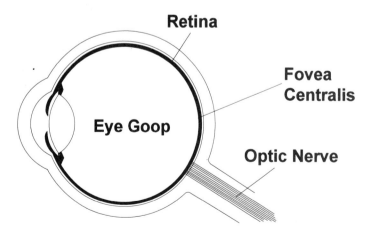

Figure 8.4  Diagram of the eye

*Cones:* Visual cells that are sensitive to color, not to light and dark. There are about 7 million per eye.

*Fovea centralis:* An area covering 1° of arc at the back of the eye. The fovea has the highest density of cones (about 10,000 per square millimeter) and the most direct connections to the optic nerve—each foveal cone has its own nerve fiber. (Rods and cones in the rest of the eye are connected in groups to nerves.) The high density and direct connections give the fovea the highest resolving power of any part of the retina. Since vision is most acute here, you instinctively move your eyes until the image you want to look at falls on the fovea.

*Blind spot:* The interface between the retina and the optic nerve. There are no rods or cones on the nerve, so no light is gathered at that point. However, you are never aware of the blind spot because the brain closes the visual field across the blank area automatically. Indeed, you can't find your own blind spot without specialized testing equipment (see Figure 8.5).

The area on which you can focus the fovea is about 1 inch at 20 inches (1° angle of view). You are aware of text or images within a circle about a foot in

**Figure 8.5  Find your blind spot: Cover one eye and stare straight ahead at a blank wall, while holding a spoon at arm's length. Move the spoon slowly back and forth, an eighth of an inch at a time, until the bowl of the spoon disappears.**

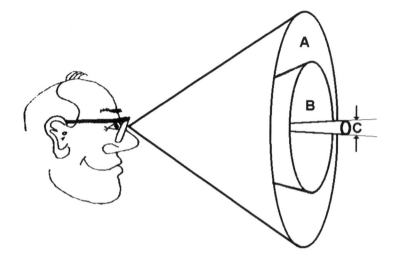

**Figure 8.6 Visual field: cone A is an angle of about 70°, cone B is about 40°, and cone C is about 1°**

diameter (1° to 40°), but can perceive only movement outside that circle (41° to 70°).

The rules for contrast on the screen, or between the screen and its immediate surrounding, take into account the size of the visual field (see Figure 8.6) as well as the dazzle effect described in Environmental Contrast (Grandjean, 1987, p. 41).

• Surfaces in the middle of the visual field should not have a brightness contrast of more than 3:1.

• Contrasts between the central and marginal areas should not exceed 10:1.

• The working area should be brighter in the middle and darker in the surrounding field.

• Excessive contrasts are more troublesome at the sides than at the top of the visual field.

### Color inside the Eye of the Beholder

Once you've picked the overall background for your program, you're ready to pick the color scheme for the windows, buttons, and icons in your software. However, colors have some odd characteristics, due to interactions between the physiology of the eye and the physics of light. In short, different wavelengths of color come into focus at different points in the eye.

Since yellow and green wavelengths come into focus at the retina, they require the least accommodation (the reason for so many yellow and green monochrome monitors a few years ago). Red wavelengths, on the other hand, come into focus a little behind the retina and therefore seem to "pop out" of the background. Since blue wavelengths come into focus in front of the retina, blues seem to fade into the background. (See Color Insert Figure 8.7.)

So, when you choose colors, remember that:

- Your eyes cannot focus clearly on blue, which is why it is such a good background color and such a bad foreground color.

- Nor can your eyes focus well on red, but red has the advantage (if you need it) of "moving forward" in the visual field.

- Yellow and green are just as visible in the periphery as they are as in the center of the visual field.

- Black and white are equally visible throughout the visual field (Horton, 1991, p. 228).

Other interesting effects include (Horton, 1991, pp. 227–228):

- For most colors, hue seems to change as luminance increases or decreases. However, saturated blue, green, and yellow remain constant throughout the range of luminance. Use them when constancy is important.

- Staring at a large patch of a saturated color for a long time shifts color perception towards its complement. For example, when you look up after working on a bright red figure, everything will look greenish. Called the "McCullough effect."

- In bright light, red seems brighter than blue. In dim light, however, blue appears lighter but colorless, while red appears nearly black. In low-light situations, avoid reds. Called the "Purkinje effect."

### Local Contrast

To create that three-dimensional GUI look (see Figure 8.8), you need at least five colors:

- Background, the color of the widget itself and the background on which it is positioned

**Figure 8.8  Diagram of a widget**

- Foreground, the color of labels and lines for buttons, icons, and other objects (usually black or white)
- Selected-mode, the color used when the item is selected
- Top shadow, for the bezel on the top of the widget
- Bottom shadow, for the bezel on the bottom of the widget

*Note:* On all development platforms, the standard light source is above and to the left of the objects.

Some decisions may have been made for you. For example, Shiz Kobara, a senior interface designer at Hewlett-Packard and one of the people responsible for the Motif visual design standard, points out that Motif has a color algorithm that can automatically calculate the correct top and bottom shadow and the select color (used to indicate that the widget has been selected) based on the background (Kobara, 1991, pp. 14–18). The algorithm adjusts the brightness of the shadows and also flips the foreground color from white to black, or vice versa, so that it contrasts well with the background. (However, a developer can override this algorithm easily.)

If your development system has no guidelines of its own (or if you're developing a development system), you may want to copy the Motif scheme. See Table 8.1 for details.

## Gray Replacements for Colors

Depending on your customer profile and/or operating system, you might want to set up a gray-scale interface and gray-scale or monochrome icons and pictures.

### Gray Widgets

In *Visual Design with OSF/Motif,* Kobara describes a scheme for designing gray-scale widgets (Kobara, 1991, pp. 20–21). You may be able to adapt his suggestions to your development system. *Note:* The percentages in Table 8.2 are about 30 percent apart.

**Table 8.1  Motif Color Recommendations**

| | |
|---|---|
| Background | Use midrange colors, 155–175 on the RGB scale (i.e., no red, green, or blue value should be higher than 175). A too-bright background will wash out the top shadow; a too-dark background will make the bottom shadow very dark and nearly invisible. |
| Foreground | Motif sets it automatically to either black or white, depending on the lightness or darkness of the background.<br><br>If you pick a midrange value, don't depend on the algorithm. Check the contrast between foreground and background visually—you may need to pick a darker or lighter background color. |
| Select | About 15 percent darker than the background color, halfway between the background and the bottom shadow. Calculate the color by multiplying the background color's RGB value by 0.85.<br><br>*Note:* For Motif buttons, the select color is a resource and is set automatically. Scales, scroll bars, and other similar widgets use the select color automatically in their troughs (the color is inherited from their parent objects). For lists, text, or other recessed widgets, however, you must set the select color as the background color. |
| Top Shadow | About 40 to 50 percent brighter than the background color. Multiply the RGB values by 1.50.<br><br>*Note:* If you aren't using Motif, you may have to adjust the color and saturation by hand to prevent such things as purple shadows on a blue background. (Motif's algorithm looks for and adjusts inappropriate color combinations.) |
| Bottom Shadow | About 45 to 60 percent darker than the background color. Multiply the RGB values by 0.50. |
| Traversal Highlight | The designer sets the color for traversals (a highlight that appears when the user moves across a widget). The traversal color is the same for all widgets. "The color should match well with the overall color scheme but be bright enough to stand out from the background. Highlight color can be specified in the resource *XmNhighlightColor*" (Kobara, 1991, p. 47). *Suggestion:* Since the traversal highlight is supposed to be obvious, use the background color's complementary color or a shade thereof. For example, you might use a yellow traversal for a dark blue background. |

**Table 8.2  Motif Gray-Scale Recommendations**

| | |
|---|---|
| Background | Light gray (30 percent gray, for example, which is RGB 79, 79, 79) |
| Foreground | White (RGB 0, 0, 0) |
| Select | Dark gray (70 percent gray, RGB 181, 181, 181) |
| Top Shadow | White |
| Bottom Shadow | Black (RGB 255, 255, 255) |

### Gray Pictures

Some items only come in color—for instance, the flags that Macintosh uses to indicate keyboard choices. In this case, you may need to define a set of black and white replacements.

The default is to change light colors to white and dark colors to black. If the flag (or other picture) uses three colors, change the midrange color to 50 percent gray (or a 50 percent dither for monochrome screens). (See Table 8.3.)

But what if there is more than one flag, all using similar colors and symbols? As usual, Apple Computer has thought about this problem and has published solutions in *Macintosh Human Interface Guidelines* (Apple Computer, 1992b, p. 254).

### Monochrome Widgets

Note that a difference of opinion exists between those who would dither monochrome widgets to create the effect of three dimensions and those who would not. (See Figure 8.9.) ("Monochrome" means black and white only,

**Table 8.3  Pattern Substitutes for Colors**

| *Color* | *Pattern* |
|---|---|
| Black or blue | Black |
| Red | 50 percent gray |
| Light blue | 25 percent gray |
| Green | Diagonal stripes |
| White or yellow | White |

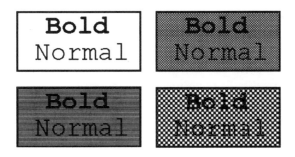

**Figure 8.9  To dither or not to dither?**

**Figure 8.10  Monochrome buttons with outline**

no gray.) In *Macintosh Human Interface Guidelines*, the authors flatly advise against dithering: "Keep black and white designs two-dimensional . . . . Don't cause unnecessary visual clutter by trying to mimic color effects, such as shadows, in black and white designs" (Apple Computer, 1992b, p. 263).

**Table 8.4  Motif Monochrome Recommendations**

| *Black Foreground* | |
| --- | --- |
| Background | White |
| Foreground | Black |
| Select | Black |
| Top Shadow | 50 percent dithered pattern |
| Bottom Shadow | Black |

| *White Foreground* | |
| --- | --- |
| Background | Black |
| Foreground | White |
| Select | White |
| Top Shadow | White |
| Bottom Shadow | 50 percent dithered pattern |

Kobara, on the other hand, demonstrates a 3-D monochrome scheme in *Visual Design with OSF/Motif* (Kobara, 1991, pp. 21–31). However, he also says that text does not show up well on dithered backgrounds, since the letters' edges bleed into the dithered dots of the background.

*Note:* To prevent the selected color from bleeding into the bottom shadow in monochrome widgets, add a contrasting outline around the label in a pushbutton (Kobara, 1991, p. 30). (See Figure 8.10.) Motif does this automatically (see Table 8.4).

*Suggestions:* If you design a monochrome interface, keep it simple and don't put labels on a dithered background (and certainly don't dither the text).

## FOREGROUND COLOR AND PATTERN

Color in the foreground parts of an application—charts, icons, toolbars, and so on—must contrast with the muted background of the application. However, bright colors bring up these issues:

- Picking meaningful colors

- Using color only for reinforcement, not for meaning—see Use Pattern for Significance, Color for Reinforcement.

- Picking colors with different gray scales—see Pick Colors with Enough Contrast.

For information on problems, see Avoiding Problems.

*Hint:* When you start to create icons and the rest of the foreground objects, avoid temptation. Don't work directly on the computer with all its multitudes of colors and brightnesses. Instead, start by sketching your pictures on a paper napkin, a cafeteria placemat, the back of an envelope—anything that keeps you working on the *shape* of the picture rather than its look and feel. Put the picture into the computer only after you're satisfied that it stands on its own (by testing it on your colleagues, friends, relatives, and clients, for example).

### Pick Meaningful Colors

Although picking culturally correct colors for the overall interface is useful (cool gray for an accounting system, hot pink for a Post-Modern game),

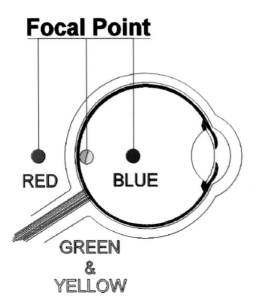

**Focal Point**

RED     BLUE

GREEN
&
YELLOW

**Figure 8.7 Wavelengths focused hither and yon**

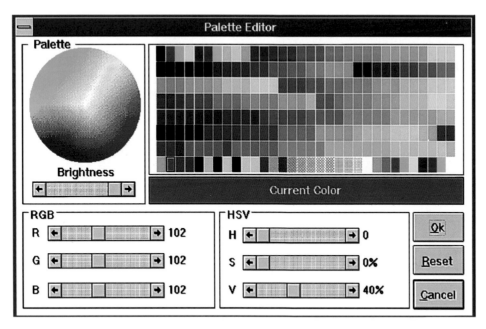

**Figure 8.12 Palette editor**

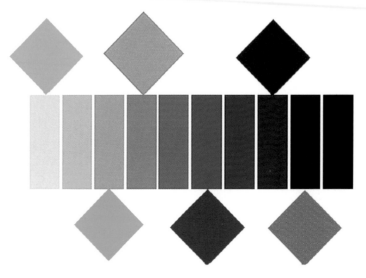

Figure 8.13  Gray-scale ruler

Figure 8.14  Which is bigger? Neither.

**Figure 8.15 Against a shade of itself versus its complement**

**Figure 8.16 Same color looks light, then dark**

**Figure 8.17 Flicker in complementary colors**

**Figure 8.18 Too much color contrast**

selecting meaningful colors for the signals *inside* your windows is even more important. There are four issues.

- *Chunking:* People can remember the significance of only seven colors, plus or minus two (see Chapter 3 for more information). In other words, don't create line charts with nine differently colored lines (*unless* the entire pattern of lines is the significant picture—for example, to indicate a noise level or a confusion level, as in Figure 8.11).

- *Actual or spurious relationships:* Since people automatically assume that items colored the same are related (Galitz, 1993, p. 429), you must color related things the same, unrelated things differently. Don't just add color, in other words. Aesthetics are not as important as sense.

  But you can take advantage of this automatic-association facility: For example, if your application has many charts, each containing the same types of data, color code the data types. In a loan-analysis program, say, you could use green for principal payments, blue for interest payments, red for defaults, and so on. As well as simplifying the situation for your clients, the programming staff won't have to reinvent the color wheel every time a new chart is added to the program.

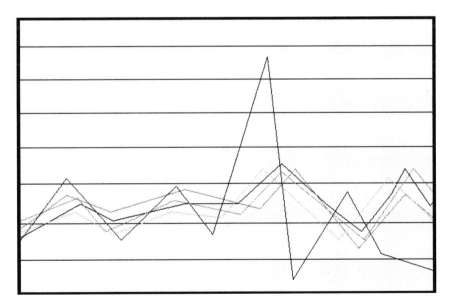

**Figure 8.11 Intentional noise and confusion**

- *Task domain expectations:* Find out how color (or pattern) is used in the area for which you're designing the program. "The designer needs to speak to operators to determine what color codes are applied in the task domain. From automobile-driving experience, red is commonly considered to indicate stop or danger, yellow is a warning, and green is go. In investment circles, red is a financial loss and black is a gain. For chemical engineers, red is hot and blue is cold. For map makers, blue means water, green means forests, and yellow means deserts" (Schneiderman, 1992, p. 327).

*Hint:* When you ask about color, ask about relative position as well. For example, color-blind individuals use "Stop on top, go below" for stoplights. If you design a dashboard with red, yellow, and green lights in the wrong order, at least 8 percent of your audience will get the lights wrong. See Color Confusions for details.

- *Cross-cultural differences:* Colors mean different things in different cultures. For example:

| | |
|---|---|
| green and orange | politically suggestive in Eire and Northern Ireland |
| red | suggests death in many African cultures |
| red, white, and blue | suggests colonialism in some countries |
| white | suggests death or mourning in some Oriental cultures (Apple Computer, 1992a, p. 219) |

## Use Pattern for Significance, Color for Reinforcement

If you always use pattern with color, you avoid most problems (except the problem of visual clutter—see Un-Design for Clarity). For example, on a line chart with one significant line, and two or three other lines, use a bright color with a solid line for the most important data, then dotted and dashed lines for the less important data.

*Suggestion:* For dotted and dashed lines, use Morse code. The first letters of the primary colors (see Table 8.5) are different from one another.

## Pick Colors with Enough Contrast

Visual acuity is worse for color than for brightness (Gregory, 1987, p. 151). If you stripped away the hue and left only the gray scale, would you still be able

**Table 8.5 Codes for Colored Lines**

| Color | Morse Code | Sample Line (3 Repeats Each) |
|---|---|---|
| Blue | — · · · | — · — · · · — · · · — · · · |
| Cyan | — · — · | — · — · — · — · — · — · — · |
| Green | — — · | — — · — — · — — · |
| Magenta | — — | — — — — — — |
| Purple | · — — · | · — — · · — — · · — — · |
| Red | · — · | · — · · — · · — · |
| Yellow | — · — — | — · — — — · — — — · — — |

to separate items visually? Picking gray-scale values in addition to hue may solve the problems caused by color confusions, black and white print-outs, and low-light or low-contrast settings on users' computers.[9]

The rule is: To create enough contrast between type, lines, or other small items, and the background, make sure that the colors' gray-scale values differ by at least 20 to 30 percent (White, 1990, p. 73).

### How to Tell if Your Selected Colors Have Enough Contrast

To check your colors, create a gray-scale ruler.

1. Pick a program with a color or palette editor (see Color Insert Figure 8.12). Open the editor and either find or create a set of nine grays and one black separated by 10 percent differences in darkness. Use white for the background. The values for each gray are:

| Gray | RGB Values | HSV Values |
|---|---|---|
| 10% | 26, 26, 26 | 0, 0%, 10% |
| 20% | 51, 51, 51, | 0, 0%, 20% |
| 30% | 79, 79, 79 | 0, 0%, 30% |
| 40% | 102, 102, 102 | 0, 0%, 40% |
| 50% | 128, 128, 128 | 0, 0%, 50% |
| 60% | 153, 153, 153 | 0, 0%, 60% |

---

[9] Keep in mind that gray scales of less than 20 percent may not print well on low-end laser printers. The print-outs will tend to show any imperfections or unevenness in the printing mechanisms.

| Gray | RGB Values | HSV Values |
|------|-----------|-----------|
| 70% | 181, 181, 181 | 0, 0%, 70% |
| 80% | 204, 204, 204 | 0, 0%, 80% |
| 90% | 232, 232, 232 | 0, 0%, 90% |
| 100% (black) | 255, 255, 255 | 0, 0%, 100% |

2.  Draw a set of gray boxes on a white background, one color of gray per box, ranging from 10 percent to 100 percent (black). See Color Insert Figure 8.13.

3.  Draw diamonds of all the colors you want to test.

4.  Drag each color sample over the gray scale, squinting as you drag it. When the color and a gray box seem to match, you've found its gray-scale value.

5.  Save the colors that are either 20 or 30 percent apart (separated by two or three boxes) and discard the rest.

*Note:* Some colors, because of their brightness, maintain high contrast no matter where you put them on the gray scale. However, check the size. Small areas of yellow disappear against white. Red, if used for something small (dots) or thin (lines), shrinks away to nothing against a dark background.

## AVOIDING PROBLEMS

Most computer illustrations come in full color nowadays, so the question of what colors to use is either irrelevant ("It's a picture of a face! The colors are face colors!") or too complicated to talk about here ("Remove that green cast in her face on the prepress system before sending the file to the color separator").

However, some colors, when used in blocks, do odd things in the presence of other colors. For example, bright colors like red look bigger than dark colors like black (White, 1990, pp. 15–18). In Color Insert Figure 8.14, notice that the inner red square looks larger than the inner black square.

### Problem: Comparing Widely Separated Colors

Since color perception is sharp only near the fovea, color coding is effective only within 10 to 15 degrees of the central area of vision. Widely separated colors are hard to compare, in other words, unless you lean back or step back from the computer (Horton, 1991, p. 226).

## Problem: Hues Change in Proximity to One Another

If you want a color to look like itself and stay that way, don't put it next to a contrasting color (White, 1990, pp. 16–18). (See Color Insert Figures 8.15 and 8.16.)

## Problem: Complementary Colors Flicker

Putting blocks of saturated *complementary colors* next to one another causes eyestrain. Because the cones in your eyes cannot see both colors at the same time, your focus shifts back and forth rapidly without being able to settle on either color.

Color Insert Figure 8.17 shows you what happens with orange and blue. Red and blue-green, yellow and dark blue, and purple and chartreuse (yellow-green) are also complementary colors.

## Problem: Contrasting Colors Create Intense Edges

*The edge between two bright contrasting colors* can be very intense and often distracting. To avoid this effect, you can either lighten or darken one of the colors or separate the two colored areas with a white or black line. (See Color Insert Figure 8.18.)

## Problem: Color Does *Not* Make Type Stand Out

Do not fall into the trap of thinking that color is as strong as black because it looks brighter, more cheerful, more vibrant, and so much more fun to look at. It is not. You have to compensate for its weakness, to make color as visible as black. There just has to be more of it, so you have to use fatter lines, bolder type, or larger type to overcome the problem.

Jan White in *Color for the Electronic Age* (White, 1990, p. 24).

When you switch from black text or lines to light- or bright-colored text or lines (red, orange, gold), double the width of the lines and use either bold or a larger type size. One to two points larger should be enough for 8- to 12-point type, two to four points larger for 14- to 24-point type. However, check visibility by squinting at the text. Too-light type will recede or even disappear.

The reason for color's poor showing is, again, physiological. Colored letters and numbers can only be read when they are quite close to the fixation, although color itself can be seen far from fixation. "This indicates that color is a useful aid for visual search, but actual reading takes place in a restricted visual reading field. If a reader is familiar with the significance of colors, then colors will help to locate the required information quickly, but the recognition of a word or symbol itself depends on the legibility of characters and not on their color" (Grandjean, 1987, pp. 30–31).

*Hint:* When you use a color for a hypertext link, the type looks best if you use the same type *size* but a slightly different *weight.* Also, print typesetters and designers like to have narrow versions of typefaces on hand for space emergencies. For example, what do you do if a program name changes and now it won't fit on its button? You could redraw the button *or* you could switch to the narrow version. True Helvetica (rather than Helios, Arial, or any of the other varieties) is an excellent all-around choice, since it comes in narrow, medium, bold, and heavy versions. However, these fonts may not be available in display versions.

## Problem: Most Colors Aren't Available

Although the VGA monitors required for GUIs have at least 262,144 colors, if not 16 million, you, as a developer, cannot access most of them when you are creating your interface. In other words, the platform developers' "recommendations" are actually restricted palettes.

This is not necessarily a bad thing, since some of the most painful color combinations are thereby precluded. For example, most of the 34 Macintosh colors are subtle, according to the *Macintosh Human Interface Guidelines:* "Subdued colors avoid a 'circus' effect on the screen." The rainbow colors that make up the Apple logo were also included "because those colors have a strong Apple identification." However, they are "very bright and should be used sparingly" (Apple Computer, 1992b, p. 240).

Also, not all screen components in Microsoft Windows and on the Macintosh screen can be colored. For example, on the Mac, controls such as scroll boxes, close boxes, size boxes, and so on are colored, but the title bar and scroll bars remain gray. Similarly, although Windows scroll bars, toolbars, buttons, and so on can be any color, backgrounds tend to be white.

On the other hand, keep in mind that on either system, users can change the widget colors themselves. The Macintosh guidelines suggest that if you create your own windows instead of using the standard window definition functions, use colors that are compatible with the ones on the Color control panel—gold, green, turquoise, red, pink, blue, gray, black, and white (Apple Computer, 1992b, pp. 136–137). On Windows, however, users have unlim-

**Table 8.6  RGB and HSV Values for the Basic Hues**

| Hue | Red-Green-Blue | HSV |
|---|---|---|
| White (default text background) | 255-255-255 | 240-240-240 |
| Yellow | 255-255-0 | 40-240-120 |
| Dark Yellow | 128-128-0 | 40-240-60 |
| Red | 255-0-0 | 0-240-120 |
| Dark Red | 128-0-0 | 0-240-60 |
| Magenta | 255-0-255 | 200-240-120 |
| Dark Magenta | 128-0-128 | 200-240-60 |
| Blue | 0-0-255 | 160-240-120 |
| Dark Blue (default color for title bar) | 0-0-128 | 160-240-60 |
| Cyan | 0-255-255 | 120-240-120 |
| Dark Cyan | 0-128-128 | 120-240-60 |
| Green | 0-255-0 | 80-240-120 |
| Dark Green | 0-128-0 | 80-240-60 |
| Gray (default for scroll bars, buttons, other window items) | 192-192-192 | 160-0-181 |
| Dark Gray (default color for screen background) | 128-128-128 | 160-0-120 |
| Black (default for lines, labels, cursors, etc.) | 0-0-0 | 0-0-0 |

ited color choices via the Control Panel, which offers predefined sets of colors ("Windows Default," "Arizona," "Black Leather Jacket," etc.) as well as an "anything goes" Color Palette option.

Table 8.6 lists the RGB values for the 16 colors available in Microsoft Windows. If you intend to cross hardware boundaries, you might want to restrict your palette to this minimum set of colors.

*Note:* On X systems, the *rgb.txt* file (usually located in */usr/lib/X11*)—the named color database—is an X toolkit facility on which any widget set can be built. The colors are listed by name and hexadecimal code—for example, `#000000` black, `#FCFCFC` white, `#FF0000` red, `#0000FF` blue. (Same idea, different number set.)

Keep in mind, however, that you should use the *name* rather than the code in your software. If you hard-code too many colors, you may fill up the color table. Then, although your application may look fine, the next application that the user opens may suddenly be full of, say, fuschia and bright green windows.

For details, see *X Toolkit Intrinsics Programming Manual* (Nye and O'Reilly 1990, pp. 447–451).

## REFERENCES

Apple Computer, Inc. *Guide to Macintosh Software Localization.* Reading, MA: Addison-Wesley, 1992a.

———. *Macintosh Human Interface Guidelines.* Reading, MA: Addison-Wesley, 1992b.

Banks, William W., Jr., and Jon Weimer. *Effective Computer Display Design.* Englewood Cliffs, NJ: Prentice-Hall, 1992.

Barnhart, Robert K. *Hammond Barnhart Dictionary of Science.* Maplewood, NJ: Hammond, 1986.

Fowler, Susan L. "Banking on a New Interface." *I.D.*, September/October 1993, pp. 70–72.

Galitz, Wilbert O. *User-Interface Screen Design.* Boston, MA: QED Publishing Group, 1993.

Grandjean, Etienne. *Ergonomics in Computerized Offices.* New York: Taylor & Francis, 1987.

Gregory, Richard L. (editor). *Oxford Companion to the Mind.* New York: Oxford University Press, 1987.

Hackman, Richard J., Garry L. Holtzman, and Penny E. Walter, "Color Vision Testing for the U.S. Naval Academy." *Military Medicine.* vol. 157, December 1992.

Horton, William. *Illustrating Computer Documentation.* New York: John Wiley & Sons, 1991.

Kobara, Shiz *Visual Design with OSF/Motif.* Reading, MA: Hewlett-Packard/Addison-Wesley, 1991.

Krantz, Les. *What the Odds Are.* New York: HarperPerennial, 1992.

Kunz, Jeffrey R. M., and Asher J. Finkel. *The American Medical Association Family Medical Guide.* New York: Random House, 1987.

Marcus, Aaron. *Graphic Design for Electronic Documents and User Interfaces.* Reading, MA: ACM Press/Addison-Wesley, 1992.

Milhaven, Kathleen R. "Visual Communication and Color Blindness." *Proceedings, Thirty-Sixth International Technical Communications Conference.* 1989.

Millerson, Gerard. *Lighting for Video.* 3d ed. Oxford: Focal Press (imprint of Butterworth-Heinemann, Ltd.), 1991.

Nye, Adrian, and Tim O'Reilly. *X Toolkit Intrinsics.* Sebastopol: CA: O'Reilly & Associates, 1990.

Rosch, Winn L. *The Winn Rosch Hardware Bible.* New York: Brady, 1989.

Sawyer, Philip W. (editor). "45 Questions to Test Your Ad IQ." *Starch Tested Copy.* vol. 4, no. 10. November 1992, pp. 1–4

Schneiderman, Ben. *Designing the User Interface*, 2d ed. Reading, MA: Addison-Wesley Publishing Co. 1992.

Slatin, Peter. "Darkness Made Visible." *I.D.* September/October 1993, pp. 81–82.

Edward R. Tufte. *Visual Design of the User Interface.* Armonk, New York: IBM Corporation, 1989.

White, Jan V. *Color for the Electronic Age.* New York: Watson-Guptill Publications, 1990.

## RESOURCES

## Color and Light

Smith, Robb. *Amphoto Guide to Filters.* Garden City, New York: American Photographic Book Publishing Co., 1979. An excellent reference for types of filters and the effects you can get.

Stroebel, Leslie. *Photographic Filters: A Programmed Instruction Handbook.* Dobbs Ferry, NY: Morgan & Morgan, 1974. This book teaches you, in the best pedagogical fashion, exactly how filters work with colors. It has an extensive bibliography, a glossary, and plastic filters in a pouch in the back (used for some of the exercises). Contact the publisher at: 145 Palisade Street, Dobbs Ferry, NY 10522.

## Color, Pattern, and Design

Chijiiwa, Hideaki. *Color Harmony: A Guide to Creative Color Combinations.* Rockport, MA: Rockport Publishers, 1991. Distributed through North Light Books, 1507 Dana Avenue, Cincinnati, OH 45209. Pages and pages of color swatches, in combination, plus a lucid description of color theory. This book is also available in Great Britain, the Philippines, Thailand, Canada, Singapore, and Turkey.

Tufte, Edward R. *Envisioning Information.* Cheshire, CT: Graphics Press, 1990. *The Visual Display of Quantitative Information.* Cheshire, CT: Graphics Press, 1983. How the pros do design. Once you've mastered the basics, go here.

White, Jan V. *Color for the Electronic Age.* New York: Watson-Guptill Publications, 1990. Not about interface design at all, but clear and practical about color in general. Also includes an appendix that compares color specification systems (Munsell, Pantone, Natural, and CIE Notation).

## Color Standards

ANSI offers these color-coding standards:

- *Color Coding of Discrete Semiconductor Devices,* ANSI/EIA 236 Revision C
- *Colors for Identification and Coding* (includes 1988 supplement, 359-A-1) ANSI/EIA 359-A
- *Safety Color Code,* ANSI Z535.1-1991

For more information, or to order these publications, contact American National Standards Institute, Attn.: Customer Service, 11 West 42nd Street, New York, NY 10036; voice: 212-642-4900; fax: 212-302-1286.

Outside the United States:

American Technical Publishers, Ltd., 27/29 Knowl Piece, Wilbury Way, Hertfordshire, SG4 0SX, England

Japanese Standards Association, 1-24, Akasaka, Minato-ku, Tokyo 107, Japan

Standards Council of Canada, 45 O'Connor Street, Suite 1200, Ottawa K1P 6N7, Ontario, Canada

## Programming Information

Kobara, Shiz. *Visual Design with OSF/Motif.* Reading, MA: Hewlett-Packard/Addison-Wesley, 1991. Although Kobara's book is about Motif and X Windows, his design ideas are useful, no matter what your orientation.

## Visual Impairment and Adaptive Technology

*American Foundation for the Blind* runs the National Technology Center (NTC), a resource for visually impaired people and their families, rehabilitation professionals, educators, researchers, manufacturers, and employers.

NTC has three divisions:

- Research and Development Laboratory, in which engineers develop or adapt consumer products to include voice or tactile output (for example, an audible carpenter's level, talking thermometer, talking blood pressure meter).

- Evaluations Laboratory, which tests new and existing products and equipment, such as Braille translation software, laptop computers with speech output, and synthetic speech access systems.

- Information Systems, which maintains databases of information on consumer products designed for visually impaired people. The databases include brief descriptions of the products and manufacturers' names and addresses. Also part of Information Systems is the Careers and Technology Information Bank (CTIB), which contains data from over 1,300 visually impaired people who use adaptive equipment in a variety of jobs. Individuals listed in the CTIB may serve as evaluators of adapted equipment or as sources of information for firms developing adaptive technology.

For more information, contact: Director, National Technology Center, American Foundation for the Blind, 15 West 16th Street, New York, NY 10011; 212-620-2080; fax: 212-620-2137.

As well as offering rehabilitative services to partially and legally blind individuals, the *Center for the Partially Sighted* prescribes and offers training in visual aids. The Center helped Citibank reprogram its touch-screen automatic teller machines so that blind and partially sighted customers could use them. For more information, contact the Center for the Partially Sighted,

919 Santa Monica Boulevard, Suite 200, Santa Monica, CA 90405; 310-458-3501; fax: 310-458-8179.

*The Trace Research and Development Center* at the University of Wisconsin offers software, telephone communication devices, and computer-access software. Contact: Trace R&D Center, University of Wisconsin-Madison, S-151 Waisman Center, 1500 Highland Avenue, Madison WI 53705; 608/263-2309; TDD 608/263-5408.

Greg Goodrich at the Veterans Administration's *Western Region Blindness Center* maintains a comprehensive database of literature about low-vision computer access. For the current copy of the bibliography generated from the database, contact Gregory L. Goodrich, Ph.D., Western Blind Rehabilitation Center, U.S. Dept. of Veterans Affairs Medical Center, 3801 Miranda Avenue, Palo Alto, CA 94304; 415-493-5000.

# 9

# Multimedia

*What is multimedia?*

The word "multimedia" is like the word "transportation." Transportation can be a car, a bus, a boat, a plane, a bicycle, a truck, or even a rocket ship. Likewise, multimedia can be a game, a demo disk, an interactive training program, an information kiosk, a trade-show presentation, an electronic encyclopedia, a virtual-reality system, an interactive advertisement (see the April 1994 *New Media* for more on this new field), or anything else that entertains or educates.

Multimedia has actually existed for quite a long time. Television is one of the early uses of multimedia—what is television but a radio with some pictures attached? Movies are an even earlier version of multimedia—moving pictures, after all, are strips of film with a sound track synchronized to the picture's action—two forms of media used in one presentation.

However, multimedia (at least as far as computer users are concerned) refers to anything that lets users interact with the software and that uses more than one method of conveying information. For instance, let's say you're at the mall and you're trying to find a particular store. You walk up to one of the interactive information kiosks and ask it for some data by touching the pictures on the screen. The kiosk answers with a video clip showing you the store you want, a sound clip explaining how to get there, and a printed map of the floor plan of the mall. There might also be some written information on the screen as well as background music. Four or five different types of media in one presentation equal—multimedia!

Although an individual multimedia application can contain any number of technologies—music, audio, video, illustration, and so on—it will probably be delivered in one of two ways:

- *On CD-ROM:* CD-ROM distribution requires a computer with a CD-ROM drive. The medium is a compact disk (like the ones used for music). CD-ROMs can be used to distribute enormous amounts of text as well as pictures and video clips (approximately 680 megabytes per disk).

- *On CD-I:* CD-I requires a television and a CD-I player (the "I" stands for "interactive"). CD-I also uses compact disks.

The difference between CD-ROM and CD-I is the market, according to Andrew Bonime of Infotainment, a New York City "new media" firm. "If your product is designed for the consumer market," he said at the Book Pub-World '93 Exposition and Conference in February 1993, "go with CD-I. A CD-I player costs less than $600, while a computer outfitted with a CD-ROM drive costs $3,000 to $5,000." (On the other hand, the number of households owning PCs with CD players increased nearly fourfold in 1993 to 1.9 million, according to Link Resources Corp., a market research firm. The total should reach 8.6 million households by 1995; Fox, 1994, p. 9.)

The CD-I system has another advantage besides price, however—it was designed with 16 channels. The developers thought these channels would be used to hold the text in different languages, but they could also be used to hold different levels of information—child, teenager, and adult, for example.

Then why use CD-ROM systems? The reason is that students or researchers with access to CD-ROM drives can move the information directly from the CDs into their own electronic papers or articles, an advantage associated with big dollar signs. Norm Bastin, senior vice president of Compton's New Media, Inc., admitted that his company sold 150,000 copies of the Compton's Interactive Encyclopedia in 1992. With a street price of $169.95 and after subtracting the $6 million Bastin said that Compton's spent rewriting the encyclopedia for multimedia, gross revenues must have been about $19 million.

## HOW TO CREATE A MULTIMEDIA APPLICATION

You can create a multimedia application in either of two ways:

- Make all the pieces yourself.
- Pull it together from existing material.

Both approaches have their problems. To create the entire presentation yourself, you need a team that includes interface designers (graphic artists with expertise in computer design), writers, film makers, and musicians as well as programmers. You also need access to a good lawyer who can set up clear, enforceable contracts with each member of the team.

If your company decides to put the application together from existing material, then you will have to deal with the issue of intellectual property rights. See What Do Rights Have to Do with It?.

### Planning and Coordination

Multimedia includes two elements that don't normally appear in other software applications: a story or sequence and the coordination of a large crew of people with very different skill sets and vocabularies. If you decide to go with new material, you will need to write a treatment and a script and create storyboards. The purpose of the treatment is to make sure that all members of the team understand the presentation and their roles in creating it. The purpose of the script is to make sure that the story is complete. The purpose of the storyboard is to give everyone the same visual idea of what the presentation will look like.

#### Treatments and Scripts

The treatment contains the practical information—the length of the presentation, the budget, the market, and so on.

The script (also called "screenplay") is essentially the specification. It contains these details:

- *Camera instructions,* including long shots, medium shots, close-ups, and other more specialized shots and angles, each of which has an emotional component.

- *Composition:* By controlling the composition, you arrange the elements in a scene so that the viewer sees what you intend him or her to see. Lighting and location are both part of composition.

- *Continuity*—the visual flow from one shot to the next.

- *Editing instructions,* which show how the shots will be put together into scenes and then how the scenes will be put together into a complete story (Shelton, 1993, p. 658).

Although narration, conversation, voice-overs, or subtitles can be part of a presentation, keep in mind that text is rarely the most important part. In fact, Pennsylvania State University studies suggest that 70 to 80 percent of the information should be conveyed visually, not through spoken or written text (Shelton, 1993, p. 659).

Information on writing scripts and treatments is widely available. See Storyboards and Screenwriting for recommended books.

## Storyboards

A storyboard is a series of sketches (or photographs) that represent the individual scenes in a film, video, or multimedia production. (See Figure 9.1.)

Storyboards were probably invented at the Walt Disney Studio in the early 1930s. The cartoonists there would draw rough sketches of the planned animation and pin them to a bulletin board in the sequence they were

**Figure 9.1  A typical storyboard frame**

supposed to appear in the feature. This helped the cartoonists visualize the story line and gave them a common vision of the finished product.

Storyboards are not just drawings, however. They may also contain dialog, sound-effect notations, music notes, and indications of camera angles and movement.

Also, storyboards are not just used to make cartoons—most feature films and advertising films use storyboards to help visualize camera angles and movement. Steven Spielberg, for instance, has been known to storyboard feature films from beginning to end. His storyboards are especially useful to the special-effects crew, who have to prepare scenes that have no parallel to any other scenes on earth (Shay, 1993, p. 149).

*Note:* You can get pads of storyboard paper at any art supply store.

## What Do Rights Have to Do with It?

Adding a film or television clip to CD-ROM software can be more trouble than actually producing something new. Jill Alofs runs Total Clearance in Mill Valley, California, which does permissions work. In a typical job, for a five-second clip from *Star Wars* for an unspecified product, she had to pursue permission from nine sources: actors, Screen Actors Guild, stunt performers, stunt coordinators, music publisher, musician's union, director, scriptwriters, and holders of rights to the film as a whole.

From the *New York Times Magazine*, Sunday, June 12, 1994, p. 22.

Since the author, producer, or publisher of an existing work owns the reproduction rights, you must pay a license fee to use it in your application. Software is licensed the same way, so there should be no difficulty, right?

The problem is finding the owner of the rights. At Book PubWorld '93, Barbara Shulman, a rights attorney with Stroock & Stroock & Lavan, New York City, pointed out that acquiring the rights to the various pieces of an electronic book—film, music, written material, and so on—is time-consuming and can be very difficult. When you want to use a piece of a film or video, she said, you might have to get permission not only from the producers, directors, and actors but from anyone involved in the scene—the writers, musicians, camera operators, stunt men and women, and so on. Getting all of the licenses may take as long as programming the entire project.

If your firm is creating a book from scratch, Shulman said, try to acquire the rights on a work-for-hire basis. In other words, hire the team members outright or else write the contract so that the contractor's work actually belongs to you. Otherwise, you may find out later that you bought a one-time license and cannot reuse the material without further negotiations and payments to its creators.

However, you may be able to bypass many of these problems if your multimedia project uses materials that are in the public domain—in other words, copyright-free. According to Jon A. Baumgarten of Proskauer, Rose, Goetz, and Mendelsohn, these materials are usually in the public domain:

- *Works of the U.S. government:* State, local, municipal, and foreign works or works by contractors are, however, fully protected by copyright.

- *Works without copyright marks,* depending on when the material was published—works published before January 1, 1978, without a copyright are generally in the public domain, unless the omission was corrected in a later edition or version of the work.

Never assume that a work is in the public domain, however. To publish the King James version of the Bible, for example, you need a license from the British Crown, which owns the rights in perpetuity.

For help finding copyright owners, contact the Library of Congress or hire a law firm with expertise in copyright law and permissions.

The next few sections contains sources for creative people and their work, plus related reference books. For books on multimedia development from a hardware or software point of view, see Multimedia Development Books.

## ART AND ILLUSTRATION

Before looking outside your company for an artist, cartoonist, or graphics illustrator, look inside. For example, the people pasting up the company's marketing brochures are probably creative artists when they're not working on your materials. (Yes, you do have to pay them extra to do illustrations or cartoons.)

Also, make sure that both parties agree as to who owns the rights to the creative work itself and to any cartoon or animated character developed for your presentation.

If you must have a particular "look and feel" that your in-house resources can't handle, then hire an artist, buy clip art, or license a particular artwork. The following are a variety of resources.

### Artists' Organizations

The *American Society of Artists* provides a reference service on arts and crafts. For more information, contact the American Society of Artists, P.O. Box 1326, Palatine, IL 60078; 312-751-2500.

The *Artists Equity Association, Inc.*, is a national nonprofit center that will answer questions, provide counseling, conduct seminars, distribute publications, and make referrals. Services are provided free to members. For more information, contact the Artists Equity Association, Inc., P.O. Box 28068, Central Station (920 F Street NW), Washington, DC 20038; 202-628-9633.

The *Artists Foundation* is a public nonprofit organization that provides referrals, conducts seminars, and distributes publications. Services are provided free, except for distribution and seminars. For more information, contact the Artists Foundation, 110 Broad Street, Boston, MA 02110; 617-482-8100.

One of the primary goals of the *Graphic Artists Guild* is to "promote and maintain high professional standards of ethics and practice and to secure the conformance of all buyers, users, sellers, and employers to established standards." As part of this role, the Guild publishes the Graphic Artists Guild Handbook: Pricing and Ethical Guidelines, 7th ed., (1991) North Light Books/F&W Publications, 1507 Dana Avenue, Cincinnati, OH 45207; 513-531-2222. If you're a buyer, use this book to estimate costs for illustrations, computer art, animation, cartoons, and so on. If you're a seller, use this book to write contracts and make sure that you aren't being underpaid. For information about the Guild, contact Graphic Artists Guild, 11 West 20th Street, 8th Floor, New York, NY 10011-3704; 212-463-7730.

The *National Association of Women Artists* answers inquiries, provides advisory and referral services, and distributes publications. Services are provided free of charge. Contact: National Association of Women Artists, 41 Union Square, New York, NY 10003; 212-675-1616.

## Directories of Artists and Illustrators

The annual directories for artists who wish to sell their work also contain lists of artists' organizations that you can use to find them. These directories are available in most general bookstores, art supply stores, and public libraries.

- A new *Artist's Market* is available every year, with fresh information for artists about where to sell artwork, how to find an agent, and so on. The Resources section contains more than eight pages of artists' organizations in all geographical areas and styles of art. The book also contains a section on where to buy and sell clip art.

- Use the subject index in the *Guide to Literary Agents & Art/Photo Reps* to find an artist or photographer familiar with your topic. The *Guide* also contains a short list of organizations for writers, graphic artists, and photographers.

- *Humor and Cartoon Markets* by Bob Staake contains animation and art/design studios, syndicates, agents and representatives, and organizations of interest to anyone who wants to buy or sell humorous cartoons, illustrations, or written material.

All three directories are published by F&W Publications, 1507 Dana Avenue, Cincinnati, OH 45207; 513-531-2222. Distributed in Canada by McGraw-Hill, 300 Water Street, Whitby, Ontario, Canada, L1N 9B6. Distributed in Australia by Kirby Books, Private Bag Number 19, P.O. Alexandria, NSW 2015.

The *Creative Black Book* is used by advertising agencies to locate still photographers, illustrators, and stock agencies. New this year is the *Black Book on CD-ROM*, which lets you search through portfolios of artists and photographers. For more information, contact the multimedia product manager at 212-702-9700.

## Clip Art

"Clip art" is copyright-free artwork that you can reproduce in your publications and software. (Art directors and designers with limited budgets or short deadlines have been using clip art for years.) However, you cannot use someone else's clip art to create your own clip-art collection, and there may be other restrictions.

*Afrocentric Klips* offers several clip art diskettes for the PC or Macintosh with images of people "other than just white males." For more information, contact Afrocentric, P.O. Box 4375, Chicago, IL 60680; 312-463-6269.

*Compact Designs, Inc.*, offers PROclaim, a CD-ROM clip art library that includes 250 ready-to-use QuickTime video clips as well as animations, drawings, color photographs, music, and sound effects. For Macintosh only. For more information, write to Compact Designs, Inc., P.O. Box 8535, Gaithersburg, MD 20898; 310-869-3919.

*Culture Clips* offers images of African, Asian, and Hispanic people of all ages. The images are in EPS format and are usable on either the PC or the Macintosh. For more information, contact H&A Graphics, 3401 Woolsey Drive, Chevy Chase, MD 20815; 301-656-9628; fax: 301-718-4906.

*Dover Publications, Inc.*, offers spot illustrations, symbols, and patterns, as well as designs, borders, alphabets, type fonts, in over 700 copyright-free clip art books. Design styles range from Celtic and ancient Egyptian to Islamic and native American to Victorian and Art Deco. Especially useful: *Handbook of Pictorial Symbols* by Rudolph Modley and W. R. Myers (order no. 23357-X, $8.95).

New: *The Dover Electronic Clip Art Library,* vol. 1, James Nadler, composed of one 288-page book and four 3" diskettes for the PC (order no. 99931-9) or Macintosh (order no. 99932-7), $49.95.

For the complete publications list, write for the *Dover Pictorial Archive Catalog* (59062-3): Dover Publications, Inc., 31 East 2nd Street, Mineola, NY 11501.

*Form and Function* offers a clip art disk called WraptureReels One. The clip art on this disk comes in the form of video footage, 3-D animations, bullets for business charts, and audio clips. The media are stored in several formats, including QuickTime video, PICS, MacroMind Director, and AIFF. This clip art is intended for the Macintosh only.

For more information, write to Form and Function, 1595 17th Avenue, San Francisco, CA 94112; 415-664-4010.

*Innovation Advertising and Design* offers a large assortment of clip art images on disk (either IBM or Macintosh format and some on CD-ROM). They offer a sampler collection disk ($9.95, refundable towards your next purchase) that covers all of their available products. You can also purchase clip art files one at a time.

For a complete list of available products, contact Innovation Advertising and Design at 41 Mansfield Avenue, Essex Junction, VT 05452. Phone toll-free 800-255-0562 or 802-879-1164; fax: 802-878-1768.

*MacroMind Paracomp* offers multimedia clip art disks containing video clips, buttons, textures, backgrounds, and animations. Available for both the IBM and Mac formats, these disks also include sound effects and musical pieces. Contact MacroMind Paracomp, 600 Townsend Street, San Francisco, CA 94103; 415-442-0200.

*New Vision Technologies, Inc.,* offers Publisher's Task Force, a very large collection of black-and-white and color CGM line art. The user guide contains an excellent section called "Common Legal Questions Regarding the Application and Use of Presentation Task Force Clip Art."

For more information, contact New Vision Technologies, Inc., P.O. Box 5436, Station F, Nepean, Ontario, Canada K2C 3M1; 613-727-8184; fax: 613-727-8190.

*WordPerfect Corporation* offers three clip art packs—the "Business Pack," the "Holiday/Leisure Pack," and the "Government/Education Pack." Each pack contains over 400 images including templates, graphic aids, icons, maps, and cartoons.

For more information, write to WordPerfect Corporation, Attn.: Information Services, 1555 N. Technology Way, Orem, UT 84057-2399; 801-225-5000; fax: 801-222-5077.

## Cartoons

If you see a published cartoon you'd like to use in your application, find the artist's name and the syndicate handling his or her work (see Figure 9.2). Call the syndicate for price information and their requirements for a reproduction request. If there is no syndicate, contact the publication in which you found the cartoon. Rights to cartoons published in the *New Yorker*, for example, are handled by the *New Yorker*. (You can sometimes buy the cartoon or cover art outright, by the way, although the artist may retain reproduction rights.) Following are some of the largest cartoon syndicates.

*Cartoonists & Writers Syndicate*, 67 Riverside Drive, New York, NY 10024; 212-362-9256.

*Creators Syndicate*, 5777 West Century Blvd., Suite 700, Los Angeles, CA 90045; 213-337-7003.

*King Features Syndicate*, North American Syndicate, 235 East 45th Street, New York, NY 10017; 212-682-5600.

*Los Angeles Times Syndicate*, Times Mirror Square, Los Angeles, CA 90053; 213-237-7987, 800-528-4637.

*Newspapers Enterprise Association, Inc., and United Feature Syndicate*, 200 Park Avenue, New York, NY 10166; 212-692-3700, 800-221-4816.

**Figure 9.2  Finding the artist and syndicate** (© 1992 Bill Watterson, Universal Press Syndicate)

*Sandhill Arts* offers cartoons about business issues by nine well-known cartoonists (including such *New Yorker* artists as Leo Cullum, Sid Harris, and Al Ross). The cartoons are available for Macintosh (EPS) and PC (CGM). For more information, contact Sandhill Arts, P.O. Box 7298, Menlo Park, CA 94026; 800-854-0717, 415-327-0845; fax: 415-854-9739.

*Tribune Media Services, Inc.*, 64 East Concord Street, Orlando, FL 32801; 407-839-5600, 800-322-3068.

*Universal Press Syndicate*, 4900 Main Street, Kansas City, MO 64112; 816-932-6600.

*Washington Post Writers Group*, 1150 15th Street NW, Washington, DC 20071; 202-334-6375.

## Maps

If you need maps for your application, start with the federal government—federal maps may be copyright-free. Two government sources are:

- The *Library of Congress Geography and Map Division*, which has the largest collection of maps in the world, many of which can be reproduced. For more information, contact the Library of Congress Geography and Map Division, First and Independence Avenue SE, Washington, DC 20540; 202-707-6277.

- The *National Cartographic Information Center*, which offers topographic maps, charts, aerial and satellite photographs, satellite imagery, and geodetic control data. Contact the National Cartographic Information Center, Geological Survey, Department of the Interior, 507 National Center, Room 1-C-107, 12201 Sunrise Valley Drive, Reston, VA 22092; 703-860-6045.

Inexpensive maps may be available from state, province, and county governments as well. However, government maps are generally geological, land title, or tax maps, which may not be what you need. For specialized maps, see the following list of sources.

*Arrow Map, Inc.*, creates many maps of the Northeastern United States, as well as other parts of the country. For more information, contact Arrow Map, Inc., Myles Standish Industrial Park, 25 Constitution Drive, Taunton, MA 02780; 508-880-2880.

*Cartesia Software* offers county maps in *MapArt Vol. 2*, plus *U.S. Metro Area Maps* for 25 cities, including waterways, city limits, parks, and interstates. Also available are *Global Perspective Maps, U.S. & International,* and *World Data Bank.* Contact Cartesia, P.O. Box 757, S. Main Street, Lambertville, NJ 08530; 800-334-4291, 609-397-1611; fax 609-397-5724.

*Clip-Art Maps* offers *USA State-by-State, World Maps,* and *World Hot Spots.* Contact Bruce Jones Design, 31 St. James Avenue, Suite 1060B, Boston, MA 02116; 800-843-3873 or 617-350-6160; fax: 617-350-8764.

*DeLorme Mapping Company* has maps available for much of the Northern and Eastern United States, For more information, contact DeLorme Mapping Company, P.O. Box 298, Freeport, ME 04032; 800-227-1656, 207-865-4171.

*GeoSystems* offers the Worldwide Electronic Map Dataset, which provides the following: worldwide coverage down to street level in major cities; political boundaries, mountain ranges, bodies of water, cities, and roadways; latitude/longitude of map corners; place/name gazetteer. For more information, contact GeoSystems, 227 Granite Run Drive, Suite 100, Lancaster, PA 17601; 717-293-7473; fax: 717-293-7467.

*Hagstrom Map Company* offers business maps, road maps and atlases, foreign maps and language guides, nautical and aeronautical maps, and more. For more information, contact Hagstrom Map Company, Inc., 46-35 54th Road, Maspeth, NY 11378; 718-784-0055.

*Rand McNally* offers international and U.S. maps and guides, globes, atlases, travel videos, language help, and more. For more information, contact Rand McNally, 8255 North Central Park Avenue, Skokie, IL 60076; 708-329-8100. New York City location: 150 East 52nd Street (between Lexington and Third), New York, NY 10022; 212-758-7488.

## Reference Books

Although you might not want to draw illustrations or cartoons yourself, it helps to know what's involved. Following are some recommended books.

### Art and Illustration

The classic book on drawing is *The Natural Way to Draw* by Kimon Nicolaïdes (1969). Available in most bookstores or from Houghton Mifflin Company, Boston, MA.

## *Cartoons*

Gautier, Dick. *The Career Cartoonist* (1992), *The Creative Cartoonist*, and *Drawing and Cartooning 1,001 Faces* (1993), New York: Perigee Books (Putnam Publishing Group)—200 Madison Avenue, New York, NY 10016; 800-631-8571. These books are priceless.

Ishinomori, Shotaro. *Japan, Inc.: Introduction to Japanese Economics*. Berkeley, CA: University of California Press, 1988. The Japanese have a much different take on cartooning than most westerners. For example, they are happy to learn about economics using comic books.

McCloud, Scott. *Understanding Comics: The Invisible Art*, Northampton, MA: Kitchen Sink Press, 1993. Highly entertaining and highly recommended. Contact the publisher at: 320 Riverside Drive, Northampton, MA 01060.

Scott, Randall W. *Comic Books and Strips: An Information Sourcebook*, Phoenix, AZ: The Oryx Press, 1988. Lists comic books, periodicals and serials, books about comics, books that reprint comics, periodicals and journals, and library collections. Includes author, title, and subject indexes. Contact the publisher at: 4041 North Central Avenue, Suite 700, Phoenix, AZ 85012-3397.

## *Maps*

Harris, Sherwood (editor). *The New York Public Library Book of How and Where to Look It Up*. New York: Prentice Hall, 1991. See p. 160 for libraries with extensive map collections.

Makower, Joel (editor). *The Map Catalog: Every Kind of Map and Chart on Earth and Even Some above It*. New York: Vintage Books, 1986. Includes land, sky, and water maps, as well as lists of federal, state, and international map agencies. (A more recent edition is available.)

## MUSIC AND SOUND

To include sound or music, you can do any of the following:

- Get a license for an existing piece of music
- Hire a composer to write new music
- Create the music yourself with an automatic composition program
- License music from a music library
- Use a music and sound clip service

Before adding music to your presentation, there are a few things to consider. First, do you really need music? Music can be used to set a mood, to build excitement, to grab attention, or just to fill a void between visual frames. Second, can you find the right music? An otherwise perfect presentation can be ruined by the wrong selection. Using Verdi's "Anvil Chorus" in an interactive shoe-display kiosk might send shoppers marching to the doors, although it might work fine in the pots and pans department.

If you decide to have music, plan for it early: If you want to use existing music, you'll need time to get permission to use musical pieces from the publishers of the music. If you intend to have music written specially for your presentation, the composer needs time to write, debug, and record the music.

You may be able to use an "automatic composition" program, which lets you write your own musical pieces based upon a variety of musical styles and composers (Yavelow, 1992, p. 18). Since you're basically writing the music yourself, you don't have to worry about copyright infringement, and each piece of music is unique and fresh (though not necessarily good).

If you want to use a piece of music that is absolutely not covered by copyright, it must have been published before January 1, 1915 (Zimmerman, 1990, p. 22). However, probably few tunes from that era will fit into the presentation you're working on right now.

Following are lists of organizations and individuals that specialize in providing music and sound effects for industry.

## Musicians

Before you look outside your company for a composer or musician, ask around inside. Many programmers are also professional-level musicians. (Also, for some unknown reason, mathematicians are often musically inclined.)

The *American Federation of Musicians* represents union musicians. For more information or referrals, contact the American Federation of Musicians, 1500 Broadway, New York, NY 10036; 212-869-1330.

*Lettumplay* promotes noncommercial jazz performances, study groups, and outreach programs. They maintain a musical archive as well as a museum. They provide consulting services and conduct seminars and workshops. There is a fee for their services. For more information, contact Lettumplay, 418 Seventh Street NW, Washington, DC 20005; 202-724-4493.

The *Musicians National Hot Line Association* is a nonprofit employment organization for musicians and related occupations. The Association has a national employment information center and an education center for musicians, a database searching and matching facility, and a national hotline. The Association also makes referrals, but their services are primarily for musicians. For more information, contact the Musicians National Hot Line Association, 277 E. 6100 Street, Salt Lake City, UT 84107; 801-268-2000.

## Music Libraries and Clips

*AirCraft Music Library* offers a cross-section of recently produced contemporary American and global music tracks. You pay an annual fee that covers frequent CD updates and a cross-reference catalog service. For more information, contact the AirCraft Music Library, 162 Columbus Avenue, Boston MA 02116; 800-343-2514.

*Associated Production Music* offers a collection of over 300 CDs and 800 LPs, categorized by musical style and usage. Customers also have access to the APM "Hitline," which lets you preview musical selections right over the phone. For more information, contact Associated Production Music, 6255 Sunset Boulevard, Suite 820, Hollywood, CA 90028; 800-543-4276; in California: 213-461-3211; Hitline: 800-328-9797.

*Audio Action* offers fresh, original production music from around the world, "from the traditional to the outrageous." All tracks are offered on CD-ROM. For more information, contact Audio Action, 4444 Lakeside Drive, Suite 340, Burbank, CA 91505; 800-533-1293; in California: 818-845-8020; fax: 818-845-8039.

*Capitol/OGM Production Music* offers 10-, 30-, and 60-second-long versions and variations of several musical styles. For more information, contact Capitol/OGM Production Music, 6922 Hollywood Boulevard, Suite 718, Hollywood, CA 90028; 800-421-4163.

*Creative Support Services* offers hundreds of musical selections as well as sound effects on CD-ROM, reel-to-reel, cassette tape, DAT, and VHS hi-fi. Multiple library and educational discounts are available. Call for a free cassette or CD demo. For more information, contact Creative Support Services, 1950 Riverside Drive, Los Angeles, CA 90039; 800-468-6874; in California: 213-666-7968.

*FirstCom/Music House/Chappell* offers over two hundred hours of music and sound effects on CD-ROM. For more information, contact FirstCom/Music House/Chappell, 13747 Montfort Drive, Suite 220, Dallas, TX 75240; 800-858-8880, 214-934-2222, fax: 214-404-9656.

*Gefen Systems* offers the M & G Library Software, which is a database program for production music libraries. All libraries are cross-referenced by musical style, tempo, and category. The software is both IBM and Macintosh compatible. For more information, contact Gefen Systems, 6261 Variel, Suite C, Woodland Hills, CA 91367; 818-884-6294.

*Manhattan Production Music* offers dozens of CD-ROMs with original production music in such styles as jazz, rock, news and sports, and industrial. For more information, contact Manhattan Production Music, 355 West 52nd Street, New York, NY 10019; 212-333-5766.

*Network Music* offers a large selection of music on CD-ROM with fresh releases each month. They have a category called "Multimedia," which includes tracks designed specifically for use in business settings, meetings, and conventions. They also have thousands of sound effects available. For more information, contact *Network Music*, 15150 Avenue of Sciences, San Diego, CA 92128; 800-854-2075.

*NFL Films* offers the "NFL Films Library," available on CD-ROM, which contains hundreds of musical selections. Also available are personalized scores, editing, mixing, and sound transfers. For more information, contact NFL Films, 330 Fellowship Road, Mt. Laurel, NJ 08054; 609-778-1600.

*The Production Garden* offers thousands of music tracks and sound effects, and a knowledgeable and friendly staff ready to help with any questions and problems you might have. For more information, contact The Production Garden, 15335 San Pedro, Suite A, San Antonio, TX 78237; 800-247-5317.

*PROMUSIC, Inc.*, offers hundreds of CD-ROM selections, with 10 to 15 new selections added each month. They also offer music library management software for either IBM or Macintosh. For more information, contact PROMUSIC Inc., 941-A Clintmoore Road, Boca Raton, FL 33487; 407-995-0331.

*Screen Music International* offers over 25 hours of live orchestral music from the classical masters including Brahms and Beethoven (listen to the last four digits of their phone number). Also available are IBM and Macintosh databases and original scores. For more information, contact Screen Music International, 11684 Ventura Boulevard, Studio City, CA 91604; 818-985-9997.

*Signature Music Library* offers musical selections that are "especially suited for corporate and institutional productions." Call for a free CD demo. For more information, write to Signature Music Library, P.O. Box 98, Buchanan, MI 49107; 800-888-7151.

*SoperSound Music Library* claims to have the widest selection of "buy-out" production music available. Their selection runs from classical arrangements to high-tech industrial to folk, pop, and new-age music. Tracks are available on CD-ROM, DAT, cassettes, quarter-inch reel-to-reel, and records. For more information, write to SoperSound Music Library, P.O. Box 498, Palo Alto, CA 94302; 800-227-9980; in California, Alaska, or Hawaii: call collect 415-321-4022.

*Sound Ideas* offers a complete music and sound-effects library that is kept up to date with regular new releases. For more information, contact Sound Ideas, 105 West Beaver Creek Road, Richmond Hill, Ontario, Canada L4B1C6; 800-387-3030.

*TRF Music* offers thousands of musical clips on CD-ROM, tapes, and LPs. For more information, contact TRF Music, 747 Chestnut Ridge Road, Chestnut Ridge, NY 10977; 914-356-0800.

*Valentino Inc.,* offers the Valentino Music and Sound Effects Library. Call for a free catalog and CD demo. For more information, write to Valentino Inc., P.O. Box 534, Elmsford, NY 10523; 800-223-6278.

*Zedz Music* offers unique musical tracks and styles with limited distribution to assure your exclusivity. Call or write for a free demo. For more information, contact *Zedz Music,* 49 Hanover Street, Malden, MA 02148; 617-324-1989.

## Oral History

Oral history is an undeveloped area in multimedia, although it has been used in a few films. For example, Aardman Animations, an English claymation firm, uses oral history as the basis for some of their videos. (In claymation, the animators use figures made of modeling clay, which are moved a tiny bit for each individual frame of the video. After the frames are put together, the figures appear to move.) The most famous Aardman Animations piece is "Creature Comforts," a set of interviews with animals in an

English zoo. The tape containing these pieces, plus a documentary about the firm, is available in the United States from Expanded Entertainment, P.O. Box 25547, Los Angeles, CA 90025.

Nevertheless, a wealth of oral-history archives are available—check your local public and college libraries. Plus, you can easily interview people about the topic of your presentation yourself.

The *Columbia University Oral History Collection* has thousands of pages of edited transcripts of oral interviews on such subjects as national affairs, international relations, arts, welfare, business and labor, law, medicine, education, and religion. The original tapes are also available. For more information, contact the Butler Library, Columbia University Oral History Collection, P.O. Box 20, New York, NY 10027; 212-854-2273, -4012, or -7083.

Oral history tapes and transcripts are also available from:

- The *Library of Congress Motion Picture, Broadcasting, and Recorded Sound Division,* James Madison Memorial Building, Room 338, 101 Independence Avenue SE, Washington, DC 20540; 202-707-5840.

- The *National Archives and Records Administration, National Audio Visual Center,* 8700 Edgeworth Drive, Capitol Heights, MD 20743-3701; 301-763-1896.

- *New York Public Library, Donnell Library Center, Media Center,* 20 West 53rd Street, New York, NY 10019; 212-621-0609.

## Reference Books

### Music

Harris, Sherwood (editor). *The New York Public Library Book of How and Where to Look It Up.* New York: Prentice Hall, 1991.

Sadie, Stanley (editor). *The New Grove Dictionary of Music and Musicians.* 6th ed. 20 vols., New York: Macmillan, 1980.

### Speech

Elster, Charles Harrington. *There Is No Zoo in Zoology.* New York: Collier Books, Macmillan Publishing Company, 1988. Help with pronunciations.

Frank, Milo O. *How to Get Your Point across in 30 Seconds or Less.* New York: Simon and Schuster, 1986. This book contains information on how to develop verbal "hooks"—the most interesting and pithy ways to describe a situation.

*Pronouncing Dictionary of Proper Names*, 900 pp., $68 print. Contains 23,000 entries, including hard to pronounce names of places, celebrities, political and historical figures, companies and products, biblical names, and literary references. Contact Omnigraphics, Inc., Penobscot Bldg., Detroit, MI 48226; 800-234-1340. Also available in an electronic version. Call Frank Abate at 203-388-6664 for details.

## PHOTOGRAPHS

If your application requires location shots, note that city and state or province chambers of commerce or tourism bureaus are often happy to send you copyright- and cost-free photos.

Also, most photos taken by the U.S. government are in the public domain—those spectacular NASA photos of the back side of the Moon and the trips to Jupiter fall into this category, for example. Don't assume anything is copyright-free, however—check before using the photo.

If copyright-free photos don't meet your needs, hire a photographer or use stock photos. Listings follow.

### Photographers

The *American Society of Picture Professionals* is an organization of photographers, agents, designers, picture editors, researchers, librarians, curators, and historians. The society answers questions, provides reference services, distributes publications, and makes referrals. Some services are free. For more information, contact the American Society of Picture Professionals, P.O. Box 5283, Grand Central Station, New York, NY 10163-5283.

The *Professional Photographers of America* publishes a directory of photographers and can help you find other sources of information. Contact the Professional Photographers of America, 1090 Executive Way, Des Plaines, IL 60018; 312-372-3411.

### Photo Sources

*After Image* offers a collection of over 400,000 photos. Services are available to those seeking copyright release to publish photos. For more information, contact After Image, 3807 Wilshire Boulevard, Suite 250, Los Angeles, CA 90010; 213-480-1105.

*Animals Animals/Earth Scenes* offers a unique collection of animals and earth scenes (surprise!). Call for a free catalog. For more information, contact Animals Animals/Earth Scenes, 580 Broadway, Suite 1111, New York, NY 10012; 212-925-2110. There's a second location at 17 Railroad Avenue, Chatham, NY 12037; 518-392-5500.

*Archive Photos Stock Photo Library* and *Archive New Media* have over five million still photos and moving pictures spanning more than a century of photography. Subjects include places, newsreels, lifestyles, historical events, and movies. Photos are available in black and white or color; also available on CD-ROM. For more information, contact Archive Photos, 530 West 25th Street, New York, NY 10001; 800-285-4851, 212-675-0115, 212-620-3980; fax: 212-645-2137.

*The Comstock Encyclopedia of Stock Photography* offers thousands of photos on such topics as vacations and travel, sports, people, business metaphors, and much more. Photos are available on paper, CD-ROM, and via an online service. For more information, contact Comstock, The Comstock Building, 30 Irving Place, New York, NY 10003; 800-225-2727, 212-353-8600; fax: 212-353-3383.

*Culver Pictures Inc.*, offers over nine million historical stock photos, old prints, and historical illustrations as well as portraits, scenes, inventions, sports, and science. Also available are early theater, vaudeville, opera, and movie stills. For more information, contact Culver Pictures Inc., 150 West 22nd Street, Suite 300, New York, NY 10011; 212-645-1672; fax: 212-627-9112.

*Direct Stock* has tens of thousands of photographs available in many styles and subject matter. For more information, contact Direct Stock, 10 East 21st Street, New York, NY 10010; 212-979-6560; fax: 212-254-1204.

*D'pix, Inc.*, offers photos of backgrounds, designs, and textures, all available on diskette or CD-ROM (for Macintosh only). For more information, write to D'pix, Inc., P.O. Box 572, Columbus, OH 43216-7192; 800-238-3749, 614-299-7192; fax: 614-294-0002.

*The Image Bank, Inc.*, represents many outstanding photographers and markets photographs in over 65 locations throughout the world. They deal mainly in commercial advertising photography. For more information, contact The Image Bank, Inc., Williams Square, Suite 700, 5221 North O'Conner Boulevard, Irving, TX 75039; 214-432-3900, fax: 214-432-3960.

*Photo Researchers* has "hundreds of thousands" of photos of every imaginable subject and style. One subset is scientific photos—research, earth, astronomy and space, medicine, and so on. For more information, contact *Photo Researchers,* 60 East 56th Street, New York, NY 10022; 800-833-9033, 212-758-3420; fax: 212-355-0731.

*SUPERSTOCK, Inc.,* offers well over three hundred thousand photos of every conceivable subject. For more information, contact SUPERSTOCK, Inc., 11 West 19th Street, New York, NY 10011; 800-828-4545 (call for a catalogue); fax: 212-633-0408. There's another location at The Penthouse, 99 Osgood Place, San Francisco, CA 94133; 415-781-4433; fax: 415-781-8985.

## VIDEO, FILM, AND ANIMATION

If you have no videographers or film makers in-house (some home film makers can be quite good, especially after they read *John Hedgecoe's Complete Video Course: A Step-by-Step, Self-Instruction Guide to Making Great Videos* listed in Reference Books below), try the local arts college or the communications or art departments of the closest university. Students can sometimes be cajoled into doing your project as part of a work-study program or for extra credit.

If, on the other hand, you need a seriously professional job, use the following resources to find a film maker or videographer or, possibly, a usable clip.

*Note:* If you're creating a management or business application, you might want to look at the Video Arts business training videos for ideas and inspiration. These videos are educational and very funny—as well they might be, since many of them were written by and star John Cleese (post-*Monty Python*). For a catalog, contact Video Arts, 8614 W. Catalpa, Chicago, IL 60656; 800-553-0091.

### Film Makers and Videographers

Unless you live in a major metropolitan center, finding film makers and videographers may require some creative searching. In your phone company's *Yellow Pages,* look under "Audio-Visual Consultants," "Motion Picture

Producers and Studios," and "Video Production Services." If your *Yellow Pages* doesn't contain these types of listings, ask a recent bride (or her parents) who videotaped her wedding. Wedding photographers and videographers often have classical art and film educations that they would be happy to use for your project.

You can also contact local chapters of film and video trade unions. In the United States, contact the Screen Actors Guild (SAG), the American Federation of Television and Radio Artists (AFTRA), and the International Alliance of Theatrical Stage Employees & Motion Picture Machine Operators of the United States and Canada (IATSE).

For names, addresses, and phone numbers of independent film and video producers, plus trained animals, props, old cars, equipment, music, and everything else you can think of, get a copy of the *Motion Picture TV and Theatre Directory*. This semiannual directory, in its sixty-eighth edition in 1994, contains listings from all over the United States. For more information, contact Motion Picture Enterprises Publications, Inc., P.O. Box 276, Tarrytown, NY 10591-0276. The directory costs $8.95 plus $3.00 shipping and handling (New York state residents add 99¢ for sales tax).

Canada has some of the best documentary film makers in the world. For names and more information, contact Telefilm Canada, 2 Bloor Street, Toronto, Ontario, Canada M4W 3E2; voice: 416-973-6436.

For the slickest videographers and film makers, look to the advertising industry. Available now from the publishers of the *Creative Black Book* is *Spot Check,* which advertising agencies use to find the names of the production houses and film makers who have made particular TV advertisements. For more information, contact the Creative Black Books multimedia product manager at 212-702-9700.

## Film and Video Organizations

*Film/Video Arts* provides film and video training, conducts seminars, makes referrals, lends material and equipment, and provides postproduction facilities and financial assistance. For more information, contact Film/Video Arts, 817 Broadway, New York, NY 10003; 212-673-9361.

The *International Communications Industries Association* answers questions, makes referrals, and conducts annual conventions and exhibits of the latest communication technology. For more information, contact the International Communications Industries Association, 3150 Spring Street, Fairfax, VA 22031; 703-273-7200.

*Northwest Film Study Center* provides film and video resource information, sponsors exhibitions, and offers advisory and referral services. For more information, contact the Northwest Film Study Center, 1219 Southwest Park Avenue, Portland, OR 97208; 503-221-1156.

The *Recording Industry Association of America* is a trade association that will answer questions, provide references, and distribute publications. Most services are free. For more information, contact the Recording Industry Association of America, 888 Seventh Avenue, New York, NY 10106; 212-765-4330.

The *University Film and Video Association* is an international organization concerned with film. They answer your questions and provide referral and advisory services. Most services are free. For more information, contact the University of Southern Illinios, Department of Cinema and Photography, University Film and Video Association, Carbondale, IL 62901; 618-453-2365.

The *Videotape Production Association* answers questions, provides advisory and referral services, and provides speakers for meetings. Most services are free. For more information, contact the Videotape Production Association, 63 West 83rd Street, New York, NY 10024; 212-986-0289.

## Video Clips

If you don't need to shoot your own video clips, use commercial video clips or video available from public agencies and sources. For example:

The *Donnell Library Center* in New York has a general collection of films, recordings, and other media. For more information, contact the New York Public Library, Donnell Library Center, Media Center, 20 West 53rd Street, New York, NY 10019; 212-621-0609.

The *Library of Congress Motion Picture, Broadcasting, and Recorded Sound Division* houses an international collection of over 100,000 films and 1.6 million sound recordings, including radio from the 1920s to the present and television from 1948 to the present. For more information, contact the Library of Congress Motion Picture, Broadcasting, and Recorded Sound Division, James Madison Memorial Building, Room 338, 101 Independence Avenue SE, Washington, DC 20540; 202-707-5840.

The *National Audio Visual Center* is a repository of all unclassified audio-visual materials produced by or for federal government agencies. The Center answers questions and rents or sells materials. For more information, contact the National Archives and Records Administration, National Audio Visual Center, 8700 Edgeworth Drive, Capitol Heights, MD 20743-3701; 301-763-1896.

## Hardware, Software

Following are short lists of hardware and software used to develop multimedia projects. For more detailed information, you might want to subscribe to the multimedia periodicals listed in Multimedia.

### Software

*Adobe Systems, Inc.*, offers Premiere Version 2 for Macintosh. Premiere software lets you combine video, audio, animation, and still images for desktop presentations. For more information, contact Adobe Systems, Inc., 1585 Charleston Road, P.O. Box 7900, Mountain View, CA 94039-7900.

*Asymetrix Corporation* offers Compel!, which lets you incorporate sound, video, and animation into your presentations. You can build simple slide shows to complex, interactive multimedia presentations with Compel! For more information, contact Asymetrix Corporation, 110 110th Avenue NE, Suite 700, Bellevue, WA 98004; 800-448-6543, 206-462-0501; fax: 206-462-0501.

### Hardware

*Intel Corporation* offers the Smart Video Recorder, which lets you create, edit, and incorporate PC-video into your presentations. For more information, contact Intel Corporation, 5200 North East Elam Young Parkway, Hillsboro, OR 97124-6497; product information: United States and Canada: 800-538-3373; in Europe: +44-(0)793-431155; worldwide: 503-629-7354.

*RasterOps Corporation* offers a wide assortment of video and color boards for PCs, Macintosh, and Sun stations. For more information, contact RasterOps Corporation: 800-729-2656.

*Videomail, Inc.*, offers the DigiTV, a digital TV board for the PC, which lets you watch TV on your PC. For more information, contact Videomail, Inc., 568-4 Weddell Drive, Sunnyvale, CA 94089; 408-747-0223.

## Reference Books

### Animation

In the United States, the word "animation" brings up images of Saturday morning children's cartoons (although the double entendres in some of the older cartoons can, when you watch them as an adult, be a bit of a shock). However, animation can be used to dramatic and heart-wrenching effect. One example is *When the Wind Blows*, a 1987 80-minute film directed by Jimmy T. Murkami, produced by John Coates, and available from International Video Entertainment.

Following are some recommended books on animation.

Gray, Milton. *Cartoon Animation: Introduction to a Career.* San Diego, CA: A Lion's Den Publication, 1991. Contact: Al Lowenheim, Publisher, 4845 Ronson Court, San Diego, CA 92111; 619-496-8550.

Noake, Roger. *Animation Techniques: Planning and Producing Animation with Today's Technologies.* Secaucus, NJ: Chartwell Books, 1988. Lots of information about the techniques that have been used to create animation, from drawing on film stock to computer programs. Includes many color illustrations and case studies. Not a how-to book, however. Contact the publisher at: Chartwell Books, Inc., 110 Enterprise Ave., Secaucus, NJ 07094.

Singer, Bob. *How to Draw Animation Storyboards.* Las Vegas: CB Publications/Bill Barry Enterprises, 1992. Contact the publisher at: 3800 S. Decatur Boulevard, Suite 248, Las Vegas, NV 89103; voice: 702-253-9583; fax: 702-253-6128.

White, Tony. *The Animator's Workbook.* New York: Watson-Guptill Publications, 1988.

### Film and Video

Hedgecoe, John. *John Hedgecoe's Complete Video Course: A Step-by-Step, Self-Instruction Guide to Making Great Videos.* New York: Fireside Books, 1989.

Katz, Steven D. *Film Directing Shot by Shot: Visualizing from Concept to Screen.* Studio City, CA: Michael Wiese Productions, 1991. Contact the publisher at: 3960 Laurel Canyon Boulevard, Suite 331, Studio City, CA 91604.

Konigsberg, Ira. *The Complete Film Dictionary.* New York: NAL Penguin, 1987.

Lipton, Lenny. *Independent Film Making.* New York: Fireside Books, 1972. Out of print but available in libraries and used-book shops.

Monaco, James, *How to Read a Film: The Art, Technology, Language, History, and Theory of Film and Media.* New York: Oxford University Press, 1981.

Weiskamp, Keith. *How to Digitize Video.* New York: John Wiley & Sons, 1994. According to the promotion piece, the book is "the complete hands-on guide to capturing and running digital moves on a PC or Mac. The authors show how to digitize footage from existing video tapes, laser discs, and other analog media." Includes a CD-ROM with QuickTime videos that can be played on either PCs or Macintoshes.

### Storyboards and Screenwriting

Field, Syd. *Screenplay: The Foundations of Screenwriting: A Step-by-Step Guide from Concept to Finished Script.* New York: Dell Publishing, 1982.

Shay, Don, and Jody Duncan. *The Making of Jurassic Park.* New York: Ballantine Books, 1993. The last section of the book is the set of storyboards for the film.

## RESOURCES

## Copyright

Following are organizations, government agencies, articles, and books related to copyright issues.

### Organizations

*The Authors Guild, Inc.,* has always fought for better copyright terms for its members. The Guild is currently working on an authors' electronic rights project. Contact them at 330 West 42nd Street, New York, NY 10036-6902; 212-563-5904; fax: 212-564-8363.

*The Interactive Multimedia Association* is the primary trade organization for multimedia developers. (See Multimedia and Design Organizations). One of the IMA's services is the Intellectual Property Project, from which is expected the *IMA Guide to Intellectual Property in the Multimedia Age.* For more information, contact Interactive Multimedia Association, 3 Church Circle, Suite 800, Annapolis, MD 21401-1933; voice: 410-626-1380; fax: 410-263-0590.

*Volunteer Lawyers for the Arts* offers legal help to artists, writers, musicians, and other creative people, provided that they meet the low-income requirements. VLA also publishes useful business-form books, legal guides, and sample contracts (no income requirements). Contact VLA at 1 East 53rd Street, 6th Floor, New York, NY 10022; 212-319-2787.

### Government Agencies

*Library of Congress,* Information Section, LM-455, Copyright Office, Washington, DC 20559. Ask for information about copyrights.

*Register of Copyrights,* Copyright Office, Library of Congress, Washington, DC 20559. Call 202-707-9100 for forms or 202-707-3000 for information.

### Articles and Publications

Smith, Eric. *Copyright Industries in the U.S. Economy.* Washington, D.C.: International Intellectual Property Alliance, 1990. Contact the publisher at: 1300 Nineteenth Street, NW, Suite 350, Washington, DC 20036; fax: 202-872-0546.

Divoky, Diane. "Copyrights And Wrongs: You Don't Need a Lawyer to Avoid Legal Conflicts." *Publish,* September/October 1986, p. 62.

Sims, Calvin. "Wounded by Patent Piracy . . . U.S. Laws Offer Less Protection Than Those Of Major Trading Partners." *New York Times,* May 13, 1987, p. D-1.

Horowitz, Joy. "Hollywood Law: Whose Idea Is It, Anyway?" *New York Times,* March 15, 1992, p. 2-1.

Andrews, Edmund L. "Trademark Bill Passed By House." *New York Times,* October 20, 1988, p. D-1.

### Books

Dorr, Robert C., and Christopher H. Munch (editors). *Protecting Trade Secrets, Patents, Copyrights, and Trademarks*. 1990. Reprint. Colorado Springs, CO: Wiley Law Publications, 1992.

Heller, Steven, and Julie Lasky. *Borrowed Design: Use and Abuse of Historical Form*. New York: Van Nostrand Reinhold, 1993.

Lee, Lewis C., and J. Scott Davidson. *Managing Intellectual Property Rights*. Colorado Springs, CO: Wiley Law Publications, 1993. According to the marketing literature, contains answers to all of your intellectual property questions. Ideal for engineers, business managers, corporate attorneys, business executives, intellectual property attorneys.

Remer, Daniel, and Stephen Elias. *Legal Care for Your Software: A Step-by-Step Guide for Computer Software Writers and Publishers*. 3d ed. Berkeley, CA: Nolo Press, 1987. If you don't already have this book on your shelf, you should.

University of Chicago Press. *The Chicago Manual of Style*. 14th ed. Chicago: The University of Chicago Press, 1993. Chapter 4, "Rights and Permissions," includes sample permission letters and a cogent description of the *fair use* doctrine, which "allows authors to quote from other authors' work or to reproduce small amounts of graphic or pictorial material for the purposes of review or criticism or to illustrate or buttress their own points. Authors invoking fair use should transcribe accurately and give credit to their sources. They should not quote out of context, making the authors of the quoted passage seem to be saying something opposite to, or different from, what was intended" (p. 146).

## Multimedia Conferences

In a field as new as multimedia and interactive computing, conferences and expositions are sometimes the best source of new information. Following are a few of the conferences we've heard about.

The 1994 *Electronic Books International Conference* was, according to its sponsors, "the world's first annual conference on the emergence of electronic books and their impacts on traditional information media, markets, and applications." For information on the world's second conference, contact

Meckler, Artillery House, Artillery Row, London, England SW1P 1RT; voice: 071-976-0405; fax: 071-976-0506.

*IEEE Computer Society's Technical Committee on Multimedia Computing* sponsors the annual International Conference on Multimedia Computing and Systems. For more information, contact IEEE Computer Society, 1730 Massachusetts Avenue, NW, Washington, DC 20036-1992.

Ziff Institute sponsored the *Interactive '94 Conference and Expo* in San Jose, California, for corporate developers and users of interactive multimedia and training programs. For information on upcoming conferences, contact Ziff Institute, 25 First Street, Cambridge, MA 02141-9819; voice: 800-34-TRAIN or 617-252-5187.

*The Intermedia Conference and Exposition on Multimedia and CD-ROM* is for "anyone in publishing, education, entertainment, training, or any information-intensive field" who wants to know more about multimedia. For information, contact Intermedia Customer Service, Reed Exhibition Companies, 999 Summer Street, Stamford, CT 06905; 203-352-8250.

ACM, in cooperation with the IEEE Communications Society, sponsored *Multimedia '94: The International Conference and Exposition on Multimedia.* For future conferences, contact ACM (see Multimedia and Design Organizations) or the conference management company: Multimedia Conference, Danieli & O'Keefe Associates, Inc., 490 Boston Post Road, Sudbury, MA 01776; voice: 800-524-1851; fax: 508-443-4715; e-mail: Elisa_van_ Dam.DOK@ Notes.compuserve.com.

*NAB MultiMedia World,* sponsored by the National Association of Broadcasters and the International Multimedia Association, offers an "in-depth look at the emerging relationships between multimedia and broadcast communications." Contact NAB at 1771 N Street NW, Washington, DC 20036-2891; 202-429-5400.

*The Virtual Reality '94 Conference and Exhibition* included the Virtual Reality Venture Capital Forum and the Virtual Reality Video Festival as well as various workshops and sessions. For information on future conferences, contact Mecklermedia, 11 Ferry Lane West, Westport, CT 06880; voice: 800-632-5537 or 203-226-6967; fax: 800-858-3144 or 203-454-5840; e-mail: meckler@jvnc.net on Internet, 70373,616 on CompuServe, or Meckler on AppleLink.

*VRST'94: The Conference on Virtual Reality Software and Technology,* was a high-quality forum for innovative virtual reality research and development, according to its sponsors. The conference is designed to bring together researchers, developers, and users of VR for a four-day program. Since the field of VR is still evolving, the scope of the conference is broad. Among the areas that VRST seminars cover are:

- Software architectures for VR
- VR interaction and navigation techniques
- Tools and techniques for modeling VR systems
- Distributed VR systems
- Motion tracking
- Telepresence and telerobotics
- Spatial audio
- VR input and output devices
- Innovative applications of VR
- Human factors of VR
- Evaluation of VR techniques and systems

For more information, contact: Dr. Gurminder Singh, Institute of Systems Science, National University of Singapore, Kent Ridge, Singapore 0511; tel: (65) 772 3651; fax: (65) 774 4998; e-mail addresses: Gsingh@iss.nus.sg, Gsingh.CHI@xerox.com.

## Multimedia and Design Organizations

*ACM,* Association for Computing Machinery, has these multimedia-related special interest groups:

- SIGGRAPH, graphics
- SIGCHI, computer-human interaction
- SIGLINK, hypertext and hypermedia
- SIGMULTIMEDIA

Also available: SOUND, a new electronic forum for the exchange of information on software, algorithms, hardware, and applications for digitally generated or manipulated audio signals.

For more information, contact ACM, 1515 Broadway, New York, NY 10036; voice: 212-626-0500; fax: 212-944-1318; e-mail: ACMHELP@ACMVM.Bitnet. In Europe: ACM, Avenue Marcel Thiry 204, 1200 Brussels, Belgium; voice: 32 2 774 9602; fax: 32 2 774 9690; e-mail: ACM_EUROPE@ACM.ORG.

The membership of the *Association for Software Design* is primarily software interface designers. Contact the Association for Software Design at 2120 Bonar Street, Berkeley, CA 94702; voice: 800-743-9415; e-mail: asd-members@pcd.stanford.edu.

*IICS*, the International Interactive Communications Society, was formed in 1985 as the professional organization of the interactive and multimedia technologies community. Membership is approximately 2,000 with 20 local chapters in the United States, Canada, Japan, and Europe. Contact IICS Executive Office, 14657 Southwest Teal Boulevard, Beaverton, OR 97007; voice: 503-579-4427; fax: 503-579-6272.

*IMA:* The mission of the Interactive Multimedia Association is "to promote the development of interactive multimedia applications and reduce barriers to the widespread use of multimedia technology." IMA sponsors projects on intellectual property and multimedia compatibility and publishes a bimonthly trade journal called *Interactive Multimedia News*. The journal is one of the best sources of information on copyright, trademark, and patent law as it relates to multimedia. Contact IMA at 3 Church Circle, Suite 800, Annapolis, MD 21401-1933; voice: 410-626-1380; fax: 410-263-0590; Brian Marquardt, compatibility project director: 71431,3312 or 6330855@mcimail.com; Brian Kahin, intellectual property project director: kahin@delphi.com.

*MDG*, Multimedia Development Group, offers networking and client-referral programs; seminars and workshops; member product showcases; an online BBS; a membership directory; and access to capital sources, market research, and professional services. Contact MDG at 2501 Mariposa Street, San Francisco, CA 94110; voice: 415-553-2300; fax: 415-553-2403.

The *Trade Show Bureau* offers research information on what makes tradeshow exhibits memorable. Contact the Trade Show Bureau at 1660 Lincoln Street, Suite 2080, Denver, CO 80264; voice: 303-860-7626; fax: 303-860-7479.

## Multimedia Development Books

Aston, Robert, and Joyce Schwarz (editors). *Multimedia: Gateway to the Next Millenium.* Cambridge, MA: AP Professional, 1994.

Aukstakalnic, Steve, and David Blatner. *Silicon Mirage: The Art and Science of Virtual Reality,* Peachpit Press, Berkeley, CA: 1992 (ISBN 0-938151-82-7).

Durand R. Begault, *3-D Sound for Virtual Reality and Multimedia Applications.* Cambridge, MA: AP Professional, 1994.

Badgett, Tom, and Corey Sandler. *Creating Multimedia on Your PC.* New York: John Wiley & Sons, 1994. Contains specific instructions for Action! and IconAuthor, as well as overview and design information. Also includes a short clip video, music, and art directory.

Caffarelli, Fabrizio, and Deirdre Straughan. *Publish Yourself on CD-ROM: Mastering CDs for Multimedia.* New York: Random House, 1992. Includes a CD-ROM with an authoring program. Watch out for the bad translations in the authoring program documentation. However, the rest of the book is excellent.

Fisher, Scott. *Multimedia Authoring: Building and Developing Documents.* Cambridge, MA: AP Professional, 1994.

Krueger, Myron W. *Artificial Reality II.* Reading, MA: Addison-Wesley, 1991.

Laurel, Brenda. *Computers as Theatre.* Reading, MA: Addison-Wesley, 1991.

Luther, Arch C. *Authoring Interactive Multimedia.* Cambridge, MA: AP Professional, 1994.

Radecki, Steven. *Multimedia with Quicktime.* Cambridge, MA: AP Professional, 1993.

Watkins, Christopher D., and Stephen R. Marenka. *Virtual Reality Excursions.* Cambridge, MA: AP Professional, 1994. Includes 3-D glasses.

Wexelblat, Alan. *Virtual Reality: Applications and Explorations.* Cambridge, MA: AP Professional, 1993.

Wodaski, Ron. *Multimedia Madness!* Carmel, IN: Sams Publishing, 1992.

Yager, Tom. *The Multimedia Production Handbook for the PC, Macintosh, and Amiga.* Cambridge, MA: AP Professional, 1993.

## Multimedia Periodicals

*Advanced Imaging: Solutions for the Electronic Imaging Professional.* Published monthly by PTN Publishing Co., 445 Broad Hollow Road, Melville, NY 11747.

*CD-ROM Today: The Leading Guide to PC and Mac Multimedia.* Published bimonthly by GP Publications, Inc., 23-00 Route 208, Fair Lawn, NJ 07410; 201-703-9505.

*Computer Pictures: For Creators and Designers of Digital Graphics, Multimedia, and Prepress Production.* Published bimonthly by Montage Publishing, Inc., 701 Westchester Avenue, White Plains, NY 10604.

*Multimedia Solutions.* Published bimonthly by IBM Multimedia Solutions, 4111 Northside Parkway, Internal Zip: HO4L1, Atlanta, GA 30327; fax: 404-238-4298.

*Multimedia Today: The Sourcebook for Multimedia* publishes regular and comprehensive lists of resources. Included (from vol. ii, issue 2, November 1993) are:

- *Multimedia production tools:* animation; desktop presentations; development and other tools; drawing and painting programs; image processing; media catalogs; modeling and rendering; music software; special effects and clip art; video editing and production.

- *Multimedia peripherals:* accelerators and file compression/decompression; audio/video controllers; cameras; digitizers and frame grabbers; encoders/decoders and scan converters; input devices; monitors; multimedia systems; multimedia upgrade kits; music hardware; optical drives; projection; scanners; video processors; other.

- *Multimedia and CD-ROM titles*

There are over 1,400 total listings. For more information, or to get a listing for your own company or product, contact Redgate Communications Corporation, 660 Beachland Boulevard, Vero Beach, FL 32963, 407-231-6904; fax: 407-231-7872.

*Multimedia Week: The Executive Report on Business Opportunities in the Multimedia Marketplace.* Published weekly by Phillips Business Information, Inc., 1201 Seven Locks Road, P.O. Box 61130, Potomac, MD 20854; 310-424-3338.

*Multimedium!,* a quarterly reference guide and product directory for Microsoft Windows multimedia projects, is available from Affinity Publishing at 206-281-0089; fax: 206-281-1799.

*New Media.* Published monthly by HyperMedia Communications Inc. (HCI), 901 Mariner's Island Blvd., Suite 365, San Mateo, CA 94404; 415-573-5170.

*Publish: The Magazine for Electronic Publishing Professionals,* is directed to desktop publishing professionals, but each issue contains an article or two on multimedia and interactive documents. If you're entering the multimedia field from the direction of graphic arts or text, contact Publish, 501 Second Street, San Francisco, CA 94107; voice: 415-978-3280; fax: 415-495-2354; e-mail: PUBLISH.MAG on AppleLink, Publish on MCI Mail, 76127,205 on CompuServe, and publish on the Well.

*Videography* covers all areas of video production. The December issue is a buyer's guide of production houses, hardware, and software. For subscription information, contact Videography at 2 Park Avenue, Suite 1820, New York, NY 10016; 212-779-1919.

*Wired*, the most fashionable computer magazine, is published monthly by Wired Ventures Ltd., 544 Second Street, San Francisco, CA 94107-1427; voice: 415-904-0660; fax: 415-904-0669; e-mail: editor@wired.com (ISSN 1059-1028).

## Online Resources

### CompuServe

CompuServe's photography forum is PHOTOFORUM. Look for:

- Overviews of the copyright process in Library 12, "Stock/ProFiles," ASMPCO.TXT
- Starting a stock photo business in JIMPIC.CO, Library 12
- Tips on getting model and property releases in MODELR.THD, Library 13, "Business/Marketing"

### Microsoft

Microsoft has created the Multimedia Developer Relations group (MMDRG) to support multimedia developers. Contact MMDRG in the WINMM forum on CompuServe or e-mail specific questions to MMDINFO@microsoft.com.

## Schools Offering Multimedia

The *Brooks Institute* is a private college with a strong concentration on the visual arts. For more information on the Advanced Imaging Group at Brooks Institute, write to Brooks Institute Advanced Imaging Group, 801 Alston Road, Santa Barbara, CA 93108-9987; 805-966-3888.

' The *Center for Creative Imaging* offers short-term classes and seminars for professional photographers on all aspects of photography, both digital and traditional. For more information, contact the Center for Creative Imaging, 51 Mechanic Street, Camden, ME 04843; 800-428-7400.

The *Massachusetts Institute of Technology's Media Laboratory* is the source of many hardware, software, and intellectual breakthroughs in multimedia and virtual reality. For lists of current projects ad publications, contact the Media Laboratory, Communications and Sponsor Relations, 20 Ames Street, Room E15-234, Cambridge, MA 02139; 617-253-0338; fax: 617-258-6264.

*New York University* offers an Interactive Telecommunications Program through the Tisch School of the Arts. Course offerings include "Simulations and Presentations," "Virtual Space I: 3D Modeling and Imaging," "Issues in Interactive Media," "Copyright, Intellectual Property and the New Technologies," and "Local Area Networks." For more information, contact The Interactive Telecommunications Program, Tisch School of the Arts, Institute of Film and Television, 721 Broadway, Fourth Floor, New York, NY 10003; 212-998-1880.

The *Georgia Institute of Technology* offers an extensive series of courses dealing with various multimedia subjects. For more information, contact the Continuing Education Department at Georgia Institute of Technology, P.O. Box 93636, Atlanta, GA 30377; fax: 404-894-8925.

The *University of Maryland at College Park* sponsors many multimedia projects, research laboratories, classes, and an annual symposium. Contact the Human-Computer Interaction Laboratory, University of Maryland, College Park, MD 20742; voice: 301-405-2104; e-mail: hcil-info@cs.umd.edu.

For Internet ftp access to information about the HCIL, connect as follows:

```
% ftp ftp.cs.umd.edu
```

Log in as anonymous and use your e-mail address as the password. Change directories:

```
cd pub/hcil
```

Look through the files, if desired, using `ls -l`. Download the files that interest you with get (individual files—`get filename`) or `mget` (more than one file by name—`mget file1 file2 file3...`).

The *University of New South Wales* offers multimedia at both undergraduate and postgraduate levels. Contact Eric Gidney, School of Media Art, The University of New South Wales, P.O. Box 259, Paddington NSW 2021, Australia; fax: +61 2 550 2140; e-mail: e.gidney@unsw.edu.au.

The *University of Notre Dame* offers courses in multimedia. Contact the Department of Art, Art History, and Design, University of Notre Dame, Notre Dame, IN 46556-5639. You can also call John Sherman, design instructor, at 219-631-7175; e-mail: john.f.sherman.1@nd.edu.

## Software Standards and Tools

### Apple Computer

Some of the tools and resources available for Apple systems are:

- *Apple Media Tool* for fast prototyping and production of multimedia projects by nonprogrammers.
- *Apple Media Tool Programming Environment*, which lets programmers add functionality to Apple Media Tool projects that were prototyped by nonprogrammers.
- *Apple Multimedia Information Mailing*, a quarterly subscription package on multimedia topics.
- *Author's Solution for Interactive Electronic Books*, which lets sophisticated users create online books. Includes HyperCard and the Voyager Expanded Book Toolkit.
- *QuickTime Developer's Kit*, which includes compression and fine-tuning tools for QuickTime on Macintoshes.
- *QuickTime for Windows Development Kit*, which lets programmers add QuickTime support to Microsoft Windows applications.
- *QuickTime Movie Exchange Toolkit*, which lets programmers convert video created on IBM RS6000, DEC VAX, SGI, Sun-4, Cray YMP, and MS-DOS to Macintosh format.
- *Sound Manager Developer's Kit*, which lets programmers add high-quality audio to applications.
- *The CD-ROM Developer's Lab*, a comprehensive multimedia reference guide on CD-ROM.

Contact ADPA, Apple Computer, Inc., P.O. Box 319, Buffalo, NY 14207-0319; voice: 800-282-2732 United States, 800-637-0029 Canada, 716-871-6555 international; fax: 716-871-6511.

## IBM

IBM, *CUA Guide to Multimedia User Interface Design*, 1992 (part no. S41G-2922-00). To order, call IBM Publications at 800-879-2755. Credit cards are accepted. Make sure you write down your requisition order number.

## MPC

For information about the Multimedia PC specifications, contact Managing Director, Multimedia PC Marketing Council, Inc., 1730 M Street NW, Suite 707, Washington, DC 20036; 202-331-0494.

### Scientific Visualization Standards

Joel Welling of the Pittsburgh Supercomputing Center wrote a set of "Truth-in-Packaging Guidelines for Scientific Visualization," which he published on the Internet in 1993.[1] They are as follows.

I proposed these guidelines for discussion by the NSF Supercomputing MetaCenter Visualization community in June of 1993, as a result of a meeting at the San Diego Supercomputing Center in April of that year.

They are a result of my own experience and discussions at that meeting. The goal of the guidelines is to avoid misunderstanding of the scientific content of high-end scientific visualizations. It's worth pointing out that these ideas apply to end-product, packaged-for-release visualizations, not for the visualizations that scientists use in their own work, as they presumably know the content of that work already.

1.  Units, time scales, and other quantitative data should be provided, either within the visualization or in the accompanying titles or narration.

2.  Camera motion, color maps, and other visualization parameters should not be deliberately chosen to conceal or minimize a weakness or error in the data.

---

[1] Copyright Joel Wellington, 1993: Permission is granted for the free distribution of these guidelines, so long as attribution is given. For more information, contact Joel Welling, Pittsburg Supercomputing Center, 4400 Fifth Avenue, Pittsburgh, PA 15213; e-mail: welling@psc.edu.

3. The limits of the resolution of the calculation should be visible, either by showing the computational grid or by using a shading scheme that shows the resolution. The appearance of the final visualization should not give the impression that the calculation is more or less accurate than it is.

4. If smoothing is used to improve the quality of the data for visualization, the fact should be noted, and unsmoothed results should be presented for comparison.

5. Visualizations based on "massaged" data should mention the type and extent of the massaging.

6. Visualizations that are not based on a physical model, for example those constructed "from scratch" using modeling and choreography software, should not give the impression that they are based on a physical model.

7. If it is possibly ambiguous, the visualization or narration should note which data come from physical measurements and which are computer generated. It is the goal of good scientific writing to allow an informed reader to reproduce the results a well-written paper presents. This is a lot to ask of an animated visualization without an associated text document, but it is reasonable to hope that a scientifically literate viewer familiar with the field of science involved can gain a rough understanding of the methods and limits of a scientific work from viewing a visualization of that work.

### Standards Ignored

For an amusing demonstration of what happens when you ignore Welling's rules, see Wayne Lytle's video clip, "The Dangers of Glitziness and Other Visualization Faux Pas," on the ACM SIGGRAPH Video Review #91 and 92. To order or for more information, contact First Priority, P.O. Box 576, Itasca, IL 60143-0576; 800-523-5503 or 708-250-0807. The tape costs $50 plus $10 for shipping and handling for ACM members or $60 plus $10 shipping and handling for nonmembers.

## REFERENCES

Fox, Robert. "News Track: On the CD-ROM Front." *Communications of the ACM,* June 1994, vol. 37, no. 6, p. 9.

Shay, Don, and Jody Duncan. *The Making of Jurassic Park.* New York: Ballantine Books, 1993.

Shelton, S. M. "Script Design for Information Film and Video." *Technical Communication,* vol. 40, no. 4, pp. 655–663.

Yavelow, Christopher. "Be a Composer, Save Big Money." *New Media,* July 1992, pp. 18–19.

Zimmerman, Barbara. "Corporations Pay the Piper for Music Copyright Violations." *AV Video, October 1990, pp. 22–27.*

# Credits

Following is a list of the software and hardware vendors that either gave or lent us products during the writing of this book.

## SOFTWARE

*Alpha Software Corporation,* 168 Middlesex Turnpike, Burlington, MA 01803. *Alpha Four Version 2.1.*

*askSam Systems,* P.O. Box 1428, Perry, FL 32347; voice: 800-800-1997 or 904-584-6590; fax: 904-584-7481. *askSam for Windows.*

*Asymetrix Corporation,* 110 110th Avenue N.E., Suite 700, Bellevue, WA 98004; voice: 800-448-6543; fax: 206-637-1504. *Multimedia ToolBook.*

*Autodesk,* 11911 N. Craig Parkway South, Bothell, WA 98011. *AutoCAD, Autodesk Animator,* and *AutoSketch.* Many of the vector-based illustrations in this book were created using AutoCAD and AutoSketch.

*Cognetics Corporation,* 51 Everatt Drive, Suite 103B, P.O. Box 386, Princeton Junction, NJ 08550. *HyperTies.*

*Davidson & Associates, Inc.,* P.O. Box 2961, Torrance, CA 90509. *Headline Harry.*

*Frame Technology Corporation,* 1010 Rincom Circle, San Jose, CA 95131. *Framemaker for Windows.*

*ICOM Simulations, Inc.,* 648 South Wheeling Road, Wheeling IL 60090. *Rightpaint, Sherlock Holmes,* and *Squeegee.* Many of the bitmap-based illustrations for this book were created using Rightpaint.

*Intuit,* 155 Linfield Avenue, P.O. Box 3014, Menlo Park, CA 94026-3014; voice: 415-329-2776. *Quicken 2.0 for Windows.*

*NTERGAID Inc.,* 2490 Black Rock Turnpike, Suite 337, Fairfield, CT 06430. *HyperWriter.*

*Ventura Software, Inc.,* 15175 Innovation Drive, San Diego, CA 92128. *Ventura Publisher for Windows* and *Ventura Database Publisher.* Please note that these products were asked for and sent to us in early 1993, before Ventura was acquired by Corel Corporation.

*Vividus Corporation,* 651 Kendall Avenue, Palo Alto, CA 94306. *Cinemation.*

*Warner New Media,* 3500 Olive Avenue, Burbank, CA 91505. *The View from Earth.*

## HARDWARE

*International Business Machines Corporation,* IBM United States, Department NC2/H04L1, 4111 Northside Parkway, Atlanta, GA 30327. *IBM Ultimedia System.* Thanks to IBM for the use of a complete Ultimedia System for a few months to evaluate and test different CD-ROMs and software packages. This system was so impressive that when the time came to send it back, we missed it so much that we went out and got one for ourselves.

# Glossary

**Accelerators:**  A type of keyboard shortcut that uses function keys, [Ctrl] key or [Option] key sequences, or keys marked with a function name (for example, "Help" or "Cut"). Unlike mnemonics, users can access an option with an accelerator key at any time.

**Achromatic color:**  Black, white, or gray—colors without saturation. Sometimes also used to describe dull colors.

**Action (menu option):**  A command; an option that does something without asking for additional user input. *Save* is a common action.

**Alert message:**  A message that conveys information and asks for a response. Also called "note," "prompt," "attention panel," or simply "message."

**Alert modal:**  See *System modal.*

**Application modal:**  See *Movable modal.*

**Application window:**  The place in which the main interaction between a user and a program or object occurs. Also called "primary window" or "main window."

**Area chart:**  A type of chart that shows cumulative totals (numbers or percentages) over time. Also called "surface," "component part," "belt," or "mountain" chart.

**ASCII:**  American Standard Code for Information Interchange. A character set containing 94 printable characters and 34 other characters such as space, bell, shift-in, tab, and so on. The original ASCII set is sufficient for English and most European languages. Extended ASCII sets are used to represent other writing systems such as Hebrew, Cyrillic, and Arabic.

**Bar chart:**  A chart that shows observations over time using horizontal or vertical bars that do not touch (see *Histogram*). Also called "column chart."

**Bidirectional text:**  A writing system in which text is entered and displayed from right to left except for numbers and roman-alphabet words, which are entered and displayed from left to right. Hebrew and Arabic use bidirectional writing systems. Sometimes abbreviated as "bidi."

**Button:**   See *Checkbutton, Pushbutton,* and *Radio button.*

**CD-I:**   "Compact disk interactive." A read-only compact disk, like the ones used for music, used to distribute multimedia applications for systems composed of a television and a CD-I player.

**CD-ROM:**   A read-only compact disk used to distribute computer-based multimedia applications. CD-ROMs can hold enormous amounts of text as well as pictures and video clips (approximately 680 megabytes per disk).

**Character-based interface:**   An interface that uses the computer's built-in character set to display data, graphics, and program elements such as commands, labels, and menus. See also *Graphical user interface.*

**Checkbutton:**   A button used for setting more than one option at the same time. Checkbuttons usually come in sets. See also *Radio buttons.*

**Chroma:**   A synonym for "saturation."

**Code page:**   Also "code space." A specification of code points for each character in a graphic character set. Code pages have two forms: the hardware code page built into the computer's read-only memory and the software-based character sets that can be used to override the hardware code page. The software code pages contain the character sets used in various languages. Although different operating systems offer different code pages, code pages seem to be converging on ISO and Unicode standards. See *ISO 10646* and *Unicode.*

**Combination box:**   A text box or field with an attached list. Users can either type an entry in the field or select an entry from a list. The list can be a standard list, visible at all times below the text field, or a drop-down list, with a down arrow button used to open it. Also called "combo box" or "drop-down combination box."

**Command line:**   An area at the top or bottom of the application window that lets expert users type commands and access operations more directly than they can using menus.

**Complementary colors:**   On the standard color wheel, complementary colors lie directly opposite each other. They are called complementary because, between them, they contain all the colors of the spectrum. The standard pairs are red and green, orange and blue-green, yellow and dark blue, yellow-green and purple, and bright green and magenta.

**Context-sensitive help:**   The type of help that appears when a user asks for help on a particular screen object. Macintosh "balloon" help is one of the better-known examples. Generally contains the "need to know" information—what this item is, how it works, or how to change it. Also called "object help."

**Contrast:** The greater the contrast, the better the visibility. Black on white has the strongest contrast. However, contrasting colors can cause optical illusions along the edges where they meet.

**Control menus:** The menus that control the operations of the windows themselves. On Microsoft Windows and Motif systems, control menus are indicated by a spacebar or hyphen in the window's upper-left corner.

**Control panel:** An array of options designed to be accessed quickly and repeatedly. It is generally used to hold toolbars, palettes, rulers, and ribbons. It is not used for controls or virtual instruments as its name might imply. *Note:* Apple Computer uses "Control Panel" to refer to a menu that contains utility programs. Control panels are called "floating windows" or "miniwindows."

**Controlled circulation magazine:** A trade magazine. If you work in the trade, you receive the magazine for free.

**Cursor:** A character or shape that marks the point at which the user last made an entry and where he or she will make the next entry. There are two types of cursors: a text cursor, which is an upright bar, and a selection cursor, which is a dotted outline around the selected object.

**Desktop:** The physical screen itself. The desktop is a background to, and is often completely covered by, application windows. Also called "workplace" or "root window."

**Development platform:** A system for relatively fast application development that may be tied to a particular operating system (MS-DOS, OS/2, UNIX, System 7, and so on) and/or to a particular programming language (ANSI C, C++, Visual BASIC, COBOL, and so on). Platforms generally contain libraries of common routines and subroutines, application program interfaces (APIs), and user-interface development systems. Development platforms are offered by operating-system and windowing-system developers, such as Microsoft, IBM, and NeXT. Platforms optimized for certain industries or uses are also available from independent software-development firms.

**Dialog box:** A window in which the computer can present several alternatives, ask for more information, or warn the user that an error has occurred. Same as "secondary window" or "panel."

**Dithering:** Also called "texture mapping." A type of optical illusion. If you put pixels of two or more colors next to one another, the human eye automatically combines them into a third color.

**Ear-cons:** Aural icons. When the user runs the mouse over the icon, it makes a sound.

**Em dash:** A long dash used in standard English to connect two parts of a sentence or to enclose a phrase. In NeXT software, used to set off parts of titles. An em dash is the width of the letter M. En dashes are the width of the letter N.

**Enabling:**   The process of preparing software so that it can be used by more than one culture or region, primarily by separating the text of messages, buttons, menu items, and so on, from the code. An enabled software application doesn't necessarily look or act differently from one that is not. However, in a correctly enabled application, all of the text can be switched from one natural language to another by having the program use a different message file. Also called "internationalization," which is abbreviated for some unknown reason as "I18N" ("I," 18 characters, "N").

**Error message:**   A message that indicates either a user or a system error. A user (or "program") error appears when the program detects a slip or a mistake. A system error occurs when something is wrong with the hardware or software system.

**FEP:**   "Front-end processor." A method used to enter ideographs, such as Japanese Kanji characters, using a roman keyboard. The most common FEP method accepts the first few letters of a roman representation of a Japanese, Korean, or Chinese word, presents a set of likely ideographs, and lets the user pick the one he or she wants.

**Focus:**   Used in the sense of "having focus." The active window or object. When a window has focus, the user's next keystroke will be entered on this window. On windows or dialog boxes, focus is generally indicated with a particular border color. In fields, it is indicated with a blinking cursor. On menu items or other selectable objects, it is indicated with a highlight. On buttons, it can be indicated with a box.

**Frequency polygon:**   A type of chart that shows frequency distributions (the count for each interval during which data were collected) using a curved, unbroken line.

**Graphical user interface (GUI):**   An interface style in which nearly all screen objects are pictures. The user is expected to interact with these screen objects using a mouse. See also *Character-based interface.*

**Grayscale:**   A system in which all of the hues are replaced with various shades or brightnesses of gray. Not the same as monochrome.

**Hazard message:**   A type of message defined by a national or international standards body that warns of potential injury or death to a person or damage to a piece of equipment.

**Histogram:**   A chart that shows frequency distributions (the count for each interval during which data were collected). Unlike the bars in bar charts, bars in histograms touch. Also called "step chart."

**Hot zone:**   The area of a button or icon that recognizes and reacts to a mouse click.

**Hotspot:**   The pixel on a mouse pointer that acts as the user's finger when the pointer is over a hot zone.

**HSV:** Hue, saturation, value (in some Macintosh programs, HSL—hue, saturation, lightness). A system available on some palette editors as an alternative to the RGB color-definition system. Matches the widely used Munsell method of color notation. See also *Hue, Saturation,* and *Value.*

**Hue:** What is normally called "color." Hues are designated by such names as red, green, yellow, blue, and so on. Hue is a function of wavelength.

**Hypertext:** Nonsequential retrieval of a document's text. The reader can take his or her own routes through a hypertext document by jumping from link to link.

**Icon:** A picture on the desktop that represents either a proprietary application or a system resource such as deletion (a common "delete" icon is a picture of a wastebasket). Selecting the icon starts the operation.

**Iconize:** To shrink a window to an icon. Synonymous with "iconify" and, on some platforms, with "minimize."

**Ideogram, ideograph:** Pictures representing entire words, as per the writing systems used in Japan, China, and Korea.

**Internationalization:** See *Enabling.*

**ISBN number:** The International Standard Book Number, which is used to facilitate ordering books by computer. For example, this book's ISBN number is 0-12-263590-6.

The number has four parts:

| | |
|---|---|
| 0 | The first digit is the language of the area of origin—0 means that the book was published in an English-speaking country, 4 means it was published in a Spanish-speaking country, and so on. |
| 12 | The second group of numbers represents the publisher. |
| 263590 | The third group of numbers represents the book's title. This number is assigned by the publisher. |
| 6 | The last number is the check digit, which alerts the inputter to errors in the previous numbers. |

**ISO 10646:** The International Standards Organization document that describes the ISO version of the Unicode character set. It contains both 16-bit (double-byte) and 32-bit (quadruple-byte) representations of characters. The 16-bit version provides up to 65,536 unique characters, which accommodates all Chinese, Korean, and Japanese characters if the characters that look alike use the same representation. (These three languages use the same characters to represent different sounds and, sometimes, different meanings.) The 32-bit version, which provides up to 4.3 million characters, accommodates separate sets of Chinese, Korean, and Japanese characters. See also *Unicode.*

**LCD:**   Liquid crystal display. The soft-surfaced panels with black lettering on gray backgrounds used to display messages from the processors embedded in fax machines, office copiers, and other machinery.

**Line chart:**   A chart that uses lines to show trends.

**Locale model:**   Implementing one set of attributes for each country or culture. The user must explicitly switch from one locale to another to access the correct character set.

**Localization:**   The process of adapting software to a particular culture or region. Localization usually means translating all user-interface text; allowing input and output in the local language; displaying dates, times, and monetary units in the local formats; and so on. Abbreviated as "L10N" ("L," 10 characters, "N.")

**Machine-readable information (MRI):**   An IBM term. The messages, audio output, animation, windows, help files, tutorials, icons, and so on, that pass between a user and an application. Presentation control information—the variables that determine color, intensity, loudness, window size, and so on—is also considered to be part of the machine-readable information.

**Main window:**   See *Primary window.*

**Maximize:**   Enlarge the window to its maximum size. The maximum size of some windows is the entire screen. For others, the maximum size is a size defined by the application's developers.

**Mega-icon:**   Icon that fills the entire screen. Often used for multimedia operations.

**Mi-cons:**   Moving icons. Changes in state (accessed, selected) are indicated with icon movements.

**Minimize:**   Replace a window with an icon representation of itself. *Note:* In NeXTStep applications, windows are miniaturized (shrunk into smaller versions of themselves) rather than minimized into icons.

**Mnemonics:**   A type of keyboard shortcut used primarily for menus, but mnemonics can also be used for buttons and other input devices on panels. Mnemonics are single letters or numbers, selected by programmers, that are indicated by underlines. If the menu or panel containing the desired option doesn't have focus, users must press [Alt], [Meta], or other defined key, then the underlined letter. If the menu or panel does have focus, the user simply presses the underlined letter.

**Modal:**   A dialog-box state in which only certain actions are available to the user. See also *Modeless, Movable modal, Semi-modal,* and *System modal.*

**Modeless:**   A state in which all actions are available. Used for toolbars and find-and-replace panels.

**Monochrome:**  Black and white, period. No grays except those created by dithering. However, also used to refer to monitors with one color (usually amber, green, or orange) on a black background.

**Movable modal:**  Lets the user switch to and work in another application. Useful for requesting input; for doing short, simple tasks; and for actions that are done infrequently. Synonymous with "application modal."

**Multilingual model:**  Implementing a character set that contains characters for many cultures or regions. The user does not have to switch between character sets when he or she needs to switch languages. Unicode and ISO 10646 are examples of standards that use the multilingual model.

**Multimedia:**  Any computer-based system that lets users interact with the software and that uses more than one method of conveying information.

**National language:**  The language of a particular country or culture. Portuguese, Swahili, Arabic, and Chinese are examples of national languages.

**Object:**  In object-oriented programming, a self-contained program unit that contains both data and procedures.

**Option menu:**  A menu on a button. When the user selects the button, the list of options appears. The label of the button changes to show the name of the last selection.

**Palette:**  A type of toolbar. Usually a set of color- or pattern-selection buttons.

**Pictograms:**  Pictures that represent programs, like icons, but which have no activity associated with them.

**Pie chart:**  Circular snapshot of proportional relationships. Also called "circle," "cake," and "sector" chart.

**Platform:**  See *Development platform.*

**Pointer:**  A small picture that moves around the screen as the user moves the mouse. An icon for mouse movement.

**Pop-up menus:**  Expert user menus that appear when the user clicks a particular mouse button on an active area. Pop-up menus contain often-used commands and shortcuts.

**Primary window:**  See *Application window.*

**Progress indicator:**  A type of status message that is used to indicate time delays. Progress indicators can be "elapsed time" messages, "percent complete" messages, or progress-indicator bars, which are long rectangular bars (horizontal or vertical) that start out empty but are filled as the operation proceeds.

**Pull-down menu:** The menu that appears when a user selects a menu title from the menu bar at the top of an application window. What most people think of when they think of menus.

**Pushbutton:** A button that lets a user do an action. Pushbuttons usually resemble actual buttons. Also called "action" or "command" button.

**Radio button:** A button that lets users select one of a group of mutually exclusive choices. See also *Checkbuttons*.

**Reference help:** Online help in book format. Generally contains the "nice to know" information—which formula is being used, how this procedure is affected by government regulations, or what this word means.

**Resource:** Any widget or application variable whose value can be set using the development platform's resource manager.

**Resource files:** Files in which window sizes and shapes, cursors, fonts, color maps, menu labels, and other such items are kept. Each resource has a unique ID within its resource file. Resource files are used to isolate interface objects and settings from program code.

**Restore:** If a window has been minimized or iconized, the restore button or control-menu option restores the window to full size. If the window has been maximized, the restore button or option restores the window to its normal size, provided that the normal and maximized sizes are not the same.

**RGB:** Red, green, blue. Three wavelengths of light—red, green, and blue—create all of the visible hues. Computer monitors use light, not pigment, to create colors. By adjusting the amounts of red, green, and blue light, you can create any of the colors available on the monitors.

**Ribbon:** A type of toolbar that contains additional, secondary settings and commands.

**Ruler:** Onscreen measurement aid. Most programs with rulers let users change the unit of measurement (from inches to picas, say, or from miles to meters).

**Saturation:** Also "purity" or "chroma." The intensity or vividness of a color. Red is more saturated than pink; navy blue is more saturated than sky blue. The purer the hue, the more visible it is at a distance. The subtler the value (the shade or tint), the more difficult it is to see.

**Scatterplot:** A chart on which each data point is the intersection of two variables plotted against the two axes. Also called "scattergram" and "XY scatter."

**Script:** In multimedia productions, the script (also called "screenplay") specifies camera angles, composition of scenes, visual flow from one scene to the next, and the text that appears or is spoken.

**Segmented bar chart:** A chart that uses bars divided into proportional segments to show proportional relationships over time.

**Semimodal:** Microsoft Windows only. The user can do certain operations outside the dialog box as a way of responding to the dialog box's message. In a spreadsheet, for example, the user might specify ranges by selecting cells with the mouse as well as with controls inside the dialog box.

**Slider button:** A sliding bar used to represent a value on a scale. The user or application can move the slider up and down or left and right on the scale.

**Spectrum:** Red, orange, yellow, green, blue, indigo, violet. The mnemonic is *Roy G. Biv.*

**Spin button:** A small square button marked with up and down or left and right buttons. Spin buttons can be used to display long lists of choices that increase or decrease in constant units—for example, type sizes.

**Status bar:** An area at the bottom or top of the application window that contains, at a minimum, page or window identification. It can also contain status messages, mode indicators (CAPS, NUM, etc.), and descriptions of buttons and menu options as the user highlights each one.

**Status message:** A running commentary on an application's activity. For example, as a program loads, the status message might be "Loading database . . . ." Status messages appear in the application window's status bar.

**Storyboard:** A series of sketches (or photographs) that represent the individual scenes in a film, video, or multimedia production.

**Subject matter expert:** An in-house guru or expert who supplies, then reviews, technical material before it is released to the end-user population. Abbreviated as "SME" and pronounced "smee."

**Submenu:** A second or third level on a pull-down menu. For example, a *Fonts* option on a *Format* menu might lead to a submenu of typefaces and sizes. Also called "cascades" in Microsoft and Motif systems and "hierarchical menus" in Macintosh and NeXTStep systems.

**System modal:** A mode in which the user can work only inside the dialog box and must respond to the dialog box before doing anything in any application. Used for system warning messages and alert boxes. Synonymous with "alert modal."

**Tear-off or "tacked" menus:** Menus that can be kept open and continuously available. Functionally, they are more like control panels or toolbars than menus.

**Toolbars:** Small windows or boxes that provide constant access to important tools—for example, a set of drawing tools in a paint program or a set of text-formatting buttons for a word-processing program. Toolbars float above the application window at all times (as long as the user doesn't close them). The Motif guidelines call toolbars or palettes "panels"; the Macintosh guidelines call them "utility windows," "palettes," or "miniwindows"; and the NeXTStep guidelines call them "floating windows."

**Translation:**   In the software industry, an operation that converts data from one format to another (from ASCII to EBCDIC, for example, or from dBASE to FoxPro). It is *not* used to mean "transforming from one natural language to another."

**Treatment:**   For multimedia productions, a report or specification containing information on the length of the presentation, the budget, the intention, the market, and so on.

**Unicode:**   The name of the international 16-bit character set and encoding method developed by members of the Unicode Consortium. See *ISO 10646.*

**Value:**   Also "lightness." The amount of white or black mixed into the hue. Some hues are inherently lighter or darker than others—yellow, for instance, is very light while violet is very dark. The related word "shade" usually describes a darkened hue, produced by adding black (actually, subtracting white). The word "tint" describes a light hue, produced by adding white.

**Wait pointer:**   A pointer in the shape of an hourglass or watch that indicates that a process is occurring.

**Widget:**   A user interface object in graphical user interfaces, especially in X Windows systems. Any basic object in a programming toolkit.

**Writing system:**   A method of putting symbols that represent words on paper or other storage media. "Roman" (English, French, Italian, and so on), "ideographic" (Chinese, Korean, Japanese), and "bidirectional" (Arabic, Hebrew) are examples of writing systems.

**X:**   "An over-sized, over-featured, over-engineered, and incredibly over-complicated window system developed at MIT and widely used on UNIX systems," according to the *New Hacker's Dictionary,* edited by Eric Raymond and published by MIT Press in 1991 (p. 388).

# Index